Wiley AP*
English Language
& Composition

by Geraldine Woods

WILEY

John Wiley & Sons, Inc.

Wiley AP* English Language & Composition

Published by
John Wiley & Sons, Inc.
111 River St.
Hoboken, NJ 07030-5774
www.wiley.com

For general information on our other products and services, please contact our Business Development Department in the U.S. at 317-572-3205.

Library of Congress Control Number: 2012952212

ISBN 978-1-118-49017-4 (pbk); ISBN 978-1-118-49003-7 (ebk); ISBN 978-1-118-49018-1 (ebk); ISBN 978-1-118-49020-4 (ebk)

Manufactured in the United States of America

10 9 8 7 6 5 4 3 2 1

Publisher's Acknowledgments

Project Editor: Tracy L. Barr

Executive Editor: Lindsay Sandman Lefevere

Technical Reviewer: Elizabeth Brown

Sr. Project Coordinator: Kristie Rees

Cover Photo: © aleksandar velasevic / iStockphoto.com

About the Author

Geraldine Woods has taught and tutored every level of English from 5th grade through AP for the past three decades. She's the author of more than 50 books, many published by Wiley: *English Grammar For Dummies*, *English Grammar Workbook For Dummies*, *Research Papers For Dummies*, *College Admissions Essays For Dummies*, *SAT For Dummies*, and *Punctuation: Simplified and Applied*.

Author's Acknowledgements

Many talented people helped me with this book: Robin Aufses, Ben Casnocha, Sam Goodman, Karen Ellen Johnson, Tom Katzenbach, Christopher Witcombe, and Don Yates. I owe a debt of gratitude to them all. I'd also like to thank Tracy Barr and Lindsay Lefevere of Wiley, as well as my technical reviewer, Elizabeth Brown of William Henry Harrison High School in West Lafayette, Indiana.

WILEY

Table of Contents

Introduction to the AP Exam and the AP Course

1

An Overview of the Exam

WHAT TO EXPECT FROM THE AP ENGLISH LANGUAGE AND COMPOSITION EXAM

KEY CONCEPTS
■ Exam format and content
■ Test scores and score reports
■ Ways to prepare before the exam date
■ Things to do before, during, and after the exam

People who favor traditional education usually want schools to focus on "the three Rs" — reading, 'riting, and 'rithmetic. Traditionalists, therefore, love the AP English Language and Composition exam because it covers two-thirds of these basic areas: reading and writing. This exam, as well as the course that may be attached to it, concentrates on your skills as a writer and as a reader of other people's writing.

In this chapter, I show you typical AP English Language and Composition questions and tell you what you need to know about scoring, timing, and guessing. I also cover how to find out when and where the test is held, what it costs, how scores are reported, and other practical information.

WHAT TO EXPECT FROM THE AP ENGLISH LANGUAGE AND COMPOSITION EXAM

The AP English Language and Composition exam is probably easier than many of the tests you've already taken, although it looks a bit intimidating. (It comes in a plastic, shrink-wrapped package with multicolored booklets and instructions.) The test boils down to two parts:

■ **Multiple Choice:** You have one hour to answer approximately 55 questions (the number varies a bit from year to year) based on five or six reading passages. Each question is followed by five possible answers lettered A–E. You bubble your answers with a number two pencil onto an answer sheet.

■ **Free Response:** This section throws three writing assignments at you, all essays, tucked into a little green booklet. You get a 15-minute reading period during which you can check out all the questions, read the passages supplied, and take notes in the question booklet. Then the test proctor lets you open the pink answer booklet and write for two hours — approximately 40 minutes per essay.

The test itself takes 3 hours and 15 minutes. As you plan for test day, add a 10-minute break between the multiple-choice and free-response sections and about 45 minutes for getting settled and bubbling registration information on the answer sheet — a little less if your school holds preregistration sessions. (More about registration and the logistics of test day appears in "Practical Considerations" later in this chapter.)

A moving target

Many high school English teachers see the AP English Language and Composition exam as a moving target. The test has changed several times in the last few years, and it may change again in the future. Why hop around so much? The AP test writers are likely responding to what today's college teachers want to see in a well-prepared student writer. The AP English Language and Composition course is roughly the equivalent of "Freshman Comp" or "Composition 101," and the exam is designed to show whether you've learned enough to get credit in that college class. More than in the past, such courses now stress the use of sources and argument. So it's not surprising that in 2007 the College Board added a synthesis essay to determine whether students can handle research material.

Other changes in the test are detectable only if you read a few decades' worth of AP questions. An extended survey reveals, for example, that paired-passage essays haven't shown up for a while. They may be gone for good, or, as some AP teachers believe, they're due for a comeback. Passages drawn from the web are on the upswing, and specialized vocabulary to describe writing style seems to be increasingly important. Not to worry: This book covers all the bases, so you'll be ready no matter what shows up on test day.

EXAM QUESTIONS, UP CLOSE AND PERSONAL

On the AP English Language and Composition exam, you encounter questions about *what* a writing passage says and *how* the passage says it. You also get a chance to argue, analyze, and synthesize. This section takes a closer look. First up is content — what sort of reading passages you'll meet. Next is format — the types of multiple-choice and essay questions facing you.

Preview of AP passages

The AP test makers aim to include a good selection of quality literature in every test — the sort of reading assigned in college courses. The vast majority of passages are nonfiction selections from essays, speeches, letters, biographies or memoirs, and *exposition* (explanation) or description from a variety of sources. Though the AP English Language and Composition test is officially the province of the English Department, subjects range from history to arts to politics to science to just about anything you can imagine. The test makers occasionally dip into fiction — usually with a descriptive or a narrative passage. Once in a great while a speech from a play appears. The AP doesn't have a required reading list, so you won't see any questions that assume you've read a particular book. In fact, everything you need — except good writing and reading skills — is given to you by the test makers. Poetry never shows up on the exam, unless it's a quotation from a Shakespearean character.

In every exam, the AP test makers include something old and something new. You will probably see a 17th- or 18th-century passage, a little from the 19th century, and some modern works from the 20th or 21st century. Striving for diversity, the AP test makers generally include a couple of passages written by women or people of color. Works from any English-speaking country, as well as an occasional translation, are possible selections. At least one passage has source citations (footnotes, parenthetical references, or a bibliography).

> The AP test doesn't always include identifying information about a particular passage (the title, author, or date and circumstances of publication). If you see such information, *pay attention*. You may learn something that will help you answer the questions.

Every AP exam presents you with a range of reading difficulty, from "not so bad" to "what in the world does this mean?" Luckily, the hardest passages tend to be accompanied by relatively easy questions. Sadly, the reverse is also true. Selections that are simpler to decode are attached to tougher multiple-choice or essay questions. Don't assume that a passage with simple vocabulary or *syntax* (grammatical structure) is a piece of cake. Such passages may have subtle points, a nuanced tone, or a complex attitude. Don't speed too quickly through an "easy" passage.

The multiple-choice section

You've probably sat down a million times in your English classes to read a piece of great writing and discuss its style and content with your classmates. Instead of requiring discussion, the AP test makers have poured tons of possible comments about a passage into ovals labeled A, B, C, D, and E. Your mission is to find the oval that matches what you think is the right answer.

Some of the multiple-choice questions evaluate standard reading-comprehension skills such as vocabulary, inference, decoding the text, and so forth. About half the questions you encounter on the AP English Language and Composition test concern writing style: how the words are put together on the page and why the author made particular style choices. You may be queried about the passage as a whole or about only one or two words. Because content and style are closely related in good literature, style questions sometimes overlap with content questions. Fortunately, you don't have to label the questions, just answer them correctly.

Following is an array of typical AP multiple-choice questions.

Vocabulary-in-context questions

A number of AP questions test whether you understand the meaning of a particular word or phrase in the context of the passage.

Check out this example:

> **1.** In line 12, "drip" may best be defined as
>
> > (A) a guy with a plastic pocket protector
> > (B) a type of coffeemaker
> > (C) a sound that water makes
> > (D) what spaghetti sauce does when you eat too quickly
> > (E) the normal state of an infant's mouth

To answer this type of question, you have to go back to line 12. If a biographer is explaining why Supermodel Sue rejected a once-in-a-lifetime chance to attend a flea circus, (A) is probably the answer. If someone's preparing breakfast, go for (B).

One particular challenge of "vocabulary-in-context" questions is that most of the choices are actual definitions of the word they're asking you to define. Don't jump on an answer too quickly. Be sure the definition fits the way the word is used in the passage.

Specialized vocabulary questions

Like every other subject area, English has its own specialized vocabulary that describes elements of writing. These terms may appear in either the question or the answer choices.

Take a look at this example:

> **1.** Which technique does the author employ in lines 18–23?
>
> > (A) figurative language
> > (B) apostrophe
> > (C) synecdoche
> > (D) allusion
> > (E) parallel structure

For specialized vocabulary questions, the answer is outlined in neon lights if you know the terms. If you don't, you're flying blind. (I review these terms in Chapters 3 through 5.)

Antecedent questions

Another type of question lurking on the AP exam involves *pronouns,* words that replace nouns. Usually you have to explain what a pronoun means by finding the word it refers to — its *antecedent*.

Take a look at this example:

1. The antecedent of "that" (line 54) is

   (A) Massachusetts (line 42)
   (B) sunbathing (line 48)
   (C) beach (line 49)
   (D) water (line 50)
   (E) algae (line 57)

Finding an antecedent is fairly easy. Just substitute each answer for the pronoun and see which one makes sense.

Factual questions

You may occasionally be asked to identify a stated fact. This type of question is frequently attached to old (pre-19th century) passages. The AP test makers want to know that you can decode works from earlier centuries.

Take a look at the following example:

1. What is Mortimer's reason for leaving his dead lover?

   (A) He was too frightened to stay.
   (B) He had to bury the murder weapon.
   (C) Her husband returned home.
   (D) He had to seek help to move her body.
   (E) He had jury duty.

A variation of the factual question looks for equivalents, as in this example:

1. Which statement is the equivalent of line 42 ("And she was never seen again")?

   (A) "Nevermore would anyone stare at her scars" (line 80)
   (B) "She had been poetry-in-motion, but now she was history" (line 82)
   (C) "The 5:42 was a one-way trip" (line 88)
   (D) "Mars afforded permanent escape" (line 99)
   (E) "Everyone she knew disdained the special eclipse-proof glasses" (line 111)

To answer one of these questions, step back and examine the big picture. What point is the author making about the fact that "she was never seen again"? If the passage is about a train wreck, (C) is a good bet. If you've been reading about space travel, opt for (D).

Inference questions

Inference resides in "read between the lines" territory. These questions make you put on your Sherlock Holmes hat and find the clues pointing to the answer, which is *not* directly stated in the passage.

Check out this example:

1. Eleanor probably refused to wear the pink dress because

   (A) it clashed with her orange hair
   (B) she had worn pink on her last date with Mortimer
   (C) pink was "so-o-o last year"
   (D) the pink dress was evidence in the bank robbery
   (E) no dress was good enough for Eleanor

This example resembles a straightforward factual question, but the word "probably" tells you that you have to draw a conclusion. Spread your net wide and gather relevant information. If Eleanor turned up her nose at an Armani outfit, (E) is the answer you seek. If the passage mentions complementary colors, (A) may win.

Main idea questions

Main idea questions make you hold an umbrella over the content of the entire passage or of a portion of the passage. Like an umbrella, your answer should be wide enough to cover everything.

Here's an example:

1. What is the main idea of paragraph three (lines 69–92)?

   (A) Children riding bicycles should be encased in bubble wrap.
   (B) Bicycle riding is dangerous.
   (C) Accidents claim many lives every year.
   (D) Lola should never have opened the car door without looking both ways.
   (E) Lola should be banned from public highways.

A question like this sends you back to paragraph three. Does everything in the paragraph fit the answer you chose? If not, your answer is too narrow. Look for the most specific answer that includes everything in the designated lines.

Purpose

You have to read between the lines for questions about the author's purpose.

Here's an example of a purpose question:

1. The narrator relates the story of Adam's apple injury (lines 14–18) in order to

    (A) prove to the reader that Adam was fatally careless

    (B) qualify his statement that "Adam was a lucky guy" (line 4)

    (C) reveal the reason for Adam's fear of red, fruit-shaped objects

    (D) contrast Adam's carelessness with Olivia's timidity

    (E) persuade the reader that thrown fruit can be deadly

This example is best answered by imagining the passage *without* the story of Adam and the apple. What changes? For example, suppose Olivia seems bolder when she's not compared with Adam. In that case, Adam is there to reveal Olivia's character.

Tone and attitude questions

Still more "big picture" questions tackle tone and attitude, either of a person or character in the passage or of the author.

Look at this example:

1. The attitude of the author toward global warming may best be characterized as

    (A) detached

    (B) critical

    (C) dismissive

    (D) alarmed

    (E) distraught

This type of question is easy as long as you read carefully. If the author says that the planet simply needs more air conditioners to combat global warming, darken oval (C). If the author explains how he "howled at the moon" and "imagined the earth melting into the sky," go for (E).

Reading carefully is often the best strategy for questions about *tone*, which is the author's or character's "voice" on the page. To determine tone, pay close attention to individual word choices and to what is included or left out of the passage. Imagine that the preceding example queries you about "tone" instead of "attitude," with the same answer choices. If the passage refers to "environmental catastrophe," the author's tone is definitely not "dismissive" or "detached." Other words in the passage may help you decide which of the remaining answers works best.

> **TIP**
>
> Tone and attitude questions often come with paired answers ("detached and thoughtful," for example.) Be sure *both* adjectives work when choosing an answer.

Structure questions

Is the passage organized by time, order of importance, or something else? Structure questions ask you to perceive the skeleton of logic that holds the passage or a paragraph together.

Consider this example:

1. Which word or phrase best describes paragraph three (lines 44–56)?

    (A) comparison and contrast
    (B) chronological order
    (C) spatial order
    (D) claim and evidence
    (E) cause and effect

When you answer a structure question, ignore the details and check out the *order* in which things appear in the paragraph or passage. Determining what's where points you toward the correct answer.

Citation questions

Questions about source citations focus on footnotes, parenthetical citations, or bibliographic citations. Rest assured: You won't find any questions about whether a comma has been correctly placed. You will be asked to explain what a citation means.

In the following example, you have to explain what the citation means:

1. Which of the following statements about footnote 2 is correct?

    (A) Paris Hilton is the author of the article entitled "Dogs I Have Owned."
    (B) The article was published in a suite at the Hilton in Paris, France.
    (C) The information about Paris was provided by the Hilton Hotel chain.
    (D) The information about Paris was provided by a small dog.
    (E) The article was published in 1802 and revised in 2002.

Citations are a world unto themselves, but you can navigate them with the help of Chapter 12.

AP essays

For the essay section of the exam, first you read for 15 minutes, jotting notes in the margin of your question booklet. Then you start writing. The questions vary from year to year, but a few types are constant.

Synthesis

The synthesis essay requires you to read and digest six or seven sources about a particular issue. The sources are usually short or excerpted news stories, editorials, letters, or web postings. At least one of the sources is visual — a chart, graph, cartoon, or photo. You take a stand on the issue and support your position with references to at least three of the sources. Here's an example:

> **Prompt:** The usefulness of the $100,000 dollar bill has been questioned by government officials, but many consumers find this type of currency essential. Read the following sources carefully. Then write an essay in which you develop a position on the desirability of the $100,000 bill in the United States currency system. Synthesize at least three of the six sources to support your stance. In your essay, attribute both direct and indirect citations.

This may seem like a ridiculous question, and I am joking a little. However, a recent AP synthesis essay questioned the usefulness of the penny. One of the sources was a photo of a penny! For help with the synthesis essay, turn to Chapters 15 and 16.

Style analysis

This type of essay question usually requires reading one passage but occasionally involves two passages. You have to read the selection(s) and explain how the writing technique relates to another element. For example, the test makers may ask you to explain how the author's attitude or purpose is revealed by her *rhetorical strategy* (writing style). If you're dealing with a pair of passages, you have to compare techniques. Check out this question.

> **Prompt:** Read this excerpt from Pablo Picasso's *My Art and Peanut Butter: A Memoir*. Then, in a well-written essay, discuss how the author's attitude toward chunky nut-spreads is revealed by the rhetorical devices he employs.

The task here is that you have to analyze and discuss the effect of the techniques you identify in the passage, not simply list them. For a review of rhetorical devices, turn to Part II.

Argument

If you're a debater, this question's for you. The AP makers may provide a letter to the editor or an editorial, or they may simply provide a provocative quotation. You have to agree or disagree with the position stated in the passage or quotation. You may also adopt a stance that partly agrees, with some objections. Here's a sample question.

> **Prompt:** Bernice Woodchick once noted that "no man is an island, but quite a few are peninsulas because they're just too shy to date." Ms. Woodchick's observation has often been cited in support of computerized dating services. In a well-written essay, develop a position on the efficacy of computer matchmaking. Support your position with evidence from literature, history, or personal experience.

The crucial element of this essay is support. The graders don't care *what* you think, but they do care about *how* you think. They want to know that you can construct a convincing argument.

THE SCORE: GRADES AND REPORTS

A *psychometrician* is someone who checks the questions on every exam, looking for just the right weighting to produce reliable, standardized results that sort students the same way no matter which year they take the test. Too many easy questions, and the psychometrician toughens the formula so that more correct answers are needed for a good grade. Too many hard questions, and the exam is curved downward. Either way, the psychometricians aim to ensure that every AP score means more or less the same thing.

The score you see ranges from 1 to 5:

> **5:** Extremely well qualified (equals an A in Freshman Comp)
>
> **4:** Well qualified (in the B range for Freshman Comp)
>
> **3:** Qualified (C territory)
>
> **2:** Possibly qualified (D)
>
> **1:** No recommendation (and also no passing grade)

What do these scores mean to colleges? If they see a 3, 4, or 5, most will be happy. Some colleges don't accept anything lower than a 4. A score of 1 or 2 won't help you much, either with college admission or with placement.

> **TIP**
>
> Some colleges give you actual credit (usually two or three credits) for a good AP grade. This practice saves you money because you then have to take fewer courses to graduate. Some colleges don't give you credit but do exempt you from the Freshman Comp requirement. Some give you nothing tangible, though a good AP score always helps your chances for admission.

Multiple-choice scoring

The multiple-choice section counts for 45 percent of your total score. The good news is that you can get a bunch of multiple-choice questions wrong and still pass. For example, if you miss as many as a third of the multiple-choice questions and score 6 out of 9 on the essay section, you're in the running for a 3.

Multiple-choice questions are scored in this way:

- Every correct answer receives one point.
- Each wrong answer and each question you leave blank receives no points.
- Totals are plugged into a math formula that spits out the converted score.

Essay scoring

The essay section comprises 55 percent of your total score. Each of the three essays counts the same, and a blank answer lops a third from your essay grade. So don't spend 90 minutes on one essay, 30 minutes on another, and 0 minutes on the remaining question. Divide your two hours more or less evenly — about 40 minutes per essay.

The essays are read by college English professors and high-school English teachers who reside in a hotel for a week. A group of teachers at one table reads the responses to a single question. In other words, one table reads hundreds of synthesis essays, another table gets stacks of the analysis essay, and so on. A table leader reads and checks the work of anyone new to the process, and psychometricians (people who understand statistics) check that the essay grade is more or less in sync with the multiple-choice grade. If the scores on the two portions of the exam seem mismatched, the essay is rechecked by a table leader.

Each essay receives a score between 0 and 9, awarded to the essay as a whole. Graders don't write comments on the paper, and they don't deduct 10 percent for bad grammar or give you 30 percent for an excellent introduction. Nines are extremely rare. One grader told me that she read 1,200 essays one year and came up with only 13 nines. Here's a general guide to essay scores:

> **0:** The question was not answered.
>
> **1, 2, or 3:** The essay is overly simple and poorly written or reflects a misreading of the passage or assigned task. An essay in this category tends to repeat or summarize information from the passage or make unsupported arguments. Two is the highest score an essay can receive if the grammar and spelling are bad enough to impede the reader.
>
> **4, 5, or 6:** Essays in this slot do the job: They synthesize, analyze, or argue reasonably well, and they include a fair amount of supportive evidence. They are written with some, but not many, grammar and spelling errors, and the writing style is adequate. However, they're not as sophisticated as essays on the next rung.
>
> **7, 8, or 9:** These essays show that students have been learning what their English teachers have been teaching. They get the job done smoothly, efficiently, and properly. The content and style would rate a good grade if written in a timed, in-class situation in a college course.

After the graders attach a number to each essay, the numbers make their way to still another formula, where the three essay scores are combined and converted and mixed into one last formula, whereupon a 1, 2, 3, 4, or 5 pops out.

Score reports

About two months after the test, you receive an envelope in the mail with your AP score inside. Or, if you pay extra (currently $8), you can get an early report by phone. The toll-free number is 888-308-0013 for the United States and Canada. Outside this area, the number is 609-771-7300. Your English teacher also gets a report sometime during the summer. If you asked that your score be reported to a college, the college also hears the news in July. The first college report is free; if you want additional score reports, you have to pay $15 (or $25 if you're in a rush) for each extra college.

To access grades by phone or to request extra score reports, you need a valid credit card and your student pack. (See "Practical Considerations" in this chapter for more information on student packs.)

A few more details on score reports:

■ All the AP exams you've taken show up on the same score report — not just the most recent one (unless you cancelled a score or paid to have it withheld).

■ You can cancel a score until mid-June — an option you may want to take advantage of if you lost your way or your memory on the day of the exam. To cancel a score, speak with your teacher or your school's AP coordinator or log on to http://www.collegeboard.com. If you cancel a score, it vanishes forever. No one, including you, will ever know how you did. Don't expect a refund. You're cancelling the result, not the test.

■ You can withhold a score from a college, though you must pay $10 per college and make a written request to the College Board by mid-June. The score will still be reported to you and to your high school, and if you change your mind, you can release the score to colleges at a later date, after paying a few more bucks.

■ For a fee of $7, the College Board will send you the essays you wrote. You'll see the score written on the essay, but no comments or corrections. If you plan to take the AP exam twice (which requires waiting a whole year because the exam is given only in May), reviewing your essays with a teacher or tutor is a good idea.

Take a look at the College Board website (http://www.collegeboard.com) or call 888-225-5427 for anything to do with score reporting, cancellations, and the like.

PRACTICAL CONSIDERATIONS

Sometime in the first or second week of May, you'll take the AP English Language and Composition exam. If you're enrolled in an AP English Comp course, your teacher will probably tell you how to sign up and when and where the exam is given. If you are home-schooled or if the school you attend doesn't offer an AP program, you can still take the exam. Call 888-225-5427 for the contact information of the nearest AP coordinator (the person in charge of ordering the tests, scheduling proctors, and so forth). You will receive a special code number from the coordinator, and you'll have to bring this number and a government-issued photo ID (such as a passport or driver's license) to the exam.

TIP

> Your photo on a school identification card isn't enough on AP day if you're not taking the test in your own school, where everyone knows you. Only a government-issued ID is acceptable.

Pre-exam chores

Apart from practicing the skills tested, you have a few additional chores to complete before the AP exam. (Students with special needs have even more to do. See the next section, "Special needs," for more information.) Here's the general list:

■ **January or February:** Pick up a student bulletin. This handy pamphlet published by the College Board is probably stacked in the College Counseling or Guidance Office of your school. If you can't find one, ask a teacher, administrator, or the school's AP coordinator. The student bulletin explains when the test is given, provides an up-to-date fee schedule, and tells you the most current information about the exam.

> **TIP**
>
> A student bulletin is available for downloading from `http://www.collegeboard.com/apstudents`. No Internet access? Call 888-225-5427 for information.

■ **Early February:** Students who need accommodations on the test but haven't been certified by the College Board must submit documentation. (See "Special needs" for more information.)

■ **Mid- to late February:** Students previously certified as needing accommodations on the exam must check that the school has sent in the required forms.

■ **March:** Check your calendar. If you have a scheduling conflict (two AP tests scheduled at the same time or a state-championship game during the essay section, for example), talk with the AP coordinator by mid-March. A makeup date is available for unavoidable conflicts. Depending upon the conflict, the College Board may charge you nothing or as much as $40.

■ **Late April:** Homeschoolers and those who are taking the test in a different school should make a practice run to the exam site.

Arriving at the exam

On the day of the test, plan to arrive about 15 minutes early at the exam room. You will meet your proctor there — the teacher who supervises the test — and receive your student pack. The student pack is a small pamphlet containing labels with a number that belongs to you alone for your entire AP life. You have to fill in some information (unless your school held a preregistration session). Then you'll hear a couple of last-minute instructions, mostly concerning what can and can't be in the room. Following is what you *must* and what you *cannot* bring to the AP test.

What you must bring into the testing room

Be sure you have these items:

■ **Pens with blue or black in:** Erasable pens are okay but not the best choice because they can smudge and make reading difficult for the graders.

■ **Number two pencils:** Bring several, just to be safe.

■ **A watch:** The test room probably has a clock, but you may not be able to see it easily.

■ **A special code number, a government-issued photo ID, and your student pack:** You need these items if you're not taking the exam in your own school.

■ **Your College Board SSD Accommodations letter:** This letter is issued to students with special needs.

What you cannot bring into the testing room

Leave these things at home or in your car:

- **Highlighters or pens with ink that isn't black or blue:** The AP moguls are worried that you'll glance at the smartest kid in the school, see the highlights on his or her exam, focus more on those sections, and gain an advantage.

- **Cellphones, iPods, MP3 players, PDAs, or any sort of electronic device:** For these few hours, silence and *nothing else* flows into your ears.

- **Food or drink:** Not even water is allowed, though you can drink and eat during the break. The concern is that you'll copy something on the label.

> **TIP**
>
> If you have a medical condition that requires you to eat, drink, or take medicine during the exam, check with the AP coordinator well in advance of the test — by late February or early March.

- **Books, papers, good luck charms, or anything else:** Depending upon your proctor, you may bring a purse or backpack, which you will have to leave in the front of the room or under your seat. But make things easy on yourself: Leave your stuff in your locker or car trunk.

Special needs

If your school grants you accommodations for special needs — additional time, a computer for writing essays, Braille exams or a reader, and so forth — chances are the AP will do the same. However, don't assume anything. Take charge of the situation:

- By late January of the year you intend to take the test, talk with the AP coordinator in your school about your needs. Homeschoolers or those whose schools don't have an AP program should call 888-225-5427 for the name and location of the nearest AP coordinator.

- Before mid-February, ask the AP coordinator if your school has submitted an official College Board student eligibility form for you. The same form is applicable to the AP, the SAT, and the PSAT/NMSQT — the whole alphabet of tests that the College Board administers. However, the AP may not grant you the same accommodations that you received on another test.

- If you recently switched schools or if your need for accommodations has changed, you need a new eligibility form. You may also have to send in additional documentation. Because the College Board takes up to seven weeks to process these forms, you have to start early. Again, mid-February gives you ample time to correct any foul-ups.

- If your special need pops up at the last minute, tell the AP coordinator right away. He or she will call the College Board to request accommodations for you.

- If your special need resides in your bank account, you can apply for a reduced rate. As of this writing, the AP exam costs $89, but it drops to $53 for students who qualify for a discount. Depending upon where you live, your state or school district may subsidize more of this amount, making your out-of-pocket expense even lower.

> **TIP**
>
> The College Board website has a helpful section for students who have special needs (http://www.collegeboard.com/ssd/student/index.html). You can also contact the College Board's Services for Students with Disabilities Office at 609-771-7137 (TTY 609-882-4118).

After the College Board has reviewed your paperwork, it'll issue you an SSD Accommodations Letter. If you do not receive this letter by the beginning of April, check with your AP coordinator. You must bring the accommodation letter to the exam.

TEST DAY COUNTDOWN

Whether your AP English Language and Composition exam is a year from now or a month from now, this section helps you prepare. You can't score high on the AP test without preparation. The following information corresponds to the amount of time remaining before the exam. Jump in at the spot that matches your calendar and follow the directions at that point for optimal AP preparation.

Exam minus one year

You're starting to prepare a year early, so clearly you have the ability to think ahead, prioritize, and get the job done. That's a good sign. The following steps will help you maximize your preparation time:

- As you plan your schedule for the following academic year, look into the array of English courses available at your school. Most people who take the AP English Language and Composition exam also take the AP English course tailored to the material tested on this exam. However, the exam is open to you whether you're enrolled in an AP class or not.

  The College Board offers two tests in English — the AP English Literature and Composition exam and the AP English Language and Composition exam. Both cover college-level material, and both stress reading and writing skills. If your school offers only the literature course, you can brush up on the question format with this book and take the language exam anyway. Non-AP, advanced-level writing courses are also a good bet, as long as you preview the exam format.

- Hit the newsstand (or the Internet) and read the daily paper, or, if you're pressed for time, just read the editorials or columns. As you read, think about how the writer argues for a particular point of view.

- Every week, read some *expository* nonfiction (prose that explains something). The field doesn't matter; pick something you like. As you read how Picasso developed his style or why the Allies triumphed, notice the way in which the writer conveys information.

- As you read, keep scrap paper nearby so that you can occasionally practice annotating. (Check out Chapter 2 for more information on annotating.)

- Analyze visual sources. Peer at advertisements, paintings, photos, charts, and cartoons. Identify the surface and deeper message of what you're seeing. (Chapter 7 explains how.)

- Choose a strategy for improving your vocabulary. (See Chapter 2 for help.)

- Gather and file corrected papers and notes from your most recent English classes.

September before the exam

The start of a new school year is an excellent opportunity to hit your English class with maximum efficiency. Good study habits take you to top grades in both the course and the AP exam. I explain the best strategy for your class in Chapter 2. Here I list a few little "extras" of pre-exam preparation that pay off in a big way:

- Each week, make an effort to read one good editorial or opinion column in a quality newspaper or magazine. As you read, keep a pen handy. If you own the publication, annotate it. (Chapter 2 explains how.) If the material is from the library or on the Internet, jot down some notes about writing style. If you're reading from an electronic device, use the "add notes" function (which may have a different name).

- Continue or start consciously adding new words to your vocabulary. In school, you automatically pick up some vocabulary just by doing your homework. But by employing one of the strategies explained in Chapter 2, you can radically increase the number of words you know.

- Start or add to a file of your writing assignments and tests from current and previous English classes.

- Keep a notebook or computer file of important points about writing methods and style from the teacher or from student discussion in your English class.

- Volunteer to write for the school paper or magazine, or send letters to the editor expressing your opinion. This practice builds writing muscles and helps you with the essay portion of the AP exam.

January before the exam

Let your New Year's resolution be to do some serious exam prep, including the following:

- Start or continue with the steps listed in the preceding section.

- Set aside 30–45 minutes each week to read a chapter in this book.

- Pull out your file of tests, quizzes, and papers from your current and previous English classes. Pay close attention to the teachers' comments, especially where you lost points. Make a list of weak spots and concentrate on chapters that develop those skills.

- Dedicate a weekend morning or afternoon to the practice exam in Chapter 17 and score it with Chapter 18. Analyze your weaknesses.

- Every time you have a writing assignment (for homework or classwork, in any subject), pay attention to your writing habits. How do you gather ideas and put them in order? How do you revise? Check out Chapters 2 and 15 for tips on streamlining and improving your writing process.

- Go over a few of your writing assignments with a friendly teacher. Assess your work — what should remain the same and what should improve?

March before the exam

You still have plenty of time to prepare. Here's how:

- Start on or continue with the steps listed in "September before the exam" and "January before the exam."
- If you haven't already done so, take the first practice exam — you'll find it in Chapter 17 — and score it with Chapter 18.
- Select practice questions from the chapters addressing the type of question you find most difficult (multiple choice or essay).
- Zero in on whatever type of writing tends to stump you — writing with source material, creating an argument, or analysis. Devote 40 minutes a week to reading or writing that sort of material.

Two weeks before the exam

You can still increase your chances for a good grade on the AP. If you've been preparing all along, this section tells you how to make a strong finish:

- Review your most recent English papers (history papers work also) and make a "watch out list" of problem areas that require special attention on the exam. For example, if you tend to generalize or repeat yourself, be sure to list those faults so that your AP essays will be free of them. Go for the big picture; don't bother writing down misspelled words.
- Take the second practice exam (Chapter 19) and score it (Chapter 20).
- After taking the second practice exam, add to your "watch out list." Just writing this list focuses your energy and helps you remember what you need to do on test day.
- Check out the sections on time-saving strategy in Chapters 13 (multiple choice) and 15 (essays). The tips in those chapters help you squeeze six hours' worth of thought into half that time period.

The night before the exam

If you haven't done a lot of preparation, at least skim the first part of this chapter so you know the format of the exam. Sample a couple of questions in one of the practice tests you find in Part V of this book and evaluate your responses. Then return to this list.

If you've been preparing for a while, you're in good shape. Take these final steps:

- Read your "Watch Out" list and then STOP studying. Anything you do now will only make you more nervous.
- Do something relaxing but not too strenuous. Shoot some hoops or watch a trashy television show. Stay away from all-night gossip sessions (or all-night anythings).

- Go to bed early, after making sure you have everything you need for the exam in one spot that is *not* accessible to pets, wildlife, little brothers, or anything else likely to mess with your stuff.

- Excavate the car keys or recheck your travel arrangements. Set the alarm clock so you won't have to rush in the morning. Begin snoring.

EXAM DAY SURVIVAL

It's finally here, and like every dreaded event, the reality is less horrible than the anticipation. Here's how to get through exam day with a minimum of fuss.

The morning of the exam

The AP schedule varies a bit from year to year, so your exam may be scheduled for 8:30 a.m. or for 1 p.m., give or take a half-hour. In some schools, students who have an afternoon exam have to report to morning classes anyway. In other schools, you get the morning off if you have an afternoon AP test. Either way, try to make the experience as smooth as possible, with these points in mind:

- AP day isn't the right time for an extreme fashion statement, especially one that involves something skin-tight. You are going to spend a huge amount of time at a desk, and no one but the proctor is allowed to look at you. So unless you have to adhere to a dress code, choose sweats or something just as comfortable (and comforting). Also, go for the layered look. You don't know how hot or cold the testing room will be.

- Leave everything you don't need for the test at home or in your car. No matter what, don't bring English notes to school with you. You may be tempted to read them before you go in the testing room, but last-minute studying accomplishes very little beyond stirring up your nerves.

- Don't "lend your ear" to friends or Romans or countrymen or anyone else before the exam, unless he or she promises *not* to talk about the test or make guesses about the subject matter. Why? You don't want anyone to put you into panic mode. Resolve to discuss your favorite TV show or who is likely to win the World Series. Stay away from AP English!

- Eat a good breakfast, heavy on the protein. Sugar and carbs give you a rush and then a letdown, nicely timed to hit during the exam. Even if you're a jelly doughnut fan, opt for eggs, cheese, tofu, or meat-based items. Don't even *think* about skipping breakfast on AP day.

- Don't drink half a tub of water or coffee or anything else on the morning of the exam. The break is short and occurs only after you've been popping your brain cells for an hour. Yes, you can leave the testing room to use the restroom, but you lose time, and time on the AP is precious. Save the supersized soda for later.

- Before you leave the house, look at yourself in the mirror. Say (aloud, if you don't mind scaring your family, or silently, if you do), "I am prepared. I will give this test my best shot." Picture yourself leaving all your worries behind.

No matter how much advice I give you, you still have to tailor everything to *your* life and *your* brain. As you prepare for the AP test, factor in details only you know — that your sister's wedding is the day before the exam or that you write best when you hear a clock ticking. (In that case, buy a noisy wristwatch before test day.)

As the exam begins

Once you enter the testing room, the proctor takes over. To give you an idea what to expect and for a few additional helpful hints, scan this list:

- **Where to sit:** You may have an assigned seat. If you are allowed to choose your own seat, steer clear of anyone who's sneezing, wheezing, or making any sort of bodily noise. No distractions make for better grades! If possible, snag a chair in full view of the clock. (You brought a wristwatch anyway, right?)

- **What to do with your stuff:** You probably have to leave your purse, backpack, and everything but the required writing utensils at the front of the room.

- **Getting the student pack:** When everyone is settled, the proctor distributes the student pack, which may also be called a candidate pack, and gives out answer sheets and question booklets, which are wrapped in see-through plastic. The student pack is basic AP identification. It contains a number assigned to you, and to no one else, for every AP exam that you take — English, math, French, history, whatever. In some schools, the student pack is already on the desk when you enter the testing room. (The pack serves as a place card. Find yours and sit there. It's your assigned seat.)

After you're seated and have your student pack, the proctor will lead you through these steps for filling out the forms:

1. **Peel a label from your student pack and stick it on your answer sheet.**

2. **Fill in the answers to some questions — your name, address, and the like.**

3. **Read a bunch of legal notices and sign on a specific line to indicate that you agree to the conditions set by the College Board.** For example, you're giving the AP the right to investigate if they think you've cheated. Unless you indicate otherwise, you're giving them the right to use your essays in their publications as examples of student work. **Note:** If you'd rather no one but the grader read what you've written, you can decline to give them permission to use your work. Your score will not be affected.

   One crucial legal notice concerns the questions on the exam. Basically, you're *never* allowed to discuss the multiple-choice questions with anyone, ever, even on your 110th birthday. Multiple-choice questions take a long time to write (and I speak as someone who has written many). The College Board wants to be able to reuse questions. So keep your lips sewn shut on this topic or risk having your score cancelled. You can talk about the essay questions after a few days. (They aren't reused, probably because they're much easier to create.)

4. **Copy the form number of the test onto your answer sheet, ensuring that the graders and the grading machine will use the correct answer key.**

5. **Read a few more legal notices — more of the same conditions — and sign your name a few more times.**

After you complete the paperwork, the proctor will instruct you when to begin work on the multiple-choice section. (The essay portion stays sealed.) When the multiple-choice portion is completed, you get a short break and then come back in to complete the essay portion of the test.

> **TIP**
>
> During the exam, listen carefully to the proctor and follow every instruction, no matter how dumb. If the proctor tells you to open the green question booklet, you're in big trouble if you absent-mindedly open the pink answer booklet instead.

Break time

AP break time occurs between the multiple-choice and the essay sections of the test. You get ten minutes. Use it wisely:

- **Keep conversation to a minimum.** Someone inevitably says, "Gee, I wasn't expecting seven B answers in a row," whereupon everyone else immediately plunges into a calculation of how many B answers he or she chose. Then everyone gets nervous for absolutely no good reason. First of all, it doesn't matter how many B answers anyone got. The AP sometimes shuffles the multiple choice around, so your question book may not match someone else's. (That's why you have to copy the form number of your test onto the answer sheet.) Second, who says that someone else's answers are right?

- **Grab some food or a beverage, if you have time to do so without being late for the essay portion of the test.** Don't overindulge. You're about to face 135 minutes of reading and writing, and you don't want to waste any time on trips to the restroom.

- **Stretch, yawn, shake, or do something else that loosens your muscles.** Cramps inhibit brain power. Take care to keep your eyes closed if you're moving your head. Even the appearance of cheating can get you into trouble.

- **When the proctor says to go in, go in.** If you're late, two scenarios are possible. Either you'll hold everyone else up waiting for you, or you'll be barred from the second half of the test.

If disaster strikes

Things happen. Some may be your fault, and some may not. If the test is interrupted by, say, a fire drill, the proctor will report that fact to the College Board. If the proctor can convince the powers-that-be that no one spoke or exchanged information during the interruption, the test may resume and the scores will count. More likely, you'll have to take the test again.

If you have a problem during the test (such as getting sick), you may choose to cancel your score. You can tell the proctor immediately and fill out a cancellation form on the spot. You won't get a refund, but you won't get a bad grade either, because officially, the test didn't happen.

If you can't even make it to the test (you're in the hospital or in a car accident, for example) and you've already paid, inform the AP coordinator. You may be able to take the test at another time or (rarely) qualify for a refund.

AFTER THE EXAM

Yes, I know this chapter is about AP preparation, but I can't resist throwing in a couple of ideas for the post-AP period:

- Keep your mouth firmly sealed if anyone *ever* asks you about the multiple-choice questions. Your test will be cancelled if you talk about them.

- Ditto for the essays, though you have to keep quiet only for a few days after the test. If you talk before the essay questions are released to the public, you're in trouble.

- After the dust of the exam has settled, think about your performance on the test. You may have more APs (in different subjects) to face in the future. Before you forget, make a list of things that should — and will — be different next time. For instance, you may decide to start preparing earlier or later.

> **TIP**
>
> If you think you can do better on the AP English Language and Composition test, you can take it again a year later, as long as you are still under the age of 21 (the official age limit for the AP exam). The colleges will see both scores, but your newer and higher score will show your determination to succeed, a helpful trait when you're applying to college.

If you know you've messed up on the exam, you can request that the College Board withhold your score from the college(s) you listed. They charge $15 for each withheld score, and they must receive a written request within about two weeks of the exam. (The AP coordinator will know the exact deadline.) If you change your mind, you can later — for a fee — send the score to the college(s) of your choice. You can also cancel the score completely. Score cancellation is permanent, however.

2

Tips for Success in AP English Class

> **KEY CONCEPTS**
>
> - Annotation and note-taking of key passages
> - Reading skills and vocabulary-building
> - The components of an efficient writing process
> - The effective use of research sources in position essays
> - An approach to interpreting visual sources

Along with your AP exam score, the grades you earn in your English classes are scrutinized by college admissions officers. Fortunately for you, earning a higher grade in an English class is easy. All you have to do is hone your reading and writing skills, and good grades will follow. Plus, superior skills actually make the work go faster. Even better, the same skills that help you ace English class also lead to a stellar AP exam score.

Think of this chapter as a fitness center. Work your way through each section of this chapter, paying special attention to what trainers tend to call "problem areas."

Note: Because this book preps you for the AP English Language and Composition test, I've tailored my comments to the sort of work you do in an AP English Language course. If you're enrolled in an AP English Lit course or a non-AP English course, never fear. Everything in this chapter will help you also, though here I neglect some areas that don't show up on the AP English Language exam, such as poetry.

ANNOTATION AND NOTE-TAKING

In English class, you study the profound ideas that writers have set down through the ages. You discuss and accept or reject these ideas. Then you express your own view of the topic. In order to study, react, and express, you first have to keep track of what you've read and heard. To accomplish this task, you annotate the text and take notes in class. This section shows you how to improve both of these skills.

Annotation

Your English homework assignment is to read a portion of *Treatises on Old Age and Friendship,* a collection of essays by the ancient Roman Marcus Tullius Cicero. Because you're a good student, you skip the Internet summary and settle down to read. Then you hit your math homework, write a science report, and organize a fundraising drive for your favorite cause. Twenty hours later, you arrive at English class and open the textbook. Cicero's essay looks vaguely familiar, but so much has traveled through your brain since you last saw it that it may as well be in the original Latin (which you never learned). If only you had annotated the text!

Annotation is simply note-taking attached to a piece of writing. To annotate effectively, you have to figure out which portions of the text to spotlight. In general, annotate the following:

- Important lines   • Foreign language
- Anything confusing
- Unfamiliar words
- Everything the teacher refers to during class

Take a look at Figure 2-1 to see an example of homework annotation in action. Notice the four question marks in the left-hand margin. Three refer to vocabulary problems —"par excellence," "sagacity," and "fastidious." As you see, I box vocabulary words. You may prefer to highlight them in a different color. After consulting the dictionary, you can record the definitions in the margins of your text (if you own the book) or add them to your personal vocabulary-building file. (See "Pump Up Your Vocabulary" in this chapter for more information.) If you're reading on an electronic device, you may be able to tap on a word and see a definition. However, you may still wish to keep a record of these unfamiliar words by compiling a vocabulary file that you can study and refer to.

Another question mark indicates a confusing reference to the "Seven Sages." Check "Seven Sages" on the Internet or ask the teacher during class. Add the explanation to your annotated text or to your notebook. Now read the annotations in the right-hand margin. They remind you what's where in the passage, so if the teacher asks you to compare Cato to Laelius, you're all set. Lastly, notice the underlined "main reason" why Laelius is wise — an important statement in the passage.

If you're like most people, you may think everything in the passage seems important enough to annotate. But too much annotation is as bad as no annotation at all. Differentiate between main ideas and supportive explanations or examples when you annotate.

You are quite right, Laelius! there never was a better or more illustrious character than Africanus. But you should consider that at the present moment all eyes are on you. **?** Everybody calls you "the wise" par excellence, and thinks you so. The same mark of respect was lately paid Cato, and we know that in the last generation Lucius Atilius was called "the wise." But in both cases the word was applied with a certain difference. Atilius was so called from his <u>reputation as a jurist;</u> Cato got the name as a kind of honorary title and in extreme old age because of his <u>varied experience</u> of affairs, and his <u>reputation for foresight</u> **?** <u>and firmness,</u> and the sagacity of the opinions which he delivered in the senate and forum. *Why others called "wise"* You, however, are regarded as wise in a somewhat different sense not alone on account of <u>natural ability and character,</u> but also from your <u>industry and learning;</u> and not in the sense in which the vulgar, but that in which scholars, give that title. In this sense we do not read of any one being called wise in Greece except one man at Athens; and he, to be sure, had been declared by the oracle of Apollo also to be "the supremely wise man." For those who **?** commonly go by the name of the Seven Sages are not admitted into the category of the wise *Why Laelius is wise* **?** by fastidious critics. Your wisdom, people believe to consist in this — that you look upon <u>yourself as self-sufficing and regard the changes and chances of mortal life as powerless to</u> <u>affect your virtue.</u> *main reason*

Illustration by Wiley, Composition Services Graphics

Figure 2-1: An annotated excerpt from Cicero's *Treatise on Old Age and Friendship*.

> **TIP**
>
> If you own the book, the easiest way to annotate is to underline, highlight, or circle lines of text and jot down a few words in the margin. If you don't own the book, sticky notes and a notebook or computer file are the way to go. Place a sticky note next to the relevant line. In your notebook or in a computer file, write the page number and a comment. For an e-book, tap "add notes" or a similar command and type your thoughts.

Of course, you annotate during class also. If the teacher or another student mentions a particular point, underline or take note of its location and write a comment. (You don't need to record any student observation that draws a remark like "interesting but irrelevant" from the teacher.)

> **TIP**
>
> Highlighting is fine for homework assignments, but on the AP exam, only blue or black ink is permitted. If your annotation style relies heavily on highlighting (different colors mean different things, for example), practice annotating without a highlighter.

Note-taking

You have to record any important points made during class. Your school may allow laptops, or you may be confined to paper and pen. You can take great notes on anything if you keep a few rules in mind:

- **Listen to the teacher.** If your teacher is a minimalist who says very little during class, write most of what you hear. If the teacher blathers on and on, listen for changes in tone or volume. Most teachers emphasize crucial ideas that way. *Foreign language*

■ **Write whatever is on the board, along with explanatory comments.** You need the comments because some teachers put one word on the board and then speak for ten minutes. If you don't put an explanation next to that word, you end up scratching your head and asking, "*Doughnut? Why did I write doughnut?*"

■ **Pay special attention to anything the teacher reads aloud.** Whatever a teacher reads aloud from the text is important. Write the comment and tie it to the text by underlining or highlighting (if you own the book) or with a sticky note or a few words in your notebook or computer file. Everything in your notebook or computer file should include a page number so that you can check the text as needed. If you're working from an e-reader, highlight the text.

■ **Take notes on any student comment that is met with "good point" or "yes, and . . . ."** Some student comments are excellent; others — not so much. If the teacher indicates that a comment has merit, make note of it.

Note-taking in class is just the first step. Squeeze out a little time after class (no later than the next day) to reread what you recorded. Add ideas you didn't have time to note during class. Because two heads really are better than one, reviewing your notes with a classmate is a good idea. Your friend may have caught something you missed, and vice versa.

> **TIP**
>
> Some people like to take notes on a divided page. The right-hand portion is for the notes and the left for "main idea" comments. For example, in the right margin, you may have "Laelius is virtuous regardless of what happens — self-sufficient, knows who he is, doesn't change." In the left margin you'd write, "why Laelius is wise." The left margin is more or less a subhead for the right side of the page. Generally, the ideas in the left margin are added later, but the process can go either way. If the discussion is moving along at a fast pace, write the main idea on the left. Later, add details on the right.

CLOSE READING

To extract everything that's present in the text you read for your class, you have to expend a little effort and do what English teachers call "close reading." One of my colleagues referred to this process as "engaging in an extended conversation with the author." The conversation varies, but it probably includes this sort of exchange:

READER: Nice point about freckles. But why are you making such a big deal about the beach umbrella?

TEXT: As the beach umbrella slowly sagged into the sand, I saw my childhood slip away.

READER: Oh, now I get it. The umbrella symbolizes protection. Without protection, the child is vulnerable.

TEXT: The sunburn, according to the doctor, probably led to my mother's bout of skin cancer.

READER: So that's why you're advocating more funds for cancer research!

When you "converse" with the text, you inevitably begin to ask why. Why is this detail included? Why does the information about the beach umbrella appear in the first paragraph instead of later? Why "slip away" and not "end"? Why mention cancer? Answering these questions, you comprehend more. As an added benefit, close readers also learn a lot about writing style. A crucial element of the AP English Language and Composition exam and any advanced English class concerns the choices authors make and the effect of those choices on the reader. Such an analysis helps you answer questions about others' writing and improves your own writing as well.

The content

The material on the AP English Language and Composition exam is almost exclusively nonfiction, so I concentrate on that type of literature in this section. However, most of the reading techniques I describe here also apply to prose fiction and, to some extent, to poetry and drama also.

When you read, follow these steps to improved reading comprehension:

1. **Figure out the surface meaning.** If any words or references are unfamiliar, look them up. Untangle long sentences so that you know the subject, verb, and object or complement. (For more grammar information on subjects, verbs, or other grammar points, turn to Chapter 6.)

2. **Pay attention to punctuation.** Punctuation tells you a lot, such as which ideas are linked together, when someone's exact words appear, and when the writer injects doubt with a question mark or drama with an exclamation point.

3. **Check out the pronouns.** Can you substitute a noun for every pronoun? Pay particular attention to "this," "which," "that," and "it." If you zoom past one of those pronouns without figuring out its *antecedent* (the word the pronoun replaced), you may misinterpret the meaning.

4. **Go "between the lines."** Most writers don't state every idea because they assume that you can infer quite a lot. For instance, suppose the passage tells you that an army greatly outnumbered the opposing forces, but soldiers were hampered by an insufficient number of weapons. You may infer that some soldiers were inexperienced. Why? If there aren't enough arms to go around, some of the fighters were new recruits.

5. **Interpret figurative language.** Check for metaphors, symbols, and anything else that resides in imagination territory. When you encounter figurative language, explore its meaning. (I tell you more about figurative language in Part II.)

6. **Characterize the intended audience and purpose.** To whom is the author writing? How do you know? What sort of reaction does the author want? How does the author provoke that reaction?

7. **Restate what you've read in simpler terms.** After you finish Steps 1–6, it's time to put it all together. Talk to yourself, explaining what you've understood. Before moving on, be sure you've grasped everything.

Writing style

After you've got content under control, take a moment to think about writing style. Some elements of writing style overlap with content, of course. However, the way in which something is written — what the AP test makers call *rhetorical technique* or *rhetorical devices* — matters. Follow these steps to appreciate the author's style:

1. **Examine the structure.** What comes first, last, and in-between? Can you figure out the logical thread? A work of literature may be organized chronologically or spatially (moving through a room from right to left, perhaps). It may use comparison or a cause-effect structure, among other organizing principles.

2. **Consider word choice and tone.** An athlete may appreciate being called "muscled" but not "steroidal." "Striding" across a room differs from "strolling" or "stomping." Word choice points you toward *tone,* the "sound" of the author. (Confused about tone? Check out Chapter 3.)

3. **Identify building blocks.** Does the author rely on a ton of description or a couple of anecdotes to get the point across? Has the author drawn on source material? If so, which sources?

4. **Check out sentence length and patterns.** Victorian writers are famous for marathon sentences — some a page or more in length. Hemingway frequently employed short, stabbing sentences. The dominant pattern for all writers is subject-verb-object. Has this writer varied from that pattern? What effect does the variation have on the reader? (Chapter 6 can help you identify sentence elements.)

5. **Think about why the author made particular style choices.** Identifying the elements of an author's style isn't enough. You must consider the effect of the author's choices on the reader. To put it another way, how do style and content relate to each other?

Sounds like a lot, I know. But if you get in the habit of reading this way, you won't need much — if any — extra time. You're changing the way you read, not how much you read. Remember, if you close read, your understanding of the work will rise like a rocket (and so will your English grades!).

PUMP UP YOUR VOCABULARY

The literary works you encounter in an advanced English course prepare you well for the level of vocabulary on the AP English Language and Composition exam. But most of the new words from class readings enter your *passive vocabulary.* You recognize them when you see them in context, but you don't know them when they're alone (for example, in a multiple-choice answer). Furthermore, you can't easily plant them in a sentence of your own, where they're part of your active, usable vocabulary. And the more words you have at your disposal, the better you'll do in English class and on the AP exam.

Happily, you can move words from passive to active vocabulary with very little effort by making a personal dictionary. The dictionary can be on index cards, in a computer file, on an e-reader (if yours has the ability to compile a list), or in a notebook. To create the dictionary, follow these steps:

1. **Write down or tag the unfamiliar word and the sentence it appears in.** If the sentence is long, just write enough of the surrounding words so that the context is clear.

2. **Define the word or, on an e-reader, call up the definition.** Most words have several definitions. Concentrate on the one that fits the context of the sentence. Also, feel free to reword the definition. The dictionary is formal, but you don't have to be.

3. **Note the part of speech.** If it's a noun, you don't want to mistake it for a verb and use it incorrectly. (Check Chapter 6 for grammar help.)

4. **Jot down the word's "family."** Most dictionaries list other forms of the word, so you can pick up a whole word "family" with one shot. For example, "motivation" may be accompanied by "motivate" and "motivated." If examples are given, jot down enough to distinguish between one form and another.

5. **Review what you've written.** Yes, this is the hard part. But if you never look back at your personal dictionary or word list, you'll never remember the words in it. You don't have to devote a lot of time to this project. Once a week, spend 15 minutes flipping through your dictionary. Concentrate your energy on words you've forgotten. Read the words, the context, and the definition. The context helps you remember the meaning of the word and guides you in your own writing.

A subsection of AP-level vocabulary involves literary terminology. You can list these terms in your personal dictionary, but you don't have to. In this book, literary terms are italicized and defined immediately.

TIP

Anything that brings you into contact with words helps build your vocabulary. Do a daily crossword puzzle, play Scrabble with a strong opponent, and watch television shows in which people discuss things. Read a good newspaper or magazine. From all these sources, add words to your personal dictionary.

TIP

You can also build your vocabulary and enhance your comprehension by reading Greek myths. The stories are great, and many authors refer to them — in shorthand — in their writing. If you know Greek mythology, you can decode references to someone's "personal odyssey" or a promotion that's the "apple of discord" in an office. (Have I stumped you? Odysseus, a Greek hero, wandered for 20 years from the Trojan War back to his home in Ithaca and had many adventures along the way. So a "personal odyssey" implies a long, eventful journey — either literally or figuratively. The "apple of discord" was labeled "for the fairest" and rolled into a bunch of goddesses. You can imagine the ensuing fight!)

WRITING: PROCESS MAKES PERFECT

Every advanced English class includes a heavy dose of writing, and an AP English Language and Composition class is no exception. According to College Board guidelines, an AP English Language and Composition class teaches you to write about a variety of subjects, including "public policies, popular culture, [and] personal experiences." You're expected to write "narrative, expository, analytical, and argumentative" essays and base some of your writing on research from several sources. Furthermore, the course includes informal writing (responses to the reading, journal entries, and the like). Last — and most important — an AP English Language and Composition course must focus on writing as a process of gathering and organizing ideas, drafting, and revising.

Even if your English class doesn't carry the AP label, chances are the teacher stresses writing process. And if the teacher doesn't, you should because that's what writing is — a set of steps that carries you from idea (or assignment) to a piece of polished prose. If you short-circuit these steps, you end up with a less-than-your-best product. In this section, I take you through the process, step by step.

Gather and group ideas

When homework is hanging over your head, you want to get it over with. Understandably, you're eager to start writing so that you can move closer to the finish line. (If you're writing with a time limit on the AP exam, the pressure to pour words on the page is even higher. I address timing issues in Chapter 15.) However, you can't know what you're writing about until you get your thoughts on the paper. You see, writing is a form of thinking. (One writer once remarked that she wrote because "I don't know what I think until I've read what I said.") When you jot down every idea — good, bad, irrelevant, or crucial — you see what's in your brain. Then you can pick and choose which ideas to include in your paper.

You can accomplish a "brain dump" in any of several ways. In my experience, one of the following three methods works for everyone, and the best method is the one that fits the writer's personality. Which one is right for you? Test-drive whichever seems most attractive. If that one doesn't fit, try all three and choose the one you like best.

Listing

Very organized people love listing. Just take a blank sheet of paper or open a new file on your computer. Make a list of all your ideas on the topic. As you list, don't worry about the order in which an idea appears. You can move things around later. Also, forget about spelling and complete sentences and all the other conventions of English. Just concentrate on content. After you've listed everything that comes to mind, go back over your list. A couple of ideas won't be useful; cross them off. Then group the remaining ideas into logical subtopics. You don't have to rewrite or spend an hour cutting and pasting. Just label similar ideas with a letter — one group is A, another B, and so on. These groups are your subtopics.

Free-writing

To free-write, pour your mind onto the paper for a few minutes. Concentrate on the topic, but don't censor yourself if you drift away a bit. Just gently refocus. Though you're writing in paragraph style, for a little while don't worry about grammar, spelling, or even logic. Just write. Don't stop to think and don't go back to reread what's there until your free-writing time is up. (About 10 or 15 minutes is plenty, but even 5 minutes will do.) When your time's up, read your work. Every time you find a useful idea, underline it. When you finish reading, assess what's there. If you don't have enough to get started on the assignment, free-write again, focusing on the most interesting underlined portions of your previous free-write. Then go back and underline the new stuff.

When you have enough material, mentally sort the underlined phrases into subtopics. Label everything in one subtopic with the same letter (A, B, C, and so on).

Clustering

Some people, especially those who are visually oriented, create a cluster — a kind of word picture in which similar ideas are linked on the page. To create a cluster, write the topic in the center and circle it. Then write every idea that comes into your mind around the center. If a couple of ideas emerge at the same time, place them near each other. If a new idea pops up, place it somewhere else. When you're done, use circles and arrows to connect ideas. Then label the connected ideas, using A for one group, B for another, and so on.

Check out Figure 2-2 for a cluster based on Cicero's *Treatise on Old Age and Friendship,* which appears in Figure 2-1. Imagine that the assignment was to define true wisdom, reacting to Cicero's ideas. As you see, "inner reality" is linked to "actions" and "career." "Many definitions" connects to "Laelius different," and "Laelius different" is tied to three phrases: "inner directed," "my own definition," and "inner & outer." The letter-labels show you the logical groupings. One subtopic contrasts definitions of wisdom arising from what a person does ("actions" and "career") with a character-based definition ("inner directed"). Another potential group considers alternatives ("many definitions"). This point connects to Cicero's description of Laelius ("inner directed") and the writer's own definition of wisdom, which apparently includes both "inner & outer" qualities.

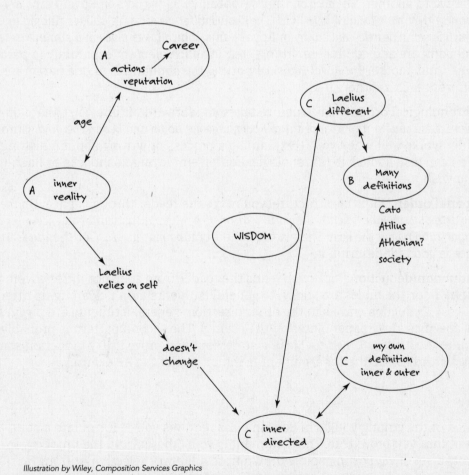

Illustration by Wiley, Composition Services Graphics

Figure 2-2: A cluster based on an excerpt from Cicero's *Treatise on Old Age and Friendship.*

Organize the information

I'm not a big fan of the traditional outline (with roman numerals, capital letters, and progressive indentations), because I tend to spend more time worrying about the format than the logic behind it. I do like an informal outline (everything I intend to say, grouped the way I want to say it, without frills) when I have time to make one. Regardless of how it looks, an outline forces me to create a logical thread to tie my ideas together. A logical thread, by the way, creates the *structure* of a piece of writing.

Many threads are possible, once you know what to look for. Consider your options when you're writing and choose the one that best fits your information:

- **Cause and effect:** This structure describes action and reaction or event and consequence: *Cutting down the cherry orchard ruined the presidential hopes of Georgie Washington because he had no way to prove his truthfulness ("I cannot tell a lie . . .").* This structure works nicely if you're arguing for or against a particular policy or explaining why something happened.

- **Comparison and contrast:** When you compare and contrast, you consider one thing relative to another: *The docs on Grey's Anatomy and the docs on Royal Pains are alike because they have tangled love-lives. The shows differ because it's always raining in Grey's, which is set in Seattle, and sunny in Royal Pains, which takes place in a summer resort.* You can compare and contrast anything, treating each element separately (a paragraph for *Grey's* and another for *Royal Pains*) or putting the similarities in one paragraph and the differences in another.

- **Chronological order:** This structure takes you forward in time: *First Marco threw a pie, then Louisa caught it and flipped it to Roger, who sat down and began chewing.* Chronological order works well when you're explaining a process or writing about a historical event. (You can also fiddle with chronological order, employing flashbacks or flash-forwards, if you wish.)

- **Spatial order:** With this structure, you move the reader through space: *On the right is the drum stand, which gently supports a drumstick. Moving eastward you encounter a drum-major, tapping out the beat. She's in front of thirty tuba players . . ..* Get the idea? This structure is good for description.

- **Induction/deduction:** Induction leads the reader from specifics (litter covers the cafeteria floor, the tables are sticky) to general (students aren't cleaning up after themselves). Deduction travels in the other direction: general (students are piggy) supported by specifics (dirty paper plates on the ceiling). The second pattern is probably the one you're most accustomed to: Make a statement and prove it. Try induction sometime; it's a sturdy structure for argument (a major part of the AP exam).

> | **TIP**
>
> Much of the writing you do in English class requires you to formulate a statement that you prove true. The statement is your "thesis," and the proof is generally a set of supporting points drawn from a literary selection or from real life. For a detailed description of how to create a thesis statement, turn to Chapter 15.

You may come up with a different organizing scheme. Good for you! Just be sure your structure supports the ideas you're conveying to the reader.

Draft and revise

When you know the content and order of your essay, it's time to draft. The computer is ideal for this task because the machine allows you to rewrite easily, but pen and paper are fine, too. (If you're writing by hand, skip lines so that you'll have room to make changes.) The point about creating a series of drafts is that the first one is *never* the last. No writer is that good! During round one, work your way through each subtopic and create an introduction and conclusion if they're appropriate to the type of piece you're writing. (Some informal tasks — journal entries or responses to the reading — don't require introductions and conclusions.)

> **TIP**
>
> If you have writer's block, leave some space and write the easiest subtopic first. You can always go back to the introduction or to another subtopic.

After the first draft is complete, reread what you wrote, changing as you go. Every writer I know hates revision, but every piece of writing needs it. Think of the piece you're working on as a custom-made suit. No matter how much you measure beforehand, when you try on the suit for the first time, it will sag in one spot or pull in another. A little adjustment pays off. It's the same thing with your paragraphs. Because you were thinking about content, you probably didn't display your very best style in the first draft. So make another draft, and, if needed, still another. Check these points:

- **Mechanics:** This includes spelling, grammar, and punctuation.

- **Sentence style:** Are all your sentences the same length? Consider combining a couple to make a longer sentence. Just be sure to use a conjunction — words such as "and," "while," "but," and the like — or a semicolon. Also look at sentence patterns. Too much of one pattern is boring. For example, if you have a series of ideas joined by "and," add a little variety by inserting a participle. You can change "He prepared dinner, and he used up all the eggs" to "Preparing dinner, he used up all the eggs." (If you're grammar-challenged, Chapter 6 is for you.)

- **Clarity:** One of the hardest tasks for any writer is differentiating between what's on the page and what's inside the writer's brain. An outside editor helps here, because no editor can read what you meant to say, only what you actually said. But you can act as an editor, too, especially if you edit a few days after writing the first draft (or a few hours). The interval between writing and editing allows you to see the work with fresh eyes. Try to spot places in which you haven't been perfectly clear.

  Many writers fall into the ambiguous-pronoun trap, explaining that "Mary told her sister that she had to text her dogwalker." Who has to text? Whose dogwalker? The way the sentence is written now, Mary may need to text or Mary's *sister* may be the one with itchy fingers. Check your pronouns and see Chapter 6 for help.

- **Redundancy:** Don't repeat yourself. Saying the same thing twice is annoying to the reader. Go back over your draft and cross out anything you've already said.

- **Specifics:** Generalities have a place in writing, but specifics make your writing come alive. Suppose you're writing about public funds and athletic arenas. Your position is that professional sports enhance the economy, so the expenditure of tax dollars is warranted. Those statements are fine. However, isn't it more interesting to read about a specific team and its recently constructed stadium? Wouldn't you want to know how much money taxpayers spent on the stadium and what they got in return?

> **TIP**
>
> *Revision* literally means "seeing again." When you see something again — really see it — you may need to tinker with it or you may have to perform major surgery. If your draft falls into the second category, don't be afraid to wield a scalpel. Sometimes the first draft is merely a way to think about the topic. The second draft (which you'll also revise) is where the writing actually occurs.

ENGLISH CLASS RESEARCH

According to the College Board, AP English Language classes must teach a "researched argument paper" that "includes the analysis and synthesis of ideas" from several sources. Furthermore, students in AP English Language courses must learn how to cite sources. (These skills are tested in the synthesis essay. See Chapter 15 for more information.) Just about all English courses, AP or not, include short research assignments as well — to find out how a word's definition has changed through the centuries, to compare critical views of a particular work, to present a position on a current issue, and the like.

As a writer and a teacher, I spend part of every day on research. I'm always glad to learn something new, so the information I dig up isn't a problem. But the path to that information sometimes contains a few potholes. A few basic skills, which I discuss in this section, smooth your way.

Where to look

When I started my writing career, I zoomed from library to library by subway, borrowing books and photocopying magazine articles in branches of the New York Public Library. I peered at microfilm (be thankful that you'll never have to know what microfilm is) and spent days turning dusty pages of decades-old newspapers. Now when I have a research project, I sit at the computer, bouncing from library to library without moving more than my mouse-click finger. When I need a magazine or newspaper article, I find it online. I still take books out of the library for research, but life has gotten much easier — in most ways.

The hard part of 21st century research is the sheer volume of information available. So much is out there that you can drown in material very quickly. To make matters worse, some of the stuff that pops up when you're researching electronically is complete drivel. Anyone can set up a web page and pretend to know something.

The first task of a researcher, therefore, is to look in places that are likely to contain quality material. Some suggestions:

- Electronic databases (JSTOR, Lexis-Nexis, Facts-on-File, and the like) provided by a school or public library generally screen out subpar material.

- Articles in nationally recognized periodicals (major newspapers such as *The New York Times* and magazines such as *Scientific American,* for example) are reliable.

- The Internet Public Library (http://www.ipl.org) is a gateway to sources that have been approved by experts in the field.

■ Websites with "edu" or "gov" in their URL (the site's "web address") are generally trust-worthy. The first type comes from an educational institution, and the second from the government.

■ Websites maintained by nationally recognized organizations are usually okay. Many of these contain "org" in their web address. I say "usually" because some organizations are nationally recognized because they hold crackpot views. Others are biased in favor of certain points of view and may not report findings or publish articles that oppose those views. When in doubt, ask your teacher or a librarian. These professionals will help you evaluate various sources.

I should say a word about Wikipedia. Lots of good material has found its way into the Wikipedia, the so-called "people's encyclopedia," which may be altered by Internet users whether they know what they're talking about or not. Recheck information you find there, if possible. Click on the source notes to read (and evaluate) the original information.

Specific search terms

After you've got the sites (which may include a catalogue of paper-and-ink sources), how do you find what you want? You search, carefully and specifically. Too broad a search is useless. Enter "climate" into a database, for example, and you'll get thousands — even millions — of hits. You have to narrow the search so the results are manageable.

Most databases and library catalogues break topics into subtopics. The general topic of climate, for example, yields a hundred or so subtopics: "climate change," "climate in the United Kingdom," and so on. Electronic databases usually have an advanced search button that brings up a screen allowing you to add some search terms ("climate" and "warming," for instance) and exclude others. If you're researching the effect of global warming on agriculture, you may search for "climate," "warming," and "agriculture."

TIP

Can't find what you're looking for? Try another term. In the preceding example, substituting "change" for "warming" may give you what you need.

Citizen whats?

The College Board says that a goal of the AP English Language course is to create "citizen rhetors." You're probably wondering what a "rhetor" is. Like much of our civilization, this concept traces its lineage to ancient Greece. Citizens there were expected to learn *rhetoric,* the art of expressing ideas clearly and persuasively. They were also expected to use their rhetorical skills to better society. Nowadays, the word "rhetoric" is often paired with the adjective "empty," with the phrase "empty rhetoric" describing writing or speeches that sound great but have no real content. A *citizen rhetor,* in the classical *and* in the AP sense, knows how to read and evaluate information, formulate a point of view, and effectively deliver the point of view to the audience or reader.

Source information

When you're writing a paper based on research, it's crucial to record where you found ideas and information and to cite your sources in the final draft. (I explain how to cite sources in Chapter 12.) If you present someone else's stuff as your own, you commit the worst academic crime — plagiarism. And in most schools, ignorance is no excuse for the law. Depending upon your school's policy, you may fail the assignment or the course or be suspended or expelled.

> **TIP**
>
> Scared? Don't be. If you're not sure what to cite or how to cite, your teacher will help. And the best strategy is simple: When in doubt, ask.

Keeping track of source material is easy. As you take notes, record this information:

- Author(s)
- Title (if it's an article, include the article title and the name of the periodical)
- Publication date, place, and company
- Page number, if possible (articles on the web may not have page numbers)
- URL or database of electronic sources and the date accessed
- Broadcast or release date (for television shows or films)
- Date of the interview or conversation (if your source is a person)

For a short paper, you may not bother to take notes and may opt to work directly from the books or articles covering your floor or from the websites saved under "favorites." Cut the time spent reviewing your sources by creating a short table of contents. As you research, note the URL or title and author of the work on a piece of paper or in a computer file. Add a phrase and a page number (if the pages are numbered) so that later you know what's where. Here's an example:

> *Kong,* p. 3 – grabs blond
>
> *Kong,* p. 122 – falls from Empire State Bldg.

> **TIP**
>
> Creating a table of contents goes even faster if you give each source a number. Then you'd write "3, p. 3 – grabs blond" if your third source is entitled *Kong.* Keep a master list of sources and the number you assigned to each.

VISUAL SOURCES

A 21st-century citizen is bombarded with advertisements, illustrations, photos, charts, and graphs — not to mention pop-ups on the computer. You should be able to interpret this material when you run across it and to use it in conjunction with your own writing whenever it's relevant. I discuss visual sources as they appear on the AP English Language and Composition exam in Chapter 7. Here I briefly explain how these sources show up in your English class and how you can get the most out of them.

Your teacher may assign a visual source or a source that includes visuals. Some graphic autobiographies, for instance, have become staples of many English classes — Marjane Satrapi's *Persepolis* and Art Spiegelman's *Maus,* for example. Or you may wish to incorporate visual sources in a research paper, particularly one that presents a point of view and doesn't simply report information. An assignment on a controversial issue, for example, may benefit from an analysis of television commercials arguing one side or the other.

When you encounter a visual source, keep these points in mind:

- **Consider the whole.** The entire source probably has an overall message or effect. Can you restate that message in your own words? If not, the source probably isn't helpful.

- **Don't neglect details.** Small elements mean a lot. For example, a public service announcement about body image begins with a shot of several girls walking across the street. One lags behind and stares at the viewer. Next a series of clips from commercials selling beauty products appears. The message is that parents should help their daughters appreciate their own beauty and not be swayed by commercials telling girls to be dissatisfied with their appearance. Many details in this sequence are effective. One stands out in my mind: The girls are crossing the street. The visual suggests danger (little kids are usually escorted across the street by adults) and sets up the idea that protection is needed.

- **Listen as well as look.** Obviously you can't listen to a chart or a still photo. But if you're working from an audio-visual source such as the public service announcement described in the preceding bullet point, the audio portion is also important. The image of the girls in the public service announcement is accompanied by a Beatles song. The line "here it comes" is repeated several times. The volume increases with each repetition, adding a sense of urgency. The underlying message — get to your daughter before the beauty industry does — is enhanced by the audio track.

- **Interpret.** Don't stay on the surface. Dig for the significance of what you're seeing. If you see a chart of homicides, for example, think about what the chart tells you and what the implications are. Is the crime rate increasing? Decreasing? Is the rate uniform for all age groups or for all areas?

Images must be cited in your source list, just as written material is. Presenting information *of any kind* without crediting the source is a plagiarism.

II

The Writer's Toolkit

3

Writing's Building Blocks: Words

KEY CONCEPTS

- Connotation
- Diction, tone, and attitude
- Figurative language
- Imagery

Writing involves more than having a great idea (though creativity is always an asset). Writing involves knowledge of *rhetoric*, the art of communicating clearly and persuasively. This chapter focuses on the smallest building blocks of writing — words and phrases and the rhetorical techniques that apply to them. As you analyze rhetoric, you improve your own writing *and* prepare yourself for the AP exam.

BEYOND THE DICTIONARY: CONNOTATION

If your word-processing program resembles mine, a couple of mouse clicks takes you to the *thesaurus*, a handy reference that provides synonyms for any given word. But the thesaurus works from dictionary definitions, so it usually deals only with the literal meaning, or *denotation*, of words. Denotation is half the story; to wring every nuance from a word and the passage it appears in, you've got to pay attention to *connotation* also. Connotation is the term for all the emotions and associations linked to a word.

To grasp the importance of connotation, examine these two statements. Which one would you like to hear as you arrive home two hours past curfew?

> Aren't you resourceful! You found the key hidden under the doormat.

> Aren't you sneaky! You found the key hidden under the doormat.

The variables in the preceding sentences — "resourceful" and "sneaky" — are both synonyms of "clever." However, the first statement isn't as likely to lead to two weeks' house arrest as the second, because "resourceful" has a positive connotation and "sneaky" a negative one. Similarly, my dictionary reports that "bright" and "cunning" may also substitute for "clever." I'm sure you can imagine a "bright" student receiving an award at graduation, while a "cunning" student gets 15 days of detention for hacking into the teachers' e-mail accounts.

Knowing connotation is crucial to using a word correctly. When you learn vocabulary from a list (not the best way to build vocabulary — see Chapter 2 for suggestions), you can't always distinguish one synonym from another. You end up calling someone "emaciated" when you mean "slim." ("Emaciated" connotes illness. "Slim" is what dieters aim for.)

Connotation is sometimes explained in the dictionary, but true understanding of connotation generally comes when you encounter the word in context, especially if you run across it several times. Thus, the reading you do for English class, your other courses, or your own interest and entertainment helps you with connotation, as do everyday conversations with literate people (those who speak or write in an educated way).

TIP

> If you're not sure of the connotation of a particular word, substitute another. Does the meaning shift? If so, you may have a clue to its connotation. For example, you can accurately call me either "old" or "experienced." I prefer the second term. In our youth-oriented media, "old" carries baggage; it connotes something out-of-date, not vigorous or relevant. "Experienced," on the other hand, connotes wisdom.

When you're reading an AP passage, either for the multiple-choice or the essay portion of the test, pay attention to connotation. Connotation is a tunnel to the deeper meaning of a passage. For example, imagine you're reading a paragraph about a "blameless" person. "Blameless" removes any suggestion of guilt, but it doesn't go beyond neutral territory. There's no blame, but there's no nobility either. Perhaps the author is hedging; you have to decide how well the "blameless" person behaved. Now imagine that you're reading a paragraph about a "worthy" person. Usually "worthy" shows up when someone merits appreciation, a reward, a promotion, or anything else that's positive. The definition, or denotation, of both "blameless" and "worthy" is decency, but the connotation of "worthy" distinguishes it from "blameless."

Here's how connotation can matter in an AP-like context. Take a look at this short passage from Harriet Jacobs's magnificent account of her escape from slavery, *Incidents in the Life of a Slave Girl, Written by Herself:*

> O, you happy free women, contrast your New Year's day with that of the poor bondwoman! With you it is a pleasant season, and the light of the day is blessed. Friendly wishes meet you everywhere, and gifts are showered upon you. Even hearts that have been estranged from you soften at this season, and lips that have been silent echo back, "I wish you a happy New Year." Children bring their little offerings, and raise their rosy lips for a caress. They are your own, and no hand but that of death can take them from you.

Notice the word "estranged." The dictionary reports that "estranged" means "separated." The connotation of "estranged," however, adds an element of bad feeling. The word leans towards "alienated" or "not on speaking terms," whereas "separated" may refer to a purely physical gap. You probably guessed this connotation because of the context, even if the word wasn't already in your vocabulary. Estranged hearts "soften at this season, and lips that have been silent echo back, 'I wish you a happy New Year.'" The message is clear: At holiday time, fences are mended.

Now take a look at "showered" in the same passage. Maybe because human beings are dependent on water, "showered" always has a positive connotation. You can be showered with gifts, as the "happy free women" are in this passage, but not with sorrows. Sorrows, however, can "rain" down on someone. Maybe these differing connotations arise from the way everyone reacts to showers (good for growing things) and rain (flooding, bad hair, squishy shoes). Showers are also natural events; in Jacobs's passage, the word "showered" implies that it's natural for "happy free women" to receive gifts.

Connotation is helpful when you're answering AP vocabulary-in-context questions. The process works in two ways. If you know the connotation, the context is clearer. If you don't know the word (connotation or even denotation), the context may help you decipher it anyway.

ANALYSIS OF DICTION, TONE, AND ATTITUDE

Diction means the words a writer chooses. You deal with diction when you analyze a writer's selection of the verb "demanded" instead of "begged" or "asked," for example. (Often, the choice of one word instead of another depends upon connotation. See the preceding section for more information about connotation.) When you move beyond one word to examine a pattern of word choices, you can characterize the diction as formal, informal, straightforward, witty, ironic, and so on.

Tone is a little more complicated to define. Tone expresses mood and attitude (a stance in relation to a particular person or situation). Tone is created by the words used (diction), the way they're put together (syntax), and the content expressed. Attitude is expressed through tone and content. In this section, I give you guidelines for examining the diction, tone, and attitude of any piece of writing to help you prepare for questions about these elements on the AP test.

Diction

Without knowing the term, you're probably already clued in to diction. In fact, I'm betting that you know how to adapt your own diction to circumstances. For instance, suppose you're talking with a teacher: "May I be excused?" you ask politely, adding that you "haven't yet completed the history research paper" he assigned. A moment later you're talking with a friend: "Gotta hit the library. I'm swamped by that history thing." These two situations illustrate the shift in diction that people make automatically, every day — in fact a hundred times a day. The first exchange is an example of formal diction; the second illustrates colloquial, or conversational, diction.

Close attention to diction pays off; diction clues you in to subtleties of meaning, the author's purpose, and a host of other things. When you're reading a passage on the AP, zero in on any unusual words. Give an extra glance to the verbs and nouns, because these words carry so much weight in writing. Look for patterns. Are all the words simple, or do you have to have the dictionary memorized to get through the paragraph? Is there any slang? Also, consider other ways the author might have said the same thing. Then try to determine how choices the author made affect meaning.

Take a peek at these two passages and analyze the diction. Passage One is an excerpt from Richard Henry Dana's *Two Years Before the Mast*. Passage Two is drawn from *Paul Volcker: The Making of a Financial Legend*, by Joseph Treaster (Wiley, 2004; reprinted with permission of John Wiley & Sons, Inc.).

Passage One:

This was a black day in our calendar. At seven o'clock in the morning, it being our watch below, we were aroused from a sound sleep by the cry of "All hands ahoy! a man overboard!" This unwonted cry sent a thrill through the heart of every one, and, hurrying on deck, we found the vessel hove flat aback, with all her studding-sails set. . . . The watch on deck were lowering away the quarter-boat, and I got on deck just in time to fling myself into her as she was leaving the side; but it was not until out upon the wide Pacific, in our little boat, that I knew whom we had lost. It was George Ballmer, the young English sailor, whom I have before spoken of as the life of the crew.

Passage Two:

Shortly after flying back to Washington from a conference in Tokyo on the international oil crisis, Carter decided to address the nation on July 5, 1979. He spent much of the Fourth of July at Camp David, the Presidential retreat in the Catoctin mountains of Maryland, working on the speech. Late in the day he canceled the talk and decided not to return to the White House.

Can you see that the diction in Passage One is much more extreme than the diction in Passage Two? Two is straightforward; the words convey little emotion. The verbs and nouns ("decided," "spent," "nation," "talk," and so on) are plain vanilla. You can imagine hearing Passage Two on the news or reading it in a textbook. Passage One has ornate diction, especially the verbs and nouns. The cry sent a "thrill" on a "black day." The narrator doesn't jump into the boat, he "fling[s]" himself in. Ballmer isn't just popular; he's the "life of the crew." This passage might show up on one of those breathless, historical re-enactment shows.

>   **TIP**
>
> Diction is related to the writer's purpose. The purpose of Passage One is to bring the reader into the experience, to convey the heartbreak of death at sea. The author of Passage Two wants to impart information. The neutrality of the language leads me to believe that the author wants readers to form their own judgments about Carter's actions.

Tone

Tone is obvious when you're listening to a real person speak aloud. But when all you have is text, the words used (diction) and the way the words are put together (syntax) help you "hear" the words and determine tone.

Context (and content) matters also. For example, imagine that you're reading a passage about a group of teenagers. Alexa tells her friend Sam that he aced a French test. Sam replies, "Right." If the passage reports that Sam studies less than a second a week and considers a D– an achievement, the word "right" is probably a wisecrack, and the tone is sarcastic. If Sam's been studying 25 hours a day, desperate to pass French, "right" may be a fist-pumped-into-the-air statement of triumph.

Here's another excerpt from Harriet Jacobs's autobiography, *Incidents in the Life of a Slave Girl, Written by Herself*. To catch the tone, take note of diction, syntax, and content:

> But to the slave mother New Year's day comes laden with peculiar sorrows. She sits on her cold cabin floor, watching the children who may all be torn from her the next morning; and often does she wish that she and they might die before the day dawns. She may be an ignorant creature, degraded by the system that has brutalized her from childhood; but she has a mother's instincts, and is capable of feeling a mother's agonies.

First, consider diction. You find "creature," "degraded," "brutalized," and "instincts." "Creature" can refer to human beings, but more often it's associated with animals. Slavery has treated this mother as if she were an animal — one that's "degraded" (pushed down) and "brutalized." This last word also connects to animals (which are sometimes called "brutes"). Also, animals are said to operate mostly on "instincts." When you add all these ideas together, you see that Jacobs's diction stresses the dehumanizing effects of slavery. Another significant word is "torn," which adds an element of violence to her description of the slave mother's situation. Tearing isn't a gentle act; Jacobs's diction emphasizes the pain of an enslaved mother, whose children may be "torn" from her at any moment.

Syntax, the way words are put together grammatically, also matters here. I discuss syntax at length in Chapter 4. Here I'll just point out that "often does she wish" is an unusual pattern. Because you expect to see "she often wishes," the rearrangement highlights "often" and emphasizes the slave mother's constant desperation.

Last, consider content. The subject is a "mother," and most people have strong reactions to that status. Love her or hate her, she's still a mother and, by definition, connected to her children. But this mother may lose her children, and all have been treated badly ("brutalized") their entire lives. The mother considers death a blessing. By referring to the system and not to a particular slave owner, Jacobs places blame on the institution of slavery, not just on one cruel slave-owner.

Add up the diction, syntax, and content. No doubt about it: Jacobs's tone is critical and passionate.

Here's another passage that provides great tone-hunting material. It's excerpted from a 19th-century book written by a missionary about his experiences with Native Americans. Zero in on diction and content:

> The iron horse rushes and shrieks where the Indian trail was once the only pathway. The picturesque garb is fast disappearing, and store clothes, often too soon transformed into rags anything but picturesque, have robbed the Indian of the interest that once clung to him.

Though the excerpt is short, the content is easy to grasp. The author compares Native American life before and after the railroad (the "iron horse") arrived. The reference to "horse" sets up a comparison, because real horses are associated with Native Americans. Diction, too, leaps out at you when you read this passage: The verbs "rushes" and "shrieks" are both extreme, so already the message is that something big has happened. A "shriek" also connotes fear or pain. Non-Native Americans, who built and operate the railway, are associated with those negative qualities, while Native Americans are linked to a simple word — "pathway." A "pathway" leads somewhere or gives you easier transit. It doesn't "rush" and "shriek." Similarly, "picturesque" clothing is contrasted to "store clothes." The "store clothes" turn into "rags." From this writer's point of view, traditional is better.

Overall, how would you characterize the tone of this passage? The words are carefully chosen; you can imagine them in a sermon (the writer's a missionary) or a lecture. Also, the writer isn't neutral. He's taking a rather extreme stand. I'd go for "formal" and "dramatic" or even "nostalgic." Also, the last few words of the passage comment that "store clothes . . . have robbed the Indian of the interest that once clung to him." Because those words depict Native Americans as a kind of living tourist attraction, the passage takes a patronizing tone at the end.

> **TIP**
>
> Tone isn't always simple or uniform. As you see in the preceding example, a tone may shift or may contain layers of meaning. The missionary expresses dismay at the changes in Native American culture because of non-Native American influence, but the dismay is expressed in a condescending way. Furthermore, some tone questions on the AP exam provide paired answers ("nostalgic and patronizing," for example). Be sure that both answers fit the passage before you make a choice.

Attitude

Once you know the tone, a tiny step takes you to the author's attitude (what the author believes or feels). In an issue-oriented passage, attitude shows up when the author or a person mentioned in the passage is in favor of or against a particular position.

Take a look at this excerpt from President John F. Kennedy's inaugural address:

> The world is very different now, for man holds in his mortal hands the power to abolish all forms of human poverty and all forms of human life. And yet the same revolutionary beliefs for which our forebears fought are still at issue around the globe — the belief that the rights of man come not from the generosity of the state but from the hand of God. We dare not forget today that we are the heirs of that first revolution.
>
> Let the word go forth from this time and place, to friend and foe alike, that the torch has been passed to a new generation of Americans, born in this century, tempered by war, disciplined by a hard and bitter peace, proud of our ancient heritage and unwilling to witness or permit the slow undoing of those human rights to which this nation has always been committed, and to which we are committed today, at home and around the world.
>
> Let every nation know — whether it wishes us well or ill — that we shall pay any price, bear any burden, meet any hardship, support any friend, oppose any foe, to assure the survival and the success of liberty. This much we pledge, and more.

Kennedy's attitude comes at you like a trumpet blast: He's in favor of human rights, and he's willing to use America's power to secure those rights around the world.

> **TIP**
>
> In a multiple-choice question, you may be given a set of adjectives ("critical," "sympathetic," "ambivalent," and the like) to characterize the attitude of the author toward a defined issue. Kennedy's attitude, as expressed in the preceding excerpt, is "favorable" or even "militant" in regard to human rights.

In a narrative or descriptive passage, the author has an attitude, as do any people or characters mentioned in the passage. The author's attitude may be complex; he or she may be nostalgic when describing the setting and critical when depicting how people act there. You determine attitude by comprehending the meaning (content) of the passage and by noticing diction, tone, and other rhetorical devices.

Here's a short narrative paragraph from Samuel Pepys's diary, written in the 17th century:

> Thanksgiving-day for victory over the Dutch. To the Dolphin Tavern, where all we officers of the Navy met with the Commissioners of the Ordnance by agreement, and dined: where good music at my direction. Our club come to 34 shillings a man, nine of us. By water to Fox-hall, and there walked an hour alone, observing the several humors of the citizens that were there this holy-day, pulling off cherries, and God knows what. This day I informed myself that there died four of five at Westminster of the plague, in several houses upon Sunday last, in Bell-Alley, over against the Palace-gate: yet people do think that the number will be fewer in the town than it was the last week.

Pepys's attitude is patriotic, as is the attitude of the celebrants in the Dolphin Tavern — the "officers of the Navy" who were dining and listening to "good music" on "Thanksgiving-day for victory over the Dutch." The citizens at "Fox-hall" are also celebrating, so it's easy to put them in the "anti-Dutch" column. Pepys reports that "people" have an optimistic attitude toward the plague ("yet people do think that the number will be fewer in town than it was the last week"). The word "yet" adds a hint of doubt; Pepys himself may not be quite so optimistic as the "people" he mentions.

Connotation and diction lead you to tone, and tone takes you to attitude. Content, of course, is related to all three rhetorical devices.

A FOCUS ON FIGURATIVE LANGUAGE

Figurative language lives in the land of imagination. Poetry is chock-full of figurative language, but nonfiction writers have passports to imagination-land also. (Not literal passports — metaphorical ones. See? I'm writing nonfiction, and I can play around with language too.) You probably know many elements of figurative language. If I listed all of the ways figurative language shows up in writing, this section would be a hundred pages long. So I've limited myself to the most common terms:

- **Metaphor:** An indirect comparison, written without "like" or "as." The famous line from the Peanuts comic strip, "happiness is a warm puppy," is a metaphor. An *extended metaphor* keeps the metaphor going. For example, if I follow the Peanuts statement with a paragraph about cuddling up with happiness and worrying that happiness will dash away when the gate is open, I'm using an extended metaphor.

- **Simile:** A direct comparison, written with "like" or "as." These similes describe the AP English Language and Composition exam: It's "as interesting as reading the phone book" and "like oozing brain cells."

- **Metonymy:** A substitute name, but not a nickname. Metonymy shows up when something associated with a person substitutes for the name of the person, as in "a spokesman for the Oval Office." In that phrase, "Oval Office" subs for the name of the current president of the United States.

- **Synecdoche:** Another substitute name. This time, the part represents the whole, as in "the hand that rocks the cradle rules the world." "Hand" subs for "mother."

- **Personification:** Human qualities given to a nonhuman. The earth is personified in this sentence: "The earth was my mother; I listen ever with my ear close to her lips."

- **Allusion:** A reference to a well-known work of art, pop culture, or history. The allusion is brief, but all the feelings associated with the referenced element come into the reader's mind. If the student-council president ends a speech with a statement that students are entitled to "life, liberty, and the pursuit of a five on the AP," the president is alluding to the Declaration of Independence, calling forth the spirit of rebellion embodied in that document. The allusion also implies that a good score on the AP is a basic human right.

- **Hyperbole and understatement:** Deliberate exaggeration and minimization, generally for a comic effect. If you have "a ton of papers to write" you're using hyperbole. If Nobel Prize names are announced and a winner responds, "Not bad," he or she is employing understatement.

- **Apostrophe:** A literary term meaning an address to an absent person or quality. "Dear Reader" and "O Melancholy" are examples of apostrophe.

Figurative language, like everything in the writer's toolkit, works only when it goes hand-in-hand with content. Good writers don't drop a metaphor into a paragraph unless the metaphor enhances meaning. When you're reading AP-level literature, the figurative language is there for a reason. Your job is not only to identify the figure of speech but also to analyze its effect.

Read this excerpt of an essay about Jonathan Swift. Check out the figurative language, and think about its effect on the passage:

> The war had transformed parties into factions, and the ministry stood between a Scylla of a peace-at-any-price, on the one side, and a Charybdis of a war-at-any-price on the other; or, if not a war, then a peace so one-sided that it would be almost impossible to bring it about. In such troubled waters, and at such a critical juncture, it was given to Swift to act as pilot to the ship of State.

This small paragraph contains two examples of figurative language. First, the author makes an *allusion* to Scylla and Charybdis, two monsters of Greek mythology that guarded the narrow body of water between Italy and Sicily. Scylla had six heads and an appetite for sailors; Charybdis was a whirlpool that sucked in ships. The allusion (if you know the myth) explains how awful the pro- and antiwar factions were in Swift's day; no choice was ideal, to put it mildly. The description of Swift as a "pilot to the ship of State" is a metaphor that works nicely with the allusion. By bringing in another nautical reference, the author illustrates how difficult Swift's task was, because piloting a ship between Scylla and Charybdis was no picnic.

Here's one more example paragraph designed to sharpen your figurative-language skills. This excerpt is from Charles Dickens's *Great Expectations*. The narrator is a young boy named Pip who is running from his home, carrying food and wine he stole. Can you identify the similes and what they contribute to the passage?

> I had seen the damp lying on the outside of my little window, as if some goblin had been crying there all night, and using the window for a pocket-handkerchief. Now, I saw the damp lying on the bare hedges and spare grass, like a coarser sort of spiders' webs; hanging itself from twig to twig and blade to blade. On every rail and gate, wet lay clammy; and the marsh-mist was so thick, that the wooden finger on the post directing people to our village — a direction which they never accepted, for they never came there — was invisible to me until I was quite close under it. Then, as I looked up at it, while it dripped, it seemed to my oppressed conscience like a phantom devoting me to the Hulks [prison ships].

The first simile is "as if some goblin had been crying there all night." A goblin is a magical, dangerous creature. Little children are especially susceptible to magical thinking, so this simile emphasizes Pip's youth. The goblin was "crying there all night." Pip's sad too, as readers know from earlier chapters of the novel. But even without reading other parts of *Great Expectations*, the simile gives an idea of Pip's mood. The next simile — "like a coarser sort of spiders' webs" — echoes the trapped situation of the narrator. Spiders catch prey in their webs, and Pip is afraid that he too will be caught. The final simile is "like a phantom devoting me to the Hulks." Pip says his conscience is "oppressed," or guilty. The simile mentions prison ships. The guilt Pip feels is strong enough to merit imprisonment.

Identifying figurative language is worth the time and effort only if you associate this rhetorical device with meaning, as I've done in the preceding paragraph.

SENSORY APPEAL: IMAGERY

The best writers (and everything you read for the AP comes from the best) are open to the world. No matter how dry the material, great writers observe carefully and later tuck some of that observation — *imagery*, in literary terminology — into their work. Just to be clear, when I talk about imagery, I mean sensory information. Imagery includes description of sights, sounds, smells, tastes, and feelings (the kind you get through your skin, not emotions). These concrete details call upon everything you've experienced through your physical body.

Imagery overlaps with figurative language (metaphors, similes, and other rhetorical devices I discuss in the preceding section). Any figure of speech that appeals to the senses may properly be called "imagery."

Time to examine imagery. Check out this excerpt from an account of an Alaskan cruise:

> On the upper deck, a lady, clad in warm cloak and thick veil, walked tirelessly to and fro. A big stump-tailed dog of the Malamute tribe at times followed at her heels, but when she had patted his head and spoken kindly to him he appeared satisfied, and lay down again with his head between his paws. Then sounds from the dancers below, the shrill laughter of the women mingled with the strum of the banjo and the wheezy accordion, seemed to disturb the dog's slumber, and he would again pace up and down at the lady's heels. At times there would come a lull in the tumult, and the click of the glasses or crash of a fallen pitcher would make a variety of entertainment for the lady and her dog on the upper deck; but the short and dusky midnight was well passed before the dancing ceased and partial quiet and order were restored.

The entire passage presents visual imagery, including the lady "in a warm cloak and thick veil" who "walked tirelessly to and fro." You see her pat his head, the dog asleep "with his head between his paws," and "short and dusky midnight" pass. The paragraph is also filled with sounds: "shrill laughter," "the strum of the banjo," "wheezy accordion," a "lull," the "click of the glasses," and the "crash" of the pitcher, followed by "partial quiet." The sense of touch is also represented by the "warm cloak," because you sense temperature through your skin.

Because the author of this travelogue is a good writer, imagery contributes to her meaning. You see the lady and wonder about her solitude and restlessness. You experience her link with the dog, who — unlike her — can rest at times. The sounds are all distant, emphasizing that the lady is alone. Everyone else ("the dancers below") seems to be having a good time (though "shrill" laughter may indicate forced merriment). The "warm cloak and thick veil" also separates the lady from others. She's wrapped in her own world, perhaps protected from the weather and from something else as well. As you see, the author zeroed in on details that convey mood and character — exactly the job of imagery.

Try your imagery-analysis skills on another travel memoir, this time Charles Dickens's account of his voyage to America. Note what you see, hear, smell, taste, and feel. (Of course, all five senses may not be present in every passage.)

> The gloom through which the great black mass holds its direct and certain course; the rushing water . . . the men on the look-out forward, who would be scarcely visible against the dark sky, but for their blotting out some score of glistening stars; the helmsman at the wheel, with the illuminated card before him, shining, a speck of light amidst the darkness, like something sentient and of Divine intelligence; the melancholy sighing of the wind through block, and rope, and chain; the gleaming forth of light from every crevice, nook, and tiny piece of glass about the decks, as though the ship were filled with fire in hiding, ready to burst through any outlet, wild with its resistless power of death and ruin. . . . My own two hands, and feet likewise, being very cold, however, on this particular occasion, I crept below at midnight. It was not exactly comfortable below. It was decidedly close; and it was impossible to be unconscious of the presence of that extraordinary compound of strange smells, which is to be found nowhere but on board ship, and which is such a subtle perfume that it seems to enter at every pore of the skin, and whisper of the hold [interior of the ship].

Did you note the "gloom," the "great black mass" of the ship surrounded by "rushing water," the lantern that's only "a speck of light" in the darkness where "some score of glistening stars" were blotted out? All this imagery is visual. Did you pay attention to the "sighing of the wind" and Dickens's "very cold" hands and feet? Those phrases stem from the senses of hearing and touch. The sense of smell is in this paragraph also, in the description of the atmosphere inside the ship, where "strange smells" get into your pores.

Dickens's imagery conveys his mood. Outside, Dickens is "filled with fire in hiding" which may "burst . . . wild." Inside, the air is "close." In this context, "close" refers to stale air, a meaning reinforced by the statement about the smells that "whisper" into your skin. You don't have to think long before you realize that Dickens's imagery illustrates how trapped he feels when he's inside the ship and how much energy and "fire" he has inside himself, just waiting to get out. Overall, Dickens's imagery creates a sense of sadness. Just look at the "gloom" and "melancholy," as well as the "cold" and the tininess of the "speck of light" in contrast to the "great black mass."

When you're reading, and especially when you're analyzing a work of literature for the AP, be attentive to imagery. Don't just notice its presence; concentrate on its effect on the meaning of the work. Besides mood, imagery may also reveal attitude, characterization, and other elements of a work of literature.

4

Sentences and Paragraphs

> ## KEY CONCEPTS
>
> - The relationship between syntax and meaning
> - Effective paragraph structures
> - The effect of point of view

ave you ever seen cotton candy made? That delicate process, in which a thread of sugar as thin as air whirls onto a stick, has always reminded me of writing. The candy emerges bit by bit, much like my own sentences. And when the stick is full, the candy-maker breaks the thread and starts a new stick, in the same way I finish one paragraph and start another. In this chapter, I examine the "threads" of sentences and paragraphs, taking a close look at the way they're made. I show you how words fit together grammatically, discuss various sentence types and patterns, and introduce the most common paragraph structures. I also briefly discuss analyzing point of view and persona.

THE SECRET OF SYNTAX

The ability to unravel *syntax* — the grammatical relationship of words to each other — is incredibly useful on the AP exam, where it's questioned in both multiple-choice and essay format. An understanding of syntax also strengthens your own writing, especially when you grasp common sentence patterns and what happens to meaning when sentences diverge from the norm.

Note: In this section, I use some basic grammar terminology. If you need a refresher, turn to Chapter 6.

Sentence patterns and variations

Think about the game "Duck Duck Goose." Children sit in a circle while one runs outside, tapping one child after another on the head and saying "Duck" — and then suddenly tapping someone as the "goose." The point of this game isn't the duck-duck pattern, it's the goose pattern-break. The variation catches everyone's attention. I mention this childhood game because writers play "Duck Duck Goose" with their sentences. Things flow along in one pattern, and then something new happens, and the reader perks up.

Subject-verb-complement: The norm

Nearly every English sentence has a subject-verb-complement configuration at its core. Think of these S-V-C sentences as the "duck duck" of the game I describe earlier:

Eleanor smacked Tracy. (*subject* – Eleanor, *verb* – smacked, *complement* – Tracy)

Tracy was annoyed. (*subject* – Tracy, *verb* – was, *complement* – annoyed)

Tracy is also a police officer. (*subject* – Tracy, *verb* – is, *complement* – police officer)

If the sentence asks a question, the common pattern places the subject between two parts of the verb:

When will Eleanor finish her jail term? (*verb* – will finish, *subject* – Eleanor, *complement* – jail term)

Of course, sentences may be much more complicated than I illustrate here. You can throw in all sorts of things — descriptions, extra explanations, and qualifiers, for example. However, even long-winded sentences almost always have a *subject-verb-complement* skeleton or the standard question pattern. (Complements, by the way, aren't essential, but they're present most of the time.)

Unusual sentence patterns

Now that you've seen ordinary "duck duck" sentences, it's time for some "goose." Check out these sentences, written in unusual word order:

Through the entire parole hearing with a smile on her face sat Eleanor. (*verb* – sat, *subject* – Eleanor, no complement)

An amazing account of her jail experience wrote Eleanor. (*verb* – wrote, *subject* – Eleanor, *complement* – account)

Tracy hated the book, did she not? (First part: *subject* – Tracy, verb – hated, *complement* – book. Second part: *verb* – did, *subject* – she, no complement)

The effect of changing the usual sentence pattern is small but significant. In the first sentence the focus is on the description of Eleanor ("Through the entire parole hearing with a smile on her face") because the description is the first thing you see. The middle sentence is similar, but in the opening, attention-getting spot, it has a complement as well as descriptions ("An amazing account of her jail experience"). The last sentence begins normally and then veers into question territory. The second half is almost a sneak attack, striking an accusatory tone.

Another variation of the normal sentence pattern starts off with a word that looks like a verb (because it expresses action or being) but acts like a description. The grammar term for this hybrid is *verbal*. You don't need to know that term for the AP exam, but you should know how verbals function. Here are two examples:

> **Appealing to the judge, Tracy requested a share in the profits.** (*verbal* – appealing to the judge, *subject* – Tracy, *verb* – requested, *complement* – share)

> **To achieve closure, Eleanor offered 10 percent.** (*verbal* – to achieve closure, *subject* – Eleanor, *verb* – offered, *complement* – 10 percent)

The descriptive verb forms ("appealing" and "to achieve") catch your attention by virtue of their location. Extra attention brings a sense of importance to the act of "appealing" in the first example and to the reason why Eleanor offered 10 percent ("to achieve closure").

 TIP

When you're analyzing an AP passage, remember that variety is a spotlight. Also, insert these elements into your own writing to make your sentences less monotonous and to showcase important ideas.

Distinctive sentence patterns

Most great writers have distinctive sentence patterns that can be identified easily. Jane Austen likes to start out in one direction and then hang a quick U-turn. Two of her gems:

> Lady Lucas was a very good kind of woman, not too clever to be a valuable neighbour to Mrs. Bennet.

> The village of Longbourn was only one mile from Meryton; a most convenient distance for the young ladies, who were usually tempted thither three or four times a week, to pay their duty to their aunt and to a milliner's shop just over the way.

See the pattern? Austen starts out with a statement that sounds positive. "Lady Lucas was a very good kind of woman" and "the young ladies . . . were tempted thither three or four times a week, to pay their duty to their aunt." Just when you're settling in for something sweet, Austen hits you with the bad stuff: Lady Lucas was "not too clever" to outshine the dumb Mrs. Bennet, and the "young ladies" were actually shopping for hats at the milliner's. The U-turn pattern heightens the humor and also underlines Austen's message that things are not always what they seem.

You can also recognize an Ernest Hemingway sentence from a mile away. Here's a tiny bit of his story "A Clean, Well-Lighted Place":

> They sat together at a table that was close against the wall near the door of the cafe and looked at the terrace where the tables were all empty except where the old man sat in the shadow of the leaves of the tree that moved slightly in the wind. A girl and a soldier went by in the street. The street light shone on the brass number on his collar. The girl wore no head covering and hurried beside him.

Hemingway's pattern is to hit you with a long sentence and then send a couple of short ones your way. This configuration places extra emphasis on the short sentences.

Periodic and loose sentences

A *complex sentence* contains at least two ideas. The main idea usually shows up in an independent clause, a subject-verb expression that makes sense all by itself. Another idea turns up in a *dependent,* or *subordinate, clause* — a subject-verb expression that isn't complete in and of itself. A *periodic sentence* starts with a dependent clause and goes on to the main idea. A *loose sentence* is the exact opposite: The main idea comes first, followed by dependent or subordinate clauses. (For a refresher on grammar terms, turn to Chapter 6.)

Look at these periodic and loose sentences:

> **When Tracy's royalty check arrived, she bought Yankee tickets.** (periodic)
>
> **The Yankees were in first place when Tracy attended a game.** (loose)
>
> **Although she has always been a Cubs fan, Eleanor watched the game on television.** (periodic)
>
> **Eleanor watched until Tracy smacked Derek Jeter.** (loose)

Why should you care whether a sentence is periodic or loose? In a carefully crafted work, the pattern affects perception of meaning. In a periodic sentence, you have to wait for the main act. You're getting some information, but you have a sense that after a couple of taps, a punch is coming. In a loose sentence, the opposite is true. You know the main idea right away, but you stick around for some extra information. In both periodic and loose sentences, the most important statement nearly always resides in the independent clause and less important information in dependent clauses *unless* the writer is purposely reversing the pattern for comic effect, as in this example:

> While the mushroom cloud ended life on earth as we know it, Felix was shaving.

Because the important information is in a dependent clause instead of in its usual place (the independent clause), Felix comes across as clueless, apathetic, pathetic, or all of the above.

TIP

Here's a trick to help you remember the difference between a periodic and a loose sentence: In a periodic sentence, you have to wait for a *period* of time before learning the main idea — unless the author's reversed the usual order, as I explain previously. In a loose sentence, you can *loosen up* right away because you know the main idea immediately.

You may see one or two multiple-choice questions about periodic or loose sentences on the AP exam. Usually these terms show up in the answer choices. If you're writing an analysis essay (see Chapter 15 for more information), you may mention periodic or loose sentences if — and only if — you relate these patterns to meaning.

Parallelism

Parallelism is the principle that brings unity and balance to a sentence. Elements of a sentence are parallel if they have the same grammatical identity (all nouns, perhaps, or all subject-verb combinations) and if they all perform the same function. Sentences are parallel if they're constructed with the same syntax.

A great example of a parallel sentence is the famous opening of Charles Dickens's *A Tale of Two Cities*:

> It was the best of times, it was the worst of times, it was the age of wisdom, it was the age of foolishness, it was the epoch of belief, it was the epoch of incredulity, it was the season of Light, it was the season of Darkness, it was the spring of hope, it was the winter of despair, we had everything before us, we had nothing before us, we were all going direct to Heaven, we were all going direct the other way — in short, the period was so far like the present period, that some of its noisiest authorities insisted on its being received, for good or for evil, in the superlative degree of comparison only.

If you inhale deeply and read that sentence aloud, you immediately hear the parallel elements. All the "it was _____" and "we had _____" clauses are balanced. In other words, they're parallel. The parallel elements place everything on the same level of importance. It wasn't "the best of times" except for a few snags. Nor was it "the worst of times" with a few redeeming features. It was both, equally. And "we" are filled in the same measure with hope and despair, goodness and evil. These qualities are unified by parallelism, and the sentence structure deems them equal in measure and importance.

Besides being a prime example of parallelism, the Dickens sentence expresses a *paradox* — something that appears to contradict itself. It's also an example of *antithesis* — a rhetorical device in which opposites are expressed in parallel elements.

Try your hand at some rhetorical analysis. Here's a passage from President John F. Kennedy's inaugural address. **Note:** Kennedy took office in 1961, during the Cold War. The expression "both sides" in the passage refers to the United States and the Soviet Union. Can you find the parallelism and determine its effect on meaning?

> So let us begin anew, remembering on both sides that civility is not a sign of weakness, and sincerity is always subject to proof. Let us never negotiate out of fear, but let us never fear to negotiate. Let both sides explore what problems unite us instead of belaboring those problems which divide us. Let both sides, for the first time, formulate serious and precise proposals for the inspection and control of arms and bring the absolute power to destroy other nations under the absolute control of all nations. Let both sides seek to invoke the wonders of science instead of its terrors. Together let us explore the stars, conquer the deserts, eradicate disease, tap the ocean depths, and encourage the arts and commerce. Let both sides unite to heed in all corners of the earth the command of Isaiah to "undo the heavy burdens, let the oppressed go free."

Kennedy's "let us . . . *verb*" sentences are parallel, and they reinforce his message: that both sides must act. The "let us" sentences place equal weight on their contents: a new start, negotiation, exploration of problems, formulation of solutions, scientific exploration and research, and freedom for the oppressed. Kennedy had a big agenda, strongly expressed. The parallelism of the long sentence ("Together let us explore . . . commerce") hammers home the message: Don't pick only the agenda items you like. Everything on his list must be addressed with the same intensity.

Kennedy's famous statement from the same speech, "Ask not what your country can do for you — ask what you can do for your country" is an example of *inverted parallelism,* also known as *chiasmus.* The two "ask" statements mirror each other, but they express opposite ideas — selfishness and selfless patriotism. You don't have to know the literary terms, but you should be able to point out their effect, which is to show the listener or reader two contrasting paths, one of which is clearly better. *Chiasmus,* by the way, comes from the Greek word "chiazein," meaning to mark with a chi. If you picture the Greek letter chi (X), you literally see several possible paths, as at a crossroads. The content and structure of Kennedy's statement reinforce each other.

Punctuation matters

When you're analyzing an AP sentence or when you're writing an essay, pay attention to punctuation. Two common punctuation marks, the semicolon and the colon, have a role in sentence patterns. A semicolon (;) links two independent clauses that are closely related in meaning. This punctuation mark, according to science writer Lewis Thomas, is a bench that you can rest on when you're climbing up a hill. Because a semicolon is a pause but not a stop, it should never be inserted between ideas that don't connect in an obvious way. For instance, it's fine to link "it was raining" and "the picnic was postponed" with a semicolon because the reader can see the cause-and-effect relationship. However, "it was raining" shouldn't be joined to "I may study archaeology" with a semicolon (or with anything else, for that matter) because the statements have nothing in common.

A colon (:) often introduces a list, but it can also join two independent clauses when the second is an explanation of the first, as in "Joshua studied far too intensely for his AP English Language test: He spent two weeks alone with nothing but an English book and a coffee pot." The second independent clause, the one that follows the colon, always begins with a capital letter.

Parallelism is such an important rhetorical technique that faulty parallelism — a sentence that aims for parallel but falls short — is a grammar error that detracts from your writing. If you have a list of items, be sure that everything on the list has the same grammatical identity. (If grammatical identity is a mystery to you, turn to Chapter 6 for help.)

PARAGRAPH CONSTRUCTION

Most paragraphs are organized around the placement of a *topic sentence,* which states the main idea of the paragraph. The topic sentence may be anywhere, but most often it's the first or second sentence. The second most common placement is last, with "middle" occurring only rarely. Some paragraphs, such as those containing dialogue, description, or narration, don't have topic sentences. Dialogue is divided by speaker; every time the speaker changes, the paragraph breaks, so no topic sentence is necessary (or appropriate). Descriptive paragraphs may list details in spatial order, moving from left to right or from up to down, and so on, without an "overview" topic sentence. Narrative paragraphs usually follow chronological order; they frequently lack a topic sentence summing up the action.

Locating the topic sentence and understanding the way in which information is organized around it come in handy on the AP exam. The exam graders expect to see well-organized paragraphs in your essay. Also, the exam makers place questions about paragraph structure in the multiple-choice section.

Topic sentence first

Paragraphs that explain (expository paragraphs) and paragraphs that present an argument almost always begin with a topic sentence. So do some narrative or descriptive paragraphs.

Here's an example of a topic-sentence-first pattern. This paragraph comes from Cecilia Cleveland's memoir, *The Story of a Summer:*

> The little play-house, that has since been removed to the croquet-ground, once stood not far from this rock, and has been used, as I said, by Gabrielle as a menagerie for her pets. A strange assortment they often were for a little girl. Inheriting her mother's exquisite tenderness of feeling towards helpless animals, Gabrielle would splinter and bandage up the little legs of any baby robin or sparrow that had met with an accident from trying its wings too early, would nurse it till well, and then let it fly away. At one time she had in the play-house a little regiment of twelve toads, a red squirrel, and a large turtle. Aunt Mary never wished her to cage her pets, as she thought it cruel; consequently they had the range of the play-house, and Gabrielle fed them very conscientiously. She ought, however, to have followed the example of St. Francis, who used to preach to animals and insects when he had no human audience, and given her pets a daily dissertation upon brotherly love and tolerance, for they did not, I regret to say, live together in the Christian harmony that distinguished Barnum's Happy Family. The result was, that one day when Gabrielle went to minister to their physical wants, she found only a melancholy débris of little legs. Her supposition was that the turtle had consumed the toads and then died of dyspepsia, and that the squirrel had by some unknown means escaped from the play-house, and returned to primeval liberty.

The topic sentence of this expository paragraph ("The little play-house . . . for her pets") immediately orients the reader to the content of the paragraph. You know right away what you're going to hear about — Gabrielle's "menagerie" (zoo). Everything that comes after that first sentence simply piles on the detail — how Gabrielle played nurse to her animals, what kind of animals were there, how some of the animals ate each other, that the turtle died, and so forth.

You may also see these patterns in a topic-first paragraph:

- **The topic sentence asserts an arguable point ("Parakeets are great pets").** The rest of the paragraph supports the point ("Parakeets can learn to talk, they're very friendly, their food is cheap," and the like).

- **The topic sentence defines a process ("Parakeet training is only possible when the bird trusts you").** The rest of the paragraph lists further steps in the process ("First, place your hand in the cage. Next, touch the bird's foot," and so on.)

- **The topic sentence explains an event ("My pet laid an egg").** Succeeding sentences describe parts of the main event ("She refused to sit on the egg, I put the egg in an incubator, the egg didn't hatch," etc.).

- **The topic sentence starts with a general description ("The cage was quite luxurious").** Subsequent sentences add detail ("Six carved perches rested on the left side," "the back wall was mirrored," and so forth).

- **The topic sentence defines a situation ("My parakeets like table scraps").** The rest of the paragraph gives examples ("One nibbled at pizza, another loved tuna fish, my current bird is crazy about lettuce," and the like.)

Topic sentence in the middle

A topic sentence plopped into the middle of a paragraph is rare, but some writers use this pattern with great success, usually to build suspense or to signal a shift of some sort.

Can you find the topic sentence and determine its role in the following paragraph, an excerpt from a memoir?

> I have said that I used to lie. I recall no particular occasion when a lie was the cause of my disgrace; but I know that it was always my habit, when I had some trifling adventure to report, to garnish it up with so much detail and circumstance that nobody who had witnessed my small affair could have recognized it as the same, had I not insisted on my version with such fervid conviction. The truth is that everything that happened to me really loomed great and shone splendid in my eyes, and I could not, except by conscious effort, reduce my visions to their actual shapes and colors. If I saw a pair of geese leading about a lazy goose girl, they went through all sorts of antics before my eyes that fat geese are not known to indulge in. If I met poor Blind Munye with a frown on his face, I thought that a cloud of wrath overspread his countenance; and I ran home to relate, panting, how narrowly I had escaped his fury.

The topic sentence, as you probably figured out, is "The truth is that everything that happened to me really loomed great and shone splendid in my eyes, and I could not, except by conscious effort, reduce my visions to their actual shapes and colors." This topic sentence perfectly describes the temperament of a writer; everything's exaggerated because that's how Mary Antin, the author, viewed life. Now examine the paragraph further. Preceding the topic sentence are a series of generalizations about her "habit" of adding "detail and circumstance" to her experiences. Following the topic sentence are two examples of Antin's exaggeration: the geese and their "goose girl" and a blind man who was frowning. The topic sentence marks a shift between general and specific.

> **TIP**
>
> When you start a "middle-topic-sentence" paragraph, you may be a little unsure about the direction the author's taking you. You may pass right over the topic sentence and only realize where it was when you reach the end of the paragraph. When you're in that situation, ask yourself *why* the author kept you in suspense. The answer to that question tells you a lot about the author's purpose — often a question in the AP multiple-choice section. For example, Antin's paragraph is designed to win you over. Lying is usually considered a moral flaw, and Antin herself calls it a "disgrace." Having established that she lies and understands the immorality of her actions, Antin goes on to justify them by explaining that she couldn't "reduce [her] visions to their actual shapes and colors." Had she begun with that statement, the reader would probably find it easier to dismiss her. But once she's got you on her side, she can hit you with her main point. Then she can continue with her life story, including the exaggerated presence of the goose girl and "Blind Munye."

A topic-sentence-in-the-middle paragraph may also have these characteristics:

- **Preceding the topic sentence may be a series of examples.** The topic sentence begins a reflection on those examples or an explanation of their significance. (This pattern is the reverse of the one in Mary Antin's comments on lying.)

- **The topic sentence may mark a shift from cause to effect.** The paragraph begins with a description of some event or circumstances. Following the topic sentence is a description of the outcome of the event or reaction to the circumstances.

- **The paragraph may present a problem and its solution.** The topic sentence links the two.

Topic sentence at the end

Some writers like to keep you in suspense, constructing paragraphs that end with the main idea.

Check out this slice from Joseph B. Treaster's *Paul Volcker: The Making of a Financial Legend* by Joseph B. Treaster (Wiley, 2004; reprinted with permission of John Wiley & Sons, Inc.). Just before this paragraph, the author describes a financial downturn during the Carter presidency. Readers learn that President Jimmy Carter asked for, and received, resignations from his cabinet and how he went about replacing some of these officials. Just after this paragraph is a discussion of Paul Volcker's appointment to the position of Chair of the Federal Reserve. Now examine the last sentence. Can you see its role in the paragraph?

> [President] Carter first turned to David Rockefeller, the chairman of Chase Manhattan Bank. When Rockefeller declined, Carter approached A.W. Clausen, the chairman of the Bank of America. Clausen also said no. Finally, Carter contacted Miller, who was in San Francisco making a speech. While finance professionals had criticized Miller, the head of the supposedly apolitical Federal Reserve, as being too sensitive to the needs of the White House and too much of a team player, the Carter administration saw those qualities as virtues. When Carter asked Miller to take charge of Treasury, he did not hesitate. Now Carter had an opening at the Fed [the Federal Reserve].

Even without my explanation of what comes before and what follows this paragraph, you can see that the paragraph builds, step by step, to the last line. First you hear that Rockefeller declined the position. Next, you learn that A. W. Clausen said no. Now you're with Miller, whose faults and/or advantages (depending upon your point of view) are listed. Lastly, you find out that Miller took the job, and — the punch line — that Miller's position gave Carter an opening at the Fed. The last sentence gives meaning to everything else in the paragraph.

A topic-sentence-ending paragraph has these qualities:

- It builds to a climax.

- It leaves the reader with a strong main idea, perhaps preparing the reader for the information that is yet to come.

- It may take the reader through a process or on a logical path. Because the reader has traveled with the author, the situation or issue is clear.

> **TIP**
>
> AP exam questions about this kind of paragraph often ask you the function of the sentences at the beginning of the paragraph. The answer, one of the multiple-choice options, is something like "to explain the opening at the Fed" (in the case of the preceding example) or "to describe the situation leading to _____" (with a few words from the topic sentence in the blank).

Transitions

Before I leave the topic of paragraphs, I should say a word about transitions. The sentence you just read, by the way, is a transition. I've been talking about paragraphs, I will be talking about transitions, and this sentence mentions both. It forms a link in the chain between one paragraph and another.

When you read AP passages (or anything else), transitions help you tag along with the author. Transitions resemble one of those talking global positioning systems. You hear, "Turn left at the next light." The driver (the author) turns left, and the passenger is ready for the new direction because the GPS (the transition) has given advance notice.

Transitions may be single words or, like the sentence at the beginning of this section, they may be multiple-word comments about what has gone before and what is about to appear. Regardless of length, they play an important role in the logical structure of the paragraph and of the piece as a whole. Here are some of the most common words or phrases used as transitions, as well as their role. Keep an eye out for them!

- **Chronological (time order):** before, after, since, while, during, along with, even as, still, continuing, going on, then.

- **Cause and effect:** because, therefore, thus, hence, consequently, as a result of, so that, in order to.

- **Contrast or change of idea:** nevertheless, by contrast, in comparison, on the other hand, opposing, rebutting, disagreeing, yet, however.

- **Continuing with the same idea:** also, further, furthermore, moreover, as well as, in addition to, not only/but also, too.

> **TIP**
>
> Transitions are important in your own writing, too. Your AP exam grader expects to see a logical structure in your free responses. Transitional words help the grader follow your logic.

THE AUTHOR'S POINT OF VIEW

For an English teacher, *point of view* has two separate but equally important meanings. Point of view may refer to the way a passage is written (using "I" or "we" or talking about a subject impersonally). The same term applies to the ideas held by the author or by people or characters in the work. In this section, I show you both roles in action.

Writing style

Pronouns are the easiest way to get a handle on point of view, when the term refers to writing style.

First-person point of view

First-person point of view is the "I-me-my" or "we-us-our" point of view. In this book, I've been using first person freely, injecting myself into almost every paragraph. I have lots of company; many memoirs, autobiographies, letters, speeches, and fictional works are written in first person. First-person point of view has several effects on the reader:

- **It's very personal.** Only one person can say "I" with that unique meaning. When you hear "I," you encounter a specific individual and see things from his or her point of view.

- **It links the reader to the author.** The reader functions as a sidekick, standing next to the hero (the "I") in the midst of the action or discussion.

- **First-person establishes a voice.** You "hear" the author talking to you.

The "I" in a work of literature or even in nonfiction isn't necessarily the author. Because authors pick and choose what to tell you — and how to tell you what they want you to know — they manipulate the reader to some extent. Therefore, literary analysis generally refers to the *persona* in the text, not to the author. The term *persona* acknowledges an element of artistic shaping. Other terms that put a bit of distance between author and subject are *narrator* (for prose works) and *speaker* (for poetry).

Second-person point of view

First-person can show up all by itself, without any acknowledgment of the reader's existence. However, sometimes it goes hand-in-hand with second-person point of view, the "you-your" construction. In this book, second-person pops up all over the place, because I'm trying to speak directly to you. Generally, second-person point of view is rare, but it does exist, particularly in letters and speeches — two formats you may encounter on the AP exam. Keep these ideas in mind when you meet up with second-person point of view:

- **Because second-person point of view connects directly with the reader, consider the intended audience when you read a second-person piece.** What is said to the reader gives some idea of the reader's personality, beliefs, and issues.

- **This point of view implies immediacy.** Whatever is discussed is happening right now, or you're being pulled into the past to experience whatever the author is describing or stating.

- **This point of view has risks too.** If the author misjudges the audience, the "you" form may alienate the reader.

Third-person point of view

With third-person point of view, the writing is about a subject, not addressed to a particular person and not from a narrator or a character. In nonfiction, the genre that dominates the AP English Language and Composition test, third-person point of view is usually straightforward. The author describes, narrates, argues, or discusses a subject without injecting any personal pronouns. (Of course, regardless of pronouns, the *content* of a nonfiction work may express deeply held, personal beliefs.) In fiction, however, the author may enter into the characters' minds and reveal their thoughts. Fictional third-person point of view comes in two varieties, limited and omniscient. In *limited third-person point of view,* the author reveals the thoughts and emotions of one character only. *Omniscient point of view* turns the author into an all-seeing voice, and all characters' ideas and emotions are fair game.

If you're analyzing a passage written in third-person point of view, these guidelines apply:

- **The passage appears objective.** Be warned, however, that all authors shape your perception by deciding what to include and exclude and by presenting their material in a particular writing style. Nothing is truly objective!

- **The passage sounds universal.** Because there's no "I," you can't pin the ideas on one particular person. The information in the passage seems separate from *a* human being and therefore seems to apply to *all* human beings.

- **Third-person point of view is the conventional style of writing for exposition (writing that explains).** In the free-response portion of the AP exam, third-person point of view is a good choice for synthesis or analysis essays. (Chapter 15 discusses these types of questions.) Argument essays may be written in third-person also, but first-person is also an option.

- **If you encounter a work of fiction (which is rare, but sometimes on the exam), pick apart anything with a third-person-limited point of view.** What do you know? What's mysterious? Keep in mind that the character doesn't necessarily understand everything that the author or the reader does. In that gap, dramatic irony thrives. Dramatic irony is a literary term for a situation in which the audience/reader knows something the character doesn't. In the ancient Greek play *Oedipus the King,* for example, Oedipus pledges to hunt down the murderer of the former king, Laius. The audience knows, but Oedipus doesn't, that Oedipus himself is the culprit.

Ideas and opinions

Frequently the free-response portion of the AP exam asks you to comment on the author's point of view — by which the exam writers mean the author's ideas and opinions. (Questions about writing style generally ask you to comment on the author's use of rhetorical devices.) Facing a question about the author's point of view, keep these points in mind:

- **Content is crucial.** The author may be arguing for a particular solution or in favor of one side of a controversial issue. What the author says tells you what he or she believes.

- **Much about the author's point of view is implied, not stated.** I haven't hung up a sign declaring that everyone should read more, but the fact that I'm an English teacher and my comments about books communicate my feelings about literature as loudly as any banner.

■ **Language matters.** If the passage refers to the "magnificent wilderness" or "wasted scrubland" in a passage about mining, you can probably guess the author's views on environmentalism. (For help with interpreting *diction*, or word choice, turn to Chapter 3.)

■ **Depending upon content and the use of first-, second-, or third-person point of view, the author may participate in or merely observe the events described in a passage.** The degree of involvement or detachment is important when you determine the author's ideas and opinions.

Here's a quick foray into point of view. Read this passage by Daniel Defoe, in which he discusses household help, and see whether you can determine his point of view.

> Women servants are now so scarce, that from thirty and forty shillings a year, their wages are increased of late to six, seven, nay, eight pounds per annum, and upwards; insomuch that an ordinary tradesman cannot well keep one; but his wife, who might be useful in his shop or business, must do the drudgery of household affairs; and all this because our servant-wenches are so puffed up with pride nowadays, that they never think they go fine enough: it is a hard matter to know the mistress from the maid by their dress; nay, very often the maid shall be much the finer of the two.

You don't have to understand the salary scale of Defoe's time see that he is *not* a fan of maids. The statement "servant-wenches are so puffed up with pride nowadays" says it all. Also, the maid is compared to the "mistress" and "very often the maid shall be the finer of the two." Defoe doesn't specifically refer to the past, but the word "now" in the first sentence implies nostalgia for the good old days, when presumably it was easier and cheaper to keep servants. Looking further, you may have noticed the term "wenches," a word for women that carries a negative connotation. Add all this up, and Defoe's point of view is clear: Maids have too many privileges.

5

Rhetorical Strategies

KEY CONCEPTS
■ The purpose of cause-and-effect essays
■ AP exam staples: Compare-and-contrast essays
■ Anecdotes as a rhetorical device
■ Classification and definition passages
■ Process and chronology works

In this chapter, I survey the most common rhetorical strategies: cause and effect, compare and contrast, anecdote and example, classification and definition, and process or chronology. Each strategy has its own quirks and conventions. **Note:** Some English teachers prefer the term "patterns of exposition," "rhetorical modes," or something else. Don't worry about the names of these strategies. Just know how they work.

Rhetorical strategies organize ideas so that the reader doesn't have to rummage through a pile of prose, hoping to bump into your point. Because ideas differ as much as clothing does, the "hangers" vary also. You wouldn't put a sweater on a clip-on hanger made for pants. Nor should you stick a compare-contrast essay into a cause-and-effect format.

Getting to know these strategies helps you create a sturdy, efficient framework for the writing you do on the essay portion of the AP exam. Understanding rhetorical strategy boosts your multiple-choice score, too, because this topic is popular with exam writers.

CAUSE AND EFFECT

Cause and effect probably entered your repertoire when you were still a toddler and faced an angry Authority Figure demanding to know *why* you had slapped your sister or painted the dog purple. You said, "She pulled my nose!" or "Rover likes purple!" or something similar. In other words, you explained the *cause* in order to justify the *effect*. Now that you're older, the *cause and effect pattern* comes in handy when you're writing.

A cause-and-effect essay is all about consequences. Something happens, or someone encounters a situation. Somebody reacts, or a new situation develops. Cause-and-effect passages frequently show up in science books, because science is all about explaining *why* things happen. It's a good strategy for history also, for the same reason.

To recognize and analyze a cause-and-effect passage, look for these qualities:

- The simplest cause-and-effect pattern identifies or describes the cause in one paragraph or in a few paragraphs, depending upon complexity. Subsequent paragraphs go into the effect.

- The cause-followed-by-effect pattern may be flipped upside down. The effects are the topic of the first paragraph or two; then the writer moves backward to explain why these effects existed.

- The two halves (cause and effect) don't have to be balanced. Depending upon the author's purpose, more weight may be given to one. In fact, sometimes the cause is just a word or a short phrase ("The Treaty of Versailles led to . . .") preceding a lengthy discussion of the effects. The reverse may also be true, with a multi-paragraph buildup to one statement ("Because of these factors, World War I began").

- Cause-and-effect passages may begin with a question, which the passage answers. The question expresses the effect ("Why is the sky blue?"), and the answer explains the cause ("The sky is blue because . . .").

- Key words include "consequently," "therefore," "thus," "hence," "as a result," "because," "the cause of," "as," and "the effect of." Don't assume that these words will be present, however. The rhetorical strategy may be expressed only through content.

Here's a passage from *The Knight,* by Alan Baker (Wiley, 2003; reprinted with permission of John Wiley & Sons, Inc.). It's a straightforward example of cause and effect.

> The eventual decline of feudalism occurred as a result of a number of factors, perhaps the most important of which was the impracticality of lords retaining a large number of knights who sat idle during the periods between wars. There was also the potentially serious problem of knights growing restless and bored waiting for the call to arms, which was their true vocation, and causing problems in the surrounding villages. The knights, too, found that the call to military service could come at the most inconvenient times, and for this reason the practice of commutation arose, whereby a knight would pay a sum of money (scutage) to his lord instead of going to war. Eventually money began to take the place of land as a symbol of power, and this gave rise to a new form of feudalism, . . . Under [the new type of feudalism], lords obtained services not by granting land to tenants, but by paying annual retaining fees and daily wages. The king thus contracted with individual earls, barons, and knights to provide a fixed number of

men at a fixed wage, should the need arise. An additional blow to the [original] form of feudalism came with the development of gunpowder, cannons, and firearms, which made castles and heavily armored mounted knights virtually obsolete. From the twelfth century onward, feudalism was further undermined by the rise of the centralized state, with its salaried officials and mercenary armies. Eventually the relationship between vassal and lord was replaced by that between subject and sovereign.

Notice that the effect — the decline of feudalism — is explored only briefly when the author describes "a new form of feudalism" and merely mentions the relationship "between subject and sovereign" that resulted from feudalism's decline. The author's attention rests mainly on the causes of the decline: "knights who sat idle" and got into trouble, money instead of land as a symbol of wealth, new weapons, "the rise of the centralized state," and "salaried officials and mercenary armies." A key phrase, "as a result of," announces the author's intentions in the first sentence. Other significant phrases are "this gave rise to" and "[a]n additional blow," as well as "further undermined."

Here's another cause-and-effect passage, an excerpt from Herman Melville's *Moby-Dick*. This great work is both a novel and a textbook on whaling, an important industry of the 19th century. In this passage Melville refers to whale oil, the fuel for lamps in this period. Melville's rhetorical strategy is subtle.

> Had you descended from the Pequod's try-works to the Pequod's forecastle, where the off duty watch were sleeping, for one single moment you would have almost thought you were standing in some illuminated shrine of canonized kings and counselors. There they lay in their triangular oaken vaults, each mariner a chiseled muteness; a score of lamps flashing upon his hooded eyes. In merchantmen [trading vessels], oil for the sailor is more scarce than the milk of queens. To dress in the dark, and eat in the dark, and stumble in darkness to his pallet, this is his usual lot. But the whaleman, as he seeks the food of light, so he lives in light. He makes his berth an Aladdin's lamp, and lays him down in it; so that in the [darkest] night the ship's black hull still houses an illumination. See with what entire freedom the whaleman takes his handful of lamps — often but old bottles and vials, though — to the copper cooler at the try-works, and replenishes them there, as mugs of ale at a vat. He burns, too, the purest of oil, in its unmanufactured, and, therefore, unvitiated state; a fluid unknown to solar, lunar, or astral contrivances ashore. It is sweet as early grass butter in April. He goes and hunts for his oil, so as to be sure of its freshness and genuineness, even as the traveler on the prairie hunts up his own supper of game.

The reader has to make the logical leaps here. Melville talks about the darkness of "merchantmen" and the "whaleman" who "lives in light." Why does the whaleman live in light? Because "he seeks the food of light." Melville also implies that access to oil and the purity of the oil are causes of brightly lit whaling ships. In contrast to *The Knight*, Melville gives equal weight in this passage to cause and effect.

> **TIP**
>
> Although the preceding passage falls into the "cause and effect" category, Melville briefly compares a "whaleman" with "merchantmen." A good writer uses the most effective means available to make a point, and, as you see in Melville's passage, rhetorical strategies often overlap.

COMPARE AND CONTRAST

It's human nature to compare and contrast. On the AP exam, compare-contrast passages show up fairly often as reading selections in the multiple-choice section. Be on the lookout for these characteristics:

- Two is a natural number in a compare-contrast passage, but three (or more) isn't a crowd. The author may compare and contrast any number of elements.

- In a stand-alone compare-contrast passage (not an excerpt from a longer work), the passage probably begins with an introduction that names the elements being compared. The conclusion renders some sort of judgment or opinion about the relative merits of these elements.

- In an excerpt from a longer work, you may not see an introduction or conclusion — just the body paragraphs.

- The simplest format for a compare-contrast passage devotes one body paragraph or section to each element. In a passage on apples and oranges, for example, you would see one section on apples and one on oranges.

- Compare-contrast essays may also divide according to qualities. For example, in an apple-orange passage, the body may be devoted to flavor, appearance, cultivation, and market — one per paragraph.

- Another structure for this type of essay devotes one body paragraph to differences and one to similarities.

> **TIP**
>
> You may have to write a compare-contrast essay yourself, if the AP exam throws a paired-passage question at you in the essay section. In that case, the analysis points in the bulleted list help you organize your work.

Check out this comparison of the diet of poor people in England with that of English sailors on a polar exploration expedition. This excerpt is taken from Scott Cookman's *Ice Blink* (Wiley, 2000; reprinted with permission of John Wiley & Sons, Inc.). This passage has no introduction or conclusion, because I sliced it out of a much longer discussion of diet. Notice how Cookman arranges the information:

> The poor in England subsisted largely on gruel (made from barley or oats), an abundance of stale bread, onions, potatoes, and occasionally bacon. In place of butter, they ate cheese (a lower-class favorite), and fish, because it was cheaper than meat. Since fuel was expensive and ovens more so, the average laborer's family had one hot meal a week, usually on Sunday when they took their suppers to the local baker's to get them cooked.
>
> The middle class diet was more substantial, but relentlessly monotonous. It consisted primarily of mutton (old, rather tough sheep's meat) and ham and bacon, which were cheap to raise, easy to cure, and kept well. To these were added potatoes and a very few vegetables, mostly cabbage, beets, and parsnips.
>
> No one drank water, because it was rightly presumed to be impure and unsafe (the great London cholera epidemic of 1854 was traced to a single public water pump). Owing to high import duties and the East India Company's virtual monopoly, tea was too expensive for most. Beer, stout, ale, and porter quenched the thirst of the poor; gin and rum were the favored spirits. Only the wealthy could afford wine.

Compared to their contemporaries ashore, able-bodied seamen in the Franklin Expedition — thanks to Barrow's foresight — ate and drank quite well. Contrary to myth, a seaman wasn't surviving on weevil-filled hardtack and putrid water. On "Discovery Service" to the polar regions, he was living high on the hog.

On a typical Monday, he got 1 pound of bread (fresh-baked if the weather and seas permitted the cook a galley fire, premade ship's biscuit if it did not). He was issued 1 pound of salt pork or beef and ½ pound of canned potatoes. He also got 2 ounces of raisins, 2 ounces of pickled vegetables, 2 ounces of suet, 2 ounces of chocolate, 1½ ounces of sugar mixed with 1 ounce of lemon juice (against scurvy), ¼ ounce of good tea, plus vinegar, mustard, salt, and pepper for seasonings, and some oatmeal or Scotch barley. Then, of course, there was the 1 gill of concentrated rum issued every day at noon.

In all, this constituted about 3 pounds of food a day, discounting the rum, tea, seasonings, and the liberal 1 ounce of tobacco issued daily. Not bad, when at home a fellow was lucky to get a stale end of bread, bowl of gruel, and some oysters. . . .

I won't go on, as Cookman does, to describe the seaman's diet on each day of the week and the perks for officers and dignitaries. However, even this small portion of *Ice Blink* makes the organizational strategy clear. Cookman divides his attention neatly between the elements being compared and takes them each in turn. Had he chosen a slightly different strategy, Cookman might have discussed quantity, healthfulness, variety, and cost in four body paragraphs, ping-ponging back and forth between land and sea.

The next example is from an early 20th-century science text. This portion has the delightful title "How to Breathe." (And you thought breathing came naturally!) Try to discern the organizational pattern. Because this section is printed in its entirety, also check whether an introduction and/or conclusion is present.

How to Breathe: Air, which is essential to life and health, should enter the body through the nose and, not through the mouth. The peculiar nature and arrangement of the membranes of the nose enable the nostrils to clean, and warm, and moisten the air which passes through them to the lungs. Floating around in the atmosphere are dust particles which ought not to get into the lungs. The nose is provided with small hairs and a moist inner membrane which serve as filters in removing solid particles from the air, and in thus purifying it before its entrance into the lungs.

In the immediate neighborhood of three Philadelphia high schools, having an approximate enrollment of over 8000 pupils, is a huge manufacturing plant which day and night pours forth grimy smoke and soot into the atmosphere which must supply oxygen to this vast group of young lives. If the vital importance of nose breathing is impressed upon these young people, the harmful effect of the foul air may be greatly lessened, the smoke particles and germs being held back by the nose filters and never reaching the lungs. If, however, this principle of hygiene is not brought to their attention, the dangerous habit of breathing through the open, or at least partially open, mouth will continue, and objectionable matter will pass through the mouth and find a lodging place in the lungs.

There is another very important reason why nose breathing is preferable to mouth breathing. The temperature of the human body is approximately 98° F., and the air which enters the lungs should not be far below this temperature. If air reaches the lungs through the nose, its journey is relatively long and slow, and there is opportunity for it to be warmed before it reaches the lungs. If, on the other hand, air passes to the lungs by way of the mouth, the warming process is brief and insufficient, and the lungs suffer in consequence. Naturally, the gravest danger is in winter.

The first paragraph sets up the comparison between nose-breathers and mouth-breathers and also explains the primary reason for the superiority of nose-breathing: purification. Paragraph two expands upon this theme, with the vision of 8,000 kids in Philadelphia living stunted, mouth-breathing lives. The third paragraph comes up with another reason — temperature. Step back a moment to consider the division of information. Each paragraph talks about both elements but focuses on a different subtopic (purity, example, temperature). The introduction is folded into the first sentence of paragraph one, and the author hasn't bothered writing a conclusion.

> **TIP**
>
> You probably noticed that the middle paragraph of "How to Breathe" is a specific example of the author's point. That paragraph could be classified as "anecdote and example," a rhetorical strategy I discuss in the next section. However, if the AP exam queried you about the overall rhetorical strategy of this piece, you should opt for the dominant strategy — compare and contrast. Though strategies sometimes overlap, one is usually more important than the others.

ANECDOTE AND EXAMPLE

Every time you open a magazine, you probably encounter the rhetorical strategy of anecdote and example. Most articles begin with an anecdote ("May had no inkling, as she watered her petunias, that disaster was about to strike her neat bungalow in Beverly Hills . . ."). The focus on one individual soon gives way to a larger point ("At least one million gardens in the United States contain killer petunia plants . . ."). Magazine writers like anecdotes because they draw the reader's interest. Who doesn't like peering into someone else's life? Examples are popular also. In fact, I've filled this book with examples — of passages similar to those on the AP exam, of AP-style questions, of rhetorical devices and strategies, and more. Examples make general principles real and understandable.

When you bump up against an anecdote or an example in a passage, place it in this context:

- The anecdote may be the first thing you see, or the author may embed anecdotes in other spots.

- Ask yourself why an anecdote appears where it does. Is it purely an attention-getter? Does the anecdote serve as proof of an assertion situated before or after the anecdote? On the AP exam, you may be asked to determine the purpose of an anecdote or example. Answering these questions helps you figure out the purpose of these elements.

- Consider the source of each anecdote or example. Are you hearing from an expert with wide-ranging knowledge or from a bystander? Is the story told from the point of view of a participant or an observer? Evaluating sources helps you identify attitude of the author or of a source — a common AP exam query.

- Key words indicating this rhetorical strategy are "include," "typical of," "for example," "for instance," "an exception to the rule," "as in," "the following," "the preceding," "sample," "testimony," "witness," "corroborate," "proof," "such as," "like," "a case in point," and "and the like." However, anecdotes and examples may appear without any of these words.

- Just because authors offer anecdotes as proof of their generalizations doesn't mean you have to accept their reasoning. You retain the right to see the anecdote or example as an exception, not a rule.

Here's a passage from Herman Melville's *Moby-Dick,* in which the narrator discusses attacks by whales. Evaluate the rhetorical strategy as you read.

People ashore have indeed some indefinite idea that a whale is an enormous creature of enormous power; but I have ever found that when narrating to them some specific example of this two-fold enormousness, they have significantly complimented me upon my facetiousness; when, I declare upon my soul, I had no more idea of being facetious than Moses, when he wrote the history of the plagues of Egypt. But fortunately the special point I here seek can be established upon testimony entirely independent of my own. That point is this: The Sperm Whale is in some cases sufficiently powerful, knowing, and judiciously malicious, as with direct aforethought to stave in, utterly destroy, and sink a large ship; and what is more, the Sperm Whale HAS done it.

First: In the year 1820 the ship Essex, Captain Pollard, of Nantucket, was cruising in the Pacific Ocean. One day she saw spouts, lowered her boats, and gave chase to a shoal of sperm whales. Ere long, several of the whales were wounded; when, suddenly, a very large whale escaping from the boats, issued from the shoal, and bore directly down upon the ship. Dashing his forehead against her hull, he so stove her in, that in less than "ten minutes" she settled down and fell over. Not a surviving plank of her has been seen since. . . . At this day Captain Pollard is a resident of Nantucket. I have seen Owen Chace, who was chief mate of the Essex at the time of the tragedy; I have read his plain and faithful narrative; I have conversed with his son; and all this within a few miles of the scene of the catastrophe.

The following are excerpts from Chace's narrative: "Every fact seemed to warrant me in concluding that it was anything but chance which directed [the whale's] operations; he made two attacks upon the ship, at a short interval between them. . . ."

Secondly: The ship Union, also of Nantucket, was in the year 1807 totally lost off the Azores by a similar onset, but the authentic particulars of this catastrophe I have never chanced to encounter, though from the whale hunters I have now and then heard casual allusions to it.

Thirdly: Some eighteen or twenty years ago Commodore J---, then commanding an American sloop-of-war of the first class, happened to be dining with a party of whaling captains, on board a Nantucket ship in the harbor of Oahu, Sandwich Islands. Conversation turning upon whales, the Commodore was pleased to be skeptical touching the amazing strength ascribed to them by the professional gentlemen present. He peremptorily denied for example, that any whale could so smite his stout sloop-of-war as to cause her to leak so much as a thimbleful. Very good; but there is more coming. Some weeks after, the Commodore set sail in this impregnable craft for Valparaiso. But he was stopped on the way by a portly sperm whale, that begged a few moments' confidential business with him. That business consisted in fetching the Commodore's craft such a thwack, that with all his pumps going he made straight for the nearest port to heave down and repair.

I chopped the list of examples considerably, in the interest of space. But the narrator goes on for a few more pages in the same vein. Although you have only a portion of this chapter, you can easily see what Melville, by means of his narrator, is doing. He announces in the first paragraph that he's not being facetious (joking) and that he's got proof: "testimony entirely independent" that the sperm whale is dangerous. Next is his first example, the wreck of Captain Pollack's ship. Did you catch the reference to this man as "a resident of Nantucket"? The narrator implies that if you doubt the story, you should go to Nantucket and check it yourself. I omitted some testimony from Owen Chace (that's where you see *ellipses,* little dots that indicate missing words), but you can see why Melville wanted Chace there — to confirm that the whale's attack was deliberate. Other examples follow: the Union and then the "American sloop-of-war" whose

Commodore tempted fate by denying whale power and getting beaten in return. The rhetorical strategy in this passage relies upon "expert witnesses"; the narrator himself isn't a participant, but he's got stories from people who were — people who can corroborate the narrator's point.

One more example of anecdote-example strategy, this time from Jack London, an American writer who described an experience in London, England. Notice how this piece (sliced from a much longer work) differs from Melville's.

> One old woman, between fifty and sixty, a sheer wreck, I had noticed earlier in the night standing in Piccadilly, not far from Leicester Square. She seemed to have neither the sense nor the strength to get out of the rain or keep walking, but stood stupidly, whenever she got the chance, meditating on past days, I imagine, when life was young and blood was warm. But she did not get the chance often. She was moved on by every policeman, and it required an average of six moves to send her doddering off one man's beat and on to another's. By three o'clock, she had progressed as far as St. James Street, and as the clocks were striking four I saw her sleeping soundly against the iron railings of Green Park. A brisk shower was falling at the time, and she must have been drenched to the skin.
>
> Now, said I, at one o'clock, to myself; consider that you are a poor young man, penniless, in London Town, and that to-morrow you must look for work. It is necessary, therefore, that you get some sleep in order that you may have strength to look for work and to do work in case you find it.
>
> So I sat down on the stone steps of a building. Five minutes later a policeman was looking at me. My eyes were wide open, so he only grunted and passed on. Ten minutes later my head was on my knees, I was dozing, and the same policeman was saying gruffly, "'Ere, you, get outa that!"
>
> I got. And, like the old woman, I continued to get; for every time I dozed, a policeman was there to rout me along again.

London's essay describes a homeless woman forced to move along all night until she finally finds refuge in a park. His own experience echoes hers. London is not only an observer but also a participant. His purpose is to call attention to the plight of the homeless, especially "a poor young man" who is too tired "to look for work" or "to do work" after a night of encounters with the police. Because his testimony comes from the inside, the reader believes him. Unlike Melville, London doesn't call upon others to prove his point; his own homeless night does the job.

CLASSIFICATION AND DEFINITION

Human beings classify and define so readily that I sometimes think the human brain comes equipped with a set of baskets. The baskets are labeled (that's definition) and items are sorted among the baskets (that's classification). To put it another way: Authors tackling huge subjects have to break those subjects down into parts (classification) and then explain what those parts are (definition). You've probably read a ton of writing with this rhetorical strategy in your science textbooks or in any textbook that deals with a lot of terminology. (Grammar texts are notorious for this!) Characteristics of classification-definition pieces include the following:

■ The author is aware of the audience. An author defines terms only when the intended reader isn't likely to know those terms already. In this book, I give the meaning of literary terms, assuming that you haven't yet memorized them.

■ Definitions are usually complicated. Don't expect to see one-word or short-phrase definitions, such as those on a vocabulary list. If the rhetorical strategy of definition is applied to an entire passage, a lot has to be explained.

- Though they're not always present, key words that help you recognize this rhetorical strategy include "definition," "type," "sort," "classify," "category," and "kind."

- The two parts of this rhetorical strategy may be separated (in different paragraphs or, if the work is full-length, in different chapters). On the AP exam, you may see only half — definition alone, usually. Classification is hard to accomplish without definition, unless the definitions are commonly known.

- The author may announce the strategy ("Loyalty may be defined as . . .") or may simply imply it ("The loyalists supported the Queen . . .").

Here's a straightforward, easy example of definition, drawn from a science text:

> A farsighted person is one who cannot see near objects so distinctly as far objects, and who in many cases cannot see near objects at all. The eyeball of a farsighted person is very short, and the retina is too close to the crystalline lens. Near objects are brought to a focus behind the retina instead of on it, and hence are not visible. Even though the muscles of accommodation do their best to bulge and thicken the lens, the rays of light are not bent sufficiently to focus sharply on the retina. In consequence objects look blurred. Farsighted-ness can be remedied by convex glasses, since they bend the light and bring it to a closer focus. Convex glasses, by bending the rays and bringing them to a nearer focus, overbal-ance a short eyeball with its tendency to focus objects behind the retina.

How many definitions did you find? I count two: the definition of "a farsighted person" and the definition of "convex glasses." The first is obvious, because the author spends several sentences discussing farsightedness. The second is subtler; convex glasses come into this paragraph only in relation to the condition they remedy (farsightedness) and what they do ("bend the light and bring it to a closer focus").

TIP

On the AP exam, you may see questions about the purpose of a particular line or section. Sometimes the answer is "to define _____" or "to clarify the meaning of _____."

Now consider a more complicated passage. This excerpt from *Moby-Dick* follows a quotation from Linnaeus, a scientist who stated that whales are not fish. (Linnaeus was correct; whales are mammals.) Here Melville argues that Linnaeus is wrong, proving nothing about the biology of whales but everything about the fact that being a good writer doesn't mean you know the facts. Read Melville's passage and figure out how he handles definition and classification.

> I take the good old fashioned ground that the whale is a fish, and call upon holy Jonah to back me. This fundamental thing settled, the next point is, in what internal respect does the whale differ from other fish. Above, Linnaeus has given you those items. But in brief, they are these: lungs and warm blood; whereas, all other fish are lungless and cold blooded.
> Next: how shall we define the whale, by his obvious externals, so as conspicuously to label him for all time to come? To be short, then, a whale is A SPOUTING FISH WITH A HORIZONTAL TAIL. There you have him. However contracted, that definition is the result of expanded meditation. A walrus spouts much like a whale, but the walrus is not a fish, because he is amphibious. But the last term of the definition is still more cogent, as cou-pled with the first. Almost any one must have noticed that all the fish familiar to lands-men have not a flat, but a vertical, or up-and-down tail. Whereas, among spouting fish the tail, though it may be similarly shaped, invariably assumes a horizontal position.

By the above definition of what a whale is, I do by no means exclude from the leviathanic brotherhood any sea creature hitherto identified with the whale by the best informed Nantucketers; nor, on the other hand, link with it any fish hitherto authoritatively regarded as alien. Hence, all the smaller, spouting, and horizontal tailed fish must be included in this ground-plan of Cetology.

Melville's strategy in this passage is to classify whales as fish and then to define a new category of fish. He rebuts Linnaeus and calls upon the authority of experts. Now for the details: Melville announces his classification — and his disagreement with Linnaeus — in the first paragraph. Melville grants Linnaeus, whom he has set up as an opponent, two biological realities: Whales have "lungs and warm blood; whereas, all other fish are lungless and cold blooded." Melville justifies his classification in the second paragraph by explaining what excludes an animal from the "fish category" (the walrus, because a walrus is amphibious). The second paragraph also contains Melville's own definition of a whale: a "SPOUTING FISH WITH A HORIZONTAL TAIL." (The capital letters are Melville's and show his strong belief.) Melville grants that fish tails are usually vertical, but spouting fish are an exception to this rule. In the third paragraph, Melville brings in the experts — the "Nantucketers" (residents of Nantucket, a whaling center) — and says that "any sea creature" they considered a whale is a whale. In essence he's saying, "They know what they're talking about. They think the whale is a fish, so it is."

PROCESS AND CHRONOLOGY

Process and chronology are natural ways of thinking (as are all the rhetorical strategies), because this rhetorical strategy explains how to get from Point A to Point B, either in action (process) or time (chronology). And that's what life is, isn't it? Moving forward. The problem is that process-and-chronology writers must lead the reader through a series of steps, and the steps have to be manageable. Leave one out, and the reader is stuck. Put too many steps in, and the reader is bored.

You've read many process-and-chronology pieces in school and, if you've ever bought any electronics, in your personal life as well. Here are some things to keep in mind when you're cracking a passage with this rhetorical strategy:

- The writing often moves forward in time, in action, or both. However, the author may digress from the main process he or she is describing to explain a subtopic, breaking the forward motion. Be alert for these breaks!

- You should be able to identify the steps and place them in order.

- The steps are usually linked by transitions. (Transitions are single words or longer statements that help the reader move from one point to the next. See Chapter 4 for more information).

- Key words associated with process and chronology include "while," "since," "then," "after," "before," "in order to," "now," "separately," "concluded," "finished," "completed," "at first," "secondly," and "last."

- Verb tense is a big deal in process-and-chronology writing. Some constructions (the helping verb "had," for example) place one action before another. For help with verb tense, turn to Chapter 6.

- Many writers employ metaphors or extended metaphors to convey information in a process-and-chronology piece. Crack the metaphor, and everything becomes clear. For example, instead of telling you to walk three yards east, turn left, and proceed for five more yards, the writer may tell you that the path is "an inverted letter L."

Time to examine process-and-chronology in action. Following is part of an account of the Spanish-American War. Notice the order of events.

> The orderly who brought the dispatch should have dashed up at a gallop, clicked his spurs, saluted and begun with "The commanding General's compliments, sir," et cetera. Instead, he dragged a very tired horse up the trail, knee-deep in mud, brought to, standing with a gasp of relief, and said, as he pushed his hat back from his forehead: "Say, is here where General McKibben is?"
>
> We stopped singing and took our feet down from the railing of the veranda. In the room back of us we heard the General raise on an elbow and tell his orderly to light a candle. The orderly went inside, drawing a paper from his pocket, and the aides followed. Through the open window we could plainly hear what followed, and see, too, for that matter, by twisting a bit on our chairs.
>
> The General had mislaid his eyeglasses and so passed the dispatch to one of his aides, saying: "I'll get you to read this for me, Nolan." On one knee, and holding the dispatch to the candle-light, Nolan read it aloud. It began tamely enough with the usual military formulas, and the first thirty words might have been part of any one of the many dispatches the General had been receiving during the last three days. And then "to accompany the commanding General to a point midway between the Spanish and American lines and there to receive the surrender of General Toral. At noon, precisely, the American flag will be raised over the Governor's Palace in the city of Santiago. A salute of twenty-one guns will be fired from Captain Capron's battery. The regimental bands will play 'The Star-Spangled Banner' and the troops will cheer. SHAFTER."
>
> There was a silence. The aide returned the paper to the General and straightened up, rubbing the dust from his knee. The General shifted his pipe to the other corner of his mouth. The little green parrot who lived in the premises trundled gravely across the brick floor, and for an instant we all watched her with the intensest attention. "Hum," muttered the General reflectively between his teeth. "Hum. They've caved in. Well, you won't have to make that little reconnaissance of yours down the railroad, after all, Mr. Nolan." And so it was that we first heard of the surrender of Santiago de Cuba.

Most of this passage is in strict chronological order: The orderly arrives, asks for the general, and "we" stop singing. The general tells his orderly to light a candle, passes the dispatch from General Shafter to an aide, who reads it aloud. Now chronological order breaks, because the dispatch describes events that *will* occur. Then the main narrative continues in chronological order: The men fall silent, the aide gives the paper to the general, who shifts his pipe. The parrot walks across the floor. The general comments on the message.

> **TIP**
>
> When chronological order *isn't* in order, something different is happening. In the preceding passage, the difference lies in the message, which tells about events that happen apart from the main narration. As always, a pattern break should catch your eye. Give that spot extra attention!

Now for a more complicated process-and-chronology piece. Here's an excerpt from *A Short History of Planet Earth,* by F. D. MacDougall (Wiley, 2002; reprinted with permission of John Wiley & Sons, Inc.). Keep your eye on the steps the passage describes.

> Where the plates [of the earth's surface] move apart, there are rifts in the earth's crust. Basalt, the most common product of melting of the earth's interior, wells up to fill them; as we have seen, this is how new seafloor is created. Most of the divergent plate

boundaries are found in the oceans. Paradoxical as it may seem at first, the rifts, which are valleys or depressions, are often at the center of ridges, which are broad topographic highs. . . . the ridges exist because of the upwelling mantle material and the heat it carries. As the newly created crust moves away from the ridge, it cools, contracts, becomes denser, and sinks to lower elevations. The depth of the ocean increases by about a factor of two, from approximately 2½ kilometers to five, from the crest of the ridges to the old parts of the seafloor far removed from the spreading region.

MacDougall has explained no fewer than four interlinked processes in this short paragraph: the creation of rifts, seafloor, oceans, and ridges. The steps are fairly easy to follow for each separate process, but because one process depends upon the other, you have to untangle them before any of them makes sense. Not an easy task, but not impossible either. Here you go: Rifts occur when the plates of the earth's surface move apart. Seafloor comes into being when (1) the earth's plates move apart and (2) basalt rushes in. Oceans show up when the sea floods into a rift. A ridge is created when (1) the earth's mantle bulges upward and (2) the crust displaced by the ridge moves outward and (3) cools and (4) contracts and (5) becomes denser and (6) sinks and (7) leaves the ridge higher than the sunken crust around it. Did you catch all that?

> **TIP**
>
> Some AP exam multiple-choice questions are little more than standard reading-comprehension queries. When you read a process-and-chronology passage, you may be asked a factual question, something like (referring to the preceding example) "According to the passage, ridges are formed when . . . ." Make a mental note of the steps in the process(es), and you can quickly locate the correct answer choice.

6

Essential Grammar Skills

KEY CONCEPTS

- Key sentence elements: verbs, subjects, complements, and descriptors
- Verb usage
- Pronouns and antecedents
- Parallel sentence structure
- Descriptive modifiers
- Punctuation rules and conventions

Mention grammar and most people run from the room, explaining why they absolutely *hate* the subject. Yet grammar is hardwired into your brain, because it's the skeleton that supports expression and communication. Furthermore, it's a huge deal on the AP English Language and Composition exam. The graders expect to see good (but not perfect!) grammar in the free-response portion of the test. Also, quite a few multiple-choice questions depend upon your ability to crack open a sentence and extract the meaning — a grammatical feat — though only a few questions contain grammar terminology. Without doubt, a quick grammar refresher is worth your time and energy. In this chapter, I address the grammatical elements most likely to trip you up on the exam and demystify some of the terms you're likely to encounter on AP Exam Day.

ELEMENTS OF A SENTENCE

Briefly, every English sentence contains these elements: a complete thought (required), a verb and a subject (also required), a complement (usually optional), and descriptions (always optional). I promise to keep the grammatical terminology to a minimum, but I have to throw some definitions at you:

- **A verb expresses action or state of being.** Add-ons (*helping verbs*) such as "has," "will," "can," "should," "does," and others alter meaning slightly by indicating *tense* (when the action or state of being happened), degree of obligation, or ability. Helping verbs also create questions. I've underlined the verbs in these sentences:

  Holly <u>spoke</u> for two hours last night. Holly <u>can ramble</u> on forever. Mort <u>is</u> impatient when he <u>must communicate</u> with Holly. "<u>Does</u> Holly ever <u>sleep</u>?" Mort <u>has</u> sometimes <u>asked</u>. "She <u>seems</u> to need no rest," he <u>added</u>.

  > **TIP**
  >
  > Did you notice that "to need" is *not* underlined in the last sample sentence? "To need" isn't a verb. It's an infinitive — a sort of verb family parent that looks like a verb but doesn't function as one. For more information on infinitives, see "The tense of verbals" in this chapter.

- **Every verb has a subject, the person or thing doing the action or existing in the state of being expressed by the verb.** To identify the subject, ask "who?" or "what?" before the verb. For instance, in the sentence "Holly spoke for two hours last night," ask "Who spoke?" The answer ("Holly") is the subject.

- **A complete thought stands alone.** Check out these two examples, one complete and one incomplete:

  Yesterday it rained. (complete)

  Because it rained. (incomplete)

  > **TIP**
  >
  > Incomplete thoughts, when they contain a subject and a verb, are usually *dependent,* or *subordinate, clauses.* The AP exam sometimes asks you the function of a specific set of dependent or subordinate clauses. Don't let the grammar lingo upset you. You don't need it in order to answer the question. Reading comprehension and logic should be enough to steer you to the correct answer.

- **A complement adds to the idea begun by the subject and the verb.** Complements are obligatory elements of a sentence if they're needed to complete a thought. Otherwise, they're optional. They come in a million shapes and sizes, but you can always locate them by asking "whom/who?" or "what?" after stating the subject and verb. For example, in the sentence "Mort is impatient," you ask, "Mort is who?" and "Mort is what?" The answer, "Mort is <u>impatient</u>," tells you that "impatient" is a complement.

- **Descriptions divide into two giant families: adjectives and adverbs.** Descriptions may be a single word, a phrase, or a clause (an expression containing a subject and a verb). Check out the underlined members of the adjective and adverb family:

  <u>Blue</u> skies <u>completely</u> covered the town <u>on the outskirts of the mountains</u>. The <u>tallest</u> mountain, <u>which was topped with snow</u>, is <u>very famous</u>.

  You don't have to distinguish between adjectives and adverbs on the AP exam, but you do have to use the words correctly! (For more about descriptive words, see "Modifiers" in this chapter.)

> **TIP**
>
> Some words look like verbs but function as adjective or adverbs. These hybrids are known as *verbals,* in grammar-speak. (Full disclosure: Verbals sometimes act as nouns, but those verbals seldom cause problems, so I ignore them here.) The tense of a verbal, as well as its placement, affects meaning. Check out "Verb Usage" for everything you need to know about tense, and "Modifiers" for information on placement.

Of course, sentences — especially in AP exam passages — may be extremely complicated, with tangles of clauses and a ton of punctuation. Sometimes they follow outdated grammar rules or break rules purposely. Regardless, most of the time, you can figure out what's what by following these easy steps:

1. **Read the entire sentence, just for comprehension**.

2. **If possible, divide the sentence into logical units**. The sentence "The book that Henry wrote last year was a best seller" has two thoughts in it: "The book was a best seller" and "that Henry wrote."

3. **As necessary, determine the grammatical identity of each part of the sentence.** Not many AP exam questions rely upon your knowing which part of the sentence is a subject and which is a verb (or a clause or something else). But some questions — those involving parallelism, for example — do require such knowledge. Working within the smaller, logical units of a sentence makes your life much simpler. For example, referring to the sentence in Step 2, you may find the subject of "wrote" more quickly when "that Henry wrote" is isolated from the rest of the sentence.

> **TIP**
>
> If you're identifying elements in a question, turn the question into a statement. The subject and verb are easier to identify in statements. For instance, suppose you're facing this sentence: "Does Martha send e-mail every day?" Change the sentence to "Martha does send e-mail every day" before picking it apart.

VERB USAGE

Every sentence pivots around its verb(s), so you should always zero in on verbs when you're faced with a complicated comprehension problem or when you're checking your own writing. Verbs can trip you up because of problems with agreement, tense, and mood. You probably won't see any questions referencing *agreement* (singular/plural issues) on the AP test, though of course your own writing should display proper agreement, matching singular subjects with singular verbs and plural subjects with plural verbs. You're more likely to encounter comprehension questions that involve interpreting tense and mood, so I concentrate on those two issues here.

Tense

Verb *tense* refers to time — past, present, and future. Most people with a good grasp of the English language already understand the basic tenses, but a couple of picky points may confuse you.

"Had" as a time clue

"Had," all by itself, expresses ownership or possession, as in "I had three sandwiches." But "had" tacked onto another verb places actions further in the past than past-tense verbs without "had." In this case, "had" creates *past perfect tense* (but you don't have to know that term for the AP test).

Here's an example of "had" in action. Imagine that a sentence describes two actions: selling tickets and learning that the tickets are counterfeit. You can explain what happened in two ways:

> When Mary learned about the counterfeit tickets, she sold 500.
>
> When Mary learned about the counterfeit tickets, she had sold 500.

The first sentence makes Mary a crook, because the two actions take place more or less at the same time. Mary knowingly sells fake tickets. The second sentence exonerates Mary, because the "had" places the ticket sales before Mary learns that they're fake. She sold 500 tickets and *then* found out that the tickets weren't legitimate. One little word — "had" — makes all the difference.

Under certain circumstances, forms of the helping verb "have" function in a similar way, placing one action before another. See "The tense of verbals" in this section for more information.

"Has" and "have" as a connection between past and present

The verbs "has" and "have," when they're not expressing ownership or possession, connect past and present. In grammatical terms, these helpers create *present perfect tense*. Again, you don't have to know the name of the tense, but you do have to know how "has" and "have" affect meaning. Take a look at these two sentences:

> Mary taught the art of counterfeiting for 20 years.
>
> Mary has taught the art of counterfeiting for 20 years.

The first sentence is firmly rooted in the past. "Mary taught," but she's not teaching now. The second sentence is completely different; it means that she taught counterfeiting in the past and she's still teaching it now.

"Will have" or "shall have" as a deadline

The helping verb "will" places actions in the future, as in "I will shred my English notes after taking the AP." "Shall" performs the same function, though it's rarely used these days. (On the AP exam, which includes many old passages, "shall" appears regularly.) A sentence with "have" tacked onto a future verb implies or states a deadline. Notice the different meanings of these two sentences:

> During the AP exam, Sam will stick a hundred seals onto his test booklets. (Taking the exam and sticking seals occur at the same time.)

> By the time the AP exam is over, Sam will have stuck a hundred seals onto his test booklets. (Seal-sticking happens before the exam ends.)

Both sentences talk about the future, but the second one places one action before another.

In the preceding examples, I made the deadline obvious by stating "by the time the exam is over." On the AP exam, the passage may be more subtle. Remember that "will have" places events at different points in the future, and interpret the meaning correctly.

The tense of verbals

The topic of verbals is thick with grammar terminology, but I promise to spare you as much as possible. Verbals are half verb, half something else (usually adjectives or adverbs). The verb half of a verbal gives it the ability to express time, because verbs have tense. The other half gives a verbal the ability to describe. I explain description problems in "Modifiers"; here I tackle tense.

The words "has," "have," and "having," when they're tacked onto a verbal, affect the time indicated. Check out some verbals in action. The verbals are underlined, and the meaning is described in parentheses:

> <u>Singing</u> "Happy Birthday to You," the waiter brought the cake to Lucy. (Two actions, singing and bringing the cake, happened at the same time.)

> <u>Having sung</u> "Happy Birthday to You," the waiter brought the cake to Lucy. (The waiter finished singing and then brought the cake.)

> It's nice <u>to meet</u> you. (I feel good about being introduced to you now.)

> It's nice <u>to have met</u> you. (This sentence implies another action, such as "I'm glad that I met you before we pronounce our wedding vows, or something like that.)

Got the picture? The plain verbals (without helping verbs "has," "have," or "having") express simultaneous actions. The verbals with helpers place one action before another.

TIP

You won't see a question about verbals on the AP exam, but your comprehension of a passage may depend upon decoding their tense.

Present tense for literature

When you write about literature (and every passage you see on the AP exam falls into that category), use present tense. Why? Because the written word is immortal. Every time I read Jonathan Swift's satire, "A Modest Proposal," he's speaking to me "live," even though he's been dead for centuries. When I open *Pride and Prejudice,* the Bennet girls are single women in search of husbands, despite the fact that most of them find mates by the end of the book. Thus, when you write about a passage in an analysis or synthesis essay, use present tense in referring to the author's words:

> Michaels advocates a uniform national curriculum. ("advocates," not "advocated")

> In the first paragraph, the author takes a critical stance. ("takes," not "took")

> **TIP**
>
> When you write about history or something you experienced or witnessed, past tense is appropriate. For example, you may say that "The seniors were given a wide range of topics" if that action took place in the past. You may also mix present and past when you write about a historical passage — present tense for statements about the passage and past tense for statements about history, as in this sentence: "The seniors were given a wide range of topics, a choice which Michaels opposes in his essay on curriculum."

Mood

Verbs have three moods — indicative, imperative, and subjunctive. The terms aren't important to the AP exam, and the first two aren't likely to cause any problems. (In case you're curious, the *indicative mood* is the one you use to make ordinary statements or to ask questions. Just about every verb in this book is in indicative mood. The *imperative mood* gives commands, as in "brush your teeth thoroughly" and similar remarks.) In terms of grammar errors and comprehension issues on the AP exam, subjunctive mood is where all the action is.

The *subjunctive mood* expresses an indirect command or a condition that's contrary to fact. Here are a few examples, with the verbs in subjunctive mood underlined:

> The proctor decreed that everyone <u>be</u> quiet during the exam. (indirect command)

> <u>Had</u> I <u>known</u> that talking was forbidden, I would have spoken more before the test. (condition contrary to fact)

> If I <u>had received</u> the memo about silence, I would have protested to the AP coordinator. (condition contrary to fact)

> If the proctor <u>were</u> fair, she would have given us 15 minutes to yell before the exam. (condition contrary to fact)

Do you see how the subjunctive can change the usual subject-verb pair? In the first example sentence, "everyone" is the subject of "be." In a normal sentence (that is, a sentence in the indicative mood), "everyone" pairs with "is," as in "everyone is here." In the fourth sentence, the subject "proctor" ordinarily partners "was." Here "proctor" links up with "were." The altered verb tips you off to the subjunctive mood.

> Sometimes the subjunctive mood doesn't alter the usual subject-verb pair, as in the second and third sentences in the preceding set of examples. The key to recognizing subjunctive in these sentences is the "would have" expression. Condition-contrary-to-fact sentences always contain these expressions.

If you run across an indirect-command subjunctive sentence on the AP exam, it probably won't cause any problems for you. This sort of sentence probably sounds right to you, and it's not likely that you'll misunderstand its meaning. A condition-contrary-to-fact statement, however, may be unfamiliar to you and may easily be misread. The first part of sentence two declares, "I didn't know talking was forbidden." The subjunctive verb in sentence three firmly states that I didn't receive the memo. Similarly, sentence four states that the proctor wasn't fair. As you see, the subjunctive mood in a condition-contrary-to-fact sentence expresses what *isn't* true. Just to be clear, notice how each sentence in this pair — containing one indicative and one subjunctive verb — differs in meaning:

> SUBJUNCTIVE: If Abby were elected, the ballot box would be in a museum. (Abby wasn't elected, and the ballot box is in the garbage.)

> INDICATIVE: If Abby was elected, the ballot box would be in a museum. (Nobody knows whether Abby was elected or not. The proof is in the ballot box. If you find it in a museum, she's president. If you don't find it there, she's not.)

Keep your eye out for condition-contrary-to-fact subjunctive statements. Remember that the meaning is reversed by the subjunctive verb.

PRONOUNS

Pronouns are small words that take the place of nouns. They solve a lot of problems by eliminating repetitions; no one wants to hear that "Roberta took Roberta's shoes to the shoemaker so that the shoemaker could fix the shoes" because "Roberta took her shoes to the shoemaker so that he could fix them" sounds better. Pronouns also get you out of some incriminating situations. ("Someone broke the window" is less likely to get your brother grounded than "Larry broke the window.")

Sadly, pronouns also cause a fair number of problems. This isn't a grammar text, so I won't explain all the rules governing pronouns. Instead, I focus on situations you may encounter: identifying pronoun antecedents (in passages provided by the test makers), providing antecedents for all your pronouns (in your own essays), and avoiding ambiguous pronouns (also in your own essays).

Antecedents

A pronoun's *antecedent* is the word a pronoun refers to. Here are a few facts about antecedents to keep in mind for the AP exam.

Pronoun-antecedent agreement

"Agreement," in English grammar, refers to singular and plural forms — singular pairs with singular, and plural with plural. Take a look at these example sentences; I've underlined the pronouns and antecedents:

> Roger wrote a 20-page essay, but he didn't do his science homework. (singular)
>
> The lab reports were very boring, so Robert blew them off. (plural)
>
> The homework that Anjelica hates is never completed. (singular)
>
> Marcy is the only one of the girls who likes English. (singular)
>
> Gene is one of the boys who like recess. (plural)

The first three sentences are straightforward. The last two sentences aren't so simple. The same pronoun, in almost the same sentence construction, is singular in one sentence and plural in another. The difference is the word "only." How many girls like English? According to sentence four, only Marcy, so "who" must refer to "one." The last sentence states that several boys like recess, so "who" refers to "boys."

> **TIP**
>
> How can you tell whether a pronoun is singular or plural? Common knowledge of the language sorts "she" from "they" and "I" from "we." But pronouns such as "who," "that," "those," "these," and "which" can be either singular or plural. A proper sentence provides a clue: the verb that's paired with the pronoun. In the preceding set, the sentence about Marcy's dislike for English pairs "who" with "likes," a singular verb. Therefore, "who" has to be singular, because singular and plural don't mix. In the sentence about Gene, "who" pairs with "like," a plural verb. Hence "who" is plural in that sentence. When you're identifying a pronoun's antecedent (a common AP exam question), check the verb to figure out whether you're searching for a singular or plural antecedent.

The no-verb rule

Pronouns are supposed to take the place of nouns and other pronouns, not verbs. Technically, this sentence commits a grammatical error:

> Ariel signed up for eight AP exams, which is a bad idea.

The pronoun "which" is supposed to sub for a noun or a pronoun, but here it appears to refer to the fact that Ariel signed up for eight AP exams.

The no-verb rule helps you when you're antecedent-hunting, because you can rule out everything but nouns and pronouns. Also, engrave the no-verb rule on your brain so that you'll remember to apply this principle when you're writing essays. One misapplied pronoun won't sink your essay, but it won't help you either.

In a multiple-choice question about antecedents, the answers may include descriptive words attached to the antecedent. Descriptions don't violate the no-verb rule, so long as the pronoun clearly refers to a noun or to another pronoun. For example, if the actual antecedents are "exam" and "proctor," a correct answer choice may be "the boring exam" or "the proctor who cried when the test was over."

Location

An antecedent is generally very close to the pronoun it replaces, usually in the same sentence. However, the pronoun and its antecedent may be several sentences apart, so long as the meaning is clear. In your own essays, try to keep these teams together. You're more likely to choose the correct pronoun if the antecedent is staring right at you. In AP exam passages, roam a little until you're sure you've picked the correct word.

Ambiguity

The goal of writing is communication, and communication falters when a pronoun is vague. Your essays suffer when you throw in a sentence like this one:

> The biographer reports that her subject says she is too passionate about conserving energy.

Who's too passionate? Did the biographer report, "My subject says I am too passionate about conserving energy"? Or does the text read, "'I am too passionate about energy,' commented Olga Centrova"? You can't tell because the pronoun "she" may refer to Olga or to the biographer. The moral of the story: Be sure the antecedent of every pronoun is clear.

TIP

A common mistake that grates on English teachers' nerves shows up in a sentence like this:

> In the passage it says that Olga hates fluorescent lightbulbs.

The pronoun "it" has no real antecedent. The passage doesn't talk, so it can't say anything. A better version of this sentence is as follows:

> According to the passage, Olga hates fluorescent lightbulbs.

As you see, sometimes the solution to a pronoun-antecedent problem is to rewrite the sentence without any pronouns at all.

PARALLEL SENTENCES

In grammar, *parallelism* is a principle that requires elements with the same function in a sentence to have the same identity. Take a look at this list: "friendly," "compassionate," "in a hurry." These are three perfectly good descriptions, but not when they're used like this:

> Tom is friendly, compassionate, and in a hurry.

The three function as *complements*, but "friendly" and "compassionate" are adjectives and "in a hurry" is a phrase. (Don't let the grammar terminology scare you. Even without the labels, you can hear the mismatch.) Here's the correct sentence:

> Tom is friendly, compassionate, and hurried.

You might also say, "friendly, compassionate, and pressed for time." The phrase "for time" doesn't affect the parallelism because "pressed," the adjective, conveys the main idea. The phrase is just an added description.

Parallel elements can be short (as you see in the preceding example) or lengthy, as in this example:

> That he was tired, that his soul was lost, that his belly was empty, and that his feet were numb with walking were all that he knew.

All the "that" statements are clauses, and they all function as subjects of the verb "were." A multiple-choice question about parallelism might ask you the purpose of the parallel elements or might identify one element and ask you what is parallel to it. In the latter type of question, the parallel element may be in a different sentence. (For more information on the way that parallel elements affect the reader's perception of meaning, turn to Chapter 4.)

MODIFIERS

Descriptive words or phrases are also called *modifiers* because they change, or modify, the meaning of whatever word they're describing. Modifiers, which are members of either the adjective or the adverb family, come in all shapes and sizes, and they move around somewhat in the sentence. Here are some examples, with the descriptive elements (the modifiers) underlined. In the first set, notice how each modifier from the adjective family changes your perception of the noun "dress." In the second set, keep your eye on the verb "wear" in all its forms and the adverbial modifier attached to it.

> The <u>blue</u> dress <u>that Mary purchased last week</u> is <u>pretty</u>. <u>Made of silk</u>, the dress seems <u>fragile</u>. The dress <u>in the closet</u>, on the other hand, is <u>sturdier</u>.

> Alex wore his suit <u>to the job interview</u> <u>to make a good impression</u>. <u>Whenever Alex is out of work</u>, he wears old clothes. Alex has <u>frequently</u> worn jeans to <u>business dinners</u>.

As you see, adjectival descriptions may appear before or after the word described or following a verb expressing state of being (usually a form of the verb "to be" or a synonym such as "seem" or "appear"). Adverbial modifiers pop up all over the place.

Though these descriptive elements roam around, they must follow some rules:

- If a sentence begins with a verbal — an element that looks like a verb but acts like a description — the action or state of being in the verbal describes the subject of the sentence. In the first example set above, "made of silk" describes "dress."

- This section is about descriptions, but I'll stretch the topic a little to fit in a good point about introductory clauses because they're similar to the introductory verbals I discuss in the preceding bullet. When a subject is implied but not stated in an introductory clause, the subject of the sentence that is stated must also be the implied subject. Here's an example:

    When driving, Ellie shifts gears roughly.

    "Ellie," the subject you see, pairs with the verb "shifts." However, "Ellie" is also the subject of "driving," or more specifically, "is driving." (The "is" and the "Ellie" are implied.) In other words, the sentence actually means "When Ellie is driving, Ellie shifts gears roughly."

- Descriptions should be near the words they modify. If you place descriptions too far away, you may end up with a meaning you didn't intend, as in this example:

    The dump truck full of garbage that we bought at the used-truck dealership has already broken down.

    As the sentence reads now, the modifier "that we bought at the used-truck dealership" modifies garbage. The truck may be a lemon, but I doubt that the writer meant to say that the dealership sold the garbage that's in the dump truck. A bit of revision fixes the sentence:

    The dump truck that we bought at the used-truck dealership is full of garbage, and it has broken down.

- All descriptions must be clear. If a description may refer to more than one thing, you have to move it. For instance, suppose you write this sentence:

    Dresses that are folded frequently have wrinkles.

    The problem lies with the word "frequently." Because of its position, "frequently" may modify "folded" or "have wrinkles." So you don't know whether folding a dress just one time causes wrinkles or whether frequent folding is necessary for wrinkling. The sentence can go either way. To solve the problem, move the description (and change it as necessary):

    Frequent folding causes dresses to wrinkle.

Check descriptions (modifiers) when you're working on your essays or decoding an AP exam passage. Modifiers add a lot of meaning to writing.

PUNCTUATION

A good understanding of punctuation can improve your AP exam score in two ways. Properly punctuated essays impress graders, and poorly punctuated work has the opposite effect. Also, punctuation affects meaning, so decoding punctuation in the passages on the exam improves your reading comprehension. **Note:** In this section I discuss commas and semicolons. For information on quotation marks, turn to Chapter 15. For an explanation of punctuation in citations (source references), see Chapter 12.

> **TIP**
>
> Many AP exam passages come from earlier time periods, when the rules of punctuation were different and many more commas and semicolons were used. Modern works tend toward an "open style," with fewer commas and semicolons. Also, British punctuation practice differs slightly from American usage. Don't be surprised to see "broken rules" in an old passage or in one by a British author.

Commas

I can't review all the comma rules here because if I did, you'd have to cart this book around with a forklift. But understanding how commas work with *essential* and *nonessential* elements of a sentence is important — and likely to show up on your AP exam.

Essential and nonessential elements have several possible grammatical identities, but generally they function as descriptions. As the names imply, an *essential element* is necessary, like the wheels on a car. Without the essential element, the meaning of the sentence changes. No commas separate an essential element from the rest of the sentence. A *nonessential element* is extra — like a sunroof or four-speaker sound system. Take the nonessential element away, and the statement says the same thing, though with less detail. Commas separate nonessential elements from the rest of the sentence. (The comma resembles a little handle that lifts a nonessential element out of the sentence.) Here are a couple of example sets, with the essential or nonessential elements underlined:

> The bus drivers <u>who failed the eye test</u> are on strike. (essential)
>
> The bus drivers, <u>who are demanding health coverage for prescription eyeglasses</u>, are on strike. (nonessential)
>
> Shakespeare's play <u>*As You Like It*</u> is a comedy. (essential)
>
> *As You Like It*, <u>a Shakespearean play</u>, is a comedy. (nonessential)

In the example set discussing bus drivers, each sentence talks about a different group. The first sentence references a subgroup; only the drivers who failed the eye test are on strike. The drivers who passed the test are working. The second sentence says that all bus drivers are on strike. The information between the commas provides a reason, but if you lift it out of the sentence, you still learn the main idea: that the bus drivers are striking. Keep an eye out for essential/nonessential information when you're decoding an AP exam passage.

The example set referring to Shakespeare's play is subtler. Shakespeare wrote more than thirty plays, so when I say "Shakespeare's play," you're waiting for me to tell you which one. Therefore, the title (*As You Like It*) is essential, because you don't know which work I'm talking about until I give the name. No commas appear because the essential element is woven into the sentence and can't be lifted out. The second sentence in the set reverses the pattern. Right away you know the title of the play I'm discussing: *As You Like It*. The attribution to Shakespeare is extra, though nice to know.

> **TIP**
>
> No grader expects perfect punctuation from a time-stressed AP test taker. However, in non-timed situations (essays or reports for your school courses), get in the habit of justifying every comma you insert. Once proper punctuation becomes second nature, you'll automatically place commas where they're needed and omit them where they're not.

Semicolons

A period ends a sentence, but a comma doesn't. A semicolon (;) is half period, half comma. Therefore, a semicolon slows the reader down more than a comma but doesn't stop the reader entirely. A semicolon tells you to wait — just a moment — because more information related to what you just read is about to appear. Related, but not exactly the same: A semicolon shifts into a new phase, but a phase that's very close in meaning to the previous one. Check out this example:

> AP exams are more than three hours long; a petition to shorten these tests is circulating.

The second half of the sentence is tied to the first half by the issue of time. The first half tells you how long you have to sit for the exam. The second half explains that students are agitating for shorter tests. The semicolon shows you a shift, but not a complete new direction.

Semicolons also show up, especially in older works, before a conjunction such as "and," "but," "nor," and "or." Usually a comma precedes a conjunction, when the conjunction links two complete sentences, as in this example:

> The petition is unlikely to influence the College Board, but the petitioners intend to try anyway.

If one of the complete sentences already contains a comma, the comma before the conjunction gets a promotion and becomes a semicolon. Why? Because the comma before the conjunction doesn't like to blend in. It has the important job of signaling the arrival of a new idea. Check out this example:

> When the petition arrives at the office, the administration will decide what to do with it; but a shorter AP is years away.

Note: Lots of very well-educated people don't know this rule, so you may not see it in action, and you may ignore it yourself, if you wish. (Reread the previous sentence. I ignored the rule! I explain it here so that you're not surprised if you encounter such a sentence on the test.)

One more point about semicolons: They separate items on a list *if* (and only if) at least one of the items has a comma in it. Here's an example:

> The narrator urges his reader to visit Paris, France; London, England; and Madrid, Spain.

7

Visual Literacy

- Analysis and interpretation of visual sources
- Underlying messages in cartoons, photos, drawings, and advertisements
- The straightforward format of tables, charts, and graphs

The synthesis essay on the AP exam includes at least one visual source: a drawing, photo, cartoon, advertisement, chart, or graph. If you choose a visual as one of your required three sources for the essay (see Chapter 15 for more information), you must know how to interpret it. This chapter helps you develop skills to handle visual material.

STEP-BY-STEP INTERPRETATION

The act of seeing is complex. By learning how to view an image and interpret related text (if present), you can appreciate the visual image on a deeper level. Think of the suggestions in this section as a pair of eyeglasses. Put them on when you're confronted with a drawing, photo, or advertisement, and the art comes into focus. (Graphs, tables, and charts are slightly different. See "How to Read Charts, Tables, and Graphs" in this chapter for more information.)

1. **Get an overall impression.** What do you see? A nobleman, smiling as he looks at his estate? A dog enjoying some treats? At first glance, keep your assessment simple and aim for the main idea.

2. **Think about what's included — and perhaps more importantly, what's missing.** The artist or photographer shapes reality by picking and choosing its content, though not always consciously. For example, if you see a homelike setting (a dining room or den, perhaps), you're probably thinking of family. If no people appear, you may perceive loneliness. Details matter, and you should be conscious of what you're actually looking at.

3. **Zero in on the picture's most important element.** The focus of the work is whatever catches your attention. It may not be in the middle of the image, despite the fact that a central location is prime real estate. The artist may manipulate light and dark or relative size to direct your eye toward one spot. Conversely, notice anything that's presented as less important, perhaps because it's shadowed, small, or hidden in the background.

   The most eye-catching aspect of a visual source is usually an image, but it may be text, with photos or drawings serving as background or secondary elements.

4. **Consider the values or priorities presented.** Once you know the relative importance of various elements in the image, you know something about the society that generated it or about the artist's individual vision. For example, suppose you're looking at a picture of a young man leaning on a 1950s car. If the focus is on the car — it takes up most of the frame or is spotlighted — you know something about the status such a vehicle conferred on its owner.

5. **Examine style.** Does the visual element mirror reality? Or are you looking at something distorted? You may be able to relate the style to the content of the image. Imagine a drawing of a young woman staring in a mirror, seeing herself as larger or smaller than she really is. The drawing suggests that she has a distorted view of her body, and that message may be the point of the artwork.

   Most people think that photos are the ultimate reality show. You point the camera, click, and record what you see. But computer software allows the photographer to change the image. Plus, sophisticated cameras create all sorts of special effects. Also, ultra-close-ups or wide-angle shots look very different from one another. No doubt about it — photos have "style" too.

6. **Look for symbolic elements.** Once upon a time, artists included specific symbols in their works — a skull to represent death, a globe to emphasize power (or travel), jewels to signify wealth, and so on. These traditional symbols still show up from time to time, as well as many contemporary references.

> **TIP**
>
> A stereotype plays upon the human tendency to generalize about large groups of people. Dumb blonds and mad scientists are stereotypes, as are many common (and often offensive) images related to race, gender, religion, and ethnicity. You probably won't detect any overt stereotypes in the visual sources on the AP exam. However, you may find subtle points about identity. I once showed a slide of a famous painting to my class. "What do you see?" I asked. They went on and on about the mythological references, the brushstrokes, the composition, and so on. After 30 minutes, one student said, "Everyone in that painting is white and male." In the time period represented by that painting, white males held pretty much all the power. That observation opened a new avenue for discussion.

7. **Check for allusions.** An *allusion* is a reference to an idea, event, or another artistic work. Allusions add meaning, whether they're verbal or visual. One memorable allusion was the basis for a political cartoon drawn after President Kennedy was assassinated. The massive statue of Abraham Lincoln that sits in the Lincoln Memorial in Washington, D.C., usually stares straight ahead, the arms resting on the chair. After the assassination, the statue was depicted with its head bowed and its face buried in its hands. Clearly, Lincoln was weeping — as was the country.

8. **Identify the intended audience.** An advertisement featuring a "new and improved cane — half off if you buy reading glasses too!" is probably *not* aimed at teenagers. You can't always tell who the audience may be, but try anyway, because the audience may help you deduce the artist's purpose.

9. **If the image contains text, examine how text and image relate to each other.** The words may alter the way you perceive nonverbal elements, and vice versa.

CARTOON ANALYSIS

Cartoons aren't just mindless entertainment; this form of visual art can have a point sharp enough to scratch whatever target it's aimed at. A traditional target is politics. Political cartoons are included in nearly every newspaper, where they make serious points about current events or policy. Figure 7-1 is a political cartoon that appeared in the 19th century, when women were denied the vote. The cartoon is entitled "The Age of Iron: Man as He Expects to Be." The artist was reacting to activists who demanded women's suffrage.

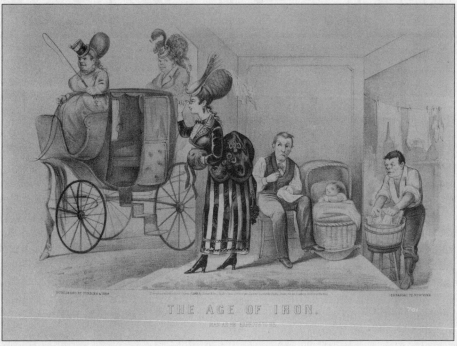

Figure 7-1: A political cartoon entitled "The Age of Iron."

The cartoon in Figure 7-1 is visual *satire,* a form that mocks a point of view or a custom. In the cartoon, traditional roles are reversed. Men sew and wash and mind the baby, while women drive off in a carriage. The eye goes immediately to the woman about to enter the carriage. She's clearly wealthy and is literally turning her back on men. The two men in the cartoon (notice they're outnumbered) are much smaller than the central female. Their clothes are light colored, in contrast to the dark dress of the carriage rider. The men have faded in importance. This image plays into fears that women's rights diminish men. Also, the carriage is inside the house — not its natural place. The message is that nature itself will be reversed if women gain the vote. An interesting aspect of this cartoon is its title. Presumably that tremendous bustle (the large hump of material the carriage passenger is wearing) is supported by something. Maybe iron? Iron is cold and hard — perhaps echoing the way the men might feel about their situation in this unnatural, upended world.

Figure 7-2 mocks the way people lock themselves into one way of thinking, ignoring other and perhaps better possibilities. Drawn in 2008, when gas prices went through the roof, it's also a comment on energy policy.

Cartoon by Sam Goodman

Figure 7-2: Cartoon entitled "Digging for Treasure."

The main message in Figure 7-2 is conveyed by the digger, who ignores the treasure chest in his search for oil. Notice the small shovel the digger's using; the absence of the heavy machinery that oil exploration requires implies that the digger will fail. Now take a close look at the hole. In the first panel, the hole blends in with other shapes. It's not emphasized. In the next three panels, the hole is darker and more prominent. The digger is sinking bit by bit into the hole, but he's still not likely to find what he's looking for. The cartoonist may be suggesting that by relying on oil we're literally digging ourselves a grave — or at least, a hole that's tough to climb out of. The cliff in the first and fourth panels reinforces this message: The digger has already fallen off a cliff. Significantly, the cliff appears higher and more dominant in the fourth panel, because the situation is more serious. In the last panel, the treasure chest (perhaps representing other sources of energy) shares the spotlight. It may be a solution, but the digger's too entranced with oil and doesn't bother opening the chest. The figure in the hat, which appears in all four panels, may be a stand-in for the audience — the public that doesn't know what's going on and more or less has to accept what they're told.

WHAT PHOTOGRAPHS REVEAL

In a recent newspaper article about a drought, I read about rainfall amounts, water rationing, and global climate trends. One month later, I can't remember anything about those factors except that the farmers and residents of the stricken area were struggling because of the lack of rain. But one thing remains absolutely clear in my mind: a photo of a bridge with a prominent "NO DIVING" sign attached to a railing. The bridge spanned a dusty, absolutely waterless trench. The photo convinced me of the crisis.

Figure 7-3, a photo by Karen Ellen Johnson, depicts an elderly woman holding fishing gear. She's standing in the shade of a tree, with a grassy stretch of land around her and a shadowed area of leaves just above her head. She's wearing a sensible hat, and her clothes are utilitarian, not fashionable. Her face is framed by the fishing poles, emphasizing the task (fishing) that she has to accomplish. Now look at her hands; they're thick and capable — what hands become after a life of hard work. No luxury or whimsy for her; she hasn't been pampered. Her legs are slightly apart, and she looks firmly set on the ground. She's not a pushover! The expression on her face reinforces the impression of strength. She gazes directly ahead, unsmiling; she doesn't have to please anyone.

Photo by Karen Ellen Johnson

Figure 7-3: Photo entitled "Fish Story, 1984—1993."

Now dig a little deeper into the photo in Figure 7-3. The subject is in a natural setting, and the vertical lines of her body and of the poles almost make her resemble a tree or, at the very least, imply a strong connection with nature. Her slightly shadowed face adds an element of mystery. The sunny patch across the middle of the photo hints at happiness. The brightest portion of the photo is at the center, where her heart is. Perhaps the photographer is emphasizing the love there, the capacity for feeling. But the darkness overhead implies that the woman has had troubles, too.

> **TIP**
>
> You may worry about reading too much into a photo. Don't! So long as you can anchor your interpretation to something that's actually present in the picture, you're fine. Artists work at least partly from their unconscious, the part of the mind that generates symbols, and symbols require interpretation.

POWERFUL ADVERTISEMENTS

Want to buy some toothpaste, a vacuum cleaner, or a box of strawberries? How about a toaster? And by the way, are you interested in purchasing a life? A new and improved version, of course! If so, you've grasped the main idea behind just about every advertisement. On the surface, an ad sells you a product, but the real message is far more subtle and much more powerful.

Check out Figure 7-4. Its purpose is to sell kitchen paint, but really it's pushing the idea that having a kitchen resembling the one in the illustration will net you a cheerful spouse, a marriage bond that extends to shared cooking, and an orderly life. The people are well dressed; nothing splatters or drips in "a kitchen like this." The husband and wife have time to talk with each other; they're smiling, not trying to figure out who was supposed to pick up the kids from soccer practice.

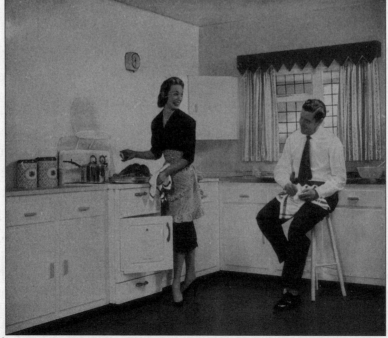

HIP/Art Resource, NY

Figure 7-4: An advertisement entitled "Who couldn't cook well in a kitchen like this? A couple happily preparing a roast."

Now turn your attention to Figure 7-5. This advertisement, printed in the late 19th century, alludes to the fact that in that era whale blubber was an ingredient in some soap products (including, presumably, Soapine). Here the emphasis is on strength. The whale dominates the image, and the oval cleaned by Soapine dominates the whale. Just in case anyone missed the point, the words "Soapine did it" are written on the clean spot. In the 19th century, whales weren't the heartwarming creatures they are today. Instead, whales were seen as strong and dangerous — qualities emphasized in this advertisement. The whale's mouth is menacing. The humans and their vessels (the ship in the background and the boat in the left foreground) are tiny in comparison to the animal. Yet the animal is vanquished by Soapine, which can overcome the whale's natural color and, by implication, the whale's strength and ability to threaten humans. The text also refers to Soapine as "The Dirt Killer." The link between dirt and illness was established (though not completely understood) in the 19th century. Soapine kills dirt, the ad implies, before the dirt can kill you.

HIP/Art Resource, NY

Figure 7-5: An advertisement for Soapine household cleaner.

Finally, take a peek at Figure 7-6. This advertisement was published in the 1920s. The text commands the reader to "Take a Kodak with you" for a day of fun at the shore. The children are frolicking, waves are relatively calm, and the clouds in the sky add contrast but not menace. The central figure is the bathing beauty on a rock. She draws your eye, but you can't see her face. She's the observer, the artist a little removed from the situation and therefore dominant, because she can shape reality with the camera she holds in the crook of her arm. The ad promises power to the photographer, plus the fun of beach-going.

HIP/Art Resource, NY

Figure 7-6: An advertisement for Kodak cameras.

HOW TO READ CHARTS, TABLES, AND GRAPHS

On the AP English Language and Composition exam, many sources may contain statistics. The synthesis essay's visual source — if it's a chart or graph — revolves around numbers. First you have to read the source correctly, and then you have to slice and dice the data until you understand its meaning and how the data supports your argument. (For more information on the synthesis essay, see Chapters 15 and 16.)

Charts and tables

A *pie chart* cuts a circle into pieces, with each piece representing a specific portion of the whole. A pie chart makes it easy to see how something is shared or distributed — whether it's approval or disapproval ratings, membership in various groups, income distribution, or something else. A *table* looks like a window with lots of panes. The headings across the top tell you one classification of information (the year, perhaps), and the headings in the left-hand column tell you another (percent of graduates going to college, for example). When you're reading a chart or table, keep these points in mind:

■ The title and caption often supply important information. For example, the caption may tell you where or how the data were collected ("Income Distribution in Glen Oaks, 2009" or the like).

■ Segments of a pie chart or numbers in a table may represent larger amounts. Here's where the title or caption comes in handy. A "6" in one slot may not represent an amount you can count on your fingers. If the caption says, "Number of Americans who believe they were kidnapped by aliens, in millions," that 6 represents 6,000,000.

- A pie chart is great for helping you see relative importance — who has a bigger stake, more members, the majority opinion, and so on.

- A table often has room for more variables than a pie chart. In a pie chart you may see a breakdown of museum-goers in 2009, for example. In a table, you may see the number of museum-goers sorted by type of museum (natural history, art, science, and so forth) during each year from 1998 to 2009.

- Pie charts are hard on the eyes, unless they're in color. (The AP exam has only black-and-white visuals, so if they throw a pie chart at you, expect to see striped or shaded sections instead of colors, as in Figure 7-7.) Sometimes the segments are labeled to help you distinguish one from another. Read those labels with extra care.

- When reading a table, use the answer sheet to isolate a line and to keep your eyes level. You don't want to mistakenly link data from one line with a label from another.

Take a look at Figure 7-7, which represents results from a fictional survey. If you were writing an essay about AP-exam stress, you could use this source to prove that no one emerges from an AP test fully sane. Figure 7-8 proves the same point, but you can get a lot more out of the data. For example, the number of students who prefer to annoy a family member rather than study remains fairly constant, while watching an octopus video was a one-time phenomenon. (Perhaps an action-hero film featured an octopus in 2007.) Pencil-point balancing and instant messaging have gained in popularity each year.

> **TIP**
>
> The caption for Figure 7-8 states that the numbers are "in thousands." If you write that in 2007, 24 people watched an octopus video when they were supposed to be studying, you're misinterpreting the chart.

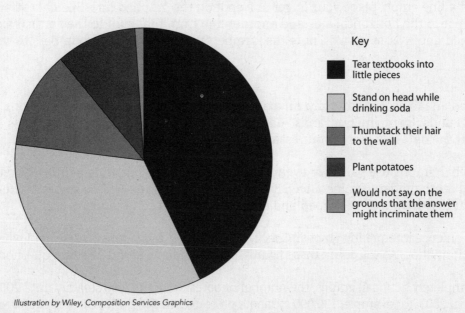

Activities Pursued Following AP Exams

Key

- Tear textbooks into little pieces
- Stand on head while drinking soda
- Thumbtack their hair to the wall
- Plant potatoes
- Would not say on the grounds that the answer might incriminate them

Illustration by Wiley, Composition Services Graphics

Figure 7-7: A pie chart.

Activity of Choice for Students Avoiding Study for the
AP Exam, 2005–2009, in thousands

Avoidance Activity	2005	2006	2007	2008	2009
Throwing spitballs at cat	9	5	4	4	2
Balancing pencil on its point	2	4	5	6	7
Instant-messaging	0	1	2	9	12
Annoying parents or siblings	5	5	5	4	5
Watching octopus videos	0	0	24	0	9

Illustration by Wiley, Composition Services Graphics

Figure 7-8: A table.

Graphs

Bar graphs feature long skinny rectangles representing amounts (of money, people, or whatever subject the graph represents). Line graphs are visually very different from bar graphs and feature spiky or curved lines indicating changes through time (in enrollment, stock prices, and so on). Both types of graphs may appear on the AP exam.

To read a bar graph, check the horizontal and vertical axis — the side-to-side and the up-and-down lines. Both will be labeled. Then look at the bars. Where is a bar situated on the horizontal axis? Its location gives you one piece of information. How high does the bar climb on the vertical axis? Now you have another piece of information.

To interpret a line graph, place your finger at a spot on the graphed line. Sketch a straight line from that spot to the horizontal axis and another line from that spot to the vertical axis. Where your sketched line crosses an axis, note the number. Now you have two numbers to work with.

> **TIP**
>
> Read all labels *very* carefully. An axis may be labeled "Funds Spent, in Billions" or "Funds Spent, in Thousands." Carelessly confusing these two labels means that the data you cite in your essay will be way off.

Sometimes bar graphs use paired or even triplet bars, each representing a different group (ninth graders and tenth graders, for instance). Bars in this sort of graph will be colored differently, with one bar lightly shaded or striped and another darkened completely.

Need some practice interpreting graphs? Check out Figure 7-9 and Figure 7-10, both of which contain the same information. As you see in these figures, lots of students found AP exam questions boring.

In these (completely fictional) graphs, the number of bored students rose steadily until 2005 and then tapered off. In 2003, for example, 130,000 students protested. In 2005, 170,000 students were bored. By 2009, only 70,000 exam-takers were yawning. If you were using one of these graphs as a source, you could make the case that the exam-writers listened to students' complaints and responded to their concerns from 2005 onward. (You could also make the case that students just gave up.)

Students Bored by AP Exam Questions, in thousands

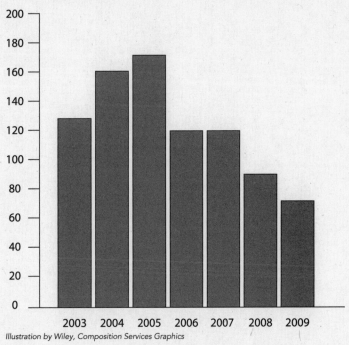

Illustration by Wiley, Composition Services Graphics

Figure 7-9: A bar graph.

Students Bored by AP Exam Questions, in thousands

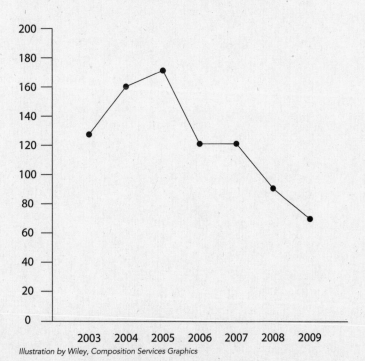

Illustration by Wiley, Composition Services Graphics

Figure 7-10: A line graph.

Types of Writing Found on the Exam

8

Four Modes of Discourse

- The purpose of narrative passages
- The use of description to reveal tone, mood, setting, and more
- The components required in argumentative passages
- The purpose of exposition

Modes of discourse is just a fancy way of saying "types of writing." The term itself isn't important; in fact, your teacher may use a different term. What's important is that you comprehend the characteristics of narrative, description, argument, and exposition. These modes of discourse often overlap, because no writer wants to be tied down unnecessarily. However, each mode comes with a set of customs (conventions). This chapter is a guide to those customs so that, when you encounter these modes of discourse on the AP exam, you'll know what to look for in every passage.

Keep in mind that you move seamlessly from one mode to another in your conversation and in your writing every day. For example, you relate how you went to the mall and, on your way to buy dog food, rescued a toddler who had jumped into a fountain (narrative). Next you go over every single detail of the perfect sports car you saw afterwards (description) and explain why you have to have that vehicle or live in social Siberia for the rest of your life (argument). Finally, you present information on car financing; a ten years' advance on your allowance plus a small, interest-free loan will cover the cost (exposition).

NARRATIVE (STORY) PASSAGES

Once upon a time, gruesome monsters — oops, I mean the AP test makers — placed a narrative, or story-telling passage, on the exam. Courageous heroes — sorry, test taker — read and analyzed the passage and . . . well, you know this story. Okay, I'm kidding about the monsters, though you *can* be a hero on the AP exam, especially if you pay attention to these characteristics of a *narrative passage:*

■ A narrative passage relates a series of events. Especially on the time-limited AP exam, you don't always get the entire story, but you should have enough information to figure out what happens.

■ Narrative mode shows up in both fiction and nonfiction, where it's prominent in memoirs and biography.

■ The events in a narrative passage are not always in chronological (time) order. The author may flash back or flash forward or may hop around the calendar.

> **TIP**
>
> Whenever you encounter a shift (a change) in time order, pay attention. Good authors shift for a reason — to highlight cause and effect, to foreshadow future events, to allow an older voice to comment on youthful habits, and so forth. Resolve to determine the reason for every shift in chronology.

■ Narrative frequently appears in *third-person point of view* (when the author talks about the events), but *first-person point of view* (the "I" narration) is a common choice also. Third-person gives the appearance of impartiality and detachment, but in reality an author always shapes material to manipulate the reader's reaction. (Go to Chapter 4 for more on point of view.)

■ In fiction, first-person point of view relies on a narrator to tell the story. The reader often knows more about the situation than the narrator does. In that gap lies *irony*.

■ In nonfiction memoirs or autobiography, first-person is the author's voice. However, all authors slant even factual material by choosing what to record, what to leave out, and how to tell the story.

■ A helpful literary term in writing about first-person narrative is *persona* — the character the author creates to represent him- or herself. This term acknowledges that the "I" in a narrative is an artistic creation. Keep in mind that the narrator may have a split personality — a younger self who experienced the events that the older self is relating or evaluating.

■ Measure the relative importance of events by comparing how many sentences the author devotes to each. What's highlighted sometimes gives you a clue to the author's purpose and attitude.

■ Narrative passages often include dialogue or report the narrator's thoughts. The diction (word choice) of direct or indirect quotations affects the reader's perception. (See Chapter 3 for more information on diction.)

Time to pick apart a narrative passage. Here's an excerpt from James Weldon Johnson's *The Autobiography of an Ex-Colored Man* in which the narrator describes a spelling bee. As you read Johnson's work, consider *how* the narrative is put together. On scrap paper or in the margins, note the events that happen, character traits of the people mentioned (including the narrator), and everything you notice about writing technique. Then compare your comments to mine, which follow the passage.

[B]y skillful maneuvering I had placed myself third and had piloted "Red Head" to the place next to me. The teacher began by giving us the words corresponding to our order in the line. "Spell 'first.'" "Spell 'second.'" "Spell 'third.'" I rattled off: "T-h-i-r-d, third," in a way which said: "Why don't you give us something hard?" As the words went down the line, I could see how lucky I had been to get a good place together with an easy word.

As young as I was, I felt impressed with the unfairness of the whole proceeding when I saw the tailenders going down before "twelfth" and "twentieth," and I felt sorry for those who had to spell such words in order to hold a low position. "Spell 'fourth.'" "Red Head," with his hands clutched tightly behind his back, began bravely: "F-o-r-t-h."

Like a flash a score of hands went up, and the teacher began saying: "No snapping of fingers, no snapping of fingers." This was the first word missed, and it seemed to me that some of the scholars were about to lose their senses; some were dancing up and down on one foot with a hand above their heads, the fingers working furiously, and joy beaming all over their faces; others stood still, their hands raised not so high, their fingers working less rapidly, and their faces expressing not quite so much happiness; there were still others who did not move or raise their hands, but stood with great wrinkles on their foreheads, looking very thoughtful. The whole thing was new to me, and I did not raise my hand, but slyly whispered the letter "u" to "Red Head" several times. "Second chance," said the teacher. The hands went down and the class became quiet. "Red Head," his face now red, after looking beseechingly at the ceiling, then pitiably at the floor, began very haltingly: "F-u--" Immediately an impulse to raise hands went through the class, but the teacher checked it, and poor "Red Head," though he knew that each letter he added only took him farther out of the way, went doggedly on and finished: "--r-t-h."

The hand-raising was now repeated with more hubbub and excitement than at first. Those who before had not moved a finger were now waving their hands above their heads. "Red Head" felt that he was lost. He looked very big and foolish, and some of the scholars began to snicker. His helpless condition went straight to my heart, and gripped my sympathies. I felt that if he failed, it would in some way be my failure. I raised my hand, and, under cover of the excitement and the teacher's attempts to regain order, I hurriedly shot up into his ear twice, quite distinctly: "F-o-u-r-t-h, f-o-u-r-t-h." The teacher tapped on her desk and said: "Third and last chance." The hands came down, the silence became oppressive. "Red Head" began: "F--" Since that day I have waited anxiously for many a turn of the wheel of fortune, but never under greater tension than when I watched for the order in which those letters would fall from Red's lips "--o-u-r-t-h." A sigh of relief and disappointment went up from the class. Afterwards, through all our school days, "Red Head" shared my wit and quickness and I benefited by his strength and dogged faithfulness.

The events in this narrative are uncomplicated and presented in strict chronological order, though you have the sense that the narrator is looking back as an adult at events he participated in as a child. The end of the passage flashes forward to "all our school days." Nearly everything in the narrative takes place within a few minutes. The narrator and the boy he calls "Red Head" are friends. Red Head stumbles over the spelling of "fourth." The narrator whispers the answer to Red Head and saves the day for his friend. The way the events unfold adds tension to a simple scene. Notice that the narrator's whisper of "u" to Red Head leads to another spelling error. When Red Head finally understands the answer, the author builds suspense by separating the "f" from the "ourth." Throughout the third and fourth paragraphs, the narrator's (and therefore the reader's) focus shifts from the class to Red Head and back several times. These shifts emphasize the antagonistic relationship between Red Head and the other kids. Because the passage is written in first person, the voice you hear is the narrator's. His outsider status (he says the spelling bee was "new" to him) allows him to observe and gives him, for a time, the appearance of objectivity. By the end of the passage, however, he sees his own fate entwined with Red Head's.

The author's use of detail reveals character. Red Head is nervous, probably because he's not a good student. His hands are "clutched tightly behind his back," and after he gets a clue from the narrator, his face turns red and he looks "beseechingly at the ceiling, then pitiably at the floor." He speaks "haltingly" and keeps at it "doggedly." Later the narrator says that Red Head "looked very big and foolish," but he rewards the narrator throughout their school days with "strength and dogged faithfulness." The narrator, on the other hand, is a better student; he says at the end of the passage that he "shared [his] wit and quickness" with Red Head. The narrator also manipulates the spelling bee line so that Red Head is next to him. Clearly, the narrator knows that Red Head will need him — and the narrator will need Red Head. (The reference to "strength" implies that Red Head is physically stronger than the narrator.) The narrator also cares for Red Head; he's often "waited anxiously for many a turn of the wheel of fortune, but never under greater tension" than while waiting for Red Head to answer. The third "character" in this narrative is the rest of the class, which comes across almost as an aggressive mob. The students raise their hands "like a flash" when Red Head makes a mistake, and "some were dancing up and down on one foot with a hand above their heads, their fingers working furiously" to attract the teacher's attention. The "joy beaming all over their faces" contrasts with the narrator's sly whisper of the right answer into Red Head's ear.

> **TIP**
>
> If you were writing about this passage for an essay or answering multiple-choice questions about it, your focus would narrow. You'd note only those details that you're asked about. Narrative passages draw questions about setting, characterization, purpose, tone, attitude, and the like.

DESCRIPTIVE PASSAGES

Every year in my writing class, I distribute raisins and ask students to describe them. Typically, each student lists four or five things about the raisins, which I write on the board. When all the lists are read aloud and duplicates crossed off, about 20 items remain. Yes, you can say 20 things about a raisin — how the outside is wrinkled and the inside is soft, that each raisin's color varies, and so on.

Description is trickier than it appears. When you're reading a descriptive passage, keep an eye out for these traits:

- **A descriptive passage must have an organizing structure — from left to right, top to bottom, older to newer aspects, and so on.** The organizing structure sometimes interacts with the author's attitude or purpose. For instance, in describing a building by moving from older features to modern additions, the author reveals an attitude toward preservation or modernization.

- **Visual ability tends to dominate the other senses, so most descriptions are heavy with visual details.** However, many descriptions include sound, smell, taste, and feel. Because they're rare, nonvisual details merit extra attention. They may make an important point about the object or the person described.

- **What's omitted may be even more important than what's included.** I remember a speech by President John F. Kennedy when he and his wife, along with Vice President Lyndon Johnson and his spouse, visited France. In response to reporters, Kennedy described his wife's elegant clothes. Then he added that no one wanted to know what "Lyndon and I are wearing." The absence of that description tells you a lot about gender roles in the early 1960s.

- **Description is often accomplished with figures of speech (imaginative language such as personification, metaphors, similes, or others).** Figures of speech sometimes add to the subtext — the underlying theme or meaning — of a work. (Check out Chapter 3 for more on figures of speech.) For example, a student of mine once described a divider in an orthodox synagogue as "a border between the nations of men and women." In orthodox Judaism, men and women worship separately. The metaphor emphasizes the separation of sexes.

- **Description may be tucked into another type of passage — a narrative or an expository piece.** Many readers skip description, letting their eyes travel to dialogue or explanation. That's a bad idea. The description contributes to your understanding of theme, purpose, tone, and other aspects of the work.

Ready for a test-drive? Read this descriptive passage and note all the sensory details you're given (information taken in through the five senses, also known as *imagery*). Then figure out what's emphasized, what's omitted, and how the words contribute to meaning. Compare your thoughts to mine, which appear after the passage.

> Mr Lamont and I walked towards an avenue of oaks, which we observed at a small distance. The thick shade they afforded us, the fragrance wafted from the woodbines with which they were encircled, was so delightful, and the beauty of the grounds so very attracting, that we strolled on, desirous of approaching the house to which this avenue led. It is a mile and a half in length, but the eye is so charmed with the remarkable verdure and neatness of the fields, with the beauty of the flowers which are planted all around them and seem to mix with the quickset hedges, that time steals away insensibly.
>
> When we had walked about half a mile in a scene truly pastoral, we began to think ourselves in the days of Theocritus, so sweetly did the sound of a flute come wafted through the air. Never did pastoral swain make sweeter melody on his oaten reed. Our ears now afforded us fresh attraction, and with quicker steps we proceeded, till we came within sight of the musician that had charmed us. Our pleasure was not a little heightened, to see, as the scene promised, in reality a shepherd, watching a large flock of sheep. We continued motionless, listening to his music, till a lamb straying from its fold demanded his care, and he laid aside his instrument, to guide home the little wanderer.

Curiosity now prompted us to walk on; the nearer we came to the house, the greater we found the profusion of flowers which ornamented every field. Some had no other defense than hedges of rose trees and sweetbriars, so artfully planted, that they made a very thick hedge, while at the lower part, pinks, jonquils, hyacinths, and various other flowers, seemed to grow under their protection. Primroses, violets, lilies of the valley, and polyanthuses enriched such shady spots, as, for want of sun, were not well calculated for the production of other flowers. The mixture of perfumes which exhaled from this profusion composed the highest fragrance, and sometimes the different scents regaled the senses alternately, and filled us with reflections on the infinite variety of nature.

When we were within about a quarter of a mile of the house, the scene became still more animated. On one side was the greatest variety of cattle, the most beautiful of their kinds, grazing in fields whose verdure equaled that of the finest turf, nor were they destitute of their ornaments, only the woodbines and jessamine, and such flowers as might have tempted the inhabitants of these pastures to crop them, were defended with roses and sweetbriars, whose thorns preserved them from all attacks.

Though Lamont had hitherto been little accustomed to admire nature, yet was he much captivated with this scene, and with his usual levity cried out, "If Nebuchadnezzar had such pastures as these to range in, his seven years expulsion from human society might not be the least agreeable part of his life."

The organization of this description follows the men's walk. They begin in an "avenue of oaks" more than a mile in length. Next they hear the sound of a flute and see a shepherd, followed by enough flowers to supply every prom in the country. When they're "within about a quarter mile of the house," they see cattle, hemmed in by some plants with thorns. Lamont, one of the walkers, ends the passage by referring to an ancient king exiled from human company. His punishment "might not be the least agreeable part of his life" if the king had had such surroundings.

Most of the details are visual, though the author makes a couple of references to scent. It would be tough to skip the sense of smell in the presence of all those flowers! The most interesting nonvisual detail, however, is the shepherd's song. As they hear the melody, the men feel transported to ancient times (the reference to "Theocritus"). This little scene sounds natural — but it's not. The shepherd is present to control nature, to "guide home the little wanderer," a lamb "straying from its fold." As you dig into the passage, you realize that this paragraph embodies the theme of the entire piece: nature is great, so long as human beings are in charge.

Notice all the references to human intervention. The avenue of oaks leads to the house, so the trees must have been planted with that route in mind. The observer sees the "neatness of the fields"; this land has been cultivated. The flowers have been "artfully planted" to make a "very thick hedge," with the cattle fields receiving special, thorned plants. The figure of speech in the first paragraph (the personification of time, which "steals away") also emphasizes human control of nature by turning a natural element (time) into a person.

Another important item in this description is what *doesn't* appear. No mosquitoes bite the shepherd, and the cattle don't smell. This is idealized nature, not a real country scene. The idealization is most intense in the last paragraph, when Lamont sees nature as a fitting substitute for the company of other people.

When you're reading a description, notice how the details create tone, mood, and setting. Analyze the elements of the description to discover purpose or attitude.

ARGUMENT PASSAGES

Argument passages on the AP exam present a sophisticated case for a particular point of view. You're asked to analyze how the author supports his or her stance, either by answering multiple-choice questions or writing an essay. Plus, you have to argue for your position in the synthesis essay and sometimes in response to another essay question as well. Happily, dissecting an argument essay is easy, as is constructing one yourself. Keep these points in mind:

- The author's position (thesis) is usually summed up in one of two places — the beginning or the end of the essay. Look in those two spots, and underline the thesis.

> **TIP**
>
> If you can't find the thesis at the beginning or the end of the essay, it may be implied instead of stated. After reading the entire passage, formulate a statement that reflects the author's stance. That statement, even though it doesn't appear in the passage, is the thesis.

- No argument works without evidence. Common types of evidence include statistics, comments from experts or authorities, or examples. An argument that relies on logic calls upon what English teachers term *logos*.

- The author may use his or her own experience or reputation in support of the thesis, saying something like "you know I don't usually criticize the administration, but this time I must speak up" or "serving 14 years on this committee has taught me that . . . ." In formal literary language, this sort of argument is called *ethos*.

- Most argument passages make a direct appeal to the reader, either via emotions ("Bert was sad when his guaranteed pay was reduced") or logic ("Bert has spent more money after the reduction, because he's overworked his credit card"). Lit-speak calls emotional appeals *pathos*.

- Effective arguments take the opposing view into account and answer any valid objections (a literary technique called *concession and reply*).

- Not every argument passage plays fair. Be on the alert for coincidence masquerading as cause and effect, sweeping generalizations, circular reasoning ("It's great because it's by Rembrandt, who's great"), and unwarranted assumptions ("Everyone knows that used cars don't work").

- A favorite — and unscrupulous — tactic in arguments is to set up a straw man and then knock him down. A *straw man* is an easy-to-disprove position, falsely attributed to the opposing side.

- Good arguments consider the audience (the readers) and attempt to connect to their concerns.

Here's a charming passage arguing the merits of the automobile. Pick it apart, inspecting how the argument works. Then scan my analysis, located at the end of the passage.

> The great point in favor of the automobile is its sociability. Once one was content to potter about with a solitary companion in a buggy, with a comfortable old horse who knew his route well by reason of many journeys. Today the automobile has driven thoughts of solitude to the winds. Two in the tonneau [back seat], and another on the seat beside you in front — a well-assorted couple of couples — and one may make the most ideal trips imaginable.

Every one looks straight ahead, there is no uncomfortable twisting and turning as there is on a boat or a railway train, and each can talk to the others, or all can talk at once, which is more often the case. It is most enjoyable, plenty to see, exhilarating motion, jolly company, absolute independence, and a wide radius of action. What mode of travel can combine all these joys unless it be ballooning — of which the writer confesses he knows nothing?

On the road one must ever have a regard for what may happen, and roadside repairs, however necessary, are seldom more than makeshifts which enable one to arrive at his destination. If you break the bolt which fastens your cardan-shaft or a link of your side-chains, you and your friends will have a chance to harden your muscles a bit pushing the machine to the next village, unless you choose to wait, on perhaps a lonely road, for a passing cart whose driver is willing, for a price, to detach his tired horse to haul your dead weight of a ton and a half over a few miles of hill and dale. This is readily enough accomplished in France, where the peasant looks upon the procedure as a sort of allied industry to farming, but in parts of England, in Holland, and frequently in Italy, where the little mountain donkey is the chief means of transportation, it is more difficult.

The question of road speed proves nothing with regard to the worth of an individual automobile, except that the times do move, and we are learning daily more and more of the facility of getting about with a motorcar. A locomotive, or a marine engine, moves regularly without a stop for far greater periods of time than does an automobile, but each and every time they finish a run they receive such an overhauling as seldom comes to an automobile.

In England the automobilist has had to suffer a great deal at the hands of ignorant and intolerant road builders and guardians. Police traps, on straight level stretches miles from any collection of dwellings, will not keep down speed so long as dangerous cobblestoned alleys, winding through suburban London towns, have no guardian to regulate the traffic or give the stranger a hint that he had best go slowly. The milk and butchers' carts go on with their deadly work, but the police in England are too busy worrying the motorist to pay any attention. Some county boroughs have applied a ten-mile speed limit, even though the great bulk of their area is open country; but twenty miles an hour for an automobile is far safer for the public than is most other traffic, regardless of the rate at which it moves.

Imagine a time when automobiles were held to ten miles per hour, and no one worried about carbon footprints. This passage refers to the early days of the automobile, but it sounds more suited to a fantasy piece about an alternate universe. However unrealistic it seems, this argument passage gets its point across easily. Right from the start, you know the author's position (pro-car) because the passage begins with the "great point in favor of the automobile," which is that you travel with companions (two in the back, the driver and one other in the front) and can talk without swiveling your head. Just in case anyone missed the point, the author hammers it again at the end of paragraph one ("one may make the most ideal trips imaginable"). The likely audience probably sees cars as newfangled inventions and yearns for "the good old days," when horses were enough.

The author's case is bolstered by supporting arguments, principally the company and the lack of head-swiveling, as I mention above, but also by the idea that there is "plenty to see, exhilarating motion, jolly company, absolute independence, and a wide radius of action." All these advantages are summed up by the author's *rhetorical question* (a question the author will answer or a question that's so obvious no answer is necessary). At the end of paragraph two, the rhetorical question indicates that nothing matches the automobile, except perhaps ballooning, which the author "knows nothing" about.

The next few arguments presented in the passage are designed to answer objections from the reader. If the car breaks down, a handy horse cart will haul it away, or you "have a chance to harden your muscles a bit pushing the machine to the next village." (The author's so pro-car that he makes a breakdown seem like a day at the gym!) If the reader contends that boats and trains are better, the author counters with the fact that "the times do move," and the automobile represents progress. The author admits that the car runs for shorter distances. After this concession comes the reply: The other means of transportation undergo extensive "overhauling" after each trip, but a car doesn't.

My favorite paragraph is the last, in which the author takes on the police, who are so busy worrying about speeding cars (at 10 or 20 miles per hour!) that they neglect "milk and butchers' carts" that presumably cause more fatal accidents, as they're described as "go[ing] on with their deadly work."

EXPOSITORY PASSAGES

When you open a textbook, refer to a user's manual, or read a letter, chances are you're reading *exposition,* a mode of discourse that explains or informs. Expository passages show up all over the AP English Language and Composition exam (and in this book as well).

>
> **TIP**
>
> In fiction or drama, the term *exposition* refers to the part of the story in which background information is delivered. In this section, I deal with nonfiction *exposition,* which conveys information of any type.

Although exposition is probably the most common mode of discourse, it's not easy to pull off. (Think about the last time you set up a new computer. How clear was the manual?) When you're reading exposition, watch out for these characteristics:

- The author generally defines new or unusual terms in an expository passage.

- If a process is involved, the steps proceed in order, each joined to the other by a transition. (For more on transitions, turn to Chapter 4.)

- Each paragraph of an expository passage has a topic sentence, conveying the main idea of that paragraph. The topic sentence may appear at the beginning (most common spot), at the end (less common), or in the middle (very rare).

- Exposition sometimes requires digressions — side points that are necessary to understand the main idea. The digression is usually linked to the main progression of ideas by a transitional word or phrase.

- Although exposition deals with facts, authors often employ *figures of speech* (imaginative language) or analogies to convey information.

- A thread of logic usually ties every aspect of an expository passage together, especially in the exposition of a process. But many expository passages resemble mosaics, with a bunch of well-explained ideas that are related to one main idea. In a mosaic passage, order isn't particularly important. Paragraphs may be moved around without muddying the message.

- The author's voice may be less important in an expository passage. In some works, you can hear the author speaking to you. In other works, the author is an impersonal voice of authority.

  Keep in mind, though, that while exposition may appear neutral, writing always has a point of view, no matter how carefully the author tries to present the facts. The act of choosing (or not choosing) information, the diction (word choice), and the emphasis on one or another point all reflect the author's bias.

Scan this selection from Roberta Larson Duyff's *American Dietetic Association Complete Food and Nutrition Guide,* 2nd Edition. (Wiley, 2002; reprinted with permission of John Wiley & Sons, Inc.). Take notes on the rhetorical techniques the author uses to convey information clearly and concisely. Then read my notes after the passage.

When did "traditional" biotechnology begin? Perhaps ten thousand years ago, as farmers raised animals and grew plants to produce food with desirable traits, higher yields, new food varieties, better taste, faster ripening, and more resistance to drought. Five thousand years ago in Peru, potatoes were grown selectively. In ancient Egypt — forty-five hundred years ago — domesticated geese were fed to make them bigger and tastier. About twenty-three hundred years ago, Greeks grafted trees, a technique that led to orchards and a more abundant fruit supply. In fact, products as commonplace as grapefruit and wine came from traditional biotechnology.

Over the years, farmers have replanted seeds or cross-pollinated from their best crops. And they've bred new livestock from their best animals. For example, within the past few decades, hogs have been bred to be leaner, in turn producing lean cuts of pork for today's consumers.

With traditional breeding, farmers changed the genetic makeup of plants and animals by selecting those with desirable traits. They then raised and selected again and again until a new, more desirable breed or food variety was established. Even in the "old days," all of this breeding resulted in genetic change.

Traditional cross-breeding takes time. Often it's unpredictable. Each time one plant pollinates another, or one animal inseminates another, thousands of genes cross together. Along the way, less desirable traits — and the genes that cause them — may pass with desirable ones. Several generations of breeding, perhaps ten to twelve years may go by before desirable traits get established and less desirable qualities are bred away.

The "new" biotechnology offers a faster and more precise way to establish new traits in both plants and animals — and so provides improved foods that are safe, nutritious, healthful, abundant, and tasty. In a nutshell, modern or "new" biotechnology refers to using living organisms — plants, animals, and bacteria — to develop products not just for food, but also for medical treatment, waste management, and alternative fuels, among others.

Modern food biotechnology started about thirty years ago, as scientists learned more about DNA (deoxyribonucleic acid), genes, and the genetic code in living things, and applied this knowledge to plant and animal breeding practices. In fact, the latest advances in food biotechnology have spawned a new vocabulary. Popular media may use "genetically modified foods" or "GM foods" to refer to these foods. Other terms, such as "genetic engineering," "gene splicing," "cell culture," and "recombinant DNA" refer to some methods of biotechnology.

This selection explains biotechnology and its traditional roots. Although it's exposition and thus appears unbiased, Duyff has a point of view tucked just under the surface. She doesn't state outright that concern about genetically modified foods is unjustified, but by showing how the genes in our food supply have always been modified, she undercuts the argument of opponents who fear "GM foods." The organization of the passage is chronological; it moves from "traditional biotechnology" to "modern food biotechnology." Along the way she takes time to define terms, briefly explain the process of selective breeding, and refer to the media coverage of biotechnology.

The passage begins with a rhetorical question, which Duyff answers immediately. Biotechnology began 10,000 years ago. Then Duyff supplies several examples of ancient biotech in chronological order, beginning with ancient Peru and then moving to Egypt and Greece. She describes the process of selective breeding, starting with the selection of "desirable traits" — including today's leaner pork — and explains how this selection happens through several generations.

Next, the author anticipates questions (and perhaps even objections) from her reader and provides answers. "Why not stick to the natural way?" is countered by the statement that selective breeding takes time and also passes along "less desirable traits." The new biotech, she states, is "faster and more precise." The last paragraph gives an overview of modern biotech, including a quick glossary of media terms for these processes.

Duyff's language is precise and plain, and most sentences follow the most common patterns (subject – verb – complement). The tone is calm and authoritative — just what you'd expect from a passage intended to inform and to allay fears.

Essay Analysis

> ## KEY CONCEPTS
>
> - Key characteristics of essays
> - Common essay structures
> - How to discern meaning from essays

In addition to writing three essays on the AP exam, you must read some, too. Essays are often attached to the multiple-choice portion of the test, and sometimes an essay is the basis for an analytical or synthesis essay question.

In this chapter, I explain what makes an essay an essay and show you how to unearth the underlying structure of each piece you read. I give you a few examples of essays in action, along with my own analysis of the way they're written, so you can compare my comments on the sample essays with your own. Along the way, you should pick up some tips that will help you improve your own essay-writing skills.

CHARACTERISTICS OF AN ESSAY

Writer Edward Hoagland called the definition of an essay a "greased pig" because both the definition and the slippery porker are hard to catch and hold onto. Aldous Huxley said that an essay was a "literary device for saying almost everything about almost anything." Not very specific definitions! Fortunately for you, coming up with a definition isn't necessary. Recognizing the basic characteristics of an essay, however, is important, because chances are you have to do so on the AP exam.

Before I tell you what's essential to an essay, I must clear up some confusion that teachers have created. Some of us call any writing that isn't poetry or fiction "an essay," as in "write a 500-word essay on the Yankees." But this assignment calls for a *report,* a simple survey of the baseball team. A report conveys information, but it doesn't consider the larger point — the significance of that information. Nor does a report hit a higher level of thinking, where some of life's most important questions reside. A report is usually impersonal — a recital of facts, without much personality or a unique voice.

A real essay, on the other hand, is an exercise in thinking things through. An essay ponders, considers, deliberates, interprets, evaluates, criticizes, or views the Big Picture. Traditionally, essays were entitled "On _____." The blank was filled with something important: "On Love," "On Freedom," "On Patriotism," and so forth. Classic essays, those following this model, are favorite AP English exam choices because (a) they're very well written so (b) they're easy to write questions about and (c) the topics are worthy of your time.

Essays in the modern age (and I'm counting the 19th century onward as "modern") have deviated from the pattern of their distinguished ancestors. They often resemble *narratives* (stories), with interpretation tacked on. You often encounter this sort of essay on the op-ed page of a newspaper. The essay begins with a news story or an account of a personal experience and then evaluates its significance or places the event in a larger context.

When you're reading an essay passage on the AP exam, keep the following characteristics in mind. Not every trait I mention here appears in any one essay, but chances are at least some do. These characteristics may become part of your own analytical essay on a passage or may help you answer multiple-choice questions on an essay:

- **The word essay comes from the French word meaning "to try."** Essays often contain an element of process, of trying out ideas and interpretations. When you're reading an essay, you may feel that you've entered into a conversation with the author. As he or she recognizes a connection or comes to a conclusion, so do you.

> **TIP**
>
> Many essays are written after the author's thought process has come to its natural conclusion. The passage may seem to present an idea that the author has always known is true. But if you look closely, you can often uncover the path the author followed to arrive at this idea.

- **Essays often resemble arguments (a mode of discourse explained in Chapter 8).** An argument presents an idea that is supported by evidence. The author may appeal to reason or emotion or may rely on a connection with the reader.

- **All essays are nonfiction, though the writer may insert hypothetical situations to make a point.** The line between reality and imagination should be clearly labeled.

- **An essay presents a voice — the persona created by the author to represent him- or herself.** Virginia Woolf called voice the "most proper but most dangerous and delicate tool" of an essay writer. Listen to the author as you read. Consider what sort of person wrote the essay and what assumptions the author made.

- **Though the author's voice is present, an essay isn't a memoir or an autobiography, even if the author relates events in his or her own life.** An essay attempts to place life experience or observation in a larger context, to answer the universal "What does it all mean?" question.

- **Essays vary greatly in structure, but they have an underlying logic. A great essay by Virginia Woolf describes a journey across London to buy a pencil.** The point isn't the pencil; it's what the writer thinks about as she walks and observes her surroundings.

- **An essay is an artistic creation.** Without slighting the efforts of scientists, journalists, bloggers, and anyone else who writes, their prose qualifies as an essay only if the writing is as much a priority as the information included.

- **Essays range from a handful of paragraphs to book length.** Naturally, you won't see book-length essays on the AP exam; short essays or excerpts are more practical.

ESSAY STRUCTURE

Writers are builders who create structures to hold their thoughts. I can't describe all the possible essay structures, simply because too many exist. Instead, in this section, I tell you the most common designs. Keep an eye out for them as you read and consider using them when you write your own essays.

Anecdote and interpretation

In this configuration, the essay begins with an anecdote. Next, the writer considers the meaning of the events related in the anecdote. Thomas L. Friedman's essay "Eastern Middle School" uses this structure. Written as an op-ed piece for *The New York Times* soon after the September 11, 2001, attacks, Friedman begins by describing his daughter's graduation from a middle school in Washington, D.C. The principal notes that the children represent 40 different countries. As these diverse graduates sing "God Bless America," Friedman muses that the terrorists see the United States as a nation without values. Friedman acknowledges America's shortcomings but says that the country's real values — respect for individual freedom and diversity — are on display at the middle-school graduation, "hiding in plain sight."

TIP

Becoming an expert at anecdote-and-interpretation essays is especially helpful because this type of essay is great for college applications.

Observation leading to conclusion

This structure is quite similar to the anecdote-and-interpretation structure. Instead of beginning with an anecdote, however, this sort of essay starts with an observation of something the writer witnessed or heard or read about. The writer then takes you through the logical ramifications, leading the reader to a concluding idea. Because this type of essay moves the reader from a specific to a generalization, it's sometimes called an *inductive* essay. ("To induce" is "to lead or to move toward a desired end.") One of my favorite essays falls into this category: "The Negro Artist and the Racial Mountain," by Langston Hughes. Writing in the 1920s, the author first quotes a poet who said, "I want to be a poet, not a Negro poet." Hughes moves from that comment to a consideration of the stereotypes facing African-American writers and the artist's obligation to his or her audience. Hughes concludes that it's more important to write without regard for one's audience and for African-American artists to be free "within ourselves."

Compare and contrast

This staple of nearly every academic area pops up in the world of essays also. Two (or perhaps more) anecdotes or observations or descriptions form the bulk of the essay. At the end, or sometimes woven throughout, are the author's observations on the significance of the similarities and differences. Amy Tan's superb essay "Mother Tongue" compares her mother's broken English to Tan's own educated speech. Her mother's efforts are dismissed by doctors and bankers, but when Tan asks for the same information, she is treated courteously. Tan also recounts her own experience switching between her "mother tongue" (the part Chinese, part English her mother speaks) and standard English, and Tan concludes that her mother tongue helped her appreciate language and become a writer.

TIP

If a comparison-and-contrast essay makes an appearance on your AP exam, mentally list the similarities and differences. Be sure to identify the author's thoughts about both. Most of the meaning lies in the interpretation, not in the description of the compared and contrasted elements.

Big ideas

A Big Idea essay — the capital letters emphasize that you're talking about something important — is a collection of statements about love or jealousy or patriotism or something else that's important and philosophical. The interesting thing about this structure, most often found in older works, is that just about every sentence in a Big Idea essay could be the topic sentence of an entire paragraph, if not the thesis of a whole other essay. If you read a Big Idea essay at your normal rate, you'll be on the floor before you're halfway to the end. This type of essay assumes that you read one sentence, walk around the block for a while thinking about the idea, and then read another. Fortunately, Big Idea essays tend to be quite short.

TIP

Naturally, walks around the block are not on the AP-exam agenda. If you encounter a Big Idea essay (most likely in the multiple-choice section), slow down. Read one sentence, pause, and restate it in your own words. Then move on to the next sentence. If you get stuck, skip the sentence and try the next one. Chances are the skipped sentence isn't crucial, and you can still comprehend most of the essay.

For a good example of a Big Idea essay, check out anything by Francis Bacon, especially "Of Studies," which discusses why you're in school (in case you need some motivation).

Thesis and proof

A thesis-and-proof essay begins with a *proposition,* an idea you put in front of the reader. Next come all the reasons why this idea is true. You've been writing thesis-and-proof essays for years, on English and history tests. The essays you write in the free-response section of the AP English Language and Composition exam may be in thesis-and-proof form. Plenty of stellar writers have used this structure with great success. Take a look at "On Lying in Bed," by British author G. K. Chesterton. This essay has one of the best first lines *ever:* "Lying in bed would be an altogether perfect and supreme experience if only one had a coloured pencil long enough to draw on the ceiling." Chesterton makes the case that life's small pleasures (such as "lying in bed") are superior to activities usually considered more important. You may not agree with him, but you have to give him credit for good writing.

TIP

When you're reading a thesis-and-proof essay, the most important task is to locate the thesis. It's usually in the first paragraph. Imagine that a defense attorney is attacking the thesis. How does the prosecutor (the essayist) respond? The prosecutor's case is the proof.

Mosaic

I call this structure "mosaic" because it resembles the art form in which little tiles are assembled to form a coherent whole. You can't grasp the overall effect of a mosaic essay until you've reached the end, when the seemingly random ideas, anecdotes, and descriptions come together and present a theme. "On Keeping a Notebook," by Joan Didion, at first puzzles the reader. Didion flips through her notebook, quoting what she's written there and commenting on the circumstances that led to each jotting. Not until the end do you realize that Didion is explaining the function of a writer's notebook and revealing how such a notebook fits into the writing process.

TIP

If you run across a mosaic essay on the AP exam, don't panic. Stick with it until the end. Mentally, step back and think: What's this all about? If no answer occurs to you, move on to another question or passage. Sometimes a little time and space are needed to make sense of a mosaic essay.

SAMPLE ESSAYS

This section presents two essay excerpts and one complete essay similar to those you may encounter on the AP exam. The structure you see in the excerpted essays may differ slightly from the ones I describe in the preceding section. But even in the excerpts, you should have enough to get a good idea of AP-style essay passages. After each essay, I list my thoughts on the rhetorical devices each author uses to convey ideas, the organizational pattern of the work, and anything else I can think of. Read with a pen in your hand, and before you read my comments, make some of your own. Then compare your observations with mine.

"Civil Disobedience"

Henry David Thoreau, a 19th-century American essayist, urges readers to resist injustice in "Civil Disobedience," excerpted here. In his essay, written in 1849, Thoreau refers to slavery in the American South, the treatment of Native Americans by the United States government, and the war between the United States and Mexico.

All men recognize the right of revolution; that is, the right to refuse allegiance to, and to resist, the government, when its tyranny or its inefficiency are great and unendurable. But almost all say that such is not the case now. But such was the case, they think, in the Revolution of '75. If one were to tell me that this was a bad government because it taxed certain foreign commodities brought to its ports, it is most probable that I should not make an ado about it, for I can do without them. All machines have their friction; and possibly this does enough good to counter-balance the evil. At any rate, it is a great evil to make a stir about it. But when the friction comes to have its machine, and oppression and robbery are organized, I say, let us not have such a machine any longer. In other words, when a sixth of the population of a nation which has undertaken to be the refuge of liberty are slaves, and a whole country is unjustly overrun and conquered by a foreign army, and subjected to military law, I think that it is not too soon for honest men to rebel and revolutionize. . . .

Under a government which imprisons unjustly, the true place for a just man is also a prison. The proper place today, the only place which Massachusetts has provided for her freer and less despondent spirits, is in her prisons, to be put out and locked out of the State by her own act, as they have already put themselves out by their principles. It is there that the fugitive slave, and the Mexican prisoner on parole, and the Indian come to plead the wrongs of his race should find them; on that separate but more free and honorable ground, where the State places those who are not with her, but against her — the only house in a slave State in which a free man can abide with honor. If any think that their influence would be lost there, and their voices no longer afflict the ear of the State, that they would not be as an enemy within its walls, they do not know by how much truth is stronger than error, nor how much more eloquently and effectively he can combat injustice who has experienced a little in his own person. Cast your whole vote, not a strip of paper merely, but your whole influence. A minority is powerless while it conforms to the majority; it is not even a minority then; but it is irresistible when it clogs by its whole weight. If the alternative is to keep all just men in prison, or give up war and slavery, the State will not hesitate which to choose. If a thousand men were not to pay their tax bills this year, that would not be a violent and bloody measure, as it would be to pay them and enable the State to commit violence and shed innocent blood. This is, in fact, the definition of a peaceable revolution, if any such is possible. If the tax-gatherer, or any other public officer, asks me, as one has done, "But what shall I do?" my answer is, "If you really wish to do anything, resign your office." When the subject has refused allegiance, and the officer has resigned from office, then the revolution is accomplished. But even suppose blood should flow. Is there not a sort of blood shed when the conscience is wounded? Through this wound a man's real manhood and immortality flow out, and he bleeds to an everlasting death. I see this blood flowing now.

This is just a thin slice of Thoreau's masterpiece, which he wrote after spending the night in jail for refusing to pay taxes that he believed would finance unjust governmental actions. (His friends bailed him out without his knowledge.) Thoreau took advantage of his time in jail to consider the nature of government and the proper relationship of citizens to the power wielded in their name. Here's my analysis of this essay excerpt:

- The last sentence of the first paragraph is its topic sentence: "I think that it is not too soon for honest men to rebel and revolutionize." This topic sentence also sets up Thoreau's main argument: One must resist an unjust government.

- The first paragraph compares the situation preceding "the Revolution of '75" (the Revolutionary War) with the current situation ("a sixth of the population . . . are slaves, and a whole country [Mexico] is unjustly overrun"). The comparison reinforces the idea of resistance to tyranny.

- The second paragraph begins with a strong topic sentence: "Under a government which imprisons unjustly, the true place for a just man is also a prison." Next Thoreau presents his proof for this statement: Prison is where fugitive slaves and Mexican prisoners are sent, and jail is "the only house in a slave State in which a free man can abide with honor." He urges readers to vote not just with paper but with their lives — their "whole influence." If everyone protests injustice, the State will yield because it cannot imprison "all just citizens." He recounts his conversation with the tax collector, whom Thoreau urges to resign.

- Thoreau's reasoning — whether you agree with him or not — is very clear. It's based on a series of assumptions: that slavery and the invasion of Mexico are great wrongs, that taxes support those actions, and that a just man must go to jail rather than give in to injustice. This is a "thesis-and-proof" essay. (See the preceding section for more information.)

- In both paragraphs of the excerpt, Thoreau employs repetitive (but slightly differing) statements. Similar syntax and diction link the statements, but in every case the variations make Thoreau's point. The first example of repetition is "such is not the case now" and "such was the case, they think, in the Revolution of '75." Thoreau contrasts the way people viewed the government in the Revolutionary period with the way they evaluate their own time period. Another example of repetition is the word "place" ("proper place today, the only place"). Repeating "place" emphasizes that jail, in Thoreau's opinion, is the "only place" for those who believe in justice. Also in paragraph two are two sentences with "put" and "out" ("to be put out and locked out of the State by her own act" and "they have already put themselves out by their principles"). The State of Massachusetts puts people "out" of society and into jail, but the prisoners have already left the unjust society by means of their just principles. Finally, Thoreau contrasts the nonviolent act of refusing to pay taxes ("not to pay their tax bills this year, that would not be a violent and bloody measure") with tax payment, which would "enable the State to commit violence."

- Thoreau's figurative language includes the metaphor of a machine and friction in paragraph one and the metaphor of blood in paragraph two. The machine represents government, and friction symbolizes the inevitable mistakes government makes. When those mistakes rise to the level of evil, Thoreau says, government becomes the friction — the evil — and must be resisted. Thoreau continues, "I say, let us not have such a machine any longer." The blood comes from a wounded conscience, but Thoreau equates it with "a man's real manhood and immortality."

■ Paragraph one contains an allusion to the Boston Tea Party, which occurred because "a bad government . . . taxed certain foreign commodities." Thoreau, had he lived in that era, would simply have avoided those commodities. In comparison to slavery and the invasion of Mexico, a tax on tea wasn't worth his time.

■ Thoreau's diction is formal, and the tone is passionate. Statements such as "Cast your whole vote, not a strip of paper merely, but your whole influence" are extreme, but he's backed them with careful reasoning.

"On Envy"

Samuel Johnson, an 18th century essayist, is famous for his quotable pronouncements on many topics, among them envy. This short essay is reprinted in its entirety. Don't be thrown off balance by some irregular spelling (which was proper in Johnson's day) or by Johnson's dense style. Read slowly, and the meaning will come through.

Envy is almost the only vice which is practicable at all times, and in every place; the only passion which can never lie quiet for want of irritation: its effects therefore are everywhere discoverable, and its attempts always to be dreaded.

It is impossible to mention a name which any advantageous distinction has made eminent, but some latent animosity will burst out. The wealthy trader, however he may abstract himself from publick affairs, will never want those who hint, with Shylock, that ships are but boards. The beauty, adorned only with the unambitious graces of innocence and modesty, provokes, whenever she appears, a thousand murmurs of detraction. The genius, even when he endeavours only to entertain or instruct, yet suffers persecution from innumerable criticks, whose acrimony is excited merely by the pain of seeing others pleased, and of hearing applauses which another enjoys.

The frequency of envy makes it so familiar, that it escapes our notice; nor do we often reflect upon its turpitude or malignity, till we happen to feel its influence. When he that has given no provocation to malice, but by attempting to excel, finds himself pursued by multitudes whom he never saw, with all the implacability of personal resentment; when he perceives clamour and malice let loose upon him as a publick enemy, and incited by every stratagem of defamation; when he hears the misfortunes of his family, or the follies of his youth, exposed to the world; and every failure of conduct, or defect of nature, aggravated and ridiculed; he then learns to abhor those artifices at which he only laughed before, and discovers how much the happiness of life would be advanced by the eradication of envy from the human heart.

Envy is, indeed, a stubborn weed of the mind, and seldom yields to the culture of philosophy. There are, however, considerations, which, if carefully implanted and diligently propagated, might in time overpower and repress it, since no one can nurse it for the sake of pleasure, as its effects are only shame, anguish, and perturbation.

It is above all other vices inconsistent with the character of a social being, because it sacrifices truth and kindness to very weak temptations. He that plunders a wealthy neighbour gains as much as he takes away, and may improve his own condition in the same proportion as he impairs another's; but he that blasts a flourishing reputation, must be content with a small dividend of additional fame, so small as can afford very little consolation to balance the guilt by which it is obtained.

I have hitherto avoided that dangerous and empirical morality, which cures one vice by means of another. But envy is so base and detestable, so vile in its original, and so pernicious in its effects, that the predominance of almost any other quality is to be preferred. It is one of those lawless enemies of society, against which poisoned arrows may honestly be used. Let it therefore be constantly remembered, that whoever envies another, confesses his superiority, and let those be reformed by their pride who have lost their virtue.

It is no slight aggravation of the injuries which envy incites, that they are committed against those who have given no intentional provocation; and that the sufferer is often marked out for ruin, not because he has failed in any duty, but because he has dared to do more than was required.

Almost every other crime is practised by the help of some quality which might have produced esteem or love, if it had been well employed; but envy is mere unmixed and genuine evil; it pursues a hateful end by despicable means, and desires not so much its own happiness as another's misery. To avoid depravity like this, it is not necessary that any one should aspire to heroism or sanctity, but only that he should resolve not to quit the rank which nature assigns him, and wish to maintain the dignity of a human being.

Not an easy essay to read, but Johnson has made some good points about envy. Check out my observations:

- This classic essay follows a Big Idea pattern. Nearly every sentence makes an important point, and Johnson includes no unnecessary elaboration. The reader's job is to flesh out every idea.

- The first paragraph lays out Johnson's thesis: Envy is everywhere. Paragraph two cites categories of people who provoke envy because of their accomplishments — the "wealthy trader," "the beauty," and "the genius." The next paragraph continues the logical thread. Because envy is everywhere, you don't notice it — unless you become a target of envy. Then you find out "how much the happiness of life would be advanced by the eradication of envy from the human heart." Paragraph four marks a shift from problem to solution. If you try hard, you can "overpower and repress" envy. Paragraph five explains that those who envy make themselves unhappy. Paragraph six goes to extremes; because envy is so bad, it's okay to use "poisoned arrows" against it. In case the reader objects to that last point, the next paragraph explains again that the object of envy has earned hatred not because "he has failed in any duty, but because he has dared to do more than was required." The conclusion slams envy out of the park: Johnson calls it a "crime," "genuine evil," and "depravity" — extreme words.

- As you see, nearly any paragraph of Johnson's essay could be expanded into an entirely separate essay about a particular aspect of envy — how it harms the envious person, how to fight envy, and so forth.

- Johnson's figurative language contributes to his message. Envy is "a stubborn weed of the mind" (a metaphor), and those who harm another's reputation because of envy gain "a small dividend of additional fame" (another metaphor).

- Paragraph two also alludes to a Shakespearean character, Shylock, of *The Merchant of Venice*. Shylock is a complicated character; the reference here is to Shylock's envy and his desire to see others fail.

- The syntax places ideas in parallel structure and balances them in importance. Here's just one of many possible examples, drawn from paragraph three: "When he that has given no provocation to malice . . . finds himself pursued . . . when he perceives clamour and malice . . . when he hears . . ." All those "when he" statements build to a strong conclusion: "he then learns" how bad envy is.

"Chimney Pot Papers"

Who loves rainstorms? Read this excerpt from "Chimney Pot Papers" to find out. This essay was written by Charles S. Brooks, a 20th century American humorist.

At this moment beneath my window there is a dear little girl who brings home a package from the grocer's. She is tugged and blown by her umbrella, and at every puff of wind she goes up on tiptoe. If I were writing a fairy tale I would make her the Princess of my plot, and I would transport her underneath her umbrella in this whisking wind to her far adventures, just as Davy sailed off to the land of Goblins inside his grandfather's clock. . . . How she labors at the turn, hugging her paper bag and holding her flying skirts against her knees! An umbrella, however, usually turns inside out before it gets you off the pavement, and then it looks like a wrecked Zeppelin. You put it in the first ash-can, and walk off in an attempt not to be conspicuous.

Although the man who pursues his hat is, in some sort, conscious that he plays a comic part, and although there is a pleasing relish on the curb at his discomfort, yet it must not be assumed that all the humor on the street rises from misadventure. Rather, it arises from a general acceptance of the day and a feeling of common partnership in the storm. The policeman in his rubber coat exchanges banter with a cab-driver. If there is a tangle in the traffic, it comes nearer to a jest than on a fairer day. A teamster sitting dry inside his hood, whistles so cheerily that he can be heard at the farther side-walk. Good-naturedly he sets his tune as a rival to the wind.

It must be that only good-tempered persons are abroad — those whose humor endures and likes the storm — and that when the swift dark clouds drove across the world, all sullen folk scurried for a roof. . . . There are many persons, of course, who like summer rains and boast of their liking. This is nothing. One might as well boast of his appetite for toasted cheese. Does one pin himself with badges if he plies an enthusiastic spoon in an ice-cream dish? . . . Of course they like it. Who could help it? This is no proof of merit. Such folk, at best, are but sisters in the brotherhood.

And yet a November rain is but an August rain that has grown a beard and taken on the stalwart manners of the world. And the November wind, which piped madrigals in June and lazy melodies all the summer, has done no more than learn brisker braver tunes to befit the coming winter. If the wind tugs at your coat-tails, it only seeks a companion for its games. It goes forth whistling for honest celebration, and who shall begrudge it here and there a chimney if it topple it in sport?

Despite this, rainy weather has a bad name. So general is its evil reputation, that from of old, one of the lowest circles of Hell has been plagued with raw winds and covered thick with ooze — a testament to our northern March — and in this villains were set shivering to their chins. But the beginning of the distaste for rainy weather may be traced to Noah. Certain it is that toward the end of his cruise, when the passengers were already chafing with the animals — the kangaroos, in particular, it is said, played leap-frog in the hold and disturbed the skipper's sleep — certain it is while the heavens were still overcast that Noah each morning put his head anxiously up through the forward hatch for a change of sky. There was rejoicing from stem to stern — so runs the legend — when at last his old white beard, shifting from west to east, gave promise of a clearing wind. But from that day to this, as is natural, there has persisted a stout prejudice against wind and rain.

But this is not just. If a rainy day lacks sunshine, it has vigor for a substitute. The wind whistles briskly among the chimney tops. There is so much life on wet and windy days. Yesterday Nature yawned, but today she is wide awake.

Doesn't Brooks make you long for a storm? Here's what I came up with after reading Brooks's essay:

■ The structure of this essay most closely conforms to "observation leading to conclusion." The excerpt begins with a description of a little girl. She's nearly blown away as she struggles down the street holding a paper bag. Next you see a man who's lost his hat to the wind. The cop and cabbie are next, and finally a teamster who's managed to stay dry. These specific observations are followed by a generalization: Good-tempered persons go out in a storm, so the baddies must be inside. Now comes the response to an anticipated reader comment: Yes, lots of people like summer rains, but that's the Weather Channel equivalent of liking toasted cheese or ice cream. As the author says, "Who could help it?" To like November rain, on the other hand, takes character. The next paragraph muses about the reasons why stormy weather "has a bad name." Perhaps this reputation stems from Noah (an allusion to the Bible story of Noah's ark), when even the animals longed for sunlight after the Flood. The excerpt (Brooks goes on for a few more pages about the wonderfulness of storms) ends with an affirmation of rainy weather: "Yesterday Nature yawned, but today she is wide awake." Storms represent nature at her liveliest.

■ Brooks's tone is fanciful. He imagines Noah's mood and alludes to Dante. (In paragraph five, "the lowest circles of Hell" is a reference to *The Divine Comedy*.) He contemplates toasted cheese and ice cream, comparing them to summer rains. He sees November's rain as "an August rain that has grown a beard."

■ Rain is only one of the examples of personification in this essay. The wind is personified too, because it's described as a force that "piped madrigals in June and lazy melodies all the summer." Nature is also personified; she "yawned" yesterday and during the storm was "wide awake."

■ By describing only cheerful people — the little girl, the man who's lost his hat, the cop, and so forth — Brooks has stacked the evidence deck in favor of his conclusion about the superiority of bad weather.

10

How to Pick Apart Memoirs and Biographies

> ### KEY CONCEPTS
>
> - Rhetorical devices common to memoirs and autobiographies
> - The relationship between autobiographical writing style and content
> - The purpose of biographies

Just about everyone is interested in other people and their life stories. You'll probably face a biographical or an autobiographical passage on the AP English Language and Composition test. Just remember that biography and autobiography (also known as *memoir,* from the French for "remember") are essentially gossip. Old gossip, maybe — well-written gossip, certainly — but gossip all the same. And because everyone loves gossip, you're probably already an expert at decoding this genre. This chapter helps you fine-tune your biography and autobiography interpretive skills.

RHETORICAL DEVICES IN BIOGRAPHIES AND AUTOBIOGRAPHIES

The AP exam is fairly short, so you won't read any life-to-death biographies. Instead, expect to see a slice of life in a biographical or an autobiographical selection. The AP test makers pick their literature carefully, but they're mostly concerned with testing your ability to understand *rhetorical devices,* the techniques that writers use to convey information. (Part II explains everything you need to know about rhetorical devices.)

Writers' approaches to biography or autobiography vary almost as much as their subjects do. The passage may be told solely from the writer's point of view, for example, or it may include quotations from letters, diaries, or friends. The tone may be critical, enthusiastic, analytical, and so on. Therefore, I can't tell you what you'll see on the exam. I can, however, explain what to look for:

- **Check point of view.** Is the subject talking? If so, the piece is written in first person, the usual point of view for autobiography. (However, some writers have been known to talk about themselves in the third person.)

  In a first-person piece, it's natural to equate the narrator with the author. However, no matter how objective they try to be, all authors shape the reader's perception through writing style and content choice. The term *persona* refers to the character the writer creates to represent him- or herself.

  In third-person point of view (the choice for biographies), does the author attempt to interpret the subject's personality, motivations, and emotions? Or does the author take a more objective stance, relying solely on verifiable material such as quotations, actions, historical records, and the like?

- **Look for descriptions, because they illuminate character.** Setting says a lot about what the subject values or about how the subject lives. A tour of my office, for example, would feature the 30 minor-league baseball pennants on the wall, all souvenirs of games I've attended. If that fact were included in my biography, the reader would know how important baseball is to me. A physical description of the subject or of people close to the subject may also reveal important information. I've never met Yao Ming, an extremely tall basketball player, but I imagine that his height has affected more than his choice of career.

- **Examine relationships, if any are presented.** You may find a paragraph about the subject's parents or best friend. What does that relationship tell you about the subject? The writer may do the work for you, analyzing the relationship, or may expect you to figure it out yourself.

- **Pay extra attention to quotations.** Technically, everything in first-person point of view is a quotation from the author. But even in first-person, quotations from others may appear. In third-person biographical passages, the subject's own words may be quoted, or you may see quotations from others. If the author included the exact words, those words are significant.

■ **Consider any anecdotes that are present.** Although AP exam passages are relatively short (500 to 800 words), one or two anecdotes may be tucked into the main narrative. What do those anecdotes add to your understanding of the subject? Often anecdotes provide contrast, showing a softer side of a hard-edged character, perhaps.

> **TIP**
>
> Anecdotes may also reveal themes. Look for common threads tying anecdotes together and to the main narrative. If the common thread is loyalty, for instance, then that quality is an important aspect of the subject.

■ **Check *tone* — a reflection of the writer's attitude.** Tone comes across partly through the author's *diction,* or word choice, but also through what the author chooses to tell you. Especially in autobiography, tone is a character clue. A passage reporting that "the police officer arrested me" is very different from one that says, "The cop hauled me down to the station." The first has a detached tone; the second has a touch of resentment. In biography, tone helps you evaluate the accuracy of the author's interpretation. If the tone is consistently critical, for example, you may want to give the subject a little more credit than the author does, to correct for any possible bias.

■ **Notice what's not in the passage.** Granted, space limitation is an important factor. However, within the passage, the author may leave out something you'd expect to find. What does that omission tell you? For example, if a passage about a subject's family mentions everyone but the mother, that fact is significant, either because the mother died young or because the autobiographer has issues. However, what a biographer omits may merely reflect who was willing to talk to the writer and who wasn't.

Rest assured that AP test makers play fair. Anything they ask you about a passage can be answered based on what's printed on the page. The significance of missing items is usually explained or implied by other material in the passage.

A FOCUS ON AUTOBIOGRAPHY

The Story of My Life, By Me. That's autobiography in a nutshell. Once you break the shell open, of course, autobiography becomes more complicated. The autobiographer may be writing to bear witness to an important historical event he or she witnessed. At times, autobiographies arise from attempts to understand the self, to make peace with people or events in the past, or to justify one's actions.

Whatever the purpose, writing style and content should complement each other, as in all good literature. As you read these autobiographical passages, keep your eyes open and your pen handy. Note the rhetorical devices I mention in the preceding section. Jot down everything you notice, as if you were preparing to write an essay. Then if you actually have to write an analytical essay about an autobiographical selection, you'll be in top shape. As a bonus, the points you note may possibly be the basis for multiple-choice questions, so you'll be prepared for those as well.

A New Yorker's story

Try your hand at this kind of text analysis. This passage, an excerpt from an article entitled "The Visit," describes a Manhattan resident's visit to a counselor near the site of the September 11, 2001, attacks on the World Trade Center.

No. Jack, our counselor, doesn't wear a white robe and sit on a rusted barrel pushed deeply into the sand for balance at the Site. Actually, he has a townhouse with a door-bell. There is nothing to distinguish his building from the others on the block. They all look new and possibly uninhabited. All are beige. All the doorbells are black. Each house has a stoop on which no one sits. There are no cars parked at the curb. I have to remind myself that I am in Manhattan.

Jack's is the first house in a row of ten. After the tenth, there is the Hudson River. The blue water is moving swiftly. He doesn't have a sign on the door. The first time we came, we skeptically compared the address in the article about the Counseling Center with the one on the townhouse. The numbers matched. It didn't look special. After all these times, it still takes faith to believe that there is someone inside who will answer the door.

I press the button and we hear nothing.

I don't doubt that someone will answer and lead us up the stairs to where Jack sits, for I realize I have made a deal. My end of the deal is that I remain defiant. I need to be defiant if I am going to survive. Jack has made that clear.

"It could be dangerous not to be defiant."

With Jack's help I have begun the process of healing, despite living in an environ-ment of promised attacks in the future, the incompetence of the FBI and the CIA, air-planes again flying over Manhattan, waiting for the first suicide bombers, politically correct random car checks, dirty bombs, being sniffed at by mean dogs that are held in check by young men in camouflage, having my bag probed by flashlights numerous times and never having my knife found, speculation about Bin Laden's kidneys, anthrax scares that become real, panic attacks, crying binges, and more.

I am learning to replace faith with defiance. Faith would be Pollyanna-ish. Things will become worse, probably.

As we wait for someone to answer the bell, I relax because there is a second part to the deal I have cut with Jack. I am allowed to have faith on this stoop and in this house. He has helped me, and he will help me more. I know that to be true. I believe that to be true. I don't have to be defiant here. I can have faith here.

To the east, across the street, there is a sign for a dentist's office, followed by two or three other buildings. Those buildings are also replicas of Jack's. Past the dentist and those other buildings is the void without shadows. I don't look at it, but that empty space is the reason we are in the neighborhood. We don't ignore it. We just don't look at it.

Last Saturday we weren't here; we were in Pennsylvania Station on our way to visit my sister for the first time since my mother's death. Since the attack, I have become a man of reasons. I no longer just visit relatives. I no longer just do anything. The terror-ists have made me anti-Nike, anti-"just do it." I have been humbled. Talk of climbing mountains just because they are there confuses me. I don't climb mountains. I take steps, very small steps. And each step is an end to itself. Each step must have a reason. I want each step to be up, but this is not necessarily true. There will be times when I wander in the wrong direction. I am just learning how to walk again. I am a human who is living in a very abnormal time.

This excerpt from "The Visit" captures the anguish so many felt after the attacks of September 11, 2001. The first-person narrative clearly conveys the fact that you're reading one person's story, but its themes are universal. Here's what I noted about the style and content of the passage:

- The heart of the passage is in the last paragraph, in which the writer states, "I take steps, very small steps." The dominant characteristic of this passage is the series of short, simple sentences. In paragraph two, for example, you see: "Jack's is the first house in a row of ten. After the tenth, there is the Hudson River. The blue water is moving swiftly." More short sentences follow, but I think you get the point. The sentences are themselves a series of "very small steps."

- Many of the sentences follow an "I – verb" pattern. One theme of this piece is that the writer can't control events, only himself. He's "made a deal," which the series of "I" statements explains.

- Most of the paragraphs are also short; in fact, two paragraphs (the third and the fifth) contain just one short sentence each. Again, the "very small steps" are mirrored by the paragraphing.

- The short-sentence pattern is broken here and there, notably in paragraph six. The content of paragraph six is a description of the writer's fears — "promised attacks," "anthrax scares," and so on. The paragraph is just one sentence long, but it's a very long sentence. The list creates a tone of anxiety and echoes the way frightened people explain what they're worried about. Furthermore, the sentence is complex because terrorism is complex; the author (and probably the reader as well) can't wrap his mind around it easily.

- Diction also connects to meaning. Most of the words are quite simple. In the last paragraph, the author says, "I have been humbled." Life has been reduced to its essentials — simplified, like the words in this passage.

- In paragraph one, the "uninhabited" houses have "stoop[s] on which no one sits." This image of emptiness is repeated in paragraph nine, where the author refers to "the void without shadows" and "that empty space" — the site of the attacks. Though the World Trade Center site is never described directly, the setting of this piece is crucial to its meaning.

- The last paragraph appears to begin a digression — a reference to a family visit. However, the visit is linked to the rest of the passage by its style ("I – verb" sentences) and content ("I take steps"). In a way, this paragraph brings the piece full circle, because visiting the counselor is a "small step."

- The author is the only "character" in the story, though he refers to "Jack," the counselor, and uses the pronoun "we" at times. The plural implies that the author is not alone in visiting the counselor. Although the "we" isn't explained here, its appearance brings in an element of universality; many New Yorkers are experiencing the same emotions.

An emigrant's story

For good measure, try another autobiographical analysis. This passage from *The Iron Puddler* was written by James J. Davis, a Welshman who emigrated to the United States because of "the problem of bread" — earning enough to feed the family. Davis writes about his childhood in this excerpt, focusing on his father and grandfather and an incident at school:

From my father I learned many things. He taught me to be skillful and proud of it. He taught me to expect no gift from life, but that what I got, I must win with my hands. He taught me that good men would bring forth good fruits. This was all the education he could give me, and it was enough.

My father was an iron worker, and his father before him. My people had been workers in metal from the time when the age of farming in Wales gave way to the birth of modern industries. They were proud of their skill, and the secrets of the trade were passed from father to son as a legacy of great value, and were never told to persons outside the family. Such skill meant good wages when there was work. But there was not work all the time. Had there been jobs enough for all we would have taught our trade to all. But in self-protection we thought of our own mouths first. All down the generations my family has been face to face with the problem of bread.

My Grandfather Davies held a skilled job at the blast furnace where iron was made for the rolling mill in which my father was a puddler. Grandfather Davies had been to Russia and had helped the Russians build blast furnaces, in the days when they believed that work would make them wealthy. Had they stuck to that truth they would not be a ruined people to-day. Grandfather also went to America, where his skill helped build the first blast furnace in Maryland. The furnace fires have not ceased burning here, and Russia is crying for our steel to patch her broken railways. Her own hills are full of iron and her hands are as strong as ours. Let them expect no gift from life.

Grandfather told my father that America offered a rich future for him and his boys. "The metal is there," he said, "as it is in Russia. Russia may never develop, but America will. A nation's future lies not in its resources. The American mind is right. Go to America."

And because my father believed that a good people will bring forth good fruit, he left his ancient home in Wales and crossed the sea to cast his lot among strangers.

I started to school in Wales when I was four years old. By the time I was six I thought I knew more than my teachers. This shows about how bright I was. The teachers had forbidden me to throw paper wads, or spitballs. I thought I could go through the motion of throwing a spitball without letting it go. But it slipped and I threw the wad right in the teacher's eye. I told him it was an accident, that I had merely tried to play smart and had overreached myself.

"Being smart is a worse fault," he said, "than throwing spitballs. I forgive you for throwing the spitball, but I shall whip the smart Aleckness [disrespect] out of you."

He gave me a good strapping, and I went home in rebellion. I told my father. I wanted him to whip the teacher. Father said: "I know the teacher is a good man. I have known him for years, and he is honest, he is just, he is kind. If he whipped you, you deserved it. You cannot see it that way, so I am going to whip you myself."

He gave me a good licking, and, strange to say, it convinced me that he and the teacher were right. They say that the "hand educates the mind," and I can here testify that father's hand set my mental processes straight. From that day I never have been lawless in school or out. The shame of my father's disapproval jolted me so that I decided ever after to try to merit his approval.

Though the author is the subject of this autobiographical piece, quite a lot of space is devoted to other people. Yet everything in the passage is linked by common themes. Now for some details:

- By telling you what he learned — "to be skillful and proud of it," "to expect no gift from life," and to "win with my hands" — the author describes himself, despite the fact that he begins by speaking of his father. These three statements recur in the passage. The second paragraph talks about the author's ancestors, who "were proud of their skill" and whose "secrets of the trade" were "a legacy of great value." The anecdote about Russia echoes "expect no gift" with the statement "Let them expect no gift from life." Finally, the whipping the father gives the author "set [the author's] mental processes straight." Repetition emphasizes these ideas and establishes the author's (and his family's) values.

- The passage contains only a few quotations, but each has a strong impact. First comes the implied quotation ("Let them expect no gift from life") and then "The American mind is right. Go to America." The teacher's comment ("Being smart is a worse fault") is strong, as is the father's "If he whipped you, you deserved it." These are people of action, not words, but the words they do use are memorable.

- The father's and the grandfather's words are quoted, but the narrator never quotes his own words. The narrator speaks as an older person, looking back at his childhood. This style of quotation is appropriate because the piece has a double subject — the boy who went through these events and the man who remembers them. Mostly you hear the adult's "voice" in the piece. However, in the schoolteacher/spitball incident, the narrator slips back into childhood: "I told my father. I wanted him to whip the teacher."

- The syntax is simple, and many of the sentences are short and emphatic: For example: "I started to school in Wales when I was four years old. By the time I was six I thought I knew more than my teachers. This shows about how bright I was." Life in Wales — and life for a small child — is straightforward. You work, you eat. If you can't find work, you're "face to face with the problem of bread."

- A few long sentences break the pattern. In paragraph two, for instance, "They were proud . . . outside the family" is relatively long. This content of this sentence is the continuity of generations — how fitting that it be long!

- This excerpt covers a lot of ground — several generations, in fact. What's missing is more about the boy's life, his activities, and friends. The second paragraph concerns life-or-death issues and states that "in self-protection we thought of our own mouths first." In that context, it's not surprising to omit childish games.

- The anecdote about the spitball brings all the themes together: the importance and authority of elders, the hand educating the mind, and the need to face life without excuses. It also brings the piece full circle, because it epitomizes what the father has taught the boy — the subject of paragraph one.

OTHERS' LIVES PRESENTED AS LITERATURE: BIOGRAPHY

The task facing biographers is both easier and harder than an autobiographer's. Biographers don't have to dig inside themselves and confront their own personality. However, biographers have to research, interview, research some more, and then make sense of someone else's character.

In this section, you find two biographical selections. Read and annotate them, noting where the information comes from and considering how reliable that information is. As always, check the style-content relationship. All of these factors may be the topic of essay or multiple-choice questions on your AP exam.

A Puritan father

The following passage is excerpted from *Daughters of the Puritans* by Seth Curtis Beech. The book contains short biographical sketches of Puritan women. (The Puritans, who colonized much of New England, followed a strict religious code.) This excerpt is from the chapter on Catharine Maria Sedgwick. (Though it's short, this excerpt presents nearly everything from that chapter.)

She could have learned some condescension and humanity from her mother who, in spite of her fine birth, seems to have been modest and retiring to a degree. She was very reluctant to have her husband embark upon a public career; had, her daughter says, "No sympathy with what is called honor and distinction"; and wrote her husband a letter of protest which is worth quoting if only to show how a well-trained wife would write her doting husband something more than a century ago: "Pardon me, my dearest Mr. Sedgwick, if I beg you once more to think over the matter before you embark in public business. I grant that the 'call of our country,' the 'voice of fame,' and the 'Honorable' and 'Right-Honorable,' are high sounding words. 'They play around the head, but they come not near the heart.'" However, if he decides for a public career, she will submit: "Submission is my duty, and however hard, I will try to practice what reason teaches me I am under obligation to do." That address, "my dearest Mr. Sedgwick," from a wife a dozen years after marriage, shows a becoming degree of respect.

We may be sure that this gentle mother would have encouraged no silly notions of social distinctions in the minds of her children. Even Mr. Sedgwick seems to have had a softer and more human side to his nature than we have yet seen. Miss Sedgwick enjoys repeating a story which she heard from a then "venerable missionary." The son of the village shoemaker, his first upward step was as boy-of-all-work of the clerk of courts. He had driven his master to the court session in dignified silence, broken on arrival by a curt order to take in the trunk. "As he set it down in the entry," says Miss Sedgwick, "my father, then judge of the Supreme Judicial Court, was coming down stairs, bringing his trunk himself. He set it down, accosted the boy most kindly, and gave him his cordial hand. The lad's feelings, chilled by his master's haughtiness, at once melted, and took an impression of my father's kindness that was never effaced."

The individual is so much a creature of his environment, that I must carry these details a little farther. Forty years in public life, Judge Sedgwick had an extended acquaintance and, according to the custom of the time, kept open house. "When I remember," says Miss Sedgwick, "how often the great gate swung open for the entrance of traveling vehicles, the old mansion seems to me much more like an hostelrie [inn] of the olden time than the quiet house it now is. My father's hospitality was unbounded. It extended from the gentleman in his coach, chaise, or on horseback, according to his means or necessities, to the poor, lame beggar that would sit half the night roasting at the kitchen fire with the servants. My father was in some sort the chieftain of his family, and his home was their resort and resting-place. Uncles and aunts always found a welcome there; cousins wintered and summered with us. Thus hospitality was an element in our education. It elicited our faculties of doing and suffering. It smothered the love and habit of minor comforts and petty physical indulgences that belong to a higher state of civilization and generate selfishness, and it made regard for others, and small sacrifices for them, a habit."

Here are some points I noted when reading this passage:

- As I'm sure you noticed, the most amazing thing about this chapter on Catharine Maria Sedgwick is that she's not really the subject of the passage. Catharine seems to have followed the Puritan ideal in learning from her "modest and retiring" mother who writes to her husband that "submission is my duty."

- A primary source for this passage is Catharine ("Miss Sedgwick"), who's quoted several times, though never about herself. The long quotation in the last paragraph about the many people staying at the family house gives Catharine Maria Sedgwick her say, but significantly, she conveys nothing about her own feelings.

- The letter that her mother wrote to her father is also a source. Though the father is described, he's never quoted directly.

TIP

A *primary source* is an original document or an interview with a participant or witness. A *secondary source* interprets primary sources.

- The sentences are quite long, and many contain both primary source information (quotations) and interpretation, such as this sentence from the first paragraph: "However, if he decides for a public career, she will submit: Submission is my duty, and however hard, I will try to practice what reason teaches me I am under obligation to do." A long sentence allows for conditions — I'll do this but . . . — and mirrors some of the conflict described.

- The diction is formal. The missionary is "venerable," not "old," and the judge gives the boy a "cordial," not a "friendly" hand. This formality coincides with the position of the judge, who has an important role in society.

- The author intrudes frequently to offer an evaluation, saying that Mrs. Sedgwick shows "a becoming degree of respect" and that the "individual is so much a creature of his environment."

- The long anecdote about the "boy-of-all-work" who melts when he shakes hands with the judge reveals the stratified society. The boy expects the "haughtiness" of his employer and sometimes gets it, but kindness from people in superior positions is a surprise and, the passage implies, an act of charity on the part of the judge.

A Boston businessman

This excerpt is from *Joseph P. Kennedy: The Mogul, the Mob, the Statesman, and the Making of an American Myth* by Ted Schwarz (Wiley, 2003; reprinted with permission of John Wiley & Sons, Inc.). The passage describes an associate of Joe Kennedy, father of President John F. Kennedy.

Galen Stone was a writer who looked at business with the emotional distance required of his profession. Upon arriving in Boston in the 1880s, Stone worked first for the *Commercial Bulletin* and then for the *Boston Advertiser*. Having no stake in the businesses or the business community itself, he learned to analyze companies, their products, their marketing, and their competition. He saw what made one company successful and a rival fail to hold its own. He could be coldly objective, yet he also understood the back room, where business and politics intertwined.

Hayden, Stone, and Company was formed in 1892. Each man [Hayden and Stone] wanted to utilize the skills of the other, though they decided that it was most practical for them to work from two different cities. Boston was no longer at the center of the American financial universe. Banking, insurance, the stock market, numerous corporate headquarters, and the like were on the move to New York City. Boston still had old money and too many businesses to ignore. By having Stone stay in Massachusetts and Hayden operate from New York, they could commute by train to confer as needed while always being available for any opportunities that might come along. Unfortunately for the longtime friends, the separation exaggerated the differences in their personalities, and they gradually found themselves acting increasingly autonomously.

Galen Stone had always been drawn to aggressive men in business. He saw in them a trait that he lacked. They could move decisively, instinctively, and usually correctly in a fraction of the time that he himself would take. Stone was the analyst, the man who needed to know everything to write a story during his days as a reporter, and still was uncomfortable if he did not have all the details to make a reasoned decision.

What went unsaid as Hayden, Stone [the firm] became respected not only for its ability to invest in new businesses, helping it to great success, but also for its stock market purchases, was that Stone was a man for whom laws would be written. He was a variation of an insider trader, the type of man who gets rich through knowledge others were unable to obtain. All other stockholders were at a disadvantage, especially the small buyer who was becoming increasingly active in the years leading up to what would become the Great Depression.

Stone used all his reporter's training to gain contacts in businesses in which he was interested or where he already had an investment. Then he would learn where the business was headed. For example, if a company was introducing a new product line, Stone would learn from marketing personnel if there were large orders pending or if the company was discovering that no one cared about the idea the owners thought would make them rich. Then he would buy stock if the company was going to prosper and quietly arrange to sell his stock if he thought the price was going to drop. More important, he did not share this information with the majority of his customers, encouraging them to buy what later would prove to be his own holdings, driving up the market value just before the problem was revealed and the stock price drastically declined.

Stock manipulation through the use of still-secret corporate knowledge was not yet illegal, though the public did not understand how the game was played and how their holdings were being endangered. Eventually, such insider trading would become illegal, but stock manipulation was merely unethical, a game a "gentleman did not play," when Joe Kennedy decided to make an appointment to see Galen Stone. Joe Kennedy probably reminded Galen Stone of his longtime friend and business partner. Joe was familiar with Stone because of his fame and because his father-in-law regularly worked with the company.

This is a tiny slice of a fine book, so you don't get much sense of the character of Joseph P. Kennedy here. The focus is on his first important business connection, Galen Stone, a former reporter and financier. Here are the important points I noted:

- Though Kennedy is mentioned only in the last paragraph, the author states that he "probably reminded Galen Stone of his longtime friend and business partner." The implication is that Kennedy would fit in nicely with Stone's business style, which was not illegal but was, the author says, "a game a 'gentleman did not play.'"

- The fact that the reference to Kennedy is located in the last paragraph means that the entire passage leads to him. He's the focal point, the reason the rest of the passage was included in the book. To put it another way: Galen Stone is important only because of what he reveals about Joseph Kennedy.

- Within Galen Stone's story, the logical thread tying everything together is his background as a reporter and how the skills he acquired in journalism helped him in business.

- Throughout this excerpt, the author cites no primary sources. The lone quotation ("a gentleman did not play") isn't attributed. The author therefore asks for the reader's trust.

- Much of the passage consists of the author's interpretation. For example, Galen Stone is said to have "emotional distance" as a reporter and to be someone who "could be coldly objective" while understanding "the back room, where business and politics intertwined." The reader has to take these statements on faith.

- The fourth paragraph begins with an unusual sentence pattern: "What went unsaid . . . was that Stone was a man for whom laws would be written." (For grammar fans, "What went unsaid" is a noun clause acting as a subject.) The noun clause works hand-in-hand with "a game a 'gentleman did not play.'" Such games have unwritten — and therefore "unsaid" — rules. Also, the paragraph emphasizes what is not said to other investors ("knowledge others are unable to obtain") — another connection to the opening noun clause.

- The mode of discourse of this piece is exposition (explanation), a fitting mode for an author who wants to explain Joseph Kennedy's life and, in this excerpt, those who influenced Kennedy in his formative years.

- The author's tone is detached and analytical. You can imagine him at a lectern, calmly explaining Galen Stone and his effect on Joe Kennedy. Though the author makes judgments ("Stone was a man for whom laws would be written"), he doesn't use extreme language and is careful to point out that Stone broke no laws.

> **TIP**
>
> When you're reading biography, consider the sources cited (if any) and the author's attitude toward his or her subject. Acknowledge the author's assumptions so that you can better evaluate his or her views on the subject.

11

Tips for Reading Letters and Speeches

THE ESSENTIAL ELEMENTS OF
LETTERS AND SPEECHES

KEY CONCEPTS

- How to determine an author's identity, tone, and voice
- Benefits of recognizing the intended audience
- Purpose conveyed by content and style

Letters and speeches are, by definition, created with an audience in mind. The audience may be one person (perhaps a letter to a friend or public official) or many (a speech to a crowd or a letter to a newspaper, for instance). Regardless of size, the identity of the audience is important. So is context, because the subject of a letter or speech generally arises from a particular experience or need.

Your task, should a letter or a speech appear on your AP English Language and Composition exam, is to understand how the writer navigated the *rhetorical triangle,* which diagrams the interaction between subject, writer, and audience. All three points of the triangle are important factors in every type of writing but particularly important in these genres. In this chapter, I explain the conventions of letters and speeches and give you a chance to practice your analytical skills.

THE ESSENTIAL ELEMENTS OF LETTERS AND SPEECHES

Not that long ago, letters were a literary form. In fact, writing a proper letter was considered a sign of an educated and well-bred person. Pen an elegant letter, and you demonstrated that you were fit for the top level of society. Compose an ill-phrased mess, and you were toast. Speeches, too, have an illustrious history.

The AP exam specializes in literary letters, those that accomplish their purpose with style. And when the exam makers question you about a speech, they pick one that stirs the spirit or informs the ignorant. Analyzing a letter or a speech is easy, as long as you know what to look for. Keep an eye out for the elements of style described in the following sections.

> **TIP**
>
> When you're analyzing a letter or a speech, check each point of the rhetorical triangle: the subject, the writer, and the recipient. If you understand how the writing connects those three, you're on your way to a top score.

The identity of the author

Letters and speeches are an extremely personal art form. Therefore, your priority is to identify the author — not just the name, but the person behind the name. "Listen" to the author's voice as you read the passage. Pretend that you have an audio version of the text playing inside your head. What sort of person do you hear? How do you know? To the extent possible, define the speaker or writer.

> **TIP**
>
> You may find it helpful to imagine that you're an actor delivering the speech or reading the letter as a *voiceover* (an unseen narrator). How would you play the role? Where would you pause, speed up, change volume? What emotions would you portray? The answers to these questions help you hear the author's voice.

Tone and voice

Voice is closely connected to *tone,* though voice tends to be a permanent expression of character and tone changes with the situation. For example, I'm a fairly easy going person, and you hear my voice when you read this book — the same voice I use to teach a class. However, my usual "I love my students" tone turns critical when a paper is long overdue. To determine tone in a letter or a speech, pay close attention to *diction* (word choice) and *syntax* (the way sentences are put together grammatically). For more information on tone, turn to Chapter 3.

> **TIP**
>
> A favorite multiple-choice question concerns *shifts,* or changes, in tone. When you locate a shift, determine why the change occurred. Often shifts are related to content.

The audience

Always try to identify the audience: the people who heard the speech when it was given or who were the intended recipients of the letter. Sometimes the introduction to the passage gives you this information, or the audience may be named in the passage itself. The identity of the audience may also be implied, not stated. Once you know the audience, consider how the writer attempts to connect. Often the writer looks for common ground — shared experiences or beliefs. Sometimes the writer supplies an anecdote to demonstrate compassion or an understanding of others' situations. Many speakers and letter writers anticipate in advance how the audience will react and address that reaction in advance.

Speeches and letters, especially public "letters to the editor," play to a mixed audience. The writer understands that some people agree and others disagree with the ideas expressed. Determine how the writer handles this situation. Often, the writer argues several points, with each idea appealing to a different group.

Assumptions the writer has made

If you know the writer and the audience of a letter or speech, you may be able to identify assumptions the writer has made. For example, suppose you're reading a letter to the editor of the school paper. The writer complains about an editorial calling for a cap on the number of AP courses in which a student may enroll but never questions whether the school should offer AP classes at all. The unspoken assumption is that AP courses should be available. (In some schools, they aren't.)

Content and style

Check content and style to determine the purpose of the letter or speech. The writer may be arguing a point, imparting information, calming a worried or vengeful audience, or doing something else entirely. As you read, continually ask why. Why has the writer made this point? Why include that anecdote? The answers help you identify the author's purpose.

The context in which the speech or letter was written

Knowing the situation in which the speech or letter was written may help you comprehend its main points as well as its nuances. Lincoln's famed speech delivered at his second inauguration reached out to a divided nation; the Civil War was about to end. A century later, Martin Luther King Jr. wrote *Letter from a Birmingham Jail* in the midst of the struggle for civil rights, at a time when racial segregation was legal. The introduction to the passage may give you information about the situation, as may the passage itself.

> **TIP**
>
> If no information about the situation is supplied, the exam writers assume that everything you need to know appears in the passage. If you're writing an analytical essay on a letter or speech, don't bring in outside information (your understanding of history, psychology, or science, for example) unless it applies directly to your analysis of the rhetorical devices in the passage. The exam graders aren't testing general knowledge. They want to know that you understand how a great speech or letter is put together.

Common stylistic choices in speeches

Because speeches rely on the audience's ears, the speaker may use repetition to ensure that a point has been made.

Speeches also frequently rely on extended metaphors. (A *metaphor* is an indirect comparison, and an *extended metaphor* continues the comparison by adding detail to the initial metaphor.) Metaphors give the audience a mental image, enhancing comprehension. For example, in his famous "I Have a Dream" speech, Martin Luther King Jr. compares justice to money in the nation's bank. He says that no check should come back stamped "insufficient funds." His message is conveyed by the metaphor: The United States has enough justice for everyone.

Common stylistic choices in letters

Letters may also employ *figurative language* to make a point. Figurative language includes metaphors, similes, symbols, and other devices that appeal to the reader's imagination. Chapter 3 explains figurative language in detail.

TIP

> Because a reader can return to a letter again and again, letters seldom employ repetition. If you find a repeated phrase, ask yourself whether the writer was careless, disorganized, or simply emphatic. A careless or disorganized letter-writer may be a character created by the author — a situation common in fiction but not unheard of in nonfiction.

PRACTICE WITH LETTERS

You may get a question on the exam that focuses on a letter. One exam asked students to comment on a letter and response between a reader and Randy Cohen, author of "The Ethicist" column for *The New York Times*. And although nonfiction is the norm, letters extracted from novels or short stories are fair game.

Prepare yourself by analyzing these two letters. Read each carefully and jot down everything you can think of about its style. Use the points in the preceding section as a guide. Also take notes on content. After each letter is a list of points I noted. Compare your ideas to mine.

The subject of the letter — war, love, civil rights, and so on — should be easy to identify. Once you know what the letter is about, consider the subject in light of the writer and recipient. How does each relate to the subject?

Jane Austen: from Isabella Thorpe

Although Jane Austen wrote fiction, her letters are fit material for the AP English exam because they're beautifully written and they match writer, subject, and audience perfectly. They're also hysterically funny. Take a look at this letter (slightly shortened), taken from *Northanger Abbey*. The letter-writer, Isabella Thorpe, is in the English resort town of Bath. The brother of the recipient, Catherine Moreland, was engaged to Isabella, but Isabella broke up with him.

My dearest Catherine, I received your two kind letters with the greatest delight, and have a thousand apologies to make for not answering them sooner. I really am quite ashamed of my idleness; but in this horrid place one can find time for nothing. I have had my pen in my hand to begin a letter to you almost every day since you left Bath, but have always been prevented by some silly trifler or other. Pray write to me soon, and direct to my own home. Thank God, we leave this vile place tomorrow. Since you went away, I have had no pleasure in it — the dust is beyond anything; and everybody one cares for is gone. I believe if I could see you I should not mind the rest, for you are dearer to me than anybody can conceive. I am quite uneasy about your dear brother, not having heard from him since he went to Oxford; and am fearful of some misunderstanding. Your kind offices will set all right: he is the only man I ever did or could love, and I trust you will convince him of it. The spring fashions are partly down; and the hats the most frightful you can imagine. I hope you spend your time pleasantly, but am afraid you never think of me. . . . I rejoice to say that the young man whom, of all others, I particularly abhor, has left Bath. You will know, from this description, I must mean Captain Tilney, who, as you may remember, was amazingly disposed to follow and tease me, before you went away. Afterwards he got worse, and became quite my shadow. Many girls might have been taken in, for never were such attentions; but I knew the fickle sex too well. He went away to his regiment two days ago, and I trust I shall never be plagued with him again. . . . The last two days he was always by the side of Charlotte Davis: I pitied his taste, but took no notice of him. The last time we met was in Bath Street, and I turned directly into a shop that he might not speak to me; I would not even look at him. . . . Such a contrast between him and your brother! Pray send me some news of the latter — I am quite unhappy about him; he seemed so uncomfortable when he went away, with a cold, or something that affected his spirits. I would write to him myself, but have mislaid his direction; and, as I hinted above, am afraid he took something in my conduct amiss. Pray explain everything to his satisfaction; or, if he still harbours any doubt, a line from himself to me, or a call at Putney when next in town, might set all to rights. I have not been to the rooms this age, nor to the play, except going in last night with the Hodges, for a frolic, at half price: they teased me into it; and I was determined they should not say I shut myself up because Tilney was gone. . . . Anne Mitchell had tried to put on a turban like mine, as I wore it the week before at the concert, but made wretched work of it — it happened to become my odd face, I believe, at least Tilney told me so at the time, and said every eye was upon me; but he is the last man whose word I would take. I wear nothing but purple now: I know I look hideous in it, but no matter — it is your dear brother's favourite colour. Lose no time, my dearest, sweetest Catherine, in writing to him and to me, Who ever am, etc.

Isabella's letter is fairly transparent and abounds with contradictions, bare-faced lies, and ill-concealed pleas. Here's what I noticed:

- The writer of the letter, Isabella Thorpe, is immediately revealed as untrustworthy. Although Catherine is supposedly "dearer" to Isabella "than all the rest," she hasn't answered two letters Catherine sent her.

- Isabella constantly contradicts herself. She says that she took "no notice" of Captain Tilney, but the "last time we met was in Bath Street, and I turned directly into a shop that he might not speak to me." She also claims to love Catherine's brother, but she can't even find his address. She says she hasn't gone out, but she describes several excursions. These contradictions create Austen's comic tone; the reader perceives the gap between what Isabella says and what she means.

- Isabella explains that Captain Tilney "was amazingly disposed to follow and tease me" before Catherine left Bath. Isabella says that "afterwards he got worse, and became quite my shadow." Though Isabella says that she wasn't taken in by Tilney, she mentions that he "was always by the side of Charlotte Davis." You don't have to be a rocket scientist to figure out that Isabella went after Captain Tilney, but Captain Tilney dumped Isabella.

- Although Isabella claims to despise Captain Tilney ("the young man whom, of all others, I particularly abhor"), she refers to a turban that "happened to become [look good on] my odd face, I believe, at least Tilney told me so at the time." Her hopes for a match with Tilney are obvious.

- Isabella, having dumped Catherine's brother, pretends that he may have gone away "misunderstanding" her. She says that he "seemed so uncomfortable when he went away, with a cold, or something that affected his spirits." Isabella hopes that Catherine will convince her brother that what happened (the dumping) didn't really happen and that Catherine's brother will take her back. Clearly, Isabella assumes that her audience — Catherine — is gullible enough to believe these lies.

- The letter is disorganized; Isabella hops from an important topic (the engagement) to the fact that "spring fashions are partly down; and the hats the most frightful you can imagine." Similarly, she moves from her social activities to the feelings of Catherine's brother to comments at a play . . . and again to fashion (Anne Mitchell's turban and the fact that Isabella wears purple because "it is your dear brother's favourite colour"). The disorganization reflects Isabella's lack of restraint. She can't follow rules of writing, nor can she follow the ethical rules that govern male/female relationships.

- Isabella's overly long, tangled sentences, such as "Pray explain . . . all to rights" or "Anne Mitchell . . . would take" mirror her botched love life.

- Isabella lies, but in terms of language, she plays it straight. She's not smart enough to employ figurative language or irony. She does take everything to extremes, however. Catherine is "dearer to me than anybody can conceive" and Tilney isn't just disliked; she "abhor(s)" him. Isabella says that she looks "hideous" in purple, not simply "unattractive." Isabella's choice of strong words adds to her characterization; she's insincere — an exaggerator who'll say anything to get her way.

Washington Irving to his publisher

Washington Irving, the famed author of *The Legend of Sleepy Hollow* and many other works, wrote a letter in 1824, excerpted here, to his publisher after completing some requested revisions.

> I am at Brighton just on the point of embarking for France. I have dragged myself out of London, as a horse drags himself out of the slough [swamp], or a fly out of a honeypot, almost leaving a limb behind him at every tug. Not that I have been immersed in pleasure and surrounded by sweets, but rather up to the ears in ink and harassed by printers' devils.
>
> I never have had such . . . altering, adding, and correcting; and I have been detained beyond all patience by the delays of the press. Yesterday I absolutely broke away, without waiting for the last sheets. They are to be sent after me here by mail, to be corrected this morning, or else they must take their chance. From the time I first started pen in hand on this work, it has been nothing but hard driving with me.

I have not been able to get to Tunbridge to see the Donegals, which I really and greatly regret. Indeed I have seen nobody except a friend or two who had the kindness to hunt me out. Among these was Mr. Story, and I ate a dinner there that it took me a week to digest, having been obliged to swallow so much hard-favored nonsense from a loud-talking baronet whose name, thank God, I forget, but who maintained Byron was not a man of courage, and therefore his poetry was not readable. I was really afraid he would bring John Story to the same way of thinking.

I went a few evenings since to see Kenney's new piece, the Alcaid. It went off lamely, and the Alcaid is rather a bore, and comes near to be generally thought so. Poor Kenney came to my room next evening, and I could not believe that one night could have ruined a man so completely. I swear to you I thought at first it was a flimsy suit of clothes had left some bedside and walked into my room without waiting for the owner to get up; or that it was one of those frames on which clothiers stretch coats at their shop doors; until I perceived a thin face sticking edgeways out of the collar of the coat like the axe in a bundle of fasces. He was so thin, and pale, and nervous, and exhausted — he made a dozen difficulties in getting over a spot in the carpet, and never would have accomplished it if he had not lifted himself over by the points in his shirt-collar.

I saw Rogers just as I was leaving town. I had not time to ask him any particulars about you, and indeed he is not exactly the man from whom I would ask news about my friends. I dined tête-à-tête with him some time ago, and he served up his friends as he served up his fish, with a squeeze of lemon over each. It was very piquant, but it rather set my teeth on edge. . . .

Farewell, my dear Moore. Let me hear from you, if but a line; particularly if my work pleases you, but don't say a word against it. I am easily put out of humor with what I do.

Because I've spent more than a few hours revising my writing, I sympathize with Washington Irving. But there's more in Irving's letter than a weary writer's complaint, as you see in this list:

- Irving begins in a humorous tone, saying he's "dragged himself out of London" the way a horse or a fly emerges from a trap. *Hyperbole* (literary exaggeration) shows up immediately, as Irving has left "a limb behind . . . at every tug." He is "up to the ears in ink" (another hyperbole). Although Irving complains, he also does the work. He comes across as responsible.

- Next, the tone becomes businesslike. Irving reports on the last sheets that "are to be sent after me here by mail, to be corrected this morning." He is serious when he says that "it has been nothing but hard driving with me" on his current writing project. Once again, the writer is revealed as a serious man; he'll accomplish his task (revision) in a timely way.

- In paragraph three, Irving again shifts from business to comedy. He recounts a dinner that took "a week to digest," not because of the food but because of an obnoxious dinner guest who didn't appreciate the poet Byron. Irving assumes that the recipient of the letter shares Irving's own admiration of Byron's work. This paragraph portrays the writer (Irving) and the recipient as poetry fans.

- Paragraph four discusses a mutual acquaintance, and again Irving turns to comic exaggeration. The acquaintance, Kenney, was so thin that he at first appears to be "a flimsy suit of clothes" without a body inside and he has to lift himself over a spot in the carpet. Though Irving mocks Kenney, the tone is affectionate. The bond between writer and recipient is strengthened here.

- Paragraph five has more of a bite to it. Rogers, another mutual acquaintance, "served up his friends as he served up his fish, with a squeeze of lemon over each." This sentence implies that Rogers was willing to use his friends' reputation as a dinner diversion — a cruel act. Irving criticizes Rogers by commenting that Rogers's actions "rather set my teeth on edge." Again, the reader sees that the writer trusts his audience (the recipient of the letter); Irving's criticism would be omitted if the relationship were shaky.

- The letter as a whole reveals a hardworking author with ethical standards. He's willing to mock people but not destroy them, and he draws a line between his own comments and Rogers's.

- Irving assumes that the recipient of the letter will understand the personalities of the people mentioned. He doesn't bother with background information. Also, the fact that personal items appear in the letter suggests that the relationship between Irving and his publisher was more than business; they were friends as well.

- The most important rhetorical device is hyperbole, but imagery — sensory details — appear in paragraph four and elsewhere. Irving wants to bring his friend into this world and share experiences with him, not simply report basic facts.

- The purpose of the letter is to inform, but Irving adds an element of entertainment. (He was a novelist, after all!)

PRACTICE WITH SPEECHES

So that you can practice your speech interpretation, I've selected two presidential addresses, given about a hundred years apart. Take a look at these two, and annotate them as you read. Then compare your comments with mine.

Lyndon Johnson: State of the Union Address

In 1964, with the nation still reeling from the assassination of President John F. Kennedy a few weeks before, President Lyndon Johnson made this speech to a joint session of Congress. His State of the Union address, which every president delivers once a year, is excerpted here.

> Let this session of Congress be known as the session which did more for civil rights than the last hundred sessions combined; as the session which enacted the most far-reaching tax cut of our time; as the session which declared all-out war on human poverty and unemployment in these United States; as the session which finally recognized the health needs of all our older citizens; as the session which reformed our tangled transportation and transit policies; as the session which achieved the most effective, efficient foreign aid program ever; and as the session which helped to build more homes, more schools, more libraries, and more hospitals than any single session of Congress in the history of our Republic....

> If we fail, if we fritter and fumble away our opportunity in needless, senseless quarrels between Democrats and Republicans, or between the House and the Senate, or between the South and North, or between the Congress and the administration, then history will rightfully judge us harshly. But if we succeed, if we can achieve these goals by forging in this country a greater sense of union, then, and only then, can we take full satisfaction in the State of the Union.

Here in the Congress you can demonstrate effective legislative leadership by discharging the public business with clarity and dispatch, voting each important proposal up, or voting it down, but at least bringing it to a fair and a final vote.

Let us carry forward the plans and programs of John Fitzgerald Kennedy — not because of our sorrow or sympathy, but because they are right. In his memory today, I especially ask all members of my own political faith, in this election year, to put your country ahead of your party, and to always debate principles; never debate personalities. . . .

This budget, and this year's legislative program, are designed to help each and every American citizen fulfill his basic hopes — his hopes for a fair chance to make good; his hopes for fair play from the law; his hopes for a full-time job on full-time pay; his hopes for a decent home for his family in a decent community; his hopes for a good school for his children with good teachers; and his hopes for security when faced with sickness or unemployment or old age.

Unfortunately, many Americans live on the outskirts of hope — some because of their poverty, and some because of their color, and all too many because of both. Our task is to help replace their despair with opportunity. This administration today, here and now, declares unconditional war on poverty in America. I urge this Congress and all Americans to join with me in that effort.

It will not be a short or easy struggle, no single weapon or strategy will suffice, but we shall not rest until that war is won. The richest Nation on earth can afford to win it. We cannot afford to lose it.

As you see from this small excerpt, Johnson knew how to capture his audience. Here's what I gleaned from this passage:

- Parallelism is a dominant rhetorical device. (*Parallelism* occurs when elements of the sentence performing the same function have the same grammatical identity.) Notice all the "as the session" statements in paragraph one, the "if we" comments in paragraph two, and the "his hopes" statements in paragraph five. Parallel statements give each element in the list equal weight. The repetition that goes hand-in-hand with parallelism creates a sense of urgency and infuses passion. In the first paragraph, the parallelism emphasizes Congress's duty — what it must accomplish during this "session." In the second paragraph, Johnson presents two alternatives, success and failure. Failure dooms Congress in the eyes of history; success brings "full satisfaction." In the fifth paragraph, Johnson personalizes the message by bringing in "each and every American citizen" and referring to an implied representative individual with the pronoun "his."

- Although Johnson reportedly had a healthy ego, in this speech he spotlights Congress and its work. The pronoun "we" emphasizes shared responsibility. If Congress fails, so will Johnson. If it succeeds, so will the president. These two rhetorical devices are Johnson's attempt to connect with his audience, the senators, and representatives.

- The American people, listening to this speech on television, are also an audience for Johnson. His comments about the "basic hopes" of "each and every American citizen" are designed to hit the audience's major concerns — "a fair chance," "fair play," a good job, "a decent home for his family," good schools, and security. These are universal needs; Johnson, speaking in an era of racial segregation, reminds the audience that they have much in common.

■ Johnson invokes the memory of the assassinated Kennedy, but not in a morbid way. He concentrates on what is "right" (Kennedy's programs and policies), not a tribute to the dead president ("sorrow or sympathy").

■ Johnson, a career politician, assumes that politics and political victories are important to his audience. However, he asks Congress to aim higher, and he singles out "all members of my own political faith" — his party — to put the country "ahead of your party." The purpose of the speech is to inspire Congress to greater goals.

■ The famous line from this speech is Johnson's declaration of "war on human poverty." The metaphor (the war won't be waged against enemy soldiers but against socioeconomic factors) is so powerful that it's been appropriated many times since Johnson's day (war on drugs, war on terror, and so on).

■ The shift in the last paragraph is significant. Johnson begins with the "richest Nation on earth can afford to win" the war on poverty, a third-person statement. Then he moves to first-person plural ("We cannot afford to lose it"). Johnson's giving the victory to the country but failure to himself and Congress.

Abraham Lincoln: The Gettysburg Address

On November 19, 1863, President Abraham Lincoln traveled to a battlefield near Gettysburg, Pennsylvania, the site of a particularly bloody battle of the Civil War, a war that was still raging as he spoke. Though the speech is short, it is deservedly famous.

> Four score and seven years ago, our fathers brought forth upon this continent a new nation: conceived in liberty, and dedicated to the proposition that all men are created equal. Now we are engaged in a great civil war, testing whether that nation, or any nation so conceived and so dedicated, can long endure. We are met on a great battlefield of that war.
>
> We have come to dedicate a portion of that field as a final resting place for those who here gave their lives that this nation might live. It is altogether fitting and proper that we should do this. But, in a larger sense, we cannot dedicate, we cannot consecrate, we cannot hallow this ground. The brave men, living and dead, who struggled here have consecrated it, far above our poor power to add or detract. The world will little note, nor long remember, what we say here, but it can never forget what they did here.
>
> It is for us the living, rather, to be dedicated here to the unfinished work which they who fought here have thus far so nobly advanced. It is rather for us to be here dedicated to the great task remaining before us, that from these honored dead we take increased devotion to that cause for which they gave the last full measure of devotion, that we here highly resolve that these dead shall not have died in vain, that this nation, under God, shall have a new birth of freedom, and that government of the people, by the people, for the people, shall not perish from this earth.

Magnificent, isn't it? I can't read it without a lump in my throat. The sentiments, but also the rhetorical devices Lincoln employed, moved his audience as they listened on the battlefield. They touch the audience today as well. I noted these points:

- The speech begins with a reference to time, using the Biblical measure ("score" — twenty years). Thus Lincoln immediately emphasizes history and religion. The nation has endured for 87 years and, through the Civil War, it is being tested.

- The reference to "fathers" in the first sentence brings in family; the nation was created by "fathers" and hence is a kind of family and therefore should not be broken apart.

- The first paragraph begins with two long sentences and finishes with a short, factual statement: "We are met on a great battlefield of that war." The next paragraph contains a transition ("to dedicate a portion of that field") and states the purpose of the speech — to create a cemetery for those who died.

- In paragraph two, the parallel "we cannot" statements pull attention away from the audience and the speaker, because "we" can't do anything. The important deeds have already been done, by the soldiers who fought there. These parallel statements underline Lincoln's theme: the greatness of what happened at Gettysburg and the importance of those who fought there.

- Though Lincoln employs first-person plural, he never goes to singular ("I"). He submerges himself in the cause.

- Paragraph two ends with a sentence placing actions above words. What Lincoln says won't be remembered (he was wrong on that point), but the soldiers' bravery will never be forgotten.

- The last paragraph explains Lincoln's main point again: The war is "unfinished work" and "the great task remaining before us" is to win the war. Lincoln's audience, wearied and grieved by war, must not give up.

- The final sentence is very long and builds in tension and zeal. Lincoln asks his audience to rededicate itself to that "cause for which they [soldiers] gave the last full measure of devotion" — the war. He refers to "this nation, under God," which "shall have a new birth of freedom," and he states three parallel phrases that are justly famous: "government of the people, by the people, for the people." The parallelism makes all three elements equal: People make up the government, they wield power, and they act in the people's interests.

- The speech ends with a rousing affirmation of the Union. With rededication to the cause, Lincoln declares, the United States and its system of government "shall not perish from this earth."

12

Citation Essentials

- ■ Elements of citations
- ■ Parenthetical citations
- ■ Footnotes or endnotes
- ■ Unusual citations

A few years ago the College Board announced that the AP English Language and Composition exam would include multiple-choice questions on *citations* — the academic world's way of crediting sources for quotations, information, and ideas. This chapter prepares you for citation questions on the AP test. I tell you what you're likely to encounter and demonstrate book, article, and electronic citations, pointing out the minor variations in citation styles.

TYPES OF CITATION QUESTIONS ON THE EXAM

The College Board never guarantees that one AP test will resemble another in every detail, so I can't predict how many multiple-choice source-citation questions your exam will include. However, since they made their debut in 2007, the number of citation questions has been minimal: only three. Here's what you're likely to see:

- **Only multiple-choice questions:** You have to insert your own citations when you write a synthesis essay (Chapter 15 tells you how), but you won't need to comment on citations in any passage of the free-response (essay) section.

- **Questions on foot- or endnotes:** Although English teachers usually require parenthetical citations, the AP exam usually quizzes you about foot- or endnotes. In case they break with tradition and include parenthetical citations, I review them also, along with their bibliographic references.

  Keep in mind that foot- or endnotes aren't always references to the original source material. Some notes discuss side points — differing views of a historical situation or a digression that doesn't fit smoothly into the text. A multiple-choice question may ask about information in this type of foot- or endnote.

- **Two identification questions:** The multiple-choice questions generally ask you to select a true statement from a list of five options. To answer this kind of question, you need to know what each element in the citation represents — the title, editor, place or date of publication, and so forth.

- **One interpretation question:** An interpretation question asks you to evaluate the sources overall. For instance, the test makers may give you a passage with five footnotes, three of which come from the same book by Charles Weatherby. Your task is to choose the true statement from answers (A) to (E). The answer will be something like "The author relied heavily on Charles Weatherby's work."

- **MLA-style source citations:** Although the College Board says that citation questions may be from any style, English teachers prefer the format of the Modern Language Association. Thus far, MLA style has been more prominent on the AP exam than other styles. Because your time is limited, I concentrate on MLA citations. I do explain the minor differences of other styles, however.

- **Outmoded features:** Citations created now differ slightly from older citations. The exam makers know that college students sometimes have to consult older works, and thus they put some old-fashioned citations on the test. (Not to worry: I cover the old as well as the new in this chapter.)

Citation styles

Each academic subject has its own preferred way to cite sources, but the differences are miniscule. The three major styles are MLA (the Modern Language Association), APA (the American Psychological Association), and CMS (from the University of Chicago's Manual of Style). MLA style shows up in the humanities — literature and languages, history, and the like. The APA format covers the sciences (biology, chemistry, and so forth) and social sciences such as psychology and sociology. The CMS is used by all disciplines, possibly because it offers a lot of choices, and by many publishers.

One piece of good news: The exam makers will *never* ask you where to put the comma or parentheses or any other piece of punctuation. All you do is decode, not create (except when you cite sources in the synthesis essay, as I explain in Chapter 15).

ESSENTIAL ELEMENTS OF ALL CITATIONS

When you're answering a citation question, look for a short identification tag in the text, directly following the material being cited. The identification tag may be inserted in parentheses or may appear as a number placed above the line of text. The numbers correspond to footnotes or endnotes. The identification tag is tied to a more complete statement about the original source. Parenthetical citations (explained in more detail in the next section) refer the reader to a *source list* (also known as a "works cited" list). Numbers send you to foot- or endnotes. On the AP exam, the passages fit on a single page, so footnotes and endnotes appear on the same page. (In the real world, footnotes are at the bottom of a page and endnotes at the end of a chapter or a book, and all the information is repeated in a source list, with a slightly different format.)

Regardless of style, all citations contain a few essential elements, either in the foot- or endnotes or in the source list:

- **Author(s):** The author's name is usually the first thing you see. If the piece has more than one author, you see all the names or, in the case of a team effort, the principal author and the phrase "et al."

  If no author's name is available, the foot- or endnote begins with the title. If the work was written by an employee of an organization, the organization may replace the author's name.

- **Title(s):** If the citation refers to a book, the title is underlined or italicized. Article titles are placed inside quotation marks. Following the article title is the name of the book or magazine containing the article. The book or magazine name is underlined or italicized.

- **Publishing information (book):** For citations to a book, the place of publication (New York, Berlin, London, and so forth), the name of the company, and the date of publication appear — generally in that order.

- **Publishing information (magazines and journals):** Citations to a magazine include the date of the issue (month and year for a monthly publication, month and day and year for a weekly publication). Citations to a journal are a little more complicated. Most journals assign a volume number, which normally corresponds to the number of years the journal has been published. Within one year, each issue has a number also. A colon separates the volume number from the issue number. The volume number always precedes the issue number. For example, a journal citation containing "8:2" came out in the second issue of volume 8. Journals often add dates to the volume and issue numbers, and some journals drop the issue number entirely.

  Scientific material is date sensitive; the treatment for tuberculosis in 1950 is quite different from the treatment today, for example. Therefore, citations for a science passage place the date of publication toward the beginning of the citation, right after the author's name.

- **Page number(s):** If the whole work is referenced, you may not see a page number. However, most citations contain a page number or a range of pages. The page number is usually the last number in the citation.

- **Web address (electronic sources):** Some material on the web is simply an electronic version of a printed journal or magazine, so those citations include everything listed in the preceding bullet points *plus* the web address (the URL). Web addresses are very long and start with "www" or "http."

- **Date accessed (electronic sources):** Because the web is updated constantly, material you find one day may not be there the next. Citations including the date accessed explain to the reader when you found the information. The words "date accessed" appear, to distinguish that date from the date of publication.

Depending upon the source, you may also see an editor or translator's name, an edition number, and some other information. Most of these items are easily identifiable ("3rd ed." for "third edition" or "trans." for "translated"). Check out "Some Unusual Citation Cases" later in this chapter for examples.

PARENTHETICAL CITATIONS

In the synthesis essay (see Chapter 15), most students cite sources parenthetically. The parentheses show up directly following the material taken from the source (even in the middle of the sentence) and contain just enough words to identify the source and the page number the material appeared on. If the source is identified in the sentence, the parenthesis contains only the page number. Here are two examples, one with the name in the text and one without:

> NAME IN TEXT: Arthur Boddy's theory of comedy (22) elevates bubble gum above banana peels on the Ashworth Hilarity Scale.

> NAME NOT IN TEXT: One theory of comedy (Boddy 22) elevates bubble gum above banana peels on the Ashworth Hilarity Scale.

Both parenthetical citations tell you the same thing. On page 22 of a source written by someone named Boddy is a statement that bubble gum is funnier than banana peels.

 TIP

If more than one work by the same author is cited, an extra word — usually one word from the title — is included in the parentheses: (Boddy, *Gum* 22). If two authors have the same last name, the first initial is added to the parentheses: (O. Boddy 22).

Of course, you can't tell from the parenthetical citation exactly what Boddy wrote. For that information, you turn to the source list (which may be printed after the passage on the AP exam). The source list used to be called a *bibliography*, from the Greek word for *book*. These days researchers usually tap into electronic sources, so the term bibliography has morphed into the more neutral *list of sources, reference list,* or *works cited.* The AP English Language and Composition exam doesn't include comprehensive source lists. In a passage with foot- or endnotes, the source list probably won't appear at all. However, if the passage has parenthetical notes, a short source list will probably be included.

In a source list, here's what you might see for different kinds of sources:

■ **Citation to a book::**

> Boddy, Oliver. *The Ashworth Hilarity Scale.* New York: Comic Press, 2008.

This source citation informs you that Oliver Boddy wrote a book entitled *The Ashworth Hilarity Scale.* It was published in 2008 by Comic Press, a company located in New York.

■ **Citation to a journal article:**

> Boddy, Oliver. "Bubble Gum and Banana Peel." *Journal of Food Comedy* 4:3 (2008): 22–32.

This source cites an article entitled "Bubble Gum and Banana Peel" that was printed in a magazine entitled *Journal of Food Comedy.* The volume number is 4, and the issue number is 3. The year in parenthesis, 2008, is the year the article appeared. The article was on pages 22–32.

> **TIP**
>
> You may have noticed that the parenthetical reference in the text says "22," but the source list says "22–32." The article is ten pages long, but the "Ashworth" bubble-gum/banana rating is discussed on only one page — number 22.

■ **Citation to an article that comes from the web:**

> Boddy, Oliver. "Bubble Gum and Banana Peel." *Food Comedy-Net.* Spring 2008. Standup Comedians United. 30 September 2008 http://www.fcnscu.org/gun.html

This citation indicates that Boddy's article, still entitled "Bubble Gum and Banana Peel," was published on the Food Comedy-Net website, which was created by a group called Standup Comedians United. The article was accessed on September 30, 2008. The web address is http://www.fcnscu.org/gun.html.

Note: As interesting as these articles sound, don't go looking for them. The article, author, publisher, and web address are all fictional.

FOOTNOTES AND ENDNOTES

The format for foot- or endnotes closely follows that of the source list, which I explain in the preceding section. Here I show you some sample foot- and endnotes, with explanations. But first, here's how the foot- or endnote number appears in the text, with and without a quotation:

TEXT WITH QUOTATION: Boddy declared that bubble gum "sticks to the audience's funny bone."[3]

TEXT WITHOUT QUOTATION: Boddy wrote about the effect of bubble gum on the audience's sense of humor.[3]

Now for samples of foot- and endnote format, continuing my fictional example:

■ **Citation for a book:**

> 3. Oliver Boddy, *The Ashworth Hilarity Scale* (New York: Comic Press, 2008), 22.

This citation informs you that Oliver Boddy is the author of a book entitled *The Ashworth Hilarity Scale*, which was published by a company called Comic Press in 2008. The company is located in New York, and the information or quotation comes from page 22.

■ **Citation for an article:**

> 3. Oliver Boddy, "Bubble Gum and Banana Peel," *Journal of Food Comedy*, 4 (August 2008): 22.

In this note, you see that Oliver Boddy wrote an article entitled "Bubble Gum and Banana Peel," which was published in volume 4 of the *Journal of Food Comedy*, published in August 2008 on page 22.

■ **Citation for an electronic source:**

> 3. Oliver Boddy, "Bubble Gum and Banana Peel," *Food Comedy-Net*, http://www.fcnscu.org/gun.html (accessed August 9, 2008).

In this note, Boddy's article is still called "Bubble Gum and Banana Peel." It was accessed on August 9, 2008, at the web address listed. The website's title is italicized.

SOME UNUSUAL CITATION CASES

A few special cases show up on the AP exam from time to time: an article in a book edited by someone else, a couple of Latin terms, multiple authors, translators, revised editions, and so forth. This section takes you through the variations you may encounter.

Multiple authors

Citations to multiple authors look like this:

■ **Parenthetical citation:**

> In a ground-breaking study of the Ashworth Hilarity Scale (Boddy, Smith, and Wickham 22), bubble gum rated higher than banana peels.

■ **Foot- or endnote, book:**

> 3. Oliver Boddy, Jane Smith, and Martin Wickham, *Bubble Gum and Banana Peel* (New York: Comic Press, 2008), 22.

■ **Source list, book:**

> Boddy, Oliver, Jane Smith, and Martin Wickham. *Bubble Gum and Banana Peel*. New York: Comic Press. 2008.

■ **Source list, article:**

> Boddy, Oliver, Jane Smith, and Martin Wickham. "Bubble Gum and Banana Peel." *Journal of Food Comedy* 4:3 (2008): 22–32.

■ **Source list, electronic source:**

> Boddy, Oliver, Jane Smith, and Martin Wickham. "Bubble Gum and Banana Peel." *Food Comedy-Net.* Spring 2008. *Standup Comedians United.* 30 September 2008 http://www.fcnscu.org/gun.html.

Translators, editors, and editions

Translations and editions are fairly easy because the abbreviations "trans." and "ed." appear, as in these examples:

■ **Source list, translated book:**

> SanMiguel, Eduardo. *La Comedia de la Comida.* Trans. Eugene Partridge. London: Omnivore, 2009.

This citation tells you that the book by Eduardo SanMiguel was translated by Eugene Partridge.

■ **Source list, article in a book:**

> SanMiguel, Eduardo. "Food Fight Fun." In *The Comedy of Food,* edited by Eugene Partridge. London: Omnivore, 2009.

In this example, Mr. Partridge edited a book containing an article by Eduardo SanMiguel.

■ **Footnote, book:**

> 3. Eduardo SanMiguel, *The Tragedy of Breakfast,* 3rd ed. (New York: Omnivore, 2009), 22.

Editions may be numbered, as you see in the "3rd. ed." reference above. Sometimes "rev." replaces the number. The abbreviation "rev. ed." stands for "revised edition."

References to other citations

Sometimes a source citation refers to something that was taken from another source. Latin abbreviations were once common shortcuts in citations. If you encounter them, "ibid" means "in the same place" and refers to the preceding citation. If you see "ibid" plus a page number, it means "in the same source, but on the page mentioned." You may also see "id." or "idem," both of which mean "by the same author," if several works by one author appear in one citation. Consider this series of footnotes:

> 3. John Meringue, "Pie-Smashing," *The Comedy of Lunch,* edited by Ilene Herring, quoted in Louis Frappe, *Smashing Pumpkins and Other Vegetables* (Cambridge: Vegivore Press, 2007), 77.
>
> 4. Ibid.
>
> 5. Sally Lemon, "Apple or Pumpkin?" *Food Comedy Journal* 8 (March 2009): 77–78; id. "Pecan v. Blueberry," *Food Comedy Journal* 3 (March 2004): 4.

Footnote 3 is an article cited by another author. Footnote 4 means that the information comes from the same place as footnote 3. The citation in footnote 5 (which uses "id.") tells you that Sally Lemon wrote two articles, "Apple or Pumpkin?" and "Pecan v. Blueberry." Both were published in *Food Comedy Journal,* the first in volume 8 in the March 2009 issue, and the second in volume 3 of the same journal, which came out in March 2004. The apple/pumpkin discussion was on pages 77–78 and the blueberry reference on page 4.

IV

Exam
Strategy
and Practice
Questions

13

Strategies for Multiple-Choice Questions

This chapter focuses on the multiple-choice section of the exam and includes tips for time management and guessing. I also survey the most common types of multiple-choice questions and explain, step by step, how to deal with each.

MULTIPLE-CHOICE SECTION TIMING

The multiple-choice portion of the AP English Language and Composition exam lasts an hour and usually contains five or six passages, each accompanied by ten questions, give or take a couple. The passages vary, but most are in the neighborhood of 700 words. Practically speaking, this format means that you have to read 3,500–4,000 words in the passages alone. The average test-taker ends up with about half a minute per question. Therefore, time management is crucial.

If you approach the multiple-choice section with maximum efficiency, you can accomplish a lot. Several factors matter: an overall strategy for the multiple-choice section, the method you employ for each passage, and the advisability of guessing. I cover the first two in this section and guessing in the next section. Your approach to each type of multiple-choice question also matters. For that topic, see "Types of Multiple-Choice Questions" later in this chapter.

Planning your overall strategy

If the multiple-choice portion of your AP English Language and Composition test is typical, you will see a few standard elements. At least one of the selections will be old (17th or 18th century) with some antiquated vocabulary and tangled syntax. One selection will cover something "technical" — a process, a historical event, or little known facts. The author of one passage will probably be from a group formerly excluded from the reading list of traditional English classes — women, African Americans, Asian Americans, or Latinos. Because this exam now quizzes you on citation style, one passage will have foot- or endnotes, a bibliography, or parenthetical citations.

These passages and the questions accompanying them present varying degrees of difficulty, even though every question counts the same. So here's the golden rule: Make sure you answer all the easy questions and as many of the tough questions as possible. As you begin work on the multiple-choice section, follow this general plan:

1. **Quickly survey the passages and choose the one that looks easiest.** This step should take no more than a minute. Remember, you don't have to work on the first passage before you get to the second — or the fifth, for that matter. If a passage looks difficult, skip it and move on to one that's more user-friendly.

> **TIP**
>
> Always check that you're entering an answer in the appropriate line on the answer sheet. You don't want any answer to end up in the wrong spot.

2. **Keep moving from passage to passage, in ascending order of difficulty.** As you complete a question-set, move to the next easiest. Keep track of the clock as you work. Ideally, no question-set should take more than ten minutes. Remember, the order in which you work is not an issue. Keep moving from passage to passage, leaving the most difficult for last.

> **TIP**
>
> If you're a fast reader and are fairly sure that you'll get to all the passages on the test, you may be tempted to tackle the hardest passage first, when your brain is freshest. If that's your plan, test-drive it before the big day. Take one of the full-length practice exams (in Chapter 17 or 19) with the timer on. Then check your answers (in Chapter 18 or 20, respectively). If the "hard first, easy later" method works for you, fine. If not, opt for the easy passages first.

3. **Within one question set, answer the easy questions first.** Decide which types of questions are easiest for you to answer. How do you know? In "Types of Multiple-Choice Questions" in this chapter, I survey the most common questions. Also, when you practice in Chapter 14, analyze your responses. Notice patterns. You may, for instance, always ace main idea or attitude questions but stumble on inference or syntax. If so, you know that to maximize your score you *must* get to all the main idea and attitude questions, even if they take a relatively long time to answer. However, no matter what you've planned, if you find yourself spending more than a minute on a single question, move on.

> **TIP**
>
> Before AP test day, spend some time on problem areas. If you always have trouble with tone questions, for example, turn to Chapter 3 for a review. If you can handle technical passages but have trouble with speeches or letters, check out Chapter 11.

4. **Budget time for the hard questions.** Once you've answered the easy questions, consider the number of minutes the hard ones will take. This is an individual decision, of course, one you can make after you've worked through some practice passages and analyzed your working habits. Most people find that vocabulary-in-context, citation, and factual questions are very fast because you either know them or you don't. Usually, equivalent, syntax, and inference questions take much longer. Questions on tone, attitude, purpose, and figurative language fall somewhere in the middle.

Your ability to answer AP questions is as individual as your fingerprints. The only way you can tell how fast or slow a certain kind of question is *for you* is to try a bunch and see. Tailor your approach to your own working style and ability.

A strategy for question-sets

An efficient approach to each question-set can help you maximize your score. Follow these steps:

1. **Skim the question stems.** The *stem* is the line before the answer choices, the part that tells you what you have to do. Quickly glance at each stem so that you have a rough idea what it's asking. Then when you read the passage, you can look for relevant information. Allot about a minute for this step.

> **TIP**
>
> The AP numbers the lines in the multiple-choice passages, and many questions direct you to a particular line. As you read the stems, put a quick check mark next to any line that is connected to a question. Then you can pay special attention to that spot later.

2. **Read and annotate the passage.** *Annotating* means underlining and/or jotting down main ideas or important thoughts in the margins. In Chapter 2, I illustrate how to annotate a reading passage when you have no time limit. Annotating on the AP exam is

different. It's quick and inexact because you don't have time to ponder what you're reading. Do the following:

- **Go for anything that relates to the question stems.** For example, if you know they're asking about the author's attitude towards the environmental movement, underline whatever reveals green or anti-green sentiments. Put "E" in the margin to identify the underlined portion as environment-related. If they've queried the purpose of the last paragraph, keep "purpose" in your mind as you read and write one or two words in the margin to sum up what you found.
- **Create a "what's where" guide to the passage by noting the main idea of each paragraph in the margin.** Be brief (one word, maybe two *tops*).

I can't recommend a time limit for this step because the length and difficulty of the passage and individual reading habits vary. However, pay attention to how much time you spend on each passage when you take the practice tests in Chapter 17 and Chapter 19. Then set your own time limit for reading and annotating.

> **TIP**
>
> Abbreviations are great for marginal notes. I use *b/c* for "because," *s/b* for "should be," and A for "author." You can work out your own abbreviations.

3. **Go through the questions again, this time reading the answer choices.** If an answer pops right out at you, bubble it and move on. If you have no idea or can't decide between two or three possibilities, put a big X next to that question and leave it blank on the answer sheet.

Guessing doesn't penalize you, so you want to answer every question. I explain best guessing practices in "How to Make a Guess," a little later in this chapter.

4. **Recheck the questions you skipped.** Do this step at the end of a set of questions, *before* you read another passage. If you wait too long, you won't remember enough to work efficiently. Keep an eye on the minute-hand of your watch. If you've spent ten minutes on a question set, leave the tough questions alone and head for another passage.

Some test takers stray, answering questions on one passage while thinking back to a previous question-set. This strategy doesn't work. Whatever passage is in front of you is the *only* one that exists, as far as you're concerned, until you're finished with the question-set that accompanies it.

5. **Repeat Steps 1–4 for the remaining passages.** Keep on working until you've gone through all the passages. Remember, set a limit of ten minutes per passage.

6. **After the last passage is done, go back one more time to questions you left blank.** Now you can roam around, if you have any minutes left after the last passage. If not, don't worry. You can still get a good AP score if you answer about two-thirds of the multiple-choice questions correctly, assuming you write reasonably good essays.

> **TIP**
>
> If you tend to panic when you're taking a standardized test, focus your eyes on only one question at a time. Place the answer sheet on top of the question booklet, just below the question you're working on. Put your non-writing hand just above that question. Now all you can see is one question, and your eyes won't hop nervously all over the place.

Speeding through reading

How fast do you read? Most students I know hover around the 200-words-per-minute mark. If you can increase that average to 300 wpm and remain at the same comprehension level, you can save a lot of minutes on the AP exam. Turning 200 into 300 is fairly simple if you see reading as a sport — specifically, track.

When you're training for a race, you build strength through various exercises. You also do wind sprints. When you're training for the AP test, you build strength by increasing your vocabulary and comprehension. (Chapter 2 tells you how.) *Wind sprints,* in the world of reading, are short periods of time when you consciously force your eyes to move down the page a little faster than your comfort level. Wind-sprint for about three minutes at a time. Then stop and try to recall what you read. At first, the amount of information that sticks in your head will be small. But each time you'll retain more. Whenever you get comfortable at a certain speed, pick up the pace again. Before you know it, you'll be a faster — and better — reader.

HOW TO MAKE A GUESS

On the AP exam, you get one point for each correct answer. You receive no points for blanks, and the scorers don't deduct anything for a wrong answer. Therefore, random guessing — a blind stab at the five choices — is not a bad idea.

An even better idea is to try to narrow down your choices so you aren't considering five equal alternatives, but you may not always be able to do so. The type of question matters in this situation. Here are some considerations:

■ Your AP exam will probably contain questions in which the five answer-choices are literary terms. If you don't know the term and you're feeling time pressure, make a random guess. The passage likely doesn't contain an explanation of the term, so you'll just waste time trying to narrow down your options.

> **TIP**
>
> Literary-term questions are easy if you know what the terms mean and can readily identify the rhetorical techniques they refer to. In this book, I place literary terms in italics and defined them immediately. Pay attention to those definitions.

■ "Equivalent" questions that require you to match an answer choice to a line cited in the question-stem take a lot of time. If you immediately grasp the meaning of the phrase in the stem, it's worth your while to attempt to eliminate some wrong answers before guessing. If the line cited in the stem is tough to figure out, just make a random guess and move on.

■ Roman numeral questions give you three statements labeled I, II, and III and ask you which, if any, are true. Do you understand two of the three statements? If so, put a little effort into whittling down your options. If you grasp the meaning of only one of the statements, make a random guess.

One size doesn't fit all when it comes to specific recommendations about guessing. The best guessing strategy *for you* arises from your performance on the practice AP tests in Chapters 17 and 19 or the practice questions in Chapter 14. Notice how much time each type of question requires. The ones that take too many minutes are good candidates for random guessing.

TYPES OF MULTIPLE-CHOICE QUESTIONS

A plan of attack for the whole section and for each question-set goes only so far. You need to know how to approach each type of multiple-choice question on the AP exam. That's what this section provides.

Vocabulary

Hemingway was once asked what was hard about writing. His answer — getting the words right. The test makers want to know that you too can "get the words right," and they place a fair number of vocabulary questions on every AP exam. Most are "vocabulary-in-context" questions that query you about the meaning of a word in the context of a particular line. But vocabulary is also the key to questions about literary terminology. After all, you can't determine whether *onomatopoeia* is present if you don't know what that term means. (It's a word whose sound reflects its meaning, such as "buzz" and "murmur.")

Attack vocabulary-in-context questions this way:

1. **If you're sent to a line, reread the whole sentence or, if it's very long, the grammatical unit containing the word in question.** A vocabulary-in-context question may refer to just a portion of a larger sentence. Checking the entire sentence, however, gives you more to go on. If it's an old piece of writing, the sentence may ramble on for many, many lines. In that situation, you should focus only on the clause the word appears in. (A *clause* is a subject-verb statement, plus any descriptions relating to it. For help with grammar, check Chapter 6.)

2. **Restate the sentence or clause, substituting a word of your own for the word they're asking about.** Be sure that your substitution hasn't altered the meaning.

3. **Match your substitution to the answer choices.** You should find a match. If you don't, recheck the sentence. Perhaps you need to adjust your paraphrase.

> **TIP**
>
> Generally, one or two of the wrong answers are real definitions of the word they're querying — real, but wrong for the context. Don't grab an answer because it matches a definition you know. Look for a word that makes sense in the sentence and matches *your* word to the answer choices.

Vocabulary-in-context questions are easy to spot:

What is the meaning of _____ in line ___?

In the context of line ____, what is the best definition of _____?

In line _____, _____ may be defined as . . . .

EXAMPLE

Now that you know what they look like, it's time to try one. Read this passage from Samuel Pepys's diary, which he wrote in the 17th century. Then try your hand at a vocabulary-in-context question:

(01) It struck me very deep this afternoon going with a hackney coach from Lord Treasurer's down Holborne. The coachman I found to drive easily and easily, at last stood still, and come down hardly able to stand, and told me that he was suddenly struck very sick, and almost blind, he could not see; so I light and went
(05) into another coach, with a sad heart for the poor man and for myself also, lest he should have been struck with the plague.

1. In the context of line 4, the best definition of "light" is

  (A) featherweight
  (B) illuminated
  (C) got down
  (D) arrived
  (E) paid

Correct answer: (C). Following the steps for vocabulary-in-context questions, you can reread the entire sentence, which begins in line 2, "The coachman I found . . . with the plague." Because the sentence is very long, however, you may focus on just the portion the words appear in — from "so I light" (line 4) to "with the plague" (line 6). Restate it in your own words: "So I <u>left</u> and went into another coach, upset for the poor man and me too, in case he had the plague." Your substitution, which I've underlined, is "left." The answer matching "left" is (C), "got down," because Pepys left a coach, and the ground is lower than the passenger compartment.

Literary vocabulary questions usually ask you to identify a rhetorical technique (or "device" or "strategy") in a particular paragraph or section of the passage. Or they ask you which rhetorical technique doesn't appear. The AP-test writers capitalize DOESN'T or EXCEPT, so you know you're searching for something that isn't there. Questions about literary terms resemble these:

What is the dominant rhetorical device in lines 1–8?

Lines 1–8 may be characterized as . . . .

All of the following appear in lines 1–8 EXCEPT . . . .

Line 5 marks a shift from _____ to . . . . (The blank is filled with a literary term, such as "figurative language" or "imagery" or "narration.")

Lines 5–8 employ which of the following?

> **EXAMPLE**
>
> Here's a sample question, based on an excerpt from the autobiography of a former slave:
>
> (01) I told him that it was certainly wrong to deceive the old man, and that it was his duty to tell him of the impositions practiced by his young master. I assured him that the old man would not be slow to comprehend the whole, and that there the matter would end. William thought it might with the old man, but not with him. He said he (05) did not mind the smart of the whip, but he did not like the idea of being whipped.
>
> 2. Which of the following is the dominant rhetorical device in lines 1–5?
>
> (A) analogy
> (B) personification
> (C) hyperbole
> (D) parallelism
> (E) understatement
>
> **Correct answer: (D).** *Parallelism* is the repetition of the same sentence structure either within one sentence or in consecutive sentences. This passage contains several "that . . . subject–verb" sentences. Parallelism is also present in the last two sentences. Read them aloud and notice the balanced sound, which is characteristic of parallelism. I've underlined the parallel elements: "William thought it might <u>with the old man</u>, but not <u>with him</u>. He said <u>he did not mind the smart of the whip</u>, but <u>he did not like the idea of being whipped</u>.

In case you're interested in the other terms (and you should be), an *analogy* is a comparison, *personification* is the attribution of human qualities to a nonhuman element, *hyperbole* is exaggeration, and *understatement* is the opposite of exaggeration.

Reading comprehension

College courses assign heavy-duty reading material, and so does an AP class. And if teachers teach it, they test it. Especially in passages written in the 19th century or earlier, expect to see questions that check whether you know what happened (fact questions), whether you can decode pronouns (antecedent questions), and whether you understand the underlying meaning of a passage (inference questions).

Fact questions

Fact questions ask who did what to whom, when, why, and how. Fact questions also test whether you can identify the writer's arguments in favor of or against a proposal. You may also be queried about the meaning of that 29-word sentence in paragraph two and whether another sentence in the passage says the same thing. These questions are fairly easy, if you approach them properly:

1. **Reread the lines indicated in the question stem.** A factual question often, but not always, contains a line reference. The answer, however, may be elsewhere in the passage.

2. **If no line numbers are specified, check your annotations.** If the question refers to "interest rates," for example, go to the spot in the passage that discusses that topic.

3. **Restate the question in your own words.** For instance, suppose the question says something like "In lines 1–8, the motive for changing carriages may best be characterized as . . . ." The paraphrase is "According to lines 1–8, why did he change carriages?" The simpler wording helps you understand what you're looking for.

4. **If you can, state the answer in your own words and match it to an answer choice.** You may remember enough about the passage to come up with an answer right away. For example, you may immediately think, "He changed carriages because he was afraid of getting sick." Then all you have to do is look for a matching answer-choice.

5. **If you can't come up with a possible answer, test each answer-choice.** Follow the usual guessing rules: Try to eliminate some choices if you can. If you can't, just make a random guess.

I can't give you a formula for the wording of fact questions because they vary too much, but you'll probably recognize this type of question instantly. Just follow the preceding steps and you'll be fine.

EXAMPLE

Take a shot at this factual question, which is based on an excerpt from *Paul Volcker: The Making of a Financial Legend,* by Joseph Treaster (Wiley, 2004; reprinted with permission from John Wiley & Sons, Inc.):

(01) For years, inflation had been eroding wealth in America. By 1978, when Miller arrived at the Fed [the Federal Reserve], inflation was the number one economic problem. As chairman, Miller argued for gradualism. Like Burns and some other board members, he worried that by sharply increasing interest rates — the stan-
(05) dard medicine for inflation — the Fed would push the economy into a recession. His approach did not alleviate the problem, and through most of 1979 the economic picture grew worse, due in large part to a growing fuel crisis. Because of the revolution that led to the fall of the Shah of Iran, oil exports to the United States from Iran had slowed. A fuel shortage developed in the United States, resulting
(10) in long lines at gas stations that sometimes erupted into violence. By midyear, the cost of gas and oil shipments to the United States from the Organization of Petroleum Exporting Countries had jumped 60 percent. Increased fuel costs were slowing the economy and many economists, including those at Miller's Fed, were expecting a recession. Unemployment and inflation were rising. By June 1979,
(15) inflation was running at an annual rate of 13 percent. At the same time, the value of the dollar had been declining against other major currencies.

3. Which of the following statements about the United States economy in 1979 is true, according to lines 9–16?

   (A) The rate of inflation was increasing.

   (B) Motorists resorted to violence because of fuel shortages.

   (C) A recession had developed.

   (D) The dollar was weaker in relation to other currencies.

   (E) Inflation caused higher interest rates.

Correct answer: (D). Lines 15–16 state that "the value of the dollar had been declining against other major currencies." Thus (D) is true. The other statements aren't supported in lines 9–15, which tells you that "inflation [was] rising" (line 14) but says nothing about the "rate of inflation" cited in (A). Choice (B) is true, but it isn't a statement about the economy; it's a statement about behavior. The passage tells you that many economists were "expecting a recession" (line 14), not that one had already developed, as indicated in (C). Choice (E) is backwards: Higher interest rates are the cure for, not the cause of, inflation.

A particularly devilish type of fact question asks for equivalents. The question stem directs you to a statement in the passage, and you have to find another statement that matches it. To answer an equivalent question, follow the same procedure as for any factual question. But beware of these questions; they eat up your test minutes very quickly. If you don't get the answer in less than a minute, make a guess and move on.

EXAMPLE

Here's an example of an equivalent question, based on a passage excerpted from a speech given by Oscar Wilde:

(01) In the lecture which it is my privilege to deliver before you tonight, I do not desire to give you any abstract definition of beauty at all. For we who are working in art cannot accept any theory of beauty in exchange for beauty itself, and, so far from desiring to isolate it in a formula appealing to the intellect, we, on the contrary,
(05) seek to materialize it in a form that gives joy to the soul through the senses. We want to create it, not to define it. The definition should follow the work: the work should not adapt itself to the definition. Nothing, indeed, is more dangerous to the young artist than any conception of ideal beauty: he is constantly led by it either into weak prettiness or lifeless abstraction: whereas to touch the ideal at all you
(10) must not strip it of vitality. You must find it in life and re-create it in art.

4. Which of the following statements is equivalent to "we . . . cannot accept any theory of beauty in exchange for beauty itself" (lines 2–3)?

(A) "I do not desire to give you any abstract definition of beauty at all" (lines 1–2)

(B) "desiring to isolate it in a formula appealing to the intellect" (line 4)

(C) "a form that gives joy to the soul through the senses" (line 5)

(D) "We want to create it, not to define it" (lines 5–6)

(E) "The definition should follow the work" (line 6)

Correct answer: (D). The original statement can be paraphrased as "we can't take the ideas people have about art instead of art (or beauty) itself." Choice (D) matches perfectly, because when you "define" something, you talk about it, and talking expresses ideas. The art (or beauty) is a creation.

A new fact question that accounts for approximately three of the multiple-choice questions on every AP exam concerns source citations. For more information about citations, see Chapter 12. And relax: The test makers don't ask you to create a citation, just to recognize elements of citations they show you, so you can demonstrate that you know the difference between a book and an article or which number refers to the page and which to a volume. They may also query the overall purpose or effect of the citations.

EXAMPLE

Here's an example, based on these endnotes from Joseph Treaster's book entitled *Paul Volcker: The Making of a Financial Legend* (Wiley, 2004; reprinted with permission of John Wiley & Sons, Inc.):

28. Paul A. Volcker Jr. interview, 2003.
29. Paul Volcker and Toyoo Gyohten, *Changing Fortunes* (New York: Times Books, 1992), p. 164.
30. Paul A. Volcker Jr. interview, 2003.

5. Which of the following statements is true, according to the citations for this passage?

(A) Much of information comes from an interview conducted by Paul A. Volcker Jr.
(B) Paul Volcker and Toyoo Gyohten wrote an article entitled *Changing Fortunes*.
(C) Volcker and Gyohten's article was published in *The New York Times*.
(D) The article that Volcker and Gyohten wrote is on page 164 of a book entitled *Changing Fortunes*.
(E) The author relied on primary source material.

Correct answer: (E). *Changing Fortunes* is a book, not an article, because it's italicized. (Article titles are enclosed in quotation marks.) Endnotes 28 and 30 refer to an interview with Mr. Volcker, not by him. These two facts rule out answers (A) through (D). You know that (E) is right not only because it's the only remaining choice but also because an interview with Volcker, as well as something he co-wrote, is cited. *Primary sources* come from the subject being studied.

Antecedents

Pronouns are handy little guys. They take the place of nouns (and occasionally of other pronouns) and help you avoid saying things like "Henry went to Henry's car and drove to Henry's house." The *antecedent* of a pronoun is the word the pronoun replaces. In the tangled world of AP reading comprehension, uncovering the antecedent (usually of "that," "which," or "it") is a favorite task. This method helps:

1. **Locate the pronoun they're questioning.** The test makers tell you which line the pronoun appears in.

2. **Reread the sentence the pronoun appears in and take a quick peek at the sentences surrounding the pronoun.** Antecedents don't always reside in the same sentence as their pronouns. Don't forget that an antecedent sometimes *follows* the pronoun it replaces.

3. **Restate the sentence the pronoun appears in, substituting a noun for the pronoun they're asking about.** Be sure you haven't altered the meaning.

4. **Find an answer choice that matches your substitution.** The answer given may vary a bit in wording (sometimes modifiers are included), but it should be there.

The wording of an antecedent question is straightforward: It asks, **"What is the antecedent of _____?"** or leaves an unfinished statement, as in the following example.

> **EXAMPLE**
>
> Read this passage from *The Knight*, by Alan Baker (Wiley, 2003; reprinted with permission from John Wiley & Sons, Inc.):
>
> (01) It is easy to see that feudalism was, at its center, defined by the localization of political, military, and economic power in the hands of lords and their vassals, who exercised that power from their castle headquarters, each of which held complete sway over the district in which it was situated. The resulting hierarchy resembled (05) a pyramid, with the lowest vassals at the base and the king, of course, at the summit. This was not the case in every nation, however; in Germany, for instance, the summit of the pyramid did not reach the king, being occupied instead by the great princes.
>
> 6. The antecedent of "This" (line 6) is
>
>   (A) pyramid (line 5 or 7)
>   (B) hierarchy (line 4)
>   (C) feudalism (line 1)
>   (D) king (line 5)
>   (E) princes (line 7)
>
> **Correct answer: (A).** What wasn't the case in every nation? The fact that the power structure resembled a pyramid. Hence "pyramid" is the closest answer, and (A) is what you want.

Inference

An inference question pushes you into the blank spaces "between the lines." The answer is implied by various clues in the passage but not directly stated. When you encounter an inference question, try this approach:

1. **Restate the question in your own words.** Now you know what they're looking for.

2. **Go back to the line numbers specified or check your annotations for the topic being asked about.** Now you know where to look for evidence.

3. **Think about the information you're given and stretch it to the next logical level.** In the excerpt from *The Knight* in the preceding section, the author tells you that in Germany "the summit of the pyramid did not reach the king, being occupied instead by the great princes." The logical conclusion is that the princes had the same powers as kings did in other countries.

4. **Match your conclusion to the answer choices.** If you don't find a match, recheck the passage to see which choice makes sense in light of the evidence there.

The wording of inference questions varies greatly. You may see these patterns:

> Lines ___ to ___ imply that . . . .
>
> The _____ in paragraph two suggests that . . . .

_____ probably _____ because . . . .

From _____, you can infer that . . . .

EXAMPLE

Test-drive this inference question, based on another excerpt from *The Knight*.

(01) The results of feudalism were mixed, to say the least. On the negative side, it meant that the state had a relationship with the heads of groups rather than directly with individuals farther down the social scale. Under a weak king, these men claimed sovereignty for themselves, and fought among themselves rather than allowing the (05) state to judge their claims. This resulted in the private wars that scarred the medieval landscape. The overlords claimed numerous rights for themselves, including that of issuing private coinage, building private castles, and the power to raise taxes. Each of these manorial groups tried to be self-sufficient and to consolidate its possessions.

7. According to the passage, what is the advantage of a powerful king?

  (A) He has a direct relationship with members of the lower social classes.
  (B) He helps keep the peace.
  (C) He takes sides in the wars between nobles.
  (D) He allows private coinage.
  (E) He sets low tax rates.

Correct answer: (B). The passage tells you about the disadvantages of a "weak king" (line 3). To answer this question, therefore, all you have to do is flip the information provided. A powerful king does what a weak one can't. Because a weak king allows nobles to claim "sovereignty for themselves" (line 4) and fight, a strong king keeps sovereignty for himself and keeps the peace.

TIP

One type of inference question asks for the main idea of the passage or a portion. To answer a main-idea question, create a title with a good, glovelike fit. You don't want floppy cloth in the finger area (too big) or bare palms (too small). Match your title to one of the answer choices, and you're home free.

Theme, attitude, and purpose

These three types of questions force you to take a step back and look at the Big Picture — the passage as a whole. A *theme* is an important idea considered in a literary work. By now in your academic life, you've probably discussed the themes of appearance and reality, loyalty, betrayal, love, and about a million others. A theme isn't a topic. For example, suppose you read a piece about soup kitchens in the Depression. "Soup kitchens in the Depression" is the topic. Themes of the piece may be generosity, greed, or poverty as ennobling (or debilitating). Attitude questions ask you to characterize the viewpoint or emotions of the author or of someone appearing in the selection. Purpose questions ask you to figure out *why* the author wrote the piece.

To deal with a question about theme, step back from the piece and conjure up a kindly teacher. What's the teacher talking about? What sort of discussion can you imagine about the selection? The answers point you toward the theme. Look back for a moment at the excerpt from Oscar Wilde's lecture on art. Imagine the teacher throwing out these questions: What is beauty? Must art be beautiful? You have your themes: beauty, art, and the relationship between the two.

To determine attitude or purpose is a little harder. You have to examine the words used (the *diction*), opinions expressed, and what's left unsaid. Take these steps when you run up against an attitude question:

1. **If a character or person in the piece is the focus, review what he or she says and does.** Also check how others interact with the character or person the question queries you about.

2. **If the question concerns the author's attitude or purpose, reread your annotations.** Your notes will remind you of the content of the piece. What does that content tell you? If you find five reasons why carbon-based fuels are harming the world, the author's attitude is probably "pro-environment" or "critical" of the major car companies. The purpose may be to rally people to the author's cause or to inform the reader of the perils of a large carbon-footprint.

3. **Imagine yourself talking with the character, person, or author.** What would that person say? In your mind, conjure up a little speech. The way it sounds is a clue to attitude; the response you have to the speech is a clue to its purpose.

4. **Check the answer choices and see which one fits the speech.**

This step may be easier if you imagine yourself reporting the speech for the school paper. What would the headline be? "Cut SUV Production" or "SUVs Are Cool"? Now you know whether the author's attitude is anti- or pro-SUV and whether the purpose is to urge that production of large vehicles be curtailed or promoted.

The answer choices for attitude questions may be single words or pairs of words. If you're faced with a pair, be sure both words fit.

Questions about theme, attitude, and purpose are generally written in a straightforward way, such as these:

The speaker's attitude is . . . .

The purpose of paragraph two is to . . . .

Which of the following would the author favor (or oppose)?

EXAMPLE

This sample question is based on the excerpt from *The Knight* that appears in the inference discussion in the earlier section "Reading comprehension":

8. The author's attitude toward feudalism may best be described as

(A) critical

(B) admiring

(C) detached

(D) reflective

(E) philosophical

Correct answer: (A). The first sentence of the excerpt tells you that "the results of feudalism were mixed, to say the least" (line 1). Right away you know that the author's not a complete fan of feudalism, and you can rule out (B) and (C). Nor is the author pondering the meaning of feudalism or attempting to place it in a larger context, so (D) and (E) don't work. (**Note:** This example doesn't ask you about purpose, but if it did, the answer would probably be "to inform the reader about feudalism" or "to criticize the feudal system" or something similar.)

Style questions

Style questions concern writing, not content. In general, the AP asks you questions about *how* a piece is written and *why* the author wrote this way. Elements of style queried on the AP test include *diction* (word choice), *syntax* (how the words fit together grammatically), *structure* (the organizing principle of the passage), and *rhetorical modes* (the basic types of writing: narration, description, exposition, and argument). The AP-exam writers also love to query you about *shifts* (when something changes in the writing, such as point of view). Turn to Part II for a review of all these concepts.

In quality literature (the type used on the AP exam and given as assignments in AP courses), style and content work together. Expect to find questions on style that overlap with content, and vice versa.

To answer a style question, the best approach is to imagine an alternate universe. Here's what to do:

1. **Examine the lines they're asking about.** If they want to know about the structure of paragraph two, reread paragraph two.

2. **Consider the element of style they've mentioned.** If they don't name an element of style in the question stem, glance at the answer choices to see what's in the running.

3. **Read the answer choices.** Does anything strike you immediately? If not, check the most likely answers.

4. **If you're stuck, imagine a change in those lines.** If the paragraph were left out, what would be different in the passage? If you altered it (say, from narration to description), how would the passage be affected? What would happen if you moved those lines to a different spot? The answer is likely to show you what those lines do — in AP terms, how those lines function — or to a glimpse of the overall structure of the piece.

5. **Match your answer to one of the choices.** If nothing fits, go back to Step 3 and try still another alteration. If that doesn't work, take a guess and move on.

Questions about style appear in many forms, including these:

Paragraph two marks a shift from _____ to _____.

The narrator's attitude is reveal primarily by _____.

The dominant rhetorical device (or rhetorical technique) in paragraph two is ___.

The argument in favor of _____ is presented primarily by which rhetorical device?

The function of _____ is to _____.

EXAMPLE

Answer the following question to see how "stylish" you are. It's based on an excerpt from Samuel Pepys's diary.

(01) After dinner, and doing some business at the office, I to White Hall, where the Court is full of the Duke and his courtiers returned from sea. All fat and lusty, and ruddy by being in the sun. I kissed his hands, and we waited all the afternoon. By and by saw Mr. Coventry, which rejoiced my very heart. Anon he and I, from all the rest of
(05) the company, walked into the Matted Gallery; where after many expressions of love, we fell to talk of business. Among other things, how my Lord Sandwich, both in his councils and personal service, hath done most honourably and serviceably.

9. The diction in paragraph one (lines 1–7) serves to

   (A) present a favorable view of the aristocracy
   (B) criticize the aristocracy
   (C) reveal the narrator's lack of confidence
   (D) emphasize the duties of the aristocracy
   (E) show the narrator's sense of detachment

Correct answer: (A). The Duke and his courtiers are "fat and lusty" (line 2), not a bad thing in the olden days, when people starved to death. The narrator "kissed his hands" (line 3) after he "waited all the afternoon" (line 3) and talked with his friend about how Lord Sandwich "hath done most honorably and serviceably" (line 7). Suppose instead that the returnees were "thin and weak" and the narrator "ignored his arrival" or said that Lord Sandwich performed "dishonorably and ineffectually." See the change? Clearly, a favorable view is what the author presents.

TIP

Shifts are a big deal in style questions. The AP-exam makers love to point you at a specific spot in the passage and ask you to determine what changes there — the point of view, the technique (narration to description, perhaps), and so forth. To answer a shift question, check what comes before and after the designated spot.

14

Practice Multiple-Choice Questions

KEY CONCEPTS

- Questions that require you to pick apart dense material
- Questions pertaining to a variety of writing styles and genres
- Citation questions

G rab a pencil because here is where you put to work all the strategy you acquired in Chapter 13. The multiple-choice questions count for 45 percent of your final AP exam grade, so this practice is definitely worth your time. After each question in this chapter, I tell you the right answer and, more importantly, *why* it's right and why other choices are wrong.

Because in this chapter the answers and explanations mingle with the questions, you aren't practicing true AP-exam timing. (You can do so when you take the practice tests in Chapters 17 and 19.) Don't worry about the clock. This chapter is about becoming familiar with AP-style questions, not racing through a passage.

PRACTICE PASSAGE 1: FRANCIS BACON

Your first practice run is an essay by Francis Bacon entitled "Of Innovations." Bacon is much-loved by standardized-test makers because he's a master of the art of the essay, and his work is dense. It's easy to write questions about a Bacon essay because the author packed so much into each line.

EXAMPLE

Read the following excerpt from Francis Bacon's essay "Of Innovations" and answer the questions that follow.

(01) As the births of living creatures, at first are ill-shapen, so are all innovations, which are the births of time. Yet notwithstanding, as those that first bring honor into their family, are commonly more worthy than most that succeed, so the first precedent (if it be good) is seldom attained by imitation. For ill, to man's nature, as
(05) it stands perverted, hath a natural motion, strongest in continuance; but good, as a forced motion, strongest at first. Surely every medicine is an innovation; and he that will not apply new remedies, must expect new evils; for time is the greatest innovator; and if time of course alter things to the worse, and wisdom and counsel shall not alter them to the better, what shall be the end? It is true, that what
(10) is settled by custom, though it be not good, yet at least it is fit; and those things which have long gone together, are, as it were, confederate within themselves; whereas new things piece not so well; but though they help by their utility, yet they trouble by their inconformity. Besides, they are like strangers; more admired, and less favored. All this is true, if time stood still; which contrariwise moveth so
(15) round, that a forward retention of custom, is as turbulent a thing as an innovation; and they that reverence too much old times, are but a scorn to the new. It were good, therefore, that men in their innovations would follow the example of time itself; which indeed innovateth greatly, but quietly, by degrees scarce to be perceived. For otherwise, whatsoever is new is unlooked for; and ever it mends
(20) some, and pairs others; and he that is holpen[1], takes it for a fortune, and thanks the time; and he that is hurt, for a wrong, and imputeth it to the author. It is good also, not to try experiments in states, except the necessity be urgent, or the utility evident; and well to beware, that it be the reformation, that draweth on the change, and not the desire of change, that pretendeth the reformation. And lastly,
(25) that the novelty, though it be not rejected, yet be held for a suspect; and, as the Scripture saith, that we make a stand upon the ancient way, and then look about us, and discover what is the straight and right way, and so to walk in it.

1. helped

1. Which of the following is equivalent to that statement that "all innovations . . . are the births of time" (lines 1–2)?

   (A) "the first precedent . . . is seldom attained by imitation" (lines 3–4)

   (B) "Surely every medicine is an innovation" (line 6)

   (C) "All this is true, if time stood still" (line 14)

   (D) "men in their innovations would follow the example of time itself; which indeed innovateth greatly" (lines 17–18)

   (E) "whatsoever is new is unlooked for" (line 19)

Correct answer: (D). This question, like all equivalent questions, relies on your reading comprehension skills. Decoding anything written by Francis Bacon isn't easy. The passage in the question refers to "innovations" (line 1) as "the births of time" (line 2). Simply put, Bacon is saying that time is pregnant; wait long enough, and something new will arrive. Choice (D) says the same thing: "time itself . . . innovateth greatly." In other words, time creates (gives birth to) innovations.

2. The function of "Yet" (line 2) is to

    (A) qualify the point made in the first sentence (lines 1–2)

    (B) support the point made in the first sentence (lines 1–2)

    (C) contradict the point made in the first sentence (lines 1–2)

    (D) explain what hasn't come true

    (E) introduce the point made in the third sentence (lines 4–6)

Correct answer: (A). To qualify is to set conditions, as in "she was given permission to use the car, yet she had to be home by midnight." Bacon begins by saying that innovations aren't perfect when they appear, just as living creatures are "ill-shapen" at birth. The second sentence in this essay (lines 2–4) declares that you're not likely to come up with something worthwhile "by imitation" (line 4). He also says that "those that first bring honor into their family, are commonly worth more than those that succeed" (lines 2–3). In this context, to "succeed" is to "come later." Bacon isn't supporting or contradicting the "ill-shapen" nature of innovations — ruling out (B) and (C). Choice (E) isn't even close because the next sentence hops to a new concept; (E) isn't introducing anything. Instead, "Yet" tweaks or qualifies the main idea of sentence one, as (A) says.

Choice (D) may have tempted you because "yet" is often associated with deadlines, as in "you haven't done your homework yet." Keep in mind that the AP-exam writers sometimes throw in an easy vocabulary word used in an unusual way. Don't be fooled.

3. According to lines 2–6, which statements about good and ill are true?

    I. Good is seldom attained by imitation.

    II. Ill actions have a tendency to continue.

    III. Good actions are stronger at the beginning.

    (A) I only

    (B) II only

    (C) III only

    (D) none of the above

    (E) all of the above

Correct answer: (E). Bacon believes that precedent (another word for "innovation") "is seldom attained by imitation" (line 4) if the precedent "be good" (line 4). Place statement I in the winner's column. Bacon also writes that "ill" (line 4) is "strongest in continuance" (line 5). In other words, bad stuff keeps going. Therefore, II passes the test. Finally, he writes that good is "strongest at first" (line 6). Statement III is true and thus makes (E) the answer you seek.

4. Which of the following elements are NOT present in this passage?

(A) rhetorical question

(B) antithesis

(C) personification

(D) paradox

(E) allusion

Correct answer: (D). A *paradox* is an unsolvable puzzle, an important-sounding statement that makes you scratch your head, such as "the more things change, the more they remain the same." This passage has no paradoxes, so (D) is the best answer. Just to review the other choices: Bacon asks a rhetorical question (A) in lines 8–9. You're not supposed to answer the question; it's a statement in disguise. (B), *antithesis,* is the dominant device in this passage. Bacon yo-yos between extremes, talking about good and ill (lines 3–6) and people who are "hol-pen" (line 20) or helped and those who are hurt (line 21). Time is *personified* — given human traits — in line 2 when it gives birth, so (C) isn't appropriate. You can find an *allusion* (E) in line 26, when Bacon refers to scripture. (An allusion is a reference to something that's commonly known, such as a book or an event.)

5. In the context of lines 9–11, what is the meaning of "fit"?

(A) physically able

(B) mentally able

(C) appropriate

(D) matching

(E) blend in

Correct answer: (E). Here's another vocabulary-in-context question. They show up more often in old (pre-19th-century) passages because the meaning of a word tends to evolve over time, and the test writers are checking your ability to ferret out a definition that is seldom employed in modern works. As usual, a couple of the answer choices are definitions of the selected word, but only one is the definition *in context.* In lines 12–14, Bacon describes the discomfort that new ideas bring. Innovations don't "fit" at first. Old customs, on the other hand, "fit" even when they're bad customs. Substitute "blend in" for "fit" in the last two sentences, and you'll see that (E) is correct.

6. The antecedent of "they" in "they are like strangers" (line 13) is

(A) "custom" (line 10)

(B) "things which have long gone together" (lines 10–11)

(C) "confederate" (line 11)

(D) "new things" (line 12)

(E) "utility" (line 12)

Correct answer: (D). To find the antecedent, chop the pronoun "they" out of the sentence. Ask yourself, "Who are like strangers?" Only one answer maintains the original meaning of the sentence, (D) — new things.

7. The statement "All this is true, if time stood still" (line 14) has the effect of

(A) negating every point made previously

(B) validating all previous points

(C) reversing the meaning of lines 12–14 ("new things piece not so well . . . less favored")

(D) supporting the meaning of lines 12–14 ("new things piece not so well . . . less favored")

(E) introducing the concept of gradual change

Correct answer: (D). Because time doesn't stand still, the line cited in the question really means "None of this is true." Now all you've got to do is figure out what "none of this" is. (A) and (B) stretch all the way to the beginning of the passage — too far, because Bacon has made several points, and only one is tackled by the question. The smaller section (lines 12–14) mentioned in choices (C) or (D) is better. How do you know? Just look at what follows "All this is true, if time stood still" (line 14). There you read that it's just as hard to keep a custom going past its expiration date as it is to change — "forward retention of custom, is as turbulent a thing as an innovation" (lines 15–16). This statement supports innovation, making choice (D) the best answer. (E) doesn't work because the concept of gradual change comes later, in lines 17–18 ("follow the example of time itself, which indeed innovateth greatly, but quietly").

8. Which statement best reflects the author's attitude toward innovation?

(A) Innovation should always be welcomed.

(B) Innovation disrupts society.

(C) Innovations are best when they effect total change.

(D) The best innovations are gradual and necessary.

(E) The desire for change is the best motive for innovation.

Correct answer: (D). Bacon's writing style is so tight that each sentence could serve as the topic sentence of another essay. His strongest statement about innovation is a perfect match for (D): "It were good, therefore, that men in their innovations would follow the example of time itself; which innovateth greatly, but quietly, by degrees" (lines 16–18). Did I catch you with (B)? Bacon acknowledges the discomfort accompanying innovation ("new things piece not so well" — line 12), but he also explains that the lack of change is as difficult as innovation ("a forward retention of custom, is as turbulent a thing as an innovation" — lines 15–16). Therefore, (D) is the better answer.

PRACTICE PASSAGE 2: A LETTER TO PUNCH

Punch, a British humor magazine, went out of business at the end of the 20th century, but it lasted more than a hundred years — long enough to accumulate a fair amount of correspondence.

EXAMPLE

Read this letter to *Punch,* proposing a streamlined novel. Then answer the questions following the letter.

(01)   DEAR PUNCH,

I was much amused the other day, on taking my seat in the Birmingham Railway train, to observe a sentimental-looking young gentleman, who was sitting opposite to me, deliberately draw from his travelling-bag three volumes of what appeared to
(05)   me a new novel of the full regulation size, and with intense interest commence the first volume at the title-page. At the same instant the last bell rang, and away started our train, whizz, bang, like a flash of lightning through a butter-firkin.[1] I endeavoured to catch a glimpse of some familiar places as we passed, but the attempt was altogether useless. Harrow-on-the-Hill, as we shot by it, seemed to be driving pell-
(10)   mell[2] up to town, followed by Boxmoor, Tring, and Aylesbury — I missed Wolverton and Weedon while taking a pinch of snuff — lost Rugby and Coventry before I had done sneezing, and I had scarcely time to say, "God bless us," till I found we had reached Birmingham. Whereupon I began to calculate the trifling progress my reading companion could have made in his book during our rapid journey, and to devise
(15)   plans for the gratification of persons similarly situated as my fellow-traveller. "Why," thought I, "should literature alone lag in the age of steam? Is there no way by which a man could be made to swallow Scott[3] or bolt Bulwer,[4] in as short a time as it now takes him to read an auction bill?" Suddenly a happy thought struck me: it was to write a novel, in which only the actual spirit of the narration should be retained,
(20)   rejecting all expletives, flourishes, and ornamental figures of speech; to be terse and abrupt in style — use monosyllables always in preference to polysyllables — and to eschew all heroes and heroines whose names contain more than four letters. Full of this idea, on my returning home in the evening, I sat to my desk, and before I retired to rest, had written a novel of three neat, portable volumes; which, I assert, any lady
(25)   or gentlemen, who has had the advantage of a liberal education, may get through with tolerable ease, in the time occupied by the railroad train running from London to Birmingham.

I will not dilate on the many advantages which this description of writing possesses over all others. Lamplighters, commercial bagmen, omnibus-cads, tavern-wait-
(30)   ers, and general postmen, may "read as they run." Fiddlers at the theatres, during the rests in a piece of music, may also benefit by my invention; for which, if the following specimen meet your approbation, I shall instantly apply for a patent.

1. A small, covered, wooden container.
2. At full speed.
3–4. 19th century novelists.

9. The "young gentleman" (line 2) is described as "sentimental-looking" probably in order to

(A) explain why he is reading a novel

(B) give an idea of his appearance

(C) create a contrast between him and the letter writer

(D) explain the content of his reading

(E) associate novel reading with the past

Correct answer: (E). On New Year's Eve, many people get "sentimental" while singing "Auld Lang Syne" because they're looking backward, at the past. The "sentimental-looking young gentleman" (line 2) is engaged in a slow-paced, old-fashioned activity (reading a novel), which contrasts with the speed of the modern train. The entire letter, in fact, ironically places the time-consuming task of reading a novel in juxtaposition to the rapid movement of the train. The train is the future, and novel reading is the past. Hence (E) is the best answer here.

10. The novel's description as "full regulation size" (line 5) is an example of

   (A) hyperbole
   (B) understatement
   (C) personification
   (D) irony
   (E) oxymoron

Correct answer: (D). When you're bogged down with homework, it's easy to imagine that English teachers have a rule: Every novel you read has to be really, really long. Of course, novels don't follow rules, and the Author's Guild hasn't decreed a "full regulation size" for anything. So this description isn't true. Throughout the passage the letter-writer says the opposite of what he means. Instead of hoping that novel-reading will speed up, he's hoping that the pace of modern life will slow down. Saying the opposite of what you mean falls under the literary category of *irony,* making (D) your answer. The other terms don't fit: *hyperbole* is exaggeration and *understatement* the opposite of exaggeration. *Personification* gives human traits to nonhuman elements, and an *oxymoron* is a self-contradicting term (think "jumbo shrimp").

11. The comparison between the train's speed and "a flash of lightning through a butter-firkin" (line 7)

   (A) emphasizes the difference between the past and present
   (B) shows the author's approval of fast-paced activities, as represented by the train
   (C) portrays progress as a natural act
   (D) focuses on the destructiveness of a rapid train
   (E) praises the speed of the train

Correct answer: (A). Butter-firkins were wooden tubs that were probably more common when this passage was written (in the late 19th century) than they are today. A wooden container implies that the butter was made the old-fashioned way, by churning it. The train is portrayed as modern, so (A) is the best answer here. The other choices don't fit very well. Choices (B) and (E) don't work because the author isn't a fan of speed, and (D) is out because the train isn't portrayed as destroying anything. Choice (C) may have made you flash back to poetry class, when the teacher probably discussed "nature as represented by lightning" in this *simile* (direct comparison). Nevertheless, (C) is too much of a stretch.

12. The author's attempt to gain a "glimpse of some familiar places as we passed" (line 8) and the list of towns

    (A) give a sense of the train's speed
    (B) show what has been sacrificed in the interests of speed
    (C) focus on the author's memories
    (D) orient the reader to the geography of England
    (E) create an air of unreality

Correct answer: (B). The familiar places pass so quickly that the author can't even see them; they're lost because of the train's rapid movement. No doubt about it; choice (B) is best. Choice (A) isn't the answer you seek because the author's exaggeration makes it impossible to tell how fast the train is actually going. Choice (C) is too extreme; the author may have memories, but they don't appear in this letter. Nor does he care about geography or deal in "unreality," represented by (D) and (E).

13. The author's statement, "I missed Wolverton and Weedon while taking a pinch of snuff" (lines 10–11), is an example of

    (A) hyperbole
    (B) symbolism
    (C) paradox
    (D) metaphor
    (E) apostrophe

Correct answer: (A). A pinch of snuff lasts a *very* short time, even less than the sneezing that follows sticking something up your nose. (That's what you do with snuff.) It's impossible to pass two towns so quickly, so the statement is an exaggeration, also known as *hyperbole,* choice (A). *Symbolism* — choice (B) — appears when something acquires added meaning — not the case here. Nor has the author presented a self-contradicting situation, or *paradox* — choice (C). Choices (D) and (E) aren't what you want; a *metaphor* is an indirect comparison, and *apostrophe* is a comment addressed to a person or idea that doesn't appear in the passage.

14. Which of the following is true of the author's statement that he could "use monosyllables always in preference to polysyllables" (line 21)?

    (A) It suggests a better method for writing novels.
    (B) It contradicts his style in this passage.
    (C) It is one of many criticisms of traditional novels.
    (D) It is merely a guideline, not a hard-and-fast rule, for writers.
    (E) It is easily achievable.

Correct answer: (B). A quick glance at the passage reveals that the author hasn't "eschew[ed]" (line 22) or rejected polysyllabic words. In fact, he's strewn long words all over the place. In this case, (B) is your best choice. Choices (A) and (C) assume that the author is serious, but he's actually joking about his streamlined novel. Choices (D) and (E) aren't relevant.

15. The letter achieves its comic effect primarily through

   (A) the author's personality
   (B) narration
   (C) examples and anecdotes
   (D) description
   (E) exaggeration

Correct answer: (E). The whole passage is way over the top. He takes snuff and loses two towns, sneezes and loses two more, and writes a novel before bedtime. The author's personality, the narration, the examples, and the description all have one thing in common, and that's exaggeration.

16. In the context of this passage, the "[l]amplighters, commercial bagmen, omnibus-cads, tavern-waiters, and general postmen" (lines 29–30) are mentioned because

   (A) they form the potential market for a short novel
   (B) they display the diversity of British society
   (C) they represent passengers on the train
   (D) they do not like novels
   (E) they all work long hours

Correct answer: (A). Every novel needs readers, and these professions have one thing in common. All these workers may "read as they run" (line 30). Hence they have little time and are the potential market for a tiny book, an idea expressed by choice (A).

17. The tone of this passage is best described as

   (A) fanciful
   (B) serious
   (C) didactic
   (D) speculative
   (E) critical

Correct answer: (A). When you imagine this author speaking these words, what do you hear? Most of what he says he doesn't mean, so (A) is best. Choices (B), (C), and (D) are way off. ("Didactic," by the way, is the tone someone takes while lecturing.) (E) is possible, because the author is no fan of modern speed, but (A) captures the author's humor.

TIP

If your English class is typical, you read a lot of heavy material dealing with death, dishonor, war, and similar subjects. Therefore, you may be at a disadvantage when facing a comic selection. Ready yourself for the AP exam by tickling your funny bone. Read some comic classics and keep an eye out for *satire*, a type of writing that mocks society. (The letter to *Punch* falls into that category.) Notice how the comic effects are achieved.

PRACTICE PASSAGE 3: RICHARD HENRY DANA

Richard Henry Dana signed on as a sailor on the brig *Pilgrim* after enduring a bout of measles while a junior at Harvard College. He hoped to improve his eyesight, which had been damaged during the course of his illness. (The common wisdom of the day was that sea air is good for the eyes.) Dana's account of his voyage was published in 1840.

EXAMPLE

Read this excerpt from Dana's account of his voyage and answer the questions that follow.

(01) Death is at all times solemn, but never so much so as at sea. A man dies on shore; his body remains with his friends, and "the mourners go about the streets"; but when a man falls overboard at sea and is lost, there is a suddenness in the event, and a difficulty in realizing it, which give to it an air of awful mystery. A
(05) man dies on shore, — you follow his body to the grave, and a stone marks the spot. You are often prepared for the event.

There is always something which helps you to realize it when it happens, and to recall it when it has passed. A man is shot down by your side in battle, and the mangled body remains an object, and a real evidence; but at sea, the man is near
(10) you, — at your side, — you hear his voice, and in an instant he is gone, and nothing but a vacancy shows his loss. Then, too, at sea — to use a homely but expressive phrase — you miss a man so much. A dozen men are shut up together in a little bark upon the wide, wide sea, and for months and months see no forms and hear no voices but their own, and one is taken suddenly from among them, and
(15) they miss him at every turn. It is like losing a limb. There are no new faces or new scenes to fill up the gap. There is always an empty berth in the forecastle, and one man wanting when the small night-watch is mustered. There is one less to take the wheel, and one less to lay out with you upon the yard. You miss his form, and the sound of his voice, for habit had made them almost necessary to you, and
(20) each of your senses feels the loss.

All these things make such a death peculiarly solemn, and the effect of it remains upon the crew for some time. There is more kindness shown by the officers to the crew, and by the crew to one another. There is more quietness and seriousness. The

oath and the loud laugh are gone. The officers are more watchful, and the crew go
(25) more carefully aloft. The lost man is seldom mentioned, or is dismissed with a sailor's
rude eulogy, — "Well, poor George is gone! His cruise is up too soon! He knew his
work, and did his duty, and was a good shipmate." Then usually follows some allusion
to another world, for sailors are almost all believers, in their way; though their notions and opinions are unfixed and at loose ends.
(30)   They say, "God won't be hard upon the poor fellow," and seldom get beyond the
common phrase which seems to imply that their sufferings and hard treatment
here will be passed to their credit in the books of the Great Captain hereafter, —
"To work hard, live hard, die hard, and go to hell after all, would be hard indeed!"
Our cook, a simple-hearted old African, who had been through a good deal in his
(35) day, and was rather seriously inclined, always going to church twice a day when
on shore, and reading his Bible on a Sunday in the galley, talked to the crew about
spending the Lord's Days badly, and told them that they might go as suddenly as
George had, and be as little prepared.
    Yet a sailor's life is at best but a mixture of a little good with much evil, and
(40) a little pleasure with much pain. The beautiful is linked with the revolting, the
sublime with the commonplace, and the solemn with the ludicrous.
    Not long after we had returned on board with our sad report, an auction was
held of the poor man's effects. The captain had first, however, called all hands
aft and asked them if they were satisfied that everything had been done to
(45) save the man, and if they thought there was any use in remaining there longer.
The crew all said that it was in vain, for the man did not know how to swim,
and was very heavily dressed. So we then filed away and kept the brig off to
her course.

18. The dominant technique in paragraphs one and two (lines 1–20) is

(A) comparison and contrast
(B) cause and effect
(C) narration
(D) description
(E) dialogue

Correct answer: (A). These two paragraphs hop back and forth between land
and sea, pointing to (A) as the correct answer. The main idea is that death is
terrible on land, but more awful at sea. Notice how many pairs of statements
Dana makes: "A man dies on shore; his body remains" (lines 1–2) is matched by
"when a man falls overboard at sea" (lines 3–4). "A man is shot down by your
side in battle" (line 8) contrasts with "but at sea, the man is near you" (lines
9–10). True, the author does describe a general situation, but there's not
enough description to warrant choice (D). Nor is this passage truly a narrative,
answer (C), because the author doesn't tell you what happened. Choices (B)
and (E) are completely off-base.

19. What is the primary purpose of the phrase "all these things" (line 21)?

    (A) to summarize the content of paragraph three (lines 21–29)

    (B) to serve as a transition between paragraphs two and three (lines 7–20 and lines 21–29)

    (C) to emphasize the solemnity of death

    (D) to stress the immense effect of death

    (E) to prepare the reader for a list

Correct answer: (B). Paragraph two is a sad list of the effects of a death at sea, and Dana makes you experience the utter absence that such a death brings to a close-knit crew. The next paragraph discusses how the crew and their officers react to a death at sea. Therefore, this phrase links paragraph two to paragraph three, serving as a transition and making (B) the right answer. Choices (A) and (E) are off because "all these things" looks back to paragraph two more than forward to paragraph three. Answers (C) and (D) refer to death in general, and Dana is writing about the additional grief that a death at sea brings.

20. What is the best definition of "rude" in the context of line 26?

    (A) impolite

    (B) unpolished

    (C) offensive

    (D) ignorant

    (E) uninformed

Correct answer: (B). If you aren't familiar with "rude" as a synonym for "unpolished" — answer (B) — you can probably guess from the comments that follow it: "Well, poor George is gone! His cruise is up too soon! He knew his work, and did his duty, and was a good shipmate" (lines 26–27). This isn't a literary speech delivered by a practiced member of the clergy; it's a rough but heartfelt comment on a man's life. Choices (A) and (C) are definitions of "rude," but not in this context.

21. Which of the following is an "allusion" referred to in line 27?

    (A) "sailors are almost all believers" (line 28)

    (B) "their notions and opinions are unfixed and at loose ends" (lines 28–29)

    (C) "God won't be hard upon the poor fellow" (line 30)

    (D) "Our cook, a simple-hearted old African" (line 34)

    (E) "always going to church twice a day when on shore" (lines 35–36)

Correct answer: (C). This question revolves around the definition of *allusion,* a literary term that describes a reference to something well known, such as a book, event, or artwork. In lines 27–28, Dana says that sailors make an "allusion to another world," so you're looking for a reference to religion. When you search for religion, you find that all the answers work except (D). However, only one answer — (C) — quotes the sailors.

22. Paragraph five (lines 39–41) begins with "Yet." Which of the following statements describe(s) the function of this word?

    I. It qualifies the recommendation of the "old African" (line 34) to be prepared for death.

    II. It contrasts the ideal presented by the cook with the reality of a sailor's life.

    III. It excuses sailors such as George who die unprepared.

    (A) I

    (B) I and II

    (C) II and III

    (D) all of the above

    (E) none of the above

Correct answer: (D). Statement I is true; "to qualify" is "to limit," and while the cook's idea is wonderful, Dana says that "a sailor's life is at best but a mixture of a little good with much evil" (line 39). Hence Dana is limiting what the cook says. Dana is also contrasting the ideal (be prepared) with reality (they aren't prepared), so II is true. Because paragraph five (lines 39–41) tells you how much pain is involved in a sailor's life, III works also. Therefore, the answer is (D).

23. What is the "sad report" (line 42)?

    (A) man overboard

    (B) the pain of a sailor's life

    (C) the poverty of the dead sailor's possessions

    (D) the evil of most sailors' lives

    (E) the "revolting" work required of sailors

Correct answer: (A). The whole passage is about death at sea, and while Dana in this selection doesn't tell you the whole story, he refers to that death constantly. He also explains that "when a man falls overboard . . . and is lost" (line 3), death is even more tragic than death on land. (A) is the only answer that fits.

24. The tone of this passage may be characterized as

    (A) mournful and combative
    (B) defiant but philosophical
    (C) passionate and committed
    (D) emotional but informative
    (E) pedantic and dismissive

Correct answer: (D). Did (A) seem possible? Yes, Dana describes death at sea as a sad event, but he spends most of his energy explaining why losing a man from a sailing ship is worse than losing one on shore, and (A) says nothing about the informative aspect of the passage. Dana never asks, "Why do people die?" — a favorite question of philosophers — so (B) is out. (C) is too narrow and extreme for this passage, and (E) is way off base. Dana conveys emotion, but he also strives to inform, making (D) the answer you seek.

25. The author's purpose is to

    (A) inform non-sailors about life at sea
    (B) advocate a career at sea
    (C) commemorate a dead friend
    (D) criticize sailors' behavior
    (E) reveal the dangers of a sailor's life

Correct answer: (A). Everything in this passage is aimed at land-based readers, who don't understand life and death at sea. The best choice here is (A), because this passage is meant to inform, nothing more.

PRACTICE PASSAGE 4: COLUMBIAN EXPOSITION

At least one passage on the AP English Language and Composition exam is likely to be technical. A technical passage explains something — a historical event, the workings of a machine, a scientific theory, and the like. In this section is a selection from *Diamond Jim Brady: Prince of the Gilded Age,* by H. Paul Jeffers (Wiley, 2001; reprinted with permission of John Wiley & Sons, Inc.). It describes a world's fair, the Columbian Exposition, held in St. Louis in 1904.

> EXAMPLE
>
> Read this passage and try your hand at the questions based on it.
>
> (01) As in Chicago in 1893, Jim Brady found the host city of the exposition bustling with excited fair-goers and many of his associates in the railroad and steel businesses. Like the Columbian Exposition, the St. Louis extravaganza was a celebration of American industry. It had officially opened at 1:06 p.m., April 30, 1904, with
> (05) President Theodore Roosevelt using the same telegraph key in the White House with which President Cleveland had signaled the start of the Chicago fair.

At that exposition electricity had been a fascinating novelty to the people who jammed into the exhibition halls. Without it in St. Louis in 1904, the fair could not have been held. To provide lights and energize machinery and displays in eleven
(10) exhibition "palaces," the Union Light and Power Company, in collaboration with the Westinghouse Company, spent $2 million to create the largest generating plant in the world.

Writing in the May 14, 1904, edition of *The American Inventor*, Charles Alma Buers noted in enthusiastic but florid prose, "Were it not for this mysterious power,
(15) which man has brought down, as if from the sky, the greatest World's Fair ever held on the globe would lie inert; for not a wheel would turn nor a light be seen. It would repose in quietness and darkness like that which envelopes some isolated tomb. And why should not this exposition receive its 'vital spark' from electricity? Why should not this be an electrical fair? This is an age of things electrical, and
(20) to keep abreast with progress, naturally, a display of that, in science, is now most important."

Aglow and humming with this wonder, inside and out, were "The Palaces" of Electricity and Machinery, Agriculture, Education and Social Economy, Festival, Horticulture, Liberal Arts, Manufacturers, Mines and Minerology, Varied Industries, and,
(25) of most interest to Diamond Jim Brady, of Transportation.

Built to evoke the style of the nation's great railway terminals, it covered fifteen acres and measured 525 by 1,300 feet. Behind three huge arches and beneath its expansive roof was a display of old locomotives representing the long struggle for speedy transportation from stagecoaches to the Pullman Palace car. An old horse-
(30) car and the modern "trolley" stood side by side. Visitors inspected a dazzling array of automobiles, descendants of the battery-powered one Jim had ordered eleven years earlier.

Centrally displayed in the hall was an exhibit of the Cleveland, Cincinnati, Chicago & St. Louis Railway (known as the Big Four Route) of a locomotive and ten-
(35) der mounted on a turntable. It was an innovation in railroading that solved the problem of turning around an engine by driving it onto a revolving platform. In this example the turntable measured seventy-five feet across. It was built by the Chicago Bridge and Iron Works and supported the 162 tons of the American Locomotive Company engine and tender, capable of pulling ten freight cars at sixty
(40) miles an hour.

Second only to the turntable in the interest of visitors was the private railway coach that had been used by Abraham Lincoln during the Civil War. It was housed in a separate building devoted to a museum displaying other Lincoln relics, including a log cabin advertised as being the actual one in which the president had
(45) been born. Constructed by the government in a workshop in Alexandria, Virginia, the coach was furnished in rich tapestries and plushly upholstered chairs and sofas. It had made its first runs over the lines of the Pennsylvania and the Baltimore & Ohio. Lincoln had used it during his second campaign in 1864 and had addressed trackside crowds from the platform at the end of the car.

(50) Should a visitor want to experience a train ride without leaving St. Louis, the fair offered "The Scenic Railway." The climax of the ride was a precursor to the roller coaster in which passengers found themselves screaming and holding on for dear life as the track took three dips in quick succession at a swift speed. As with future roller coasters, most people immediately lined up to do it again.

26. What is the dominant rhetorical strategy of paragraph one (lines 1–6)?

   (A) cause and effect
   (B) comparison and contrast
   (C) narration
   (D) description
   (E) definition

Correct answer: (B). The first paragraph moves back and forth between the Chicago fair and the Columbian Exposition. In fact, the first five words of the paragraph are the tip off: "As in Chicago in 1893" (line 1). Right away you know you're in comparison-and-contrast territory, which steers you to the correct answer, (B).

27. In the phrase "At that exposition" (line 7), what is the antecedent of "that"?

   (A) Chicago (line 1)
   (B) host city (line 1)
   (C) extravaganza (line 3)
   (D) Columbian Exposition (line 3)
   (E) fair (line 6)

Correct answer: (E). An *antecedent* is the word a pronoun replaces. A pronoun replaces a noun or another pronoun, not a whole set of ideas, and is generally placed near its antecedent. In this passage, "that" refers to "the Chicago fair" (line 6). The closest answer is (E), "fair."

28. The quotation marks surrounding "palaces" (line 10) most likely indicate that

   (A) the word was used by Jim Brady
   (B) the buildings were anything but palatial
   (C) exposition officials called the buildings palaces
   (D) the writer thinks the label was misapplied
   (E) the writer wishes to distance himself from the term

Correct answer: (C). Everyone knows that quotation marks surround a direct quotation of someone's speech or writing. Answers (A) and (C) fall into this category. But quotation marks have other uses, too. Sanitizing quotation marks place a space between a term and the view of the writer — a function expressed by (B), (D), and (E). So which one works here? Choice (C). Why? You can rule out the sanitizing function, because the rest of the passage is heavy on the exciting details of the fair, including "huge arches" (line 27), "expansive roof" (line 28), and "a dazzling array of automobiles" (lines 30–31). The author's view doesn't contradict the idea of "palaces." Now you're down to (A) and (C). Who names buildings at a fair? The most likely candidate, and your answer, is (C) — the exposition officials.

29. In lines 14–21, the author includes a quotation in order to

    (A) illustrate the reaction of people who visited the fair

    (B) show how his own view of the fair differs from that of Charles Alma Buers

    (C) bring the past alive

    (D) provide an example of "florid prose" (line 14)

    (E) continue the comparison with the Chicago fair of 1893

Correct answer: (A). I must tell you that (C) drives English teachers up a wall. It's the sort of general statement that applies to just about any sentence concerning something that happened before this exact minute. Because it applies to everything, it means almost nothing. Therefore, (C) isn't the answer. The quotation praises electricity and doesn't contradict the author's admiration of the fair, so (B) drops away. True, the style of the quotation is flowery, but "florid prose" is a description of the quotation. The quotation isn't there to illustrate "florid." Rule out (D). Moving on to (E): Electricity was present at both Chicago and St. Louis, but the quotation isn't necessary to illustrate this point. The author could simply have stated that fact. The only reason for the quotation is to show a contemporary view, which means that (A) is correct.

30. The pronoun "that" (line 20, last sentence in the quotation) refers to

    (A) isolated tomb (lines 17–18)

    (B) vital spark (line 18)

    (C) things electrical (line 19)

    (D) progress (line 20)

    (E) science (line 20)

Correct answer: (D). The fastest way to the correct answer is to restate the sentence containing "that," inserting the word(s) that makes sense. Then check your insertion against the answer list and select the closest match. My first try came out this way: "This is an age of things electrical, and to keep abreast of progress, naturally, a display of new things, in science, is now most important." What matches "new things"? Choice (D). The only other possibility is (C), but "a display of things electrical, in science, is now most important" doesn't work as well because of the phrase "in science."

31. The tone of the passage may be described as

    (A) critical but informative

    (B) contemplative and nostalgic

    (C) playful and distant

    (D) informative and appreciative

    (E) enthusiastic and exaggerated

Correct answer: (D). This tone question features two descriptions in each answer. Take care that both of them fit, because the test writers like to place a good partner with a bad one. To determine tone, look at the author's word choice and the attitude displayed toward the subject, in this case, the Columbian Exposition. The author sounds like a publicity agent for the fair. The "Palaces" are "[a]glow and humming with this wonder" (line 22). The arches are "huge" (line 27) and much is made of the heavy train cars that are spun on a turntable. The roller coaster sounds like fun. You get a lot of information and a positive view — making (D) the best answer. Why don't the other choices work? (A) doesn't work because the passage isn't critical; nor is it "contemplative" — answer (B) — because the author makes no attempt to ponder or evaluate the fair. (C) is out because the author isn't "distant"; he's a cheerleader. (E) goes because he doesn't exaggerate.

32. Which statement describes the rhetorical function of the last sentence of paragraph five ("Visitors inspected a dazzling array of automobiles, descendants of the battery-powered one Jim had ordered eleven years earlier" — lines 30–32)?

    (A) It contrasts with the information in paragraph six (lines 33–40).
    (B) It is an elaboration of the point made in the preceding sentence ("An old horse-car . . . side by side" — lines 29–30).
    (C) It provides a specific example of a point made in paragraph four ("Aglow and humming . . . Transportation" — lines 22–25).
    (D) It focuses the reader's attention on Jim Brady.
    (E) It creates a transition to the next paragraph (lines 33–40).

Correct answer: (C). The sentence they're asking about concerns cars, and it's plopped in the middle of information on electricity and railroads, with a short detour to horsecars and trolleys. Because cars relate only in a general way to these ideas, you can drop (A), (B), and (E). Jim Brady is mentioned, but the passage skips over him quickly, so (D) isn't the answer either. That leaves (C), which refers to a sentence that's also an entire paragraph. Tucked into that sentence is this phrase: "of most interest to Diamond Jim Brady, [the Palace] of Transportation" (line 25). What's a car? Transportation, and therefore (C) is the appropriate choice.

33. Overall, the rhetorical strategy of this passage may be characterized as

    (A) example
    (B) process
    (C) narration
    (D) argument
    (E) definition

Correct answer: (A). A *rhetorical strategy* refers to the type of writing. You determine the strategy by asking yourself, "What's the author doing here?" The passage takes you through the Columbian Exposition, giving example after example of what you'd see if you were a time-traveler to 1904. Hence (A) is the best answer.

34. Which of the following is parallel to "It was housed in a separate building" (lines 42–43)?

(A) "the private railway coach that had been used by Abraham Lincoln during the Civil War" (lines 41–42)

(B) "devoted to a museum displaying other Lincoln relics" (line 43)

(C) "advertised as being the actual one in which the president had been born" (lines 44–45)

(D) "Constructed by the government in a workshop in Alexandria, Virginia" (line 45)

(E) "It had made its first runs over the lines of the Pennsylvania and the Baltimore & Ohio" (lines 47–48).

Correct answer: (E). *Parallel structure* is a grammatical term, but parallel lines in math can help you remember what it means. Those lines resemble train tracks — they look the same and head in the same direction. With that image in mind, search for an answer that resembles "It was housed in a separate building" (lines 42–43). Choice (E) is easy, because you have two "It-verb" combinations.

PRACTICE PASSAGE 5: JAPAN IN 1800

At least one selection on the AP English Language and Composition test must have footnotes, endnotes, parenthetical citations, or a bibliography, because the AP test makers want to make sure that you understand citations. (If citations stump you, turn to Chapter 12 for assistance.) This passage is excerpted from *The World in 1800*, by Olivier Bernier (Wiley, 2000; reprinted with permission of John Wiley & Sons, Inc.).

Note: The "shogunate" was a system of government in Japan in which the "shogun" was the ruler. "Samurai" were Japanese nobles. "Franciscans" are members of a Catholic religious order.

EXAMPLE

Read this excerpt from *The World in 1800* and answer the questions that follow it.

(01) China was huge, Japan was small. China had a population of 300 million, Japan's was about 28 million. When China failed to pay attention to the rest of the world, it was out of a sense of superiority; when the Japanese government decreed the closing of Japan, it was out of fear that Japan's very identity might be lost. Of course, that closing could never be complete, nor could the country remain ex-
(05) actly as it had been in 1600 when the shogunate was established; but still Japan looked firmly inward.

Even then, it was not completely cut off from the rest of the world. It sold luxury goods to the West and copper to China. Chinese and Dutch ships entered the one permitted harbor at Nagasaki; but no one in Japan felt connected to any other
(10) country. The rest of the world might be one; Japan stood alone.

Japan, in 1800, was a country apart. Naturally, its language, history, and culture were different from those of China or the rest of East Asia; less naturally, its government relied on a complex system of power relationships, set up 200 years (15) earlier; and held to be a model of unchanging perfection. The most startling characteristic of all, though, was that, for 165 years, the Japanese islands had, deliberately and almost completely, been insulated from the outside world.

The Edict of Closing, which was promulgated in 1635, was specific and thorough. "Japanese ships," it declared, "are strictly forbidden to leave for foreign countries. (20) No Japanese is permitted to go abroad. If any Japanese returns from overseas after residing there, he must be put to death."[1] It went on to restrict all trade with China — although an occasional Portuguese ship was allowed in. The only diplomats ever seen there were Chinese, and they came rarely. As for trade, which was most often discouraged by the government, it was carried out by Chinese (25) and Dutch merchants. The former bought copper; the latter came mostly to buy lacquerwork, bronzes, silks, and porcelain. More trade came through the Ryukyu Islands, the property of the Satsuma clan, but that was largely ignored by the government.

There were three main reasons for this extraordinary state of affairs. One was to (30) prevent any outflow of gold and silver — always in short supply within the empire. If nothing were known of the outside, if no traders were permitted outside Nagasaki, then there would be no imports. The sale of luxury goods, on the other hand, brought in precious metals, and so it was allowed. The second, and even more important reason, was to prevent missionaries from entering Japan. The culture (35) and government of Japan were based on religion; if the gods suddenly were mere pagan idols, as the missionaries claimed, then the whole structure of the country was likely to be destroyed. The government therefore banned Christianity. The converts resisted in a number of places, particularly the samurai and peasants at Shimabara in southern Kyushu, adding civil unrest to the threat presented by a (40) new religion. Political fighting, now revived, was the very problem which the rulers had taken pride in solving. Even worse, the Franciscans in Manila, their headquarters in the Far East, let it be known they would ask the king of Spain to intervene; thus, to actual civil unrest, Christianity added the threat of foreign invasion. That was clearly intolerable. Just as alarming, the Christians in Shimabara defended (45) themselves so efficaciously that their fortress could be taken only with the help of Dutch warships. The Dutch, being Protestant, were naturally delighted to help put down Catholic converts.

As for Western religious publications, the government made very sure they could not be accidentally brought in. When, in the 1770s, a Dutch trading ship came into (50) the harbor at Nagasaki, "all the Prayer-Books and Bibles belonging to the sailors were collected, and put into a chest, which was nailed down . . . and left under the care of the Japanese till the time of our departure,"[2] one of the officers, Carl Peter Thunberg, noted.

The third reason for the closure was just as cogent. The Japanese ruling class (55) prized its culture; it had no wish to see it Westernized. The best way to defend it from all intrusions, it decided, was physically to prevent all non-Japanese ideas and artifacts from reaching the people. These were all strong and clearly stated motivations. Just as important, however, was the essential justification of Japan's

peculiar system of government; that it must preserve, unaltered, the settlement
(60) reached in 1600 by the first shogun of the Tokugawa family; and that the best way
to do that was to prevent any change of any kind.

[1] David J. Lu, *Japan: A Documentary History* (London, 1984), 221.
[2] Carl Peter Thunberg, *Travels in Europe, Africa, and Asia Performed Between the Years 1700 and 1779* (London, 1793), 3:11–12.

35. "China was huge, Japan was small" (line 1) is an example of

   (A) aphorism
   (B) antithesis
   (C) juxtaposition
   (D) hyperbole
   (E) repetition

Correct answer: (B). An *aphorism* is something people call an "old saying." An
aphorism doesn't actually have to be old; it just has to be something that
catches on and expresses a moral truth or principle. *Antithesis* puts contrary
ideas together in a similar sentence pattern. *Juxtaposition* means putting two
things next to each other, so one is seen in light of the other. A *hyperbole* is an
exaggeration. *Repetition,* of course, is repeating. Now that these words are in
your vocabulary, the question is easy: (B) is the answer.

36. The first sentence of paragraph two ("Even then . . . world" — line 8)

   (A) repeats the information given in paragraph one (lines 1–7)
   (B) contradicts the main idea of paragraph one (lines 1–7)
   (C) qualifies the main idea of paragraph one (lines 1–7)
   (D) quantifies the information in paragraph one (lines 1–7)
   (E) exemplifies the situation described in paragraph one (lines 1–7)

Correct answer: (C). The first paragraph compares China and Japan in a couple
of ways but comes down hard on the idea that Japan "looked firmly inward"
(line 7) because the Japanese government closed the country to outsiders. The
first sentence of paragraph two explains that the country wasn't completely
closed; a few contacts with outsiders were allowed. Therefore, "Even then . . .
world" (line 8) qualifies the main idea of paragraph one. "To qualify" in AP
terms is to explain exceptions or to set limits.

37. Which of the following is the most likely reason why the author quotes from the
"Edict of Closing" (lines 19–21)?

   (A) to show how extreme Japan's isolation was
   (B) to illustrate the Japanese system of government
   (C) to provide a change of pace for the reader
   (D) to clarify the situation of foreigners in Japan
   (E) to introduce the idea of restriction

Correct answer: (A). You take a vacation abroad, and when you return home, they kill you. That's what the quotation says. The Edict of Closing is about as extreme as a law can be, so (A) is the reason for inserting the quotation. (B) is out because the quotation doesn't deal with the government, just with its actions. Answer (C) is way too general; it sounds like a sentence students throw into an essay when they're stretching to make the required word count. You can dump (D) because the quotation deals with the Japanese, not with foreigners in Japan. Finally, (E) fails because the idea of restriction was introduced in paragraph one, not with the quotation.

38. Lines 34–47 ("The culture and government of Japan . . . Catholic converts") present

    (A) reasons why the Japanese government banned foreigners
    (B) information on Western religions
    (C) an expansion of the preceding sentence ("The second, and even more important reason, was to prevent missionaries from entering Japan" — lines 33–34)
    (D) a contradiction of the preceding sentence ("The second, and even more important reason, was to prevent missionaries from entering Japan" — lines 33–34)
    (E) an introduction to the next paragraph (lines 48–53)

Correct answer: (C). Go back to the lines designated in the question. All of them explain why Western religion, which was brought to Japan by missionaries, was a threat to the Japanese government. Hence these lines are an expansion of the sentence they follow, and (C) is your answer. The only other remotely possible choice is (E) because the next paragraph also deals with religious restrictions. However, the lines mentioned in (E) merely explain what the restriction is, not why the government felt the need to restrict foreign religion.

39. Which statement about the first citation is true?

    (A) The quotation came from an article entitled *Japan: A Documentary History.*
    (B) The quotation came from a book entitled *Japan: A Documentary History.*
    (C) *Japan: A Documentary History* was published by a company called London.
    (D) The quotation appeared on page 1984 of this source.
    (E) The publisher of this source is unknown.

Correct answer: (B). Book titles are italicized or underlined; article titles are placed inside quotation marks. London is where the book was published, not the company. (Years ago the name of the company wasn't always given. The assumption was that you could locate the company with the other information in the citation.) The number 221 is the page where the quotation may be found, and 1984 is the year of publication.

40. In the second citation, the number 3 represents

(A) the edition

(B) the page number

(C) the section of the book being quoted

(D) the number of times the book has been reissued

(E) the volume number

Correct answer: (E). Either Carl Peter Thunberg traveled a lot, or he wrote a lot about every moment of his trips, because 3 is the volume number. Keep in mind that in footnotes and endnotes, the page number is the last number cited.

41. Taken together, the citations for this passage suggest that

(A) the author researched from primary sources

(B) the author relied on secondary sources

(C) the passage is not well-supported by research

(D) the best sources for this topic are British

(E) both books and articles are useful sources for this topic

Correct answer: (A). A *primary source* is firsthand; it's produced by the culture you're studying. A *secondary source* interprets or comments on primary sources. David J. Lu's book is subtitled "A Documentary History," so chances are it includes documents from Japan — a primary source. Thunberg's travelogue was published in 1793, making it more or less contemporary to the period discussed in the passage. (Remember, the passage is from a book entitled *The World in 1800*.) The best answer, therefore, is (A). Choices (B), (C), and (E) are inaccurate. You may have fallen for the trap in (D). Yes, both books were published in London, but how do you know that these sources are the best? You don't, so (D) doesn't make the cut.

15

Strategies for the Essay Section

KEY CONCEPTS

- The logistics of writing exam essays
- Time constraints
- Crucial skills: Decoding prompts, annotating, creating a thesis, and organizing ideas
- Evidence as support for your ideas
- Essay structures and types

The AP English Language and Composition exam essay section requires reading approximately 2,000 words in about 15 minutes and writing approximately 1,500 words in two hours. You create three essays that are the basis for 55 percent of your AP exam grade. Clearly, you have to move quickly to succeed.

You achieve the necessary speed by being prepared: knowing what to expect, deciding ahead of time how to proceed, and fine-tuning your essay-writing skills. This chapter helps you accomplish all these tasks.

THE LOGISTICS OF THE ESSAY SECTION

The essay section, also known as the "free response" portion of the exam, begins when you tear the plastic wrap from a green question booklet. The proctor announces the start of a 15-minute reading period, during which you look over and annotate the three questions you find inside. Here's what you see:

- **A synthesis essay:** One synthesis essay is on every test. It includes a short introduction to the topic (in recent years, the effect of television on presidential elections and the advisability of keeping the penny coin), a *prompt* (which simply means an essay question), and six or seven sources. You have to develop your own position on the topic ("television has ruined democracy" or "save the penny," or something similar) and support that position with references to at least three sources.

- **An analysis essay:** Your exam will probably include an analysis essay. The test makers give you one passage, or occasionally a pair, and ask you to discuss how the writing style relates to content or to one specific aspect of content (characterization, attitude, purpose, and the like).

- **An argument essay:** You may be presented with an issue and asked to take a stand and defend it. Sometimes the issue is defined by a short quotation or passage.

After the reading period, you tear still more plastic wrap, this time from a pink answer-booklet. You then fill that booklet with three essay responses. As you work, keep these points in mind:

- **You don't have to do the essays in order.** Since its debut in 2007, the synthesis essay has appeared first. It's the longest, and the College Board may be suggesting that you should write it while your brain is still fresh. But if you wish, you can make the synthesis essay your second or third task.

> **TIP**
>
> The essay section differs from the multiple-choice portion of the exam. Many test takers don't have enough time to complete all the multiple-choice questions, so working from easiest to hardest makes sense, because you want to achieve as many correct answers as possible. However, you *must* get to all the essays, because omitting one earns you a zero and severely damages your final score on the AP exam. Maximizing your score revolves around writing three responses that showcase your skill and knowledge. Before you decide to work from hardest to easiest (or the reverse), write a couple of practice essays from Chapter 16. Decide what type is easy for you and what type is tough. Then take at least one of the practice exams (found in Chapters 17 and 19). Notice your energy level as you write. Can you sustain a solid effort after an hour and a half? If so, feel free to leave the toughest writing for last. If not, address the hardest essay first.

- **When you answer an essay question, put the number of the essay on the top of each page in the little box provided for that purpose.** Also indicate the page number and the total number of pages in your essay ("p. 1 of 3," for example). At the end of each essay, write a large # — journalists' traditional symbol for "the end."

- **If you run out of room in the booklet, the proctor distributes lined paper, so space is not an issue.** Consider skipping lines as you write. In a double-spaced format, you have room to tuck in an idea or make a correction.

- **Write as much as you wish on the question booklet, but be aware that graders see only the pink answer booklet and any sheets attached to it.** Before your two writing hours are up, be sure that all your brilliant ideas are reflected in the pink booklet or on attached sheets.

- **Only blue or black ink is allowed.** Erasable pens are permitted, but they tend to smear. You're better off writing in regular ballpoint ink.

- **If you want to change something, draw one neat line through it and write the correction above the deleted words.** Place a caret (^) under the line to indicate where the words should be inserted.

- **If you need to add a lot of material, place an asterisk (*) at the spot where the new material should be inserted.** Write "see insert A" next to the asterisk. At the end of the essay, write the paragraph you want to insert. Put a box around it and label it "insert A." Your grader will make every attempt to find "insert A" or even "insert B" or "C" and read your words in the proper order. However, don't use this approach too often. Instead, plan ahead what you want to write. (Chapter 2 explains how to gather ideas and put them in order before writing.)

- **As you work on the practice essays (see Chapter 16), pay attention to penmanship.** Most students are more comfortable typing on a keyboard than writing with a ballpoint pen. If your handwriting is illegible, your grader will struggle to decode your sentences.

> **TIP**
>
> If your writing isn't readable no matter how hard you try, you may have *dysgraphia,* a learning disability. Long before the AP exam date, speak with your guidance counselor or with your teacher. Dysgraphic students qualify for accommodations on test day — usually a computer on which you can type your responses.

TIME MANAGEMENT

In Chapter 2, I explain the process of essay writing — gathering ideas, creating a thesis statement, formulating supporting points and putting them in order, writing, and drafting. Chapter 2, however, refers to situations in which your time is not severely limited. The time constraints of the AP exam call for major strategic planning. Follow these steps:

1. **During the 15-minute reading period, read and annotate the questions.** (In the next section, I explain how to annotate both prompts and passages.) You can devote more time to annotation later, but even during the first run-through, you should jot down ideas and underline important sections of the text.

2. **Once you've seen all three questions, decide the order in which you'll answer them.** Don't agonize about this step. Make a decision and stick to it. If you haven't finished reading all the passages by the end of the reading period, make a decision anyway. When the writing period begins, you should know which question you're answering first.

3. **During the writing period, devote about 40 minutes to each essay.** You can go a little over or under — say two or three minutes, but no more. Remember: A blank essay earns no points at all. No matter how wonderful one of your essays is, you don't want the graders to average in a zero (for a blank essay) or a very low score (for a half-completed effort).

> **TIP**
>
> The synthesis essay contains six or seven sources, but you have to refer to a minimum of three. After the first read-through, choose the sources you'll definitely use. Spend more time on them and skim the sources you aren't going to reference.

4. **Divide the 40 minutes into prewriting, writing, and revising periods.** These slots aren't equal in length. Everyone's needs are slightly different, but a good guideline is about 7 minutes for reading and annotating (in addition to the work you did during the reading period), 28 minutes for writing, and 5 minutes for checking and revising.

Don't skip any steps in the writing process, no matter how tempted you are to write for 40 minutes straight before hopping into the next essay. The best essays come from an organized plan (the prewriting stage) and a final look (the revision stage).

YOUR WRITING PROCESS ON THE AP EXAM

By the time you're taking the exam, you've already developed a fairly sophisticated writing process. Just a bit of effort adapts your process to the AP exam, so you can streamline the way you decode a prompt, annotate, create a thesis, and organize ideas into supporting points.

Decode the prompt

Prompts are statements that "prompt" you to write. On the AP exam, they may seem fancier than the prompts your teacher assigns for class or homework. But really, they're just questions. Take a look at a few AP-style prompts. These questions were never on the exam but could have been.

■ **Argument prompt:** In recent decades some activists have promoted the idea that the United States government should make reparations to the descendants of slaves. Read the following passage, which is a letter written to *The New York Times* about this issue. In a well-organized essay, explain your own point of view on reparations.

■ **Synthesis prompt:** The question below is based on the six sources that follow it. To answer this question, you must synthesize information from these sources. Your essay must present a clear argument supported by at least three of the sources. Do *not* merely summarize the information or the point of view of the sources. Be sure to cite information, quotations, or ideas taken from these sources. You may cite them as "Source A," "Source B," or by the descriptions in parentheses.

Every two years either the summer or winter Olympic Games take place. Typically, several countries compete to host this event. The winning bid generally requires the host-city to build new sports venues such as stadiums, arenas, ski slopes, tracks, pools, and the like. The Olympics are frequently controversial; some citizens object to the use of public money for these games, while others believe that the attention of the world is worth the price. Read the following six sources and develop your own point of view on the desirability of hosting the Olympic Games. In a well-written essay explain your point of view and support your stance with references to the sources supplied.

Source A (McCullough)

Source B (Doctoroff)

Source C (International Olympic Committee)

Source D (Table of Revenue)

Source E (NBC News)

Source F (Wide World of Sports)

- **Analysis prompt:** The passage below is excerpted from an essay by Calvin Trillin. Read the passage and explain how the author conveys his attitude toward fast-food chains.

- **Paired-passage prompt:** Both passages below describe a scene in which a child confronts prejudice for the first time. Read the passages carefully and in a well-written essay, compare the rhetorical techniques the authors use to convey the effect of this experience on each child.

> **TIP**
>
> Synthesis essays always contain a statement explaining that you have to synthesize at least three of the sources and that you must cite these sources in your essay. A synthesis prompt also reminds you that summarizing or reporting isn't enough. All this information is important, but you can learn it now. Study the sample prompt so that you know the standard elements. On the exam, you can quickly move to the variables.

Decoding the prompt is so important that you should spend a couple minutes on this task. After all, if you don't know what you have to do, how can you do it? Here's how to proceed:

- **Read with your pen in hand.** You should annotate the prompt as well as the passage.

- **Underline key words.** A key word is anything that directs you to do something or that points you to a specific writing technique or feature of a passage.

- **Restate the task in your own words.** Be direct and simple: "I have to take a position on reparations for slavery. I have to write about my point of view and support it." Or, "I have to explain how the child in Passage One reacted to prejudice. I have to explain how the child in Passage Two reacted to prejudice. I have to compare the way the author of Passage One wrote about the child's reaction to the way the author of Passage Two wrote about the child's reaction." You don't need to rewrite the prompt; just underline the important stuff and "hear" the restated prompt in your mind.

Annotate the text

In Chapter 2, I explain how to annotate the text when you have no time limits. During the exam itself, you have to make every second count. Follow these steps:

1. **Keep the task firmly in your mind.** If the test makers ask you about the author's attitude toward arts education, waste no time on information about the author's gym teacher, unless you can relate gym class to the arts.

2. **After the first read-through, quickly decide what's important.** Continuing the example of the author's attitude toward arts education, imagine that you notice the extreme language with which the author praises art. She doesn't take an "interesting class"; she's enrolled in a "fascinating exploration of sculpture" that's an "adventure" equal to "an epic hero's journey." Now you know that *diction* (word choice) is something you should discuss in your essay.

3. **Reread, looking for evidence in each category you identified.** Reread and underline all the extreme words — in our example, those that praise art and perhaps those that condemn other types of learning. If you discover that an appeal to authority is an important factor, underline all references to the "Official Commission on Education in the Twenty-First Century" or whatever authority is cited.

4. **Note the main idea of each paragraph.** Don't waste many words on this task; simply write one or two words to remind you of the content of a particular paragraph. These marginal notes form a skeletal outline of the passage. When you're writing and need to find a reference, the marginal notes take you to the right spot instantly.

5. **If you come up with any ideas for a thesis or subtopics, jot down a few words in the margins.** The test makers leave room at the bottom of the page for you to take notes. Use this space to capture a fleeting idea before it vanishes. Again, don't write a lot; one or two words should be enough to boost your memory.

Figure 15-1 is an example of an annotated passage for an AP exam question. Notice that the underlining and notes are sparse, but they do the job.

sentence structure

S. not journalist — But to say this of Swift is not to say that he was a journalist. The journalist is the man <u>of the hour</u> writing <u>for the hour</u> in harmony with popular opinion. Both his text and his heads are ready-made for him. He follows the <u>beaten road</u>, and only essays <u>new paths</u> when conditions have become such as to force him along them. Such a man Swift certainly was not. Journalism was <u>not</u> his way to the goal. If anything, it was, as Epictetus might have <u>said,</u> but a <u>tavern by the way-side</u> in which he took occasion to find the means by which the better to attain his goal. If Swift's contributions to the literature of his day be journalism, then <u>did journalism spring full-grown</u> into being, and its history since his time must be considered as a history of its degeneration. But they were much more than journalism. That they took the form they did, in contributions to the periodicals of his day, is but an accident which does not in the least affect the contributions themselves. These, in reality, constitute a criticism of the social and political life of the first thirty years of the English eighteenth century. From the time of the writing of "A Tale of a Tub" to the days of the Drapier's Letters, <u>Swift dissected his countrymen with the pitiless hand of the master-surgeon</u>. So profound was his knowledge of human anatomy, individual and social, that we shudder now at the pain he must have inflicted in his unsparing operations. So accurate was his judgment that we stand amazed at his knowledge, and our amazement often turns to a species of horror as we see the <u>cuticle flapped open</u> revealing the crude arrangement beneath.

S = critic

reader reaction — <u>Nor is it</u> to argue too nicely, to suggest that our present sympathy for the past pain, our amazement, and our horror, are, after all, our own unconscious tributes to the power of the man who calls them up, and our confession of the lasting validity of his criticism.

metaphors   appeal ⟶ authority

Illustration by Wiley, Composition Services Graphics

Figure 15-1: An example of a passage annotated under exam conditions.

Write a thesis and supporting points

Once you've annotated the text, look at what you have. Does a *thesis* — the main idea you're proving — come to mind? If not, spend a minute or two (no more than that) using one of the idea-gathering techniques I describe in Chapter 2. You can cluster, free-write, or list until you have a sense of where your essay is going. Your next job is to state that direction as a thesis. Then you group your ideas into logical subtopics — the points you make in support of your thesis.

Thesis

The prompt often contains the seeds of a thesis. If you're asked to take a position on reparations for slavery, for example, your statement in favor of or against reparations (or a qualified reaction that's partially in favor and partially opposed) is your thesis. Other prompts are vague ("Discuss how the author conveys the relationship between the father and son," for example). Your thesis for this sort of essay emerges from the details you've noted in the passage. If the passage is filled with angry dialogue from the father and a description of the son's silent reaction, your thesis may be that the father's emotions have silenced the son.

A good thesis statement has the following characteristics:

- **Brevity:** Most thesis statements are fairly short, one or two sentences maximum. A common mistake is to cram too much into a thesis statement. The complexity of your ideas can be developed in the essay; you don't need to say everything in your thesis statement.

- **Clarity:** In an argumentative or synthesis essay, you know what side of the fence the writer is on (against standardized testing and in favor of keeping the penny coin, for example) after reading the thesis. You know which rhetorical techniques the essay will explore (such as nautical metaphors, diction, and syntax). You don't know every aspect of the discussion, but you've been oriented to the direction the discussion will take.

- **Specificity:** If you generalize too much, you end up with a really bad thesis statement. An essay based on the thesis that "authors use many different rhetorical devices in their writing" will flop. Your thesis should specifically address the prompt and the passage, if a passage is provided.

To help you visualize a proper thesis, here are some examples:

Although proponents of standardized testing claim that it raises skill levels, such testing makes schooling a soulless exercise instead of true education.

The humble penny is so much a part of our tradition that discontinuing this coin would do more harm than good.

In this excerpt from his autobiography, author Henry Danis employs a series of nautical metaphors to convey his sense of being carried along by the tide of history. Danis's diction and syntax reinforce this point.

In arguing for a lower voting age, the writer appeals to authority and to the emotions of his reader.

The narrator of Passage A shows her dismay at being the victim of prejudice obliquely, through figurative language. The narrator of Passage B expresses his reaction to a similar situation directly, in narrative form.

Supporting points

Your thesis is the roof that covers the information in the essay; *supporting points* (also known as *subtopics*) are the walls that hold up the roof. If you did a good job annotating the passage and/or brainstorming for ideas, coming up with supporting points is a cinch. Use this method:

1. **Review your notes and the underlined portions of the passage.** Don't spend a lot of time on this step; a couple of minutes should be enough.

2. **Look for logical groups.** If you've underlined three metaphors, you know that "metaphor" is one group. If you've written "appeal to emotion" on the bottom of the page and noted "penny proverbs" in the margin, you have another supporting point (that "a penny saved is a penny earned" and "a penny for your thoughts" would be obsolete without the coin).

3. **Label and sort your ideas.** Write "A" next to everything in one group, "B" next to everything in another group, and so forth. For instance, you may place "A" next to everything that relates to metaphor and "B" next to each example of unusual syntax. You can also connect related ideas with a line, so long as you don't obscure the text. (You may have to reread it.)

4. **Put the ideas in order.** The faster you work, the better, so don't rewrite anything. Decide which supporting point is first, which is second, and so on. Don't get hung up on your labels. Feel free to discuss the "B group" first and the "A group" later, for example.

Figure 15-2 is an example of an annotated passage in which ideas have been grouped into three supporting points: (A) sentence structure, (B) appeal to authority, and (C) metaphors. In your essay, you may deal with these points in any order you wish.

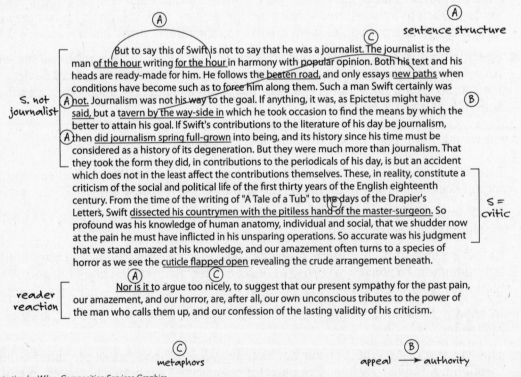

Figure 15-2: An example of annotations grouped into supporting points.

Illustration by Wiley, Composition Services Graphics

HOW TO HANDLE EVIDENCE

When you write an AP essay, you're the prosecutor, and your grader is the jury. You have to make a case in support of your thesis, and you can't do so without presenting evidence. If you're working from a text, the evidence is staring you in the face: the language and ideas in the passage. If you're arguing an issue not connected to a text (or if you're allowed to bring in your own experience or observations to supplement a text), the details you provide serve as evidence.

Quotations are great for your essay — sometimes. Why not always? Because it's fairly easy to expend too many minutes rewriting words from the passage without achieving your purpose. In this section, I explain when to quote the exact words from a passage, how to choose relevant quotations, and how to insert quotations into your text.

When to quote

If the idea rather than the wording is important to your argument, you can *paraphrase* (restate ideas in your own words) or simply refer to the passage. On the other hand, you should always quote from the text if you're discussing how something is written. Those are the general rules. Now for some specific guidelines on when to quote (and when not to quote) the text:

- **Always quote when you're analyzing diction.** How can you discuss the author's word choice if you don't examine those words directly?

- **Generally, you should quote when you're talking about syntax (the way a sentence fits together grammatically).** Why "generally" and not "always"? Because sometimes a summary does the job. For example, you may mention that the second paragraph is a series of "I-verb" statements without quoting those statements. However, sometimes you should quote to illustrate an unusual word order (for example, "Such a man Swift certainly was not" — a sentence from Figure 15-1), especially if you want to make a point about that specific sentence.

- **You should quote whenever you're trying to establish attitude — of the author or of a person/character appearing in the passage — because attitude is frequently dependent upon syntax and diction.** In New York City, for example, "You talkin' to me?" can be a declaration of war or a simple inquiry. Whatever case you're making, the quotation helps.

- **Quote when you're discussing tone.** *Tone* — the nostalgic, reflective, critical, sarcastic, ironic, or other flavor of a piece of writing — can't be examined without quotations.

- **Quote when you're discussing characterization.** *Characterization* (the way a personality is presented) is often dependent upon the specific words used in dialogue and description, so quotations help.

- **If the passage is a narrative (a story), you don't need to quote when you refer to events, unless the wording is significant.** "James demolished the opposing team" is not the same as "James defeated the opposing team," so a quotation may be useful in this instance.

- **In discussing the author's purpose, you may not need direct quotations.** A passage may present a series of reasons why the United States should sign a certain treaty. You can refer to those reasons without quoting them if you're discussing the author's intention to persuade pro-war delegates that peace is possible.

- **Anything about figurative language (metaphors, similes, symbols, and other imaginative elements) must be quoted.** You can't analyze language without examining the exact words.

- **Imagery — the sensory details the author includes — probably requires quotation.** Occasionally you can summarize by saying that "the second paragraph is dominated by imagery of the flower garden" or something similar.

Don't be tempted to quote and then translate the quotation into your own words. Students often translate when analyzing older texts, especially Shakespeare's works. They write things such as "In *Hamlet,* the title character asks, 'To be or not to be.' This sentence means that Hamlet is considering whether it is better to continue living or to die." Your reader — the AP grader — understands the text without your translation.

How much to quote

Quotations are potent elements that can support your thesis, but you can have too much of a good thing. Follow these guidelines in deciding how much to quote:

- You don't need five quotations proving the same point, unless you're saying that the author emphasized that point or that the author is fond of overkill.

- As always, budget your time. If you want to discuss three subtopics in your essay, don't quote seven examples for the first subtopic. You won't have time to make your case for the other two subtopics.

- Aim for balance. If diction is the most striking element in a passage, of course you quote more in a paragraph discussing diction than you do in a paragraph about imagery. But if the subtopics are equally important, your evidence should reflect that fact.

- Some test takers quote 20 words where 2 or 3 would be enough. For example, in one of the bullet points in the preceding section, I mentioned that "James demolished the opposing team" differs in meaning from "James defeated the opposing team." If you're discussing that difference, you probably need to quote only the verb ("demolish" or "defeat") because that's the crucial element. Similarly, if you want to make a point about syntax, you may not need an entire sentence — just the subject-verb combo, if that's what you're analyzing.

Inserting quotations into the text

First, take a look at how *not* to insert a quotation. Read this clunker:

> The author argues that Swift was not a journalist. "That they took the form they did, in contributions to the periodicals of his day, is but an accident which does not in the least affect the contributions themselves." Swift's criticisms are valid.

The quotation in the preceding example is inserted without a clear indication of the point the writer is trying to communicate. Nothing leads into it, and nothing comes out of it. Here's a better version of the preceding example:

> The author argues that Swift was not a journalist. The fact that Swift wrote for "the periodicals of his day" was "an accident" that takes nothing away from Swift's "contributions." In fact, the author sees Swift's criticisms as having "lasting validity."

Now the quotations are smoothly woven into the sentence. They should be fused to your analysis also. Notice the difference between version one and version two here:

- **Version one:** The author says that a journalist "follows the beaten road, and only essays new paths when conditions have become such as to force him along them." This quotation shows that the author has little respect for journalists.

- **Version two:** The author shows little respect for journalism because a journalist "follows the beaten road, and only essays new paths when conditions have become such as to force him along them."

Version two assumes that the reader can make a connection between the analysis (the author's lack of respect for journalism) and the quotation. Avoid the expression "This quotation shows that." It's not necessary.

Punctuating quotations properly is easy. If you have a speaker tag ("the author says," "Mr. Wilde remarks," and similar expressions), capitalize the first word of the quotation and separate it from the rest of the sentence with a comma:

> The author remarks, "Swift dissected his countrymen with the pitiless hand of a master surgeon."

> "Swift dissected his countrymen with the pitiless hand of a master surgeon," remarks the author.

Without a speaker tag, the quotation isn't separated from the rest of the sentence by a comma and the first word isn't capitalized (unless of course it's a name):

> The author remarks that Jonathan Swift "dissected his countrymen with the pitiless hand of a master surgeon."

If you omit words from within a quotation, insert three spaced dots to show the gap. If the gap is a complete sentence, you need an extra dot to represent the period:

> The author remarks, "If Swift's contributions . . . be journalism," journalism was born fully developed. (gap of a few words)

> The author states, "These, in reality, constitute a criticism of the social and political life of the first thirty years of the English eighteenth century. . . . Swift dissected his countrymen." (gap includes a complete sentence)

If you change anything in the quotation, place your words in brackets:

> "So profound was [Swift's] knowledge of human anatomy," according to the passage, that he inflicted pain.

If your punctuation skills are rusty, turn to Chapter 6 for a review.

Citations

When you're quoting in response to a single- or paired-passage essay, you don't need citations, though you should identify in the text which of the pair-members you're talking about. (Say something like "In Passage One, the child . . .") In the synthesis essay, however, you must cite whatever you glean from a source — whether you quote the source directly or refer to it indirectly. The citations may, according to the rules of the test, be to "Source A," "Source B," and so on, or they may use the names of the sources indicated in the question.

Footnotes, endnotes, and parenthetical citations are all acceptable. The easiest method for a synthesis essay is the last, because you don't have to worry about leaving space at the bottom of the page or at the end of the essay.

To cite sources parenthetically, place the source identification in parentheses after each quotation or idea you're citing. The citation is *not* part of the quotation, so it comes *after* the closing quotation marks. The citation is part of the sentence, so it precedes the period. Here's an example:

> Connolly argues that arts education is "indispensable" (Source A).

If the sentence continues, insert the citation wherever the source material ends, as in this example:

> Connolly argues that arts education is desperately needed (Source A), though he provides little evidence for that assertion.

ESSAY STRUCTURES

The AP exam graders understand that you don't have time to come up with a fancy organizational plan for your essay when you're writing with such a strict time limit. Even so, you have to organize your ideas logically. Enter structure — the basic pattern you follow when you write. In this section, I explain some standard, easily adaptable structures that work well with AP exam questions.

Deductive

I'm guessing that most essays you've written in English class are *deductive*; you begin with a thesis statement and move to proof. A deductive essay generally has this structure:

- **Introduction:** The introduction contains your thesis, supporting points, and perhaps a quotation or intriguing statement to draw the reader's attention. If the author or title is identified, place that information in the introduction.

- **Body:** In the body of your essay you analyze, argue, or otherwise explain yourself. Generally, but not always, you address one subtopic per paragraph. Here's where you provide specifics — the proof for your thesis.

- **Conclusion:** A conclusion isn't a summary or a restatement of the introduction. It's the natural last step in your argument, where you bring everything together and take the discussion to the next level.

This sort of structure is fine for any AP prompt, so long as you don't sound formulaic. You probably learned this pattern (which may have been called "the five-paragraph essay") in elementary school. But you're older now, and the graders want to see mature writing. Stay away from "this is what I will prove," "here's the proof," and "this is what I have proved." That kind of writing will earn no more than a 3 or 4 out of a possible 9 points on the AP exam.

Don't lock yourself into a five-paragraph structure just because you're accustomed to it. Use as many paragraphs as you need, and no more. If you have two subtopics, four paragraphs (intro, body paragraph 1, body paragraph 2, conclusion) may be better. If you have four subtopics, you need more than five paragraphs in your essay.

Inductive

An *inductive* essay reverses the order of a deductive essay: You begin with specifics and move to a general conclusion. Though this format may be unfamiliar, this structure is very useful, especially for argument essays. Here's the pattern:

- **Introduction:** In the introduction, you explain the issue (perhaps a description of prom night and the costs involved).

- **Body:** Here you discuss every aspect of the issue, one per paragraph. You may, for example, have a paragraph on pre-prom events, one on transportation problems, and so forth.

- **Conclusion:** Now you take a stand and state your opinion: Proms should be subsidized or simplified, for example.

Think of the inductive essay as leading — inducing — your reader to a particular stance. Make sure the path holds together logically, with no missing steps.

Compare-contrast

This structure's a natural for paired-passage essays, but you can also use it when you argue for a particular position. (In that case, you compare positions and decide which is better.) A compare-contrast essay has these components:

- **Introduction:** Here you state what you're comparing (Passage One and Passage Two or Pro and Con positions). You may include the key differences and similarities, the advantages and disadvantages, or an explanation of the two competing positions.

- **Body:** You can organize the body paragraphs in a couple of ways. You may have one paragraph addressing similarities and one addressing differences, or a paragraph about each position on an issue. More complex, but very impressive, is a paragraph about each aspect of the elements you're comparing. For example, in a literary analysis you may have a paragraph comparing diction in each of two passages, a paragraph comparing point of view, and so forth. In an argument or synthesis essay, you may have a paragraph about environmental problems, another about economics, another about social consequences — or whatever makes sense for the topic.

■ **Conclusion:** The conclusion often puts the comparison/contrast into a larger context. Yes, we should abolish the penny, as a step toward an all-electronic monetary system. Or no, we need the penny, because society tends to overlook small opportunities to save, not just in money but in energy, time, and so forth.

One danger of a compare-contrast essay is repetition. Don't ping-pong your reader back and forth, saying, for example, "In Passage One . . . while in Passage Two . . . " over and over again.

Passage order

You may opt for a fast organizational pattern when you're analyzing a passage: the order of the passage itself. With this structure, you simply work your way through the passage, discussing everything you encounter. Almost no organization is necessary, because the author of the passage already did the job. Add an introduction (orienting the reader to the title and author — if you know what and who it is — and stating the main points you'll discuss). Finish with a conclusion (a discussion of the last element in the passage or, if you wish, a "why this is significant" statement).

>
> **TIP**
>
> Be warned that a passage order essay can fall prey to repetition. The second or third time you discuss point of view, for example, you may end up saying the same thing. Vary your comments as much as possible by individualizing them. The more specific you are, the less likely you are to repeat yourself. Also, be especially careful to note when an element of content or style changes or progresses in the passage and to analyze how those questions relate to the question you're answering. Simply summarizing the passage is not enough.

TYPES OF ESSAYS

The general techniques of essay-writing serve you well no matter which question you're facing. However, each of the three major types of AP essay (synthesis, argument, and analysis) calls for a slight shift in approach.

Synthesis

The AP test writers warn you not to summarize or report the sources provided for the synthesis essay. If that's all you do, expect to earn no more than 2 points out of a possible 9. Instead, see the sources as raw material — like spools of thread. When you write a synthesis essay, you select threads from three or more sources and weave them together so that they form cloth. The cloth, in my analogy, represents your position on the issue. When you write a synthesis essay, keep these points in mind:

- **Don't discount any source right away; skim everything.** All the sources are potentially valid for the issue you're discussing.

- **The sources tend to balance out.** A couple of sources clearly favor one side of the issue, and others take the opposing view. A source may also be neutral; you can find ammunition in it for either side.

- **Most issues aren't limited to a yes or no stance.** The graders are looking for maturity, and a mature thinker acknowledges complexity. If you believe that your answer is a qualified yes or no, explain why.

- **Once you've defined a position, reread the sources most likely to be helpful.** Annotate them more fully, if necessary. But don't totally ignore sources that disagree with your position. Sometimes the opposing argument stimulates your thought processes and reveals additional reasons why your position is correct.

- **Include a concession-and-reply paragraph — or more than one paragraph, if warranted.** In "concession and reply," you acknowledge opposing points and counter them with your own argument.

- **Be sure that your argument progresses logically.** The logic is easier to follow if you provide transitional words. "Also," "on the other hand," "nevertheless," "consequently," and similar words help the reader navigate from one paragraph to the next.

- **The six or seven synthesis sources usually appear on six different pages of the question booklet.** Choose one spot to gather your thoughts after you've annotated the individual sources.

- **Cite your sources.** Cite the source for quotations, indirect references, and any ideas you gathered from a source.

How long should a synthesis essay be? About as long as the other two essays you have to write — perhaps 500 words. Although you're working from a lot of sources, you don't necessarily have to say more. Just use the material wisely. (For tips on interpreting visual sources, see Chapter 7. For help with all kinds of source material, review "How to Handle Evidence" earlier in this chapter.)

Analysis

The analysis essay asks you to pick apart a passage (or a pair of passages) and explain how the writing style works hand-in-hand with content. Do not take a laundry-list approach. It's not enough simply to state what rhetorical techniques (or devices, or strategies) appear in the passage. You have to explain what these techniques accomplish. Guidelines for an analysis essay are as follows:

- **The prompt sometimes specifies an element you should focus on: characterization, purpose, setting, attitude, and the like.** Don't lose that focus and try to analyze everything.

- **If the prompt doesn't specify an element to focus on, cast a wide net.** Look for everything that's there, and once you think you have everything, look deeper. A couple of obvious points appear in every essay, but only a few test takers find the subtleties. Graders are very impressed by a new idea. However, remember that originality isn't everything. Be sure that you don't stretch too far in your analysis. Everything you write must be supported with evidence from the passage.

■ **This type of essay requires analysis, not just reporting.** The difference is huge. Say, for example, that you find a shift from first-person to third-person point of view in the third paragraph. Why did the author make that change? How does the change affect the reader? What's gained or lost with the new point of view? What happens to the content at that point in the story? Did the content also change? These are the kinds of questions that you should ask yourself. The answers constitute an analysis of style.

> **TIP**
>
> One way to determine the effect of a particular rhetorical device is to place the passage in an alternate universe. If the writer has loaded you with *imagery* (sensory detail), rewrite the passage in your head. Without the imagery, how does the reader react? Or substitute another technique for the imagery, such as figurative language. If you're reading about wine that "tastes like old socks" instead of wine "with a musky aroma," do you change your opinion of the drink? Now you know the effect of imagery in the original passage.

■ **An analysis essay calls for more quotations than other types of essays.** Writing style is best discussed when the actual writing is put under the microscope.

Keep in mind that analysis essays also argue a case. You're not discussing the merits of civil disobedience or a national healthcare system, as you may be in an official argument essay. Instead, you're arguing that the author's use of passive voice takes the spotlight away from individuals and makes the ideas more universal or that the extended metaphor comparing justice to the banking system emphasizes the financial suffering of ex-convicts. Even though you're discussing literature, you're still proving a point.

Argument

When you're writing an argument essay in response to a quotation or to a situation described in the prompt, keep these points in mind:

■ **Not every argument divides neatly into two categories.** Typically, the prompt for an argument essay orders you to "develop a position" on a particular issue. Or the prompt asks you to react to a quotation that is itself an argument — a statement of opinion. Your position may be totally in favor, totally against, or something in between.

■ **State your position clearly.** You don't have to do so in the essay introduction, but by the time the grader has finished reading, he or she should know where you stand and *why* you feel that way.

■ **Acknowledge the opposing arguments and, if possible, provide the counter arguments.** This tactic is called *concession and reply*. Concession-and-reply paragraphs accomplish two things: They tell the grader that you've considered the opposition's point of view, and they shore up your case by taking ammunition away from the other side. A typical concession-and-reply statement resembles this one: "Curbs on hate-speech may appear to violate the first amendment, which guarantees the right to free speech. However, the first amendment has never been interpreted as giving complete freedom. Words that inflame racial, ethnic, or gender bias may be as dangerous as recklessly shouting 'fire' in a crowded movie theater."

- **In an argument essay, you're allowed to write about personal experience or observation.** Give enough information to make your point, but don't get bogged down in trivia. If you're talking about your friend's bout with cancer in an essay on national health coverage, her financial situation is relevant but her suffering probably isn't. You can mention that fighting with the insurance company added to her woes, but don't spend two paragraphs describing her chemotherapy.

- **References to literature and history are useful in an argument essay, as long as they back up your point of view.** Don't hesitate to mention Antigone in an essay about civil disobedience (she's the title character in an ancient Greek drama who defies an unjust law) or September 11 in an essay about terrorism.

> **TIP**
>
> Feel free to use a reference to literature or history even if you're not 100 percent sure of every detail. Of course you want to be accurate. But if you make a small mistake (referring, for example, to Vice President Ronald Reagan), the graders won't take off any points. They know that you'd correct yourself and write President Ronald Reagan in a final draft, after consulting a reference book.

- **As you argue your viewpoint, pretend that the reader doesn't agree with you.** Doing so can inspire you to make your strongest, most logical arguments in the effort to persuade this person.

Two hours, plus a measly 15 minutes of extra reading time, takes you from "the essay section is about to begin" to "thank goodness that's over." This chapter radically affects your mood at the endpoint. If you avoid the score-destroying methods I describe in this chapter, you'll be pleased when you put down your pen and seal your booklet.

16

Practice Essays

In this chapter, you have the opportunity to try your hand at writing AP essays. I provide sample AP-style essay questions and answer guides for each. The free-response portion of the AP exam has only three questions, but the AP has more than three sorts of prompts. Therefore, I've offered at least one of each of the possible types of essay prompts (with an extra analysis and synthesis question for good measure, since those two types will almost certainly appear on your AP test).

PRACTICE ESSAY GENERAL GUIDELINES

With AP exams, timing is an important factor. But you don't have to hit full speed right away. With the practice essays in this chapter, you can start off a little more slowly than you would on a real AP test, perfecting your essay-writing technique before you try for AP-style speed-writing. (For more on producing essays quickly, check out Chapter 15.) When you write the essays on the practice exams (in Chapters 17 and 19), keeping within the time limit is essential. But for now, it's okay to write just one essay at a time, allowing yourself a few additional minutes.

To be clear about official timing: The College Board suggests that you devote about 40 minutes to each essay. However, the essay portion of the exam begins with a 15-minute reading period, during which you can read and annotate all the questions. If you decide to mimic test conditions while writing a practice essay from this chapter, give yourself a few extra minutes (a total of 42–43 minutes) for single or paired-passage essays and 46–50 minutes for a synthesis essay. As on the real exam, write in blue or black ink on lined paper. If the College Board has granted you accommodations, adjust the timing or writing method accordingly. (For more information on special-needs accommodations, see Chapter 1.)

When the time comes to evaluate your practice essay, reread your work a couple of times. Your first task is to rate your answer according to these general guidelines:

■ Your essay should answer the question. Off-topic essays receive no points.

■ The *prompt,* or essay question, may contain more than one task, and your essay must complete *all* the required tasks. For example, you may have to (1) determine the author's tone or purpose and (2) identify the author's rhetorical devices or strategies and (3) discuss how the rhetorical devices reveal or contribute to the tone or purpose.

■ The essay should assert a *thesis,* the main idea you are proving.

■ The thesis should be supported by evidence, which may be quotations or references to the text if a passage is supplied or, if the question is more general, references to your experience or observation.

■ Evidence should be inserted smoothly into the essay.

■ In the synthesis essay, the source material should be cited properly. Be sure to cite ideas you have taken from a source, not just direct quotations.

■ The essay should be organized; the reader should be able to follow a thread of logic from introduction to conclusion.

■ The essay should display good grammar and spelling and a mature writing style. Repetitive or overly general statements weaken your essay. If grammar and spelling mistakes make your essay hard to read, the overall score can be no higher than 2. (See Chapter 1 for more information on AP scoring.)

When you've finished the general evaluation, reread your work and compare the points you made in your essay to the list of specifics following each essay question. In each list, I've placed more ideas than any test taker would ever have time to include. Don't panic if you have fewer; you can omit quite a few and still end up with a high-scoring essay. You may also think of an idea that doesn't appear on the list. Give yourself credit for doing so, as long as you can justify your assertions.

How does your essay rate overall? Consider yourself in the "excellent" category if you fulfill most of the general requirements and have included about three-quarters of the specific points. You're "good" if you drop to 50 percent of the general requirements and specific points. Moving to "fair," you have perhaps a third of the general requirements and a third of the specific points. Below these numbers, you need to work on essay writing a bit more.

ANALYSIS OF A SINGLE PASSAGE

One type of essay that nearly always appears in the free-response section of the AP exam requires you to analyze the rhetorical techniques in a single passage. Usually a single-passage question involves a selection with a distinctive writing style. The prompt settles on one element — the author's purpose, attitude, point of view, or something similar. You have to analyze the passage in terms of the selected element and the rhetorical devices (also called "techniques" or "strategies") that the author employs. Try the sample questions in the following sections.

Prompt 1 for an analysis essay

EXAMPLE

The passage below is excerpted from a nineteenth-century history of two Native American tribes, the Ottawa and the Chippewa. It was written by Andrew J. Blackbird, the son of an Ottawa chief and an interpreter of Native American languages for the government representative to those tribes. Read the passage carefully. In a well-written essay, discuss how the author's purpose is revealed through the rhetorical devices he employs.

(01)   I have seen a number of writings by different men who attempted to give an account of the Indians who formerly occupied the Straits of Mackinac and Mackinac Island (that historic little island which stands at the entrance of the strait) also giving an account of the Indians who lived and are yet living in Michigan, scat-
(05) tered through the counties of Emmet, Cheboygan, Charlevoix, Antrim, Grand Traverse, and in the region of Thunder Bay, on the west shore of Lake Huron. But I see no very correct account of the Ottawa and Chippewa tribes of Indians, according to our knowledge of ourselves, past and present. Many points are far from being credible. They are either misstated by persons who were not versed in the tradi-
(10) tions of these Indians, or exaggerated. An instance of this is found in the history of the life of Pontiac (pronounced Bwon-diac), the Odjebwe (or Chippewa) chief of St. Clair, the instigator of the massacre of the old fort on the Straits of Mackinac, written by a noted historian. In his account of the massacre, he says there was at this time no known surviving Ottawa Chief living on the south side of the Straits.
(15) This point of the history is incorrect, as there were several Ottawa chiefs living on the south side of the Straits at this particular time, who took no part in this massacre, but took by force the few survivors of this great, disastrous catastrophe, and protected them for a while and afterwards took them to Montreal, present-ing them to the British Government; at the same time praying that their brother
(20) Odjebwes should not be retaliated upon on account of their rash act against the British people, but that they might be pardoned, as this terrible tragedy was com-mitted through mistake, and through the evil counsel of one of their leaders by the name of Bwondiac (known in history as Pontiac). They told the British Govern-ment that their brother Odjebwes were few in number, while the British were in
(25) great numbers and daily increasing from an unknown part of the world across the ocean. They said, "Oh, my father, you are like the trees of the forest, and if one of the forest trees should be wounded with a hatchet, in a few years its wound will be entirely healed. Now, my father, compare with this: this is what my brother Odjebwe did to some of your children on the Straits of Mackinac, whose survivors
(30) we now bring back and present to your arms. O my father, have mercy upon my brothers and pardon them; for with your long arms and many, but a few strokes of retaliation would cause our brother to be entirely annihilated from the face of the earth!"

According to our understanding in our traditions, that was the time the British
(35) Government made such extraordinary promises to the Ottawa tribe of Indians, at the same time thanking them for their humane action upon those British rem-nants of the massacre. She promised them that her long arms will perpetually extend around them from generation to generation, or so long as there should be rolling sun.

Answer guide for the first analysis essay

First, check your answer with the general guidelines at the beginning of the chapter. Then consider these bullet points, which describe some points you could have made in your analysis of Blackbird's work.

- Blackbird's purpose is probably to inform people who don't know Native American history. He refers specifically to "persons who were not versed in the traditions of these Indians" (lines 9–10) as making mistakes about the Ottawa tribe in their accounts of a massacre. He criticizes a "noted historian" (line 13) who erred in reporting that no known "surviving Ottawa Chief" (line 14) lived on the "south side of the Straits" (line 14). The implication here is twofold. Even people who should know the truth (the "noted historian") don't. Also, no one looked for or asked about the Native American point of view.

> **TIP**
>
> If you read the prompt carefully, you noticed that helpful information is tucked into it. Andrew J. Blackbird is described as "the son of an Ottawa chief and an interpreter of Native American languages for the government representative to those tribes." Knowing that Blackbird was Native American and worked for the government tells you that the author straddled two worlds. (In the 19th century, more so than in the present day, Native Americans were still fighting for their rights and full participation in society.) Because you know that Blackbird saw two points of view, you can infer that he wished to interpret one point of view (that of Native Americans) to those who may be unfamiliar with it (non-Native Americans).

- You may express Blackbird's purpose in any of several ways: He wishes to correct the historical record. Or he wants the reader to understand that Native Americans (specifically, the Ottawa tribe) may be different from what the reader imagines. He wants to validate the historical accounts of the Native Americans.

- By acknowledging the massacre, Blackbird partially allies himself with those who may have sympathy for the victims. However, he also explains that some Native Americans helped the survivors. The message here is "not every Native American acted the same way or held the same beliefs."

- The *diction* (word choice) helps Blackbird accomplish his purpose. He refers to "our knowledge of ourselves" (line 8) and "our understanding in our traditions" (line 34). The pronouns "our" and "ourselves" emphasize his bond with Native Americans and establish his frame of reference. He has inside knowledge. The strong terms Blackbird uses to describe what happened ("great, disastrous catastrophe" [line 17], "rash act" [line 20], "evil" [line 22], and the like) are an attempt to identify with those who condemn the massacre. (Even the term "massacre" suits Blackbird's purpose, as opposed to something more neutral, such as "conflict" or "fight.")

- The quotation at the end of the first paragraph (lines 26–33) employs a simile, comparing the British to trees in a forest that will quickly repair any gaps after some trees are "wounded with a hatchet." (Notice the term "hatchet" — a word associated with Native Americans.) The simile reinforces the idea that the Native Americans are vulnerable, as plants are vulnerable. Blackbird, without using today's terminology, is calling the tribe an endangered species: "their brother Odjebwes were few in number" (line 24) and with retaliation could be "entirely annihilated from the face of the earth!" (lines 32–33).

- The quotation is not attributed. Blackbird is portraying himself as someone with inside knowledge, not calling upon an outside expert. A few times he corrects the common pronunciation of Native American names (Pontiac should be Bwon-diac), again emphasizing Blackbird's knowledge and others' ignorance.

- The long sentence in the middle of the first paragraph ("This point of history . . . Pontiac" — lines 15–23) stands out. By throwing so much information into that sentence, which English teachers call a *cumulative sentence,* Blackbird forces the reader to comprehend all the ideas in the sentence at the same time. Yes, Native Americans massacred British colonists, but Native Americans also saved lives.

- Did you notice the switch from "my father" (line 26) to "She" (line 37) in paragraph two? Both pronouns refer to Britain. The difference in pronouns emphasizes the gulf between Native Americans and British custom.

- The author states that "Indians . . . lived, and are yet living" (line 4) in Michigan. The message here is the same: Non-Native Americans may not know much, if anything, about Native American life. The author's the expert, the one who will correct misapprehensions.

You can structure this essay in a couple of ways. No matter what you choose, your introduction should define the author's purpose. Then you can devote a paragraph to each rhetorical device (one for diction, one for sentence length, one for figurative language, and so forth). Another possibility is to work your way through the passage in order, from first sentence to last, noting every rhetorical device you find. The first structure is more organized, but it takes a couple of minutes to group your ideas into subtopics, and you don't have much time. The second structure is faster to execute, but you may end up repeating yourself (going back to diction again and again, for instance). Whichever you choose, take care to explain how the rhetorical devices interact with content. Simply summarizing the passage or listing the elements of style is *not* enough.

Prompt 2 for an analysis essay

EXAMPLE

This speech, delivered by Marc Antony to a hostile crowd of Romans, appears in Shakespeare's *Julius Caesar* just after the title character has been murdered. Marc Antony refers to Brutus, one of the assassins. In a well-organized essay, analyze the rhetorical strategy Marc Antony employs to win the support of the crowd.

(01) Friends, Romans, countrymen, lend me your ears;
I come to bury Caesar, not to praise him.
The evil that men do lives after them;
The good is oft interred with their bones:
(05) So let it be with Caesar. The noble Brutus
Hath told you Caesar was ambitious:
If it were so, it was a grievous fault;
And grievously hath Caesar answer'd it.
Here, under leave of Brutus and the rest,
(10) For Brutus is an honorable man;
So are they all, all honorable men,
Come I to speak in Caesar's funeral.
He was my friend, faithful and just to me:

But Brutus says he was ambitious;
(15) And Brutus is an honorable man.
He hath brought many captives home to Rome,
Whose ransoms did the general coffers fill:
Did this in Caesar seem ambitious?
When that the poor have cried, Caesar hath wept:
(20) Ambition should be made of sterner stuff:
Yet Brutus says he was ambitious;
And Brutus is an honorable man.
You all did see that on the Lupercal
I thrice presented him a kingly crown,
(25) Which he did thrice refuse: was this ambition?
Yet Brutus says he was ambitious;
And, sure, he is an honorable man.
I speak not to disprove what Brutus spoke,
But here I am to speak what I do know.
(30) You all did love him once, not without cause:
What cause withholds you, then, to mourn for him?
O judgment, thou art fled to brutish beasts,
And men have lost their reason! Bear with me;
My heart is in the coffin there with Caesar,
(35) And I must pause till it come back to me.

Answer guide for the second analysis essay

In this speech, Marc Antony faces down the crowd and gradually brings them over to the pro-Caesar side. Brutus, an honest man despite his participation in murder, doesn't have a clue when Antony asks to speak over the body of Caesar. Brutus trusts Antony, and if you've read the play, you know that his trust is misplaced. Even in this small portion of Antony's speech you can see that Antony is a master manipulator. Your essay has to explore Antony's strategy. Here are some points you might include:

- Antony's first words are "Friends, Romans, countrymen" (line 1). By identifying himself as one of them, he creates a bond with his listeners.

- Antony begins by reassuring the crowd that he isn't going to praise Caesar, just bury him. Because the crowd is hostile (as you know from the introduction), this is a good ploy. Once again, Antony becomes less of an opponent and more aligned with the crowd.

- Antony's statement about burial is another great tactic. Every culture stresses proper disposal of human remains. Who could argue with a man who simply wants to bury a dead friend?

- Did you notice a strange verb in this passage? Antony says of Caesar's ambition, "If it were so, it was a grievous fault" (line 7). The "were" is subjunctive. Don't panic over the grammatical term (which I explain in Chapter 6). Even without knowing the grammar vocabulary, you know that "If it were so" is a way of saying that "it is not so." (Think of the old song, "If I Were a Rich Man" sung in the Broadway musical by a character who is poor.) So Antony is subtly reinforcing the idea that Caesar wasn't ambitious, and therefore his murder was unjustified. Furthermore, Antony hedges his bets. If the crowd still believes in Caesar's ambition, Caesar has already paid the price by losing his life ("And grievously hath Caesar answer'd it"— line 8). Antony implies that the crowd has no reason to hate Caesar now — or to hate Marc Antony.

■ Having established that he isn't going to praise Caesar, Antony goes on to . . . praise Caesar. But Antony hides his praise carefully. He says he's going to let the good that Caesar accomplished be "interred with [Caesar's] bones" (line 4). By mentioning "good," he subtly reminds the crowd that Caesar actually did some good things. Then Antony gives details: Caesar was Antony's "friend, faithful and just" (line 13). Caesar "brought many captives home to Rome" (line 16) and the money spent to ransom them made money for the Roman state — always good for taxpayers. "When that the poor have cried, Caesar hath wept," says Antony (line 19), appealing to the lower economic classes in the crowd. These statements appeal to logic.

■ After Antony recites the list of Caesar's good deeds, he reminds the crowd that they "all did love him once, not without cause" (line 30). Here Antony appeals to emotion. Who wants to be reminded that they've betrayed someone they loved?

■ Interspersed throughout these lines is a refrain: "Brutus says he [Caesar] was ambitious; / And Brutus is an honorable man." As Antony goes on, it becomes harder and harder to believe that Brutus is honorable or that Caesar was ambitious. Each point Antony makes about Caesar — he was a faithful friend, he brought money to Rome, he sympathized with the poor, and he turned down the crown three times — weakens Brutus's case. By the end, you can imagine Antony saying, "Brutus is an honorable man," in a sarcastic tone of voice.

■ "Did this in Caesar seem ambitious?" (line 18) and "was this ambition?" (line 25) asks Antony. A few lines later (line 31), he challenges the crowd: "What cause withholds you, then, to mourn for him?" Antony doesn't really expect an answer to these rhetorical questions, but he establishes a link to the listeners, who will respond to the questions internally.

■ Antony employs *apostrophe,* addressing a personified quality (in this case, judgment). In lines 32–33, he tells "judgment" that "thou art fled to brutish beasts, / And men have lost their reason!" The point is strong: The crowd has much in common with animals ("brutish beasts") and must regain perspective.

■ Antony's final appeal is emotional. He's crying and must cease speaking until he composes himself. He asks the crowd to "[b]ear with me" (line 33), once more calling them to his side and, implicitly, to oppose Brutus and the other murderers.

A good essay on this amazing speech doesn't have to cover everything in the preceding bullet points. If you have touched upon half of these ideas, you're in good shape. The fastest and easiest way to organize this essay is to take the passage line by line, explaining and quoting as you go. You can also divide the essay by types of argument: appeal to reason, to emotion, bonding with the crowd, and so forth.

PAIRED PASSAGES

Paired passages show up on the AP English Language and Composition exam every couple of years. This type of question contains a pair of passages, usually two approaches to one topic by two different authors. You generally have to compare and contrast one element — tone, purpose, description, or something similar — in the pair.

Prompt

Read these passages carefully. In a well-written essay, discuss the rhetorical devices each writer employs to describe scientific research.

Note: Passage A is an excerpt from *Scientific American: Inventions and Discoveries,* by Rodney Carlisle (Wiley, 2004). Passage B is excerpted from *The Big Splat, or How the Moon Came to Be,* by Dana Mackenzie (Wiley, 2003). Both are reprinted with permission of John Wiley & Sons, Inc.

Passage A

(01)   Great scientific discoveries are relatively rare. Believing that the universe was ordered by law, reflecting the fact that many early scientists had legal and theo- logical training as well as training in natural philosophy, scientists reduced their findings to laws representing simple descriptions of how the universe operates.
(05) In a number of cases the laws were named for the person who discovered them, giving credence to a kind of "great man" view of science. In a few cases several scientists simultaneously came to nearly identical formulations of the laws, often leading to bitter disputes over priority of discovery. Such simultaneity served to demonstrate that scientific discovery was not simply a matter of individual bril-
(10) liance but also a consequence of a more general process of scientific advance and progress.
    Such discoveries of the laws of nature represent a special class of work in which a cluster of natural phenomena, long observed by the human race, is ana- lyzed and reduced to a group of immutable principles that are found to govern the
(15) phenomena. In many cases the laws can be expressed in mathematical or alge- braic fashion, reducing the complexity of the world around us to a set of numeri- cal constants and immutable relationships. The fields of physics and celestial mechanics include Newton's three laws of motion, the law of gravity, Kepler's laws of planetary orbits, Pascal's principle, Boyle's law, and the four laws of thermody-
(20) namics, among others. In each of these cases, one or more natural philosophers contemplated a long-observed phenomenon and deduced a mathematical or me- chanical principle at work, reducing it to a statement with universal application.

Passage B

(01)   But where others saw only a confusing pattern of light and dark spots, Galileo understood that he was seeing a *landscape*. The Moon's detail showed up most clearly in the boundary region between the illuminated part of the Moon and the dark part. This dividing line is called the terminator, and it is the place where, to
(05) a Moon-dweller, the Sun would be seen setting or rising at any given moment. . . . Seen through the telescope, the terminator visibly moves during the course of an evening, and the changes Galileo saw in the patterns of light and dark confirmed his belief that the Moon had a rugged surface. Some bright spots would light up even before the terminator reached them; these spots would be illuminated on
(10) the side facing the Sun, and a dark shadow on the other side would persist for a while after the terminator moved by. . . . For the most part, Galileo's first descrip- tions of the Moon show admirable restraint. He resisted the temptation to give in to conjecture, and instead described exactly what he saw — not a mountain, but a

(15) shadow that behaved in such-and-such a way, until the case was clear and compelling that the shadow had to be a mountain. Galileo noticed, for example, that the dark-colored regions of the Moon seemed to be lower than the lighter regions, based on his observations of the terminator.

Answer guide for the paired-passage essay

Check your essay against the general guidelines at the beginning of this chapter. Then examine your work in light of the following standards, which are tailored to this prompt. The bullet points are more or less in descending order of importance. Your essay should contain statements similar to those in the first couple of bullets. If you have ideas from the last couple of bullets, you've come up with ideas many other test takers probably missed, which is impressive to an AP grader.

- Your essay should state how scientific research is characterized in each passage *and* discuss the rhetorical devices each author uses. Your essay should also relate content (the characterization of scientific research) to writing style (the rhetorical devices). Simply listing the rhetorical devices is not acceptable. Your essay must show how each rhetorical device contributes to the characterization of scientific research.

- A thesis statement for this essay might be something like "Both passages characterize scientific research as a process involving observation and the formulation of general principles, but Passage B focuses on an individual scientist and Passage A take a more general approach." (Many variations are possible. For more information on thesis statements, see Chapter 15.)

- The characterization of scientific research should be supported by evidence from the text. According to Passage A, scientific discovery begins in observation that is then turned into an abstract principle, or "law," which is often named for the scientist who formulated it. The laws are "simple descriptions of how the universe operates" (line 4). Discovery is "relatively rare" (line 1) and not only a result of "individual brilliance" (lines 9–10) but also "a consequence of a more general process of scientific advance" (line 10).

- Passage A is more abstract than Passage B. A couple of scientists are mentioned in Passage A, but only in the context of the name of a particular law. Instead, Passage A explains scientific discovery in general ("a cluster of natural phenomena, long observed by the human race, is analyzed and reduced to a group of immutable principles that are found to govern the phenomena" — lines 13–15) and states that "the laws can be expressed in mathematical or algebraic fashion" (lines 15–16).

- The use of passive voice in Passage A ("observed by" [line 13], "is analyzed and reduced" [lines 13–14], "are found" [line 14]) emphasizes the process, not the person conducting the process.

- In Passage B, the emphasis is on one scientist. The author employs the story of Galileo as an example of the process of scientific research. The author describes what Galileo saw ("patterns of light and dark" [line7], "the terminator visibly moves" [line 6], "[s]ome bright spots would light up even before the terminator reached them" [lines 8–9], "a dark shadow on the other side would persist for a while after the terminator moved by" [lines 10–11]). The author also states what Galileo did — a particular man who "resisted the temptation to give in to conjecture" (lines 12–13) and "described exactly what he saw" (line 13) and didn't come to a conclusion "until the case was clear and compelling" (lines 14–15).

- The verbs in Passage B are in active voice: "Galileo understood," "Galileo saw," and "Galileo noticed" (lines 1–2, 7, and 15). Active voice emphasizes the person performing the action.

- Passage A gives the impression that all scientists operate in more or less the same way. It refers only to groups, as in "scientists reduced their findings" (lines 3–4). Passage B contrasts Galileo's method of strict observation to something looser: "where others saw only a confusing pattern of light and dark, Galileo understood. . ." (lines 1–2) and "For the most part, Galileo's first descriptions of the Moon show admirable restraint" (lines 11–12) a statement implying that others did *not* show restraint.

- In Passage A, the second sentence begins with two qualifying statements ("Believing that the universe was ordered by law" [lines 1–2] and "reflecting the fact . . . natural philosophy" [lines 2–3]). These statements apply to "scientists," who "reduced their findings to laws" (lines 3–4) governing how the universe operates. The qualifying statements imply that scientists trained differently would conduct their research differently as well.

- Passage B is more fanciful. The terminator is described from the point of view of a "Moon-dweller" (line 5). This reach into figurative language mirrors the creativity of Galileo, who leapt from "a confusing pattern of light and dark spots" (line 1) to "a *landscape*" (line 2).

- Passage A has some repetitive statements. The repetition mirrors the idea that all scientific research proceeds in the same way, no matter who conducts it.

- Passage B follows Galileo's process of deduction, from observation to conclusion. The reader is left to make the generalization about science — making the reader into a scientist, because scientists deduce.

You can organize this essay in any of several ways. You can write one paragraph for A and one for B, for example. Or you could say everything about content in one paragraph, then write a paragraph on rhetorical devices, and then add another paragraph on the relationship between content and style.

> **TIP**
>
> In a paired-passage essay, you should have roughly the same amount of information about each passage. If your essay spends 350 words on Passage A and 50 words on Passage B, you're tilting too much.

ESSAY BASED ON A QUOTATION

Recent AP English Language and Composition exams have included an essay based on a short quotation. You have to agree, disagree, or partially agree with the point made in the quotation and then support your stance with evidence from literature, history, or personal observation and experience — or some combination of these.

Prompt

> **EXAMPLE**
>
> A philosopher once commented, "Wisdom is founded on memory; happiness on forgetfulness." Drawing upon your reading, observation, and experience, consider this statement. In a well-organized essay, argue your own viewpoint on the origin of wisdom and happiness. Be sure to provide support for your stance.

Answer guide for a quotation-based essay

I can't get too specific in this section, as I have with other types of essay questions, because you can approach this essay in an infinite number of ways. You have to work a little harder here to apply my comments to your own writing.

> **TIP**
>
> Ask your English teacher or a trusted adult to read your answer. You may not get an official AP-style evaluation, but you will probably learn whether you have made a logical case and supported it adequately.

As you review your quotation-based essay, keep these points in mind:

- You don't have to accept or reject the quotation. You can write a *qualified* response such as "I agree that wisdom is founded on memory, but so is happiness." Nuanced views exist, and most of your opinions likely fall into the "yes, but" or "no, although" category.

- Your answer should respond to both halves of the quotation. If you discuss only wisdom and forget about happiness (or vice versa), you haven't completed the assigned task. The essay doesn't have to divide 50-50. You may spend more time on wisdom and then link happiness to that definition, perhaps explaining that true happiness, along with wisdom, comes from weathering and remembering the tough times in life.

- The prompt asks you to "provide support for your stance." The test makers want you to think of examples that support your ideas. You may remember an example from the reading you did for English class and discuss Oedipus's hard-won wisdom at the end of Sophocles's play. You may look at a historical event (the rise of the Nazi party, for instance) and explain how remembering that era guides and improves our decisions now, making us wiser. Your own life or what you've witnessed in others' lives is another possible area to explore. You may write about a classmate whose family was thrust into a difficult situation (bankruptcy, illness, and the like). Does remembering those days confer wisdom? Or is something else needed?

- You can mix and match types of evidence. For example, you may decide to discuss a work of literature *and* a personal experience.

- If you wish, you can base your opinion on only one example, though of course you have to write more about that example than you would if you had chosen a couple of supporting points.

- No matter how many examples you use, details matter. I've referred to Oedipus and the Nazi era in preceding bullet points, but I haven't given enough information to make a strong case for my opinion. Whatever evidence you choose must be presented fully.

- You're writing an argument, and you have to take the opposing view into account. The strongest argument includes an acknowledgment of the objections that may arise and an answer to those objections. (For help with this aspect of essay writing, turn to Chapter 15.)

An argument essay may be organized around the evidence, with one section for each supporting example. Or you may devote a few paragraphs to a discussion of wisdom and a few to your ideas about happiness. Either way, the first paragraph should include the quotation and your *thesis statement,* the compact expression of your point of view. (I explain how to create a thesis statement in Chapter 15.)

AN OPINION PIECE

Although most of the AP exam is based on text, occasionally you're asked to write about an idea that isn't stated in a passage or quotation. See what you can do with the sample question in the next section.

Prompt

> **EXAMPLE**
>
> Some schools allow students to take whatever courses they wish, and some place a cap on the number of AP and honors classes or the overall number of classes in which a student may enroll. The first system gives more freedom and responsibility to the students (and their parents, if parental consent to a course-load is required). However, such freedom may fuel college-admission competition and result in overstressed and overworked students. The second is based on the idea that educators know what constitutes a healthy workload.
>
> Write an essay supporting, criticizing, or qualifying the notion of regulating student schedules. Support your opinion with well-reasoned arguments.

Answer guide for an opinion piece

This is the sort of piece that you might read in the op-ed section of your school paper. You need to indicate what you think, and you have to support your ideas. Check out these guidelines:

- The graders will look for complexity here. An essay that advocates free choice, regardless of consequences, is unlikely to impress your reader. Neither is a straight "grown-ups know best" essay.

- The best approach to this essay considers the opposing point of view and credits that view where it's warranted. For example, assume that you favor caps on classes. What's good about the pro-freedom stance? Students will learn a lot about time management if they try to take too many courses, for example, and they may develop a greater sense of personal responsibility. You can acknowledge these points while still arguing that the benefits of adult wisdom outweigh them.

- A variation on the preceding bullet point is *concession and reply*. This technique, which I explain further in Chapter 15, acknowledges the opposition and refutes it. For example, say that you're for student freedom, but you know that some hyper-competitive kids will go too far and sign up for too many classes. State that fact, and then respond. For example, you may say that students can handle freedom if they receive the proper training. Suggest that kids be counseled by older, experienced students or alumni about the drawbacks of an overpacked schedule. Or propose that students be given one week to try out a schedule before enrolling for real.

- Personal observation may be helpful here. Suppose you have a friend at a school where students have no limits. What's your friend's experience? Describe your friend's schedule. On the other hand, what was it like for you when you couldn't take the elective of your dreams because you were already over the limit in your course load? Either example or both, if used properly, can be great supporting evidence in your essay.

The structure of this essay depends upon what you're saying. Probably the easiest structure begins with an introduction stating your opinion and some supporting points. Then the body paragraphs tackle one supporting point each. The problem with this structure is that it's boring. Your grader has read thousands of similar essays. To perk things up, you might try a deductive structure, beginning with the small specific points you want to make and leading up to a big finish: your opinion. You have to put a little more thought into this kind of structure, but your product may be more interesting. If you're undecided about how to organize your thoughts, try a back-and-forth structure: "It's good because . . . on the other hand."

THE SYNTHESIS ESSAY

The synthesis essay requires you to check out six or seven sources, which include at least one visual (a chart, photo, drawing, graph, table, or something similar). You have to read them and develop a point of view. Then you *synthesize* — not summarize — three of the sources into a coherent argument. Give it a try.

Prompt for synthesis essay 1: National service

EXAMPLE

Directions: The question below is based on the six sources which follow it. To answer this question, you must synthesize information from these sources. Your essay must present a clear argument supported by at least three of the sources. Do NOT merely summarize the information or the point of view of the sources.

Be sure to cite information, quotations, or ideas taken from these sources. You may cite them as "Source A," "Source B," and so forth, or by the descriptions in parentheses.

Source A (Poster)

Source B (Yates)

Source C (Bureau of Labor Statistics)

Source D (Footnoted)

Source E (Keisling)

Source F (Casnocha)

The Question: At various times in its history, the United States has drafted young men into military service. In recent years the draft has been replaced by a system of voluntary enlistment. Many politicians and commentators have called for a mandatory national service program — a year of service to the community or in the military — for young people, both male and female. Mandatory national service has supporters and opponents. After reading the following sources carefully, develop a position regarding mandatory national service. Then write an essay in which you support your position with references to these sources.

Source A

Poster, "Uncle Sam Wants You"

I WANT YOU
FOR U.S. ARMY
NEAREST RECRUITING STATION

Art Resource/Art Resource, NY

Source B

Yates, Gary L. "Mandatory National Service: Building National Spirit and Solving Social Ills." February 2002. The California Wellness Foundation www.tcwf.org. (Reprinted with permission from Gary L. Yates, President and CEO, The California Wellness Foundation. Copyright 2008 The California Wellness Foundation. All rights reserved.)

(01) In President Bush's first State of the Union speech on January 29, he called for expanding and improving AmeriCorps, our nation's national service program, by recruiting more than 200,000 new volunteers. He also promised to revitalize the Peace Corps by doubling its membership over the next five years.

(05) Many Americans in our post-September 11 world are looking for ways to contribute to our national strength and build our sense of unity. I can think of no better way to instill patriotism and appreciation for our national diversity than through these national service programs. But the idea of national service for young adults between high school graduation and college and careers has another, often over-
(10) looked, benefit: it helps to reduce crime and violence.

As president and CEO of one of California's largest health foundations, I have long been concerned about and active in violence prevention efforts. Therefore, I think President Bush's proposal is a tremendous first step. But I think we should go further and consider mandatory national service for all U.S. citizens when they reach
(15) 18 years of age. This way we would build strong citizens and provide opportunities for improving lives, which is the surest way to reduce crime.

In crime prevention we focus on "critical hours" and "critical years." The critical hours when most youth crimes occur are between 3 p.m. and 6 p.m. We have made strides in addressing this problem with after-school programs that keep kids
(20) involved and busy before adult supervision arrives at home. Mandatory national

service would address the "critical years" problem, the after-school years between 18 and 24 when men and women are more likely to be the victims or perpetrators of crimes than at any other time in their lives.

(25) These are the years when young adults often lose the support they had from schools, after-school programs and the community. The Criminal Justice Statistics Center reports that this age group suffers from and commits the most homicides by firearms. We owe it to our young adults to keep them productive and safe from violence.

Today AmeriCorps engages more than 50,000 Americans in intensive, results-oriented service each year. Jose Hernandez, of South Central Los Angeles, is a good (30) example of how it changes lives. Growing up, Jose attended the Bresee Foundation's after-school program where he participated in positive recreational, cultural and community activities. When Jose graduated from high school, he watched many young people in his neighborhood turn to gangs and end up dead or in jail. Jose knew he wanted more and a Bresee worker recommended AmeriCorps.

(35) There, Jose served a year working at an after–school program, learning community building and communication skills. Today, three years after his AmeriCorps year, Jose is an outreach worker in his community. Jose doesn't know where he would have ended up without AmeriCorps and credits the program for teaching him to help himself as he learned how to help others.

(40) Today's economy makes the case for national service programs even stronger. California's Employment Development Department (EDD) reported that the unemployment rate for November 2001 was six percent, the highest unemployment rate in the state since September 1998. For the 23 percent of California young adults without a high school diploma and 44 percent who do not enter college im-(45) mediately after high school, this job market will make it more difficult for them to find meaningful employment.

Can you imagine if every youth in California could spend a year learning about themselves and their communities and gaining job skills in the process? As Father Greg Boyle of Los Angeles-based Homeboy Industries so eloquently puts it, "Noth-(50) ing stops a bullet like a job."

Some may question a mandatory national service for youth. Why not keep it voluntary? Perhaps the answer lies in what people do not appear to be doing amid the brisk sales of U.S. flags. Have we seen reports showing dramatic increases in voter registration or military enlistments? I haven't. I believe this is because many of our (55) youth — who have grown into today's adults — have missed out on the experience of giving back to their country. This may explain why many don't feel any need to channel their patriotism into volunteerism or make voting a life-long commitment.

I believe mandatory national service would provide a way for the youth of this nation to give something back for the freedoms they enjoy and to work side-by-side (60) with other young Americans for a common national purpose. The result would be a better understanding of the strength of our diversity and increased participation in the voting booth. For some, the military may be an option, as it was for me; for others the ability to work in a nursing home, recreation facility or day care center may be a life-altering experience. The benefits will surely be safer, healthier and (65) more civically engaged youth and adults.

Source C

"Volunteering in the United States, 2007." Bureau of Labor Statistics. Date accessed: January 23, 2008.
www.bls.gov

Source: U.S. Bureau of Labor Statistics

Table A. Volunteers by selected characteristics, September 2003 through September 2007
(Numbers in thousands)

Characteristic	September 2003		September 2004		September 2005		September 2006		September 2007	
	Number	Percent of population	Number	Percent of population	Number	Percent of population	Number	Percent of population	Number	Percent of population
Sex										
Total, both sexes	63,791	28.8	65,542	28.8	65,357	28.8	61,199	26.7	60,838	26.2
Men	26,805	25.1	27,011	25.0	27,370	25.0	25,546	23.0	25,724	22.9
Women	36,987	32.2	37,530	32.4	37,987	32.4	35,653	30.1	35,114	29.3
Age										
Total, 16 years and over....	63,791	28.8	64,542	28.8	65,357	28.8	61,199	26.9	60,838	26.2
16 to 24 years	8, 671	24.1	8,821	24.2	8,955	24.4	8,044	21.7	7,798	20.8
25 to 34 years	10,337	26.5	10,046	25.8	9,881	25.3	9,096	23.1	9,019	22.6
35 to 44 years	15,165	34.7	14,783	34.2	14.809	34.5	13,308	31.2	12,902	30.5
45 to 54 years	13,302	32.7	13,584	32.8	13,826	32.7	13,415	31.2	13,136	30.1
55 to 64 years	8,170	29.2	8,784	30.1	9,173	30.2	8,819	27.9	9,316	28.4
65 years and over...	8,146	23.7	8,524	24.6	8,712	24.8	8,518	23.8	8,667	23.8
Educational attainment (1)										
Less than a high school diploma	2,793	9.9	2,718	9.6	2,837	10.0	2,615	9.3	2,394	9.0
High school graduates, no college (2)	12,882	21.7	12,709	21.6	12,594	21.2	11,537	19.2	11,379	18.6
Some college or associate degree (3) ..	15,966	34.1	16,414	34.2	16,452	33.7	15,196	30.9	15,468	30.7
Bachelor's degree and higher (3)	23,481	45.6	23,880	45.7	24,517	45.8	23,808	43.3	23,799	41.8
Employment status										
Civilian labor force	45,499	30.9	45,896	30.9	46,872	31.1	43,579	28.5	43,405	28.1
Employed	45,499	30.9	45,896	30.9	46,872	31.1	43,579	28.5	43,405	28.1
Full time	33,599	29.6	34,237	29.6	35,225	29.8	32,951	27.3	32,714	26.9
Part time	9,539	38.4	9,649	38.5	9,669	38.2	8,910	35.5	8,994	35.4
Unemployed	2,361	26.7	2,010	25.6	1,978	26.4	1,718	23.8	1,697	23.2
Not in the labor force....	18,293	24.6	18,646	24.7	18,485	24.4	17,621	23.1	14,433	22.3

1 Data refer to persons 25 years and over.

2 Includes persons with a high school diploma or equivalent.

3 Includes persons with bachelor's, master's, professional, and doctorial degrees.

4 Usually work 35 hours or more a week at all jobs.

5 Usually work less than 35 hours a week at all jobs.

Source D

"Footnoted: Debating Mandatory National Service," *Chronicle of Higher Education,* September 28, 2007. (Copyright 2007, *The Chronicle of Higher Education.* Reprinted with permission.)

(01) September 28, 2007

Debating Mandatory National Service

Should national service, either military or civilian, be mandatory for 18-year-old Americans? That is the question being debated by the University of Chicago eco-
(05) nomics professor Gary Becker and his co-blogger, Richard Posner, who lectures at the University of Chicago Law School.

Posner kicks things off with a cost-benefit analysis of the case for universal na-tional service. As he sees it, such a program would generate significant costs: the "deadweight costs" of the necessary taxes to finance such an ambitious program,
(10) and the inefficiency costs that stem from reallocating "a year of a college gradu-ate's working life from after college to before college, when he would be less pro-ductive." In addition, "Universal national service would also have peculiar effects on the distribution of income. The unpaid national service workers would replace low-paid service workers, pushing many of them into poverty."

(15) These costs are somewhat mitigated by the potential for nurturing social solidar-ity across class lines. But Posner seems skeptical. Even if the actual motive for mandatory service is to "take rich kids down a peg by forcing them to work for a year with minimal compensation," he finds scant evidence that a year spent work-ing without pay would make one more sympathetic toward issues of distributive
(20) justice.

Becker is more emphatic: "compulsory service is a bad policy" with all the charac-teristics of a "very bad tax."

Ilya Somin takes a different tack in a post at the Volokh Conspiracy. Granting that Becker-Posner do a good job attacking such a policy on economic grounds, Somin,
(25) a professor of law at George Mason University, objects on moral grounds: It is forced labor. "Even in the unlikely event that mandatory national service could be shown to provide benefits that outweigh its costs, it would still be morally repul-sive," Somin writes. "Short of outright slavery or the murder of innocent people, it is hard to think of anything that violates individual liberty more clearly than
(30) forced labor."

Source E

Keisling, Phil. "Make National Service Mandatory for All." *Washington Monthly.* January–February 1994. www.bnet.com. (Reprinted with permission from *The Washington Monthly.* Copyright by Washington Monthly Publishing, LLC, 5471 Wisconsin Avenue, Suite 300, Chevy Chase, MD 20815. (240) 497-0321. Website: www.washingtonmonthly.com)

(01) I have become convinced that the U.S. — like most industrialized nations — should enact a mandatory system of national service. But we should go much further than the draft ever did and even further than the systems widely used elsewhere in the world.

(05) Such a system should be mandatory, not voluntary. It should be broad, not narrow, with exceptions based on inability rather than personal inconvenience. (Exceptions for prison inmates, for example, but definitely not for the college-bound or well-heeled). It should involve women as well as men, in stark contrast to our draft and the male-only service plans of most other countries. Eventually, it should ask some-
(10) thing of all Americans, just as the jury system (at least in theory) does now.

Obviously, national service would be costly and raises a host of practical and lo-gistical problems. For example, given that between 3 and 4 million Americans turn 18 each year, a full-fledged program might easily cost $50 billion a year, including living expenses, supervisory costs, and G.I. Bill-style benefits for additional educa-
(15) tion and training.

Participants would have to be properly trained and supervised. They would need to do real jobs, not make-work. Serious problems with discipline, drug and alcohol abuse, criminal behavior, and shoddy work would be inevitable. It would require the kind of well-planned, efficient government organization that most Americans
(20) consider highly doubtful if not impossible.

Considerable obstacles, to be sure. But we've risen to considerable organizational challenges before, from World War II and the sixties' space program to the recent flooding in the Midwest. And consider the costs, tangible and intangible, of not having such a system.

(25) For starters, today's military budget is higher than it would be if highly compen-sated, career-track men and women were a substantially smaller backbone of our armed services than they are today. Personnel costs — which account for a far greater share of Pentagon spending than all our low-tech and high-tech weapons and missiles put together — would be billions lower. So would retirement costs,
(30) which now run more than $11.8 billion a year.

Given current military manpower needs, only about 10 percent of the 18-to-21-year-old population would be needed in uniform. What to do with the rest?

Just think about five areas — education; public safety; health care; the rural en-vironment; the urban environment. Now think of all the work that isn't getting
(35) done — and the tremendous price we're paying for that.

The nation's infrastructure is in shambles, requiring trillions of dollars for repair and costing billions each year in lost economic opportunities. Crime and gang activity increase as our police have far too little presence in our communities. Educational achievement falls and drop-outs increase as classes get bigger and
(40) bigger, students bring more serious problems into the classroom, and teachers feel overwhelmed. Health care costs skyrocket, in part because we lack even the most rudimentary ability to provide simple, prevention-based care. Young parents go on or stay on welfare because basic child care is unavailable, too expensive, too low in quality, or all three.

(45) Just one example: It's been estimated that as many as 300,000 Americans now in nursing homes — and half of the nation's nursing home costs are financed through Medicaid — could be served in normal community settings if they had someone to assist them in their daily routines.

Community service helps not just the receiver, but the giver. Many of our young
(50) people succumb to too-early parenthood, to drug and alcohol abuse, to gangs and
violence. National service obviously won't be a panacea. But it can communicate a
powerful message that often isn't received by our younger citizens — that you can
make a difference. You matter. Society values your contribution. The self-esteem
that's built from tutoring a younger child, cleaning up a park, or talking a peer out
(55) of self-destructive behavior can be a powerful antidote to the devastating — and
expensive — trends now so prevalent in our society.

Finally, consider the less tangible but staggering costs to our society and its demo-
cratic underpinnings as our citizens become increasingly divided and isolated
from each other, not just along racial lines but class lines as well. Consider, too,
(60) the widespread ethos that encourages people to think of government as merely
a broker among interest groups — with the loudest and best-organized holding
sway — and "citizenship" as a collection of rights but not responsibilities.

Source F

Casnocha, Ben. "Mandatory National Service." *Marketplace*. Minnesota National Public Radio. Transcript of broadcast. (Copyright Ben Casnocha 2008: http://ben.casnocha.com)

(01) **KAI RYSSDAL:** It's been a while since Congress and the White House have seriously
considered a military draft, but there is a growing movement in favor of a national
service program of some kind. Younger Americans would give a year of their life to
serve the country, maybe in the military, or maybe in a community service or educa-
(05) tion corps. The most enthusiastic advocates want any such program to be mandatory.

Commentator, college freshman, and potential national service draftee Ben Casnocha says they're sending a mixed message.

BEN CASNOCHA: Listen carefully to those who hail the benefits of national service programs. "It'll improve civic engagement, build national unity, instill duty
(10) and honor in America's youth." Isn't it strange how the conversation is always
about the benefits to us?

A few years ago, a Washington University report noted that nobody has really
studied how broad service programs affect those actually being served. It suggests
that in some cases the local communities in which we are volunteering may be
(15) hurt more than helped. How so?

Say an Uncle Sam–sponsored American comes along and offers to rebuild a dilapi-
dated home in a poor area for free. What rational homeowner would say no? The
community's happy, and the subsidized volunteer feels good about himself, but
what about the local builder who was charging market rate for the service? Sorry,
(20) he's out of a job. Temporary streams of volunteers can disrupt local labor markets
over the long haul. One study of AmeriCorps, for example, suggests the positive
impact may be only short-term.

Now national service is just a sliver of the total volunteer pie. Americans volun-
teered over three billion hours last year. The vast majority of these people did so
(25) without an order from the government. They worked with private non-profits.
Since they choose to volunteer for a specific local cause, these people are better
able to create a long-term positive impact on the folks they serve.

Nevertheless, John McCain and others want to nationalize volunteerism. There's an effort underway to pump up the social pressure. Advocates want to offer various fi-
(30) nancial incentives for kids to serve "voluntarily" for the United States. McCain talks about increased "patriotism" and "serving one's country." So wait. Is McCain's plan a nationalistic morale building exercise? Are the benefits intended to flow primarily toward the servers or the served? Now what's the point of an expensive government program that doesn't quite know whom it's trying to help? Let's stick with local,
(35) community-organized service programs, and make sure those in need come first, and those who offer the services are contributing of their own volition.

Answer guide for synthesis essay 1: National service

The synthesis essay is probably the hardest of the three AP free-response questions to write, and it's also hard to evaluate. Because you can spin this answer in literally thousands of ways, I can't get too specific about what points you must make in your essay. But I can give you some guidelines about what you can extract from each source and how you can use the sources to support various positions.

Here are some potential ideas from the sources:

- Source A may look familiar, because variations of this "Uncle Sam Wants You!" poster are everywhere. The poster's popularity is a good point to make. Americans know that their country needs them, but not everyone volunteers to serve "Uncle Sam." Perhaps a law is needed to drive home the point. Or, arguing the opposite position, you can say that the poster is frequently reproduced because Americans are aware of the value of service to the nation and their communities and will volunteer when their life circumstances permit them to do so.

- Source B takes a pro-mandatory service stance, characterizing national service as a violence-prevention measure. You can use the story of "Jose" to illustrate the benefit of service and quote Father Boyle ("Nothing stops a bullet like a job" — lines 49–50) to drive home the point. The statistics on unemployment are also useful for a pro-manda-tory service essay. Yates's comments on "giving back to their country" (line 56) go well with Source A (the poster of Uncle Sam) and can be used for both pro and con posi-tions, because you can always argue that people serve their country voluntarily also.

- Source C, the chart, provides ammunition for several positions. If you're advocating for voluntary, not mandatory service, you can cite the high rate of volunteerism. More than a quarter of all Americans volunteer at any given time. Of course, you can spin that number the other way too; nearly three-fourths of Americans don't volunteer. Be-cause mandatory national service is likely to affect mostly young people, you may zero in on the percentages for 16- to 24-year-olds. As those numbers are lower than the per-centages for older groups, you can tuck this statistic into an essay arguing that young people are not as involved in national life as they should be and thus need a stronger motive to volunteer. However, because the percentage rises with age, up to the 35–44 slot, you can make a good case for choice. Young people may not volunteer in large numbers, but they will volunteer as their life circumstances permit.

- In Source C the data on educational level also support both positions, depending upon how you look at the numbers. People with more education usually earn more, so they can afford to take the time to volunteer. In a "con" essay, you can suggest that increasing support for community-service organizations will allow them to pay all volunteers a living wage (which only some volunteer organizations are able to do at present). Without financial pressure, more young people may choose to volunteer. In a "pro" essay, you can make the point that mandatory service will lead to a more tolerant society. Everyone of a certain age will have to commit to helping the community, so rich and poor and people from diverse backgrounds will have to work together and get to know each other better.

■ Another useful statistic from Source C is that part-time workers volunteer the most. In a pro-mandatory service essay, you can use this fact to back up the idea that people want to help out; they don't always have the time.

■ Source D is a gold mine if you're arguing against mandatory service because it contains a bunch of quotations to back up your case. For example, you can quote Ilya Somin's view that mandatory national service is "morally repulsive" (lines 27–28) and the worst policy "[s]hort of outright slavery or the murder of innocent people" (line 28). You can also mention that University of Chicago economics professors see mandatory service as generating more expenses and inefficiency than benefits to society, though the source doesn't contain the supporting statistics that these experts undoubtedly compiled.

■ Source E, which favors mandatory service, lists the many areas where labor is needed. The source has a great paragraph of *concession and reply* (acknowledgment and rebuttal of the opposing argument): Yes, mandatory service will be expensive and difficult to administer. However, the benefits far outweigh the problems. Use this source for arguments against mandatory service (paragraph three), or use (and cite) Keisling's answers to these arguments as stated in paragraph four. The last two paragraphs are great for pro-mandatory essays, as they explain how the giver as well as the community benefits.

■ Ben Casnocha's commentary in Source F makes a strong case against mandatory service. He points out that the benefits may be larger for the volunteer than for the community. His remarks are short on statistics but long on quotations, such as "Let's stick with local, community-organized service programs, and make sure those in need come first. . . ." (lines 34–36).

> **TIP**
>
> In a synthesis essay, it is crucial that your essay take an identifiable point of view, so be sure that you have a thesis statement in your introductory paragraph. Your opinion doesn't have to fall neatly into one category, either pro or con. You might argue, for example, that incentives should be created to entice more people to voluntary national service and legislation enacted only if these measures fail. Whatever your view, be sure the thesis statement communicates what you believe.

Organizing a synthesis essay is challenging because you have a lot of information. After an introduction containing your thesis statement and perhaps something to draw the reader's attention (a quotation or an interesting statistic, perhaps), you might devote one paragraph to each reason why national service should be mandatory (or not, if that's your position). Another possible structure for this essay is to begin by describing the situation — civic work left undone or people in need — and then move to your solution (volunteerism or mandatory service).

Keep in mind that taking information or ideas from a source without giving proper credit is absolutely forbidden. You must include citations for all quotations, statistics, *and* arguments that you've gleaned from these six sources. (For more information on citing sources, check out Chapter 12.)

Prompt for synthesis essay 2: Art

Directions: The question below is based on the six sources which follow it. To answer this question, you must synthesize, or combine, information from these sources. Your essay must present a clear argument supported by at least three of the sources. Do NOT merely summarize the information or the point of view of the sources.

Be sure to cite information, quotations, or ideas taken from these sources. You may cite them as "Source A," "Source B," and so forth, or by the descriptions in parentheses.

Source A (Johnson)

Source B (Mondrian)

Source C (Yates)

Source D (Witcombe)

Source E (Dicker/sun)

Source F (Picasso)

The Question: What is the purpose of art? To serve as a vehicle of self-expression, to create social or political change, or something else entirely? Artists and critics, as well as the general public, have answered this question in diverse and conflicting ways. Develop a position about the purpose of art, drawing upon these sources for support.

Source A

Photo, Peeling, 1976-1993, by Karen Ellen Johnson

Photo by Karen Ellen Johnson

Source B
Mondrian, Piet. "Plastic Art & Pure Plastic Art." *Circle*, 1937

(01) Although Art is fundamentally everywhere and always the same, nevertheless two main human inclinations, diametrically opposed to each other, appear in its many and varied expressions. One aims at the direct creation of universal beauty, the other at the esthetic expression of oneself, in other words, of that which one
(05) thinks and experiences. The first aims at representing reality objectively, the second subjectively. Thus we see in every work of figurative art the desire, objectively to represent beauty, solely through form and color, in mutually balanced relations, and, at the same time, an attempt to express that which these forms, colors, and relations arouse in us.

Source C
Unpublished remarks of Don Yates, art historian

(01) What is art? "It's art because I say it is," according to Robert Rauschenberg. In the end, though, a society gets the art that it needs, and you can't judge the art of one society by the standards of another or judge the art of one particular era by the standards of the same society at a different point in its history. Some moments in
(05) history call for political art; others do not. The creation of art can't help being contingent upon the society in which it's created.

However, art is always made in a political context, whether the issue of politics is avoided by the artist or not. Look at Pollock and the modernists. It's almost as though the politicization of society in the Cold War made artists bury politics, if
(10) they had a political message. In recent years art has become more overtly political, especially if you consider criticism of society as a political act. Think of Jenny Holzer and Barbara Kruger, both openly critical of society. With the emergence of the modern feminist movement and the gay-rights movement, you see strong political statements made through art.

Source D
Witcombe, Christopher L.C.E. "Art for Art's Sake." witcombe.sbc.edu/modernism/artsake.html

(01) Generally speaking, progressive modernism tended to concern itself with political and social issues, addressing aspects of contemporary society, especially in its poorer ranks, that an increasingly complacent middle class, once they had achieved a satisfactory level of comfort for themselves, preferred to ignore.

(05) Through their art, in pictures that showed directly or indirectly the plight of the peasants, the exploitation of the poor, prostitution, and so on, the progressives repeatedly drew attention to the political and social ills of contemporary society, conditions they felt needed to be addressed and corrected.

Fundamentally, the intention was to educate the public, to keep alive in the face
(10) of conservative forces the Enlightenment ideals of freedom and equality through which the world would be made a better place.

The position taken by progressive modernism came to be referred to as the avant-garde (a military term meaning "advance-guard"). In contrast to the conservative modernists who looked to the past and tradition, the avant-garde artist conscious-
(15) ly rejected tradition.

Rather than existing as the most recent manifestation of a tradition stretching back into the past, the avant-garde artist saw him- or herself as standing at the head of a new tradition stretching, hopefully, into the future. The progressive modernist looked to the future while the conservative modernist looked to the
(20) past.

The rejection of the past became imperative for the progressives with the advent of the First World War, which signalled for them the catastrophic failure of tradition. The senseless carnage of the "Great War" starkly showed that modernism's faith in scientific and technological progress as the path to a better world was
(25) misdirected. For the Dadaists, World War One also signalled the failure of all modernist art. It could be claimed that Dada in fact marks the emergence of a post-modernist cast of mind.

Today, we would characterize progressive modernism, the avant-garde, as left-leaning and liberal in its support of freedom of expression and demands of equal-
(30) ity. Since the 18th century, the modernist belief in the freedom of expression has manifested itself in art through claims to freedom of choice in subject matter and to freedom of choice in style (i.e., in the choice of brushstroke and colour). It was in the exercise of these rights that the artist constantly drew attention to the goals of progressive modernism.

(35) As the 19th century progressed, the exercise of artistic freedom became fundamental to progressive modernism. Artists began to seek freedom not just from the rules of academic art, but from the demands of the public. Soon it was claimed that art should be produced not for the public's sake, but for art's sake.

Art for Art's Sake is basically a call for release from the tyranny of meaning and
(40) purpose. From a progressive modernist's point of view, it was a further exercise of freedom. It was also a ploy, another deliberate affront to bourgeois sensibility which demanded art with meaning.

Source E

Advertisement for Glenda Dicker/sun's *African American Theater* (Wiley-Blackwell, 2008; reprinted with permission from John Wiley & Sons, Inc.)

(01) Written in a clear, accessible, storytelling style, *African American Theater* will shine a bright new light on the culture which has historically nurtured and inspired Black Theater. Functioning as an interactive guide for students and teachers, *African American Theater* takes the reader on a journey to discover how social realities
(05) impacted the plays dramatists wrote and produced.

The journey begins in 1850 when most African people were enslaved in America. Along the way, cultural milestones such as Reconstruction, the Harlem Renaissance and the Black Freedom Movement are explored. The journey concludes with a discussion of how the past still plays out in the works of contemporary play-
(10) wrights like August Wilson and Suzan-Lori Parks.

African American Theater moves unsung heroes like Robert Abbott and Jo Ann Gibson Robinson to the foreground, but does not neglect the race giants. For actors looking for material to perform, the book offers exercises to create new monologues and scenes. Rich with myths, history and first person accounts by ordinary (15) people telling their extraordinary stories, *African American Theater* will entertain while it educates.

Source F
Quotation from Pablo Picasso, artist

(01) What do you think an artist is? An imbecile who only has eyes if he is a painter, or ears if he's a musician, or a lyre at every level of his heart if he's a poet, or even, if he's a boxer, just his muscle? On the contrary, he is at the same time a political being, constantly alive to heart-rending, fiery or happy events to which (05) he responds in every way . . . painting is not done to decorate apartments. It's an instrument of war for attack and defense against the enemy.

Answer guide for synthesis essay 2: Art

These artists, editors, critics, and art-history professors have weighed in on an important topic: the purpose of art. Should it change the world or just allow the artist to express him- or herself? About a million variations of this essay are possible, but it seems likely that your thesis falls roughly into one of these categories:

- **Art is self-expression.** All those unique feelings and ideas inside need an outlet, and art provides one.

- **Art changes the world.** This definition sees art as a political act.

- **Art is beauty.** It doesn't have to be pretty, but if it's art, how it looks or sounds or reads matters.

- **Art has several purposes.** In that case, your thesis should state that art can't be pigeon-holed. "Some art is political, and other art is personal" or a similar statement works for this definition.

Because I don't know what you think, I can't comment on which of these sources you should have used, and in what way, to support your stance on the purpose of art. Instead, I'll comment on each source and what you might extract from it.

- Source A may support either the "Art is self-expression," the "Art is beauty," or even a political view of art. The photo of the hands of an elderly woman peeling oranges is beautiful, though it doesn't fit the usual Hollywood airbrushed vision of good looks. Notice the work-roughened hands and the two bowls, one containing (literally) the fruits of this woman's labor — the oranges. This photo dignifies work done with one's hands — something that society often sees as less valuable than work performed at a desk.

- Source B comes from painter Piet Mondrian, who created beautiful, multicolored grids with seemingly random squares of color. Mondrian stresses both esthetics — the creation of beauty through art — and self-expression. Your essay, if it's in the "art is beauty" camp, would benefit from a few words from Mondrian. You can include this quotation, for example: "One [inclination of an artist] aims at the direct creation of universal beauty" (line 3). If you're pulling for the self-expression team, you can quote Mondrian's view that another inclination of the artist is the "esthetic expression of one-self . . . that which one thinks and experiences" (lines 4–5).

> **TIP**
>
> Mondrian's comments work for two views of art, but if you choose to quote him, be sure that you don't misrepresent his comments. He doesn't divide artists into two separate camps but instead speaks of two "inclinations" that coexist. Yes, you can see the "direct creation of universal beauty" (line 3) in art, but Mondrian also says that "at the same time, an attempt to express that which these forms, colors, and relations arouse in us" (lines 8–9) — in other words, one's reaction to art — is present.

■ Source C is short, but it packs a punch. If your thesis is that all art is political, you find support here because Yates says that artists respond to the time in which they live, even if they do so by suppressing all political content. So, too, can you find support if you take the position that suppressed political content is *not* political at all, just a response to a social climate. Further support for the nonpolitical stance is the first painter Yates refers to — Jackson Pollock — who picked up the title "Jack the Dripper" because of his large-scale paintings that resemble a tangle of paint drips. I'm not putting these paintings down; they're quite beautiful. However, because they don't depict anything recognizable, you can easily include them in your essay as an example of totally nonpolitical art. Yates's references to the feminist and gay-rights movements support an "art-politics" connection.

■ Source D comes from an essay explaining modernism, an artistic movement. The author contrasts the early years of "progressive modernism" (line 1), which addressed "political and social issues" ignored by a "complacent middle class" (lines 1–3) with a later stage of modernism, which advocated "art is for art's sake" — freedom from what the author calls "the tyranny of meaning and purpose" (lines 39–40). How can you use this source? If your stance is "art for art's sake," you can refer to the progressive modernists' ideas about this subject (citing the essay, of course). You can, in a different essay, describe the earlier political or social stance of modernists. However, take care not to misrepresent the source. Witcombe's essay explains an evolution of ideas. If you use this source, acknowledge both viewpoints and then focus on their relationship to your own position.

■ Source E, the advertisement for a fine book about African American theater, reveals the intersection of art and a cause — in this case, social justice. The ad stresses that the plays reflect the "culture which has historically nurtured and inspired Black Theater" (lines 2–3). Like art historian Don Yates, whose comments are found in Source C, this advertisement stresses that art is a product of a particular moment in time and of a specific culture. The ad states that the text discusses "how social realities impacted the plays" (lines 4–5). Once you're in the territory of "social reality," you're only a tiny step away from social protest or commentary.

■ Picasso, the towering figure of 20th-century art, sees art as "an instrument of war for attack and defense against the enemy." He doesn't offer much material for the "art as personal expression" or "art as beauty" camps. His words powerfully support the art-politics link.

How can you organize all this information? Begin with an introduction defining your own ideas about art. Pick and choose quotations from these sources that back up your position. Divide the body paragraphs of your essay by ideas. For example, suppose you have an essay asserting that art is political, even if it is beautiful and appears to arise only from a need to express oneself. You might have a paragraph about overtly political art (Source F or Source E) and one about seemingly nonpolitical art (Source B) that nevertheless changes the way the viewer looks at reality. Then you have a paragraph about how a change in one's ideas always results in some sort of political effect. Many other variations are possible, of course. Just be sure that you don't simply summarize each source. You have to employ the ideas to bolster your case.

This point is so important that I don't mind repeating myself. You *must* cite ideas taken from these sources, even if you changed the wording, a process known as paraphrasing. Unless it's your own brainchild, you need to acknowledge the source.

V

Practice Exams and Answer Sheets

17

Practice Exam 1

No matter how much you read beforehand or how many practice sections you do, you can't match the experience of taking a complete exam, especially one taken under simulated test conditions. When you take the exam in this chapter, you experience the time constraints of the actual exam, gauge your speed on the multiple-choice and essay sections, and — after you check your answers in Chapter 18 — pinpoint areas for improvement.

BEFORE YOU TAKE THE PRACTICE EXAM

The point of this chapter is to mimic the actual exam. Here's how you can best do so:

1. **Isolate yourself.** Turn off your computer, cellphone, television, radio, MP3 player, and anything else that makes noise. Inform whoever is likely to knock on the door that you are busy and that interruptions are *not* okay.

2. **Put a clock or a timer where you can easily see it; then set the timer for one hour, the time allotted for the multiple-choice section.** If you don't have a timer, write the start and end time on a piece of paper and tape the paper to the side of the desk. When you're battling a tough question, you don't want to wonder how much time is left.

3. **Tear out the multiple-choice answer sheet at the back of this book and use it as you complete the multiple-choice portion of the test.** Even though you'll be scoring the essay by hand, grab a number 2 pencil and indicate your answers by darkening the ovals that correspond to your choices. The idea is to mimic exam conditions so you get comfortable doing what you'll do on test day. If you finish before the hour is up, recheck any questions that challenged you.

4. **Give yourself a fifteen-minute break after the multiple-choice section.** Get up and stretch. Sip some water or visit the bathroom. But don't even *think* about looking at the essay section, and don't check or change any answers from the multiple-choice section.

5. **When your break is over, turn to the essay portion of the test. Use your own loose-leaf paper (allot 3–4 pages for each essay).**

6. **Reset the timer (or check the clock and note a fifteen-minute interval) and turn to the essay questions; read and annotate as much as you wish.** Don't write anything on your loose-leaf paper during this reading period.

7. **When the reading period is finished, set the timer for two hours, the time allotted for you to write your three essays, and start writing.**

8. **Evaluate how well you did.** Check your answers (you can find the answers and explanations in Chapter 18) and then convert your raw score into an AP grade using the formula at the end of that chapter.

   Don't just consider the final score. Take a close look at the answers you got wrong. See if you can figure out what types of questions trip you up (inference, vocabulary, tone, or terminology, for example). Then go back to Part II for a review of the basics or to Part III for extra practice in your problem areas. If timing was an issue, read Chapter 1 for tips on streamlining your test approach.

> | **TIP**
>
> When you're actually taking the AP, you have to do the whole test in one morning or afternoon — a real challenge to your powers of concentration. Resist the temptation to chop the practice test into smaller units — multiple-choice after school one day and essays the next night, for example. Simulated tests work best when they actually resemble the real exam. Resign yourself to 3:15 hours of testing (plus one fifteen-minute break).

THE AP ENGLISH LANGUAGE AND COMPOSITION TEST

This test consists of two parts:

> **Section One:** Multiple choice — one hour
>
> **Section Two:** Essays — fifteen-minute reading period plus two hours for writing

At any time you may write in the margins of the exam, annotating as you wish. However, nothing but the scoring grid and the essay answer sheets will be graded. Answers or remarks written next to the question receive no credit. During the fifteen-minute reading period, you may not write on the answer sheet.

SECTION ONE: MULTIPLE CHOICE

Time: 60 minutes

This section contains five selections, each of which is followed by a set of questions. Section One has a total of 53 questions and counts as 45 percent of the exam score.

You have one hour for this section. Work carefully and quickly. Not all students will finish the multiple-choice questions. Blank answers and wrong answers receive no credit.

Do not turn to another section if you finish early.

For each multiple-choice question, choose the best answer. Fill in the corresponding oval, being sure to darken the entire oval. Do not select more than one answer. If you erase an answer, take care to do so completely. Questions with more than one answer are automatically scored as wrong.

Questions 1–10 are based on the following passage, which is an excerpt from Franklin Roosevelt's First Inaugural Address. Roosevelt took office during the Great Depression, when banks failed and millions were unemployed.

(01)   This is a day of national consecration, and I am certain that on this day my fellow Americans expect that on my induction into the Presidency I will address them with a candor and a decision which the present situation of our people impels. This is pre-eminently the time to speak the truth, the whole truth, frankly and boldly. Nor need we
(05) shrink from honestly facing conditions in our country today. This great Nation will endure as it has endured, will revive and will prosper. So, first of all, let me assert my firm belief that the only thing we have to fear is fear itself — nameless, unreasoning, unjustified terror which paralyzes needed efforts to convert retreat into advance. In every dark hour of our national life a leadership of frankness and of vigor has met with that understanding
(10) and support of the people themselves which is essential to victory. And I am convinced that you will again give that support to leadership in these critical days.

    In such a spirit on my part and on yours we face our common difficulties. They concern, thank God, only material things. Values have shrunk to fantastic levels; taxes have risen; our ability to pay has fallen; government of all kinds is faced by serious curtailment
(15) of income; the means of exchange are frozen in the currents of trade; the withered leaves of industrial enterprise lie on every side; farmers find no markets for their produce; and the savings of many years in thousands of families are gone. More important, a host of unemployed citizens face the grim problem of existence, and an equally great number toil with little return. Only a foolish optimist can deny the dark realities of the moment.

(20)   And yet our distress comes from no failure of substance. We are stricken by no plague of locusts. Compared with the perils which our forefathers conquered because they believed and were not afraid, we have still much to be thankful for. Nature still offers her bounty and human efforts have multiplied it. Plenty is at our doorstep, but a generous use of it languishes in the very sight of the supply. Primarily this is because the rulers of
(25) the exchange of mankind's goods have failed, through their own stubbornness and their own incompetence, have admitted their failure and have abdicated. Practices of the unscrupulous money changers stand indicted in the court of public opinion, rejected by the hearts and minds of men.

(30) True they have tried, but their efforts have been cast in the pattern of an outworn tradition. Faced by failure of credit they have proposed only the lending of more money. Stripped of the lure of profit by which to induce our people to follow their false leadership, they have resorted to exhortations, pleading tearfully for restored confidence. They only know the rules of a generation of self-seekers. They have no vision, and when there is no vision the people perish.

(35) Yes, the money changers have fled from their high seats in the temple of our civilization. We may now restore that temple to the ancient truths. The measure of that restoration lies in the extent to which we apply social values more noble than mere monetary profit.

Happiness lies not in the mere possession of money; it lies in the joy of achievement, in (40) the thrill of creative effort. The joy, the moral stimulation of work no longer must be forgotten in the mad chase of evanescent profits. These dark days, my friends, will be worth all they cost us if they teach us that our true destiny is not to be ministered unto but to minister to ourselves — to our fellow men.

1. All of these techniques are present in paragraph one (lines 1–11) EXCEPT

    (A) allusion

    (B) repetition

    (C) alliteration

    (D) direct address

    (E) simile

2. What is the dominant rhetorical technique in paragraph two (lines 12–19)?

    (A) general statement followed by specifics

    (B) specifics leading to a generalization

    (C) anecdotal evidence

    (D) appeal to moral principles

    (E) allusion to historical events and documents

3. Which is the most likely meaning of "withered leaves" (line 15)?

    (A) declining profits

    (B) low tax revenue

    (C) ruined or abandoned factories

    (D) low agricultural prices

    (E) outmoded financial models

4. What is the purpose of line 19 ("Only a foolish optimist can deny the dark realities of the moment")?

    (A) to urge the audience to have hope

    (B) to imply that the speaker is realistic

    (C) to refute others' views of the situation

    (D) to explain the speaker's attitude towards life

    (E) to express pessimism

5. The statement that "our distress comes from no failure of substance" (line 20) expresses the same meaning as which of the following?

   (A) "This great Nation will endure as it has endured" (lines 5–6)

   (B) "the only thing we have to fear is fear itself" (line 7)

   (C) "the savings of many years in thousands of families are gone" (line 17)

   (D) "Plenty is at our doorstep" (line 23)

   (E) "human efforts have multiplied it" (line 23)

6. A shift in the third paragraph occurs

   (A) after the first sentence — "And yet our distress comes from no failure of substance" (line 20)

   (B) after the third sentence — "Nature still offers . . . multiplied it" (lines 22–23)

   (C) within the fourth sentence — "Plenty is . . . sight of the supply" (lines 23–24)

   (D) after the fourth sentence — "Plenty is . . . sight of the supply" (lines 23–24)

   (E) after the fifth sentence — "Primarily this is because . . . have abdicated" (lines 24–26)

7. "True they have tried" (line 29) is an example of a rhetorical technique known as

   (A) transition

   (B) antithesis

   (C) paradox

   (D) concession and reply

   (E) analogy

8. The subject of "have admitted" (line 26) is

   (A) rulers (line 24)

   (B) exchange (line 25)

   (C) mankind's (line 25)

   (D) goods (line 25)

   (E) incompetence (line 26)

9. The tone of this excerpt may be described as

   (A) disillusioned and regretful

   (B) antagonistic and partisan

   (C) critical and pessimistic

   (D) pragmatic and informational

   (E) realistic and inspirational

10. The change from passive to active voice in lines 42–43 ("not to be ministered unto but to minister . . .") implies that

(A) Americans must take care of themselves before taking care of others

(B) Americans should assume responsibility for their communities

(C) the role of government is to fulfill all our needs

(D) government is not as effective as it should be

(E) the crisis will ultimately enrich Americans

Questions 11–22 are based on the passage below. Read it carefully and answer the questions that follow.

---

(01)   To account for, and excuse the tyranny of man, many ingenious arguments have been brought forward to prove, that the two sexes, in the acquirement of virtue, ought to aim at attaining a very different character: or, to speak explicitly, women are not allowed to have sufficient strength of mind to acquire what really deserves the name of virtue. Yet it
(05)   should seem, allowing them to have souls, that there is but one way appointed by providence to lead MANKIND to either virtue or happiness.

If then women are not a swarm of ephemeron triflers, why should they be kept in ignorance under the specious name of innocence? Men complain, and with reason, of the follies and caprices of our sex, when they do not keenly satirize our headstrong passions
(10)   and groveling vices. Behold, I should answer, the natural effect of ignorance! The mind will ever be unstable that has only prejudices to rest on, and the current will run with destructive fury when there are no barriers to break its force. Women are told from their infancy, and taught by the example of their mothers, that a little knowledge of human weakness, justly termed cunning, softness of temper, OUTWARD obedience, and a scru-
(15)   pulous attention to a puerile kind of propriety, will obtain for them the protection of man; and should they be beautiful, every thing else is needless, for at least twenty years of their lives.

Thus Milton[1] describes our first frail mother; though when he tells us that women are formed for softness and sweet attractive grace, I cannot comprehend his meaning, unless
(20)   . . . he meant to deprive us of souls, and insinuate that we were beings only designed by sweet attractive grace, and docile blind obedience, to gratify the senses of man when he can no longer soar on the wing of contemplation.

How grossly do they insult us, who thus advise us only to render ourselves gentle, domestic brutes! For instance, the winning softness, so warmly, and frequently recommended, that
(25)   governs by obeying. What childish expressions, and how insignificant is the being — can it be an immortal one? Who will condescend to govern by such sinister methods! "Certainly," says Lord Bacon[2], "man is of kin to the beasts by his body: and if he be not of kin to God by his spirit, he is a base and ignoble creature!" Men, indeed, appear to me to act in a very unphilosophical manner, when they try to secure the good conduct of women by attempting to keep them
(30)   always in a state of childhood. Rousseau[3] was more consistent when he wished to stop the progress of reason in both sexes; for if men eat of the tree of knowledge, women will come in for a taste: but, from the imperfect cultivation which their understandings now receive, they only attain a knowledge of evil.

Children, I grant, should be innocent; but when the epithet is applied to men, or wom-
(35)   en, it is but a civil term for weakness. For if it be allowed that women were destined by Providence to acquire human virtues, and by the exercise of their understandings, that stability of character which is the firmest ground to rest our future hopes upon, they must be permitted to turn to the fountain of light, and not forced to shape their course

by the twinkling of a mere satellite. Milton, I grant, was of a very different opinion; for he
(40) only bends to the indefensible right of beauty, though it would be difficult to render two
passages, which I now mean to contrast, consistent: but into similar inconsistencies are
great men often led by their senses:

      To whom thus Eve[4] with perfect beauty adorned:
      My author and disposer, what thou bidst
(45)   Unargued I obey; so God ordains;
      God is thy law, thou mine; to know no more
      Is woman's happiest knowledge and her praise.

These are exactly the arguments that I have used to children; but I have added, "Your
reason is now gaining strength, and, till it arrives at some degree of maturity, you must
(50) look up to me for advice: then you ought to THINK, and only rely on God."

1. English poet. 2. English essayist. 3. French philosopher. 4. In the Bible, the first woman.

11. The passage may be characterized primarily as
(A) narrative
(B) exposition
(C) argument
(D) description
(E) definition

12. What is the function of the colon in the first sentence of paragraph one (line 3)?
(A) to alert the reader that a list follows
(B) to precede a direct address to the reader
(C) to introduce an unrelated idea
(D) to define more specifically a general idea stated earlier
(E) to explain objections to an idea stated earlier

13. What purpose does the last sentence of paragraph one ("Yet it should seem . . . virtue or happiness" — lines 4–6) serve?
(A) to summarize a popular view of virtue in women
(B) to refute a popular view of virtue in women
(C) to introduce the ideas in the next paragraph
(D) to tease the reader by offering a vague but intriguing statement
(E) to define virtue and happiness

14. In paragraph two (lines 7–17), which of the following rhetorical devices is most prominent?
(A) allusions to historical or religious texts
(B) antithesis
(C) listing of factual information
(D) understatement
(E) abstract generalization

15. The most likely answer to the question in the first sentence of paragraph two ("If then women . . . name of innocence?" — lines 7–8) is

   (A) "Men complain, and with reason" (line 8)

   (B) "they do not keenly satirize our headstrong passions" (line 9)

   (C) "Behold, I should answer, the natural effect of ignorance!" (line 10)

   (D) "women are formed for softness and sweet attractive grace" (lines 18–19)

   (E) no answer appears

16. The capitalization of "OUTWARD" (line 14) implies that the author

   (A) doesn't agree that women are taught to create a facade

   (B) believes that women disobey in unnoticeable ways

   (C) wishes to emphasize the importance of concealing one's feelings and ideas

   (D) considers obedience an essential female trait

   (E) prefers that women rebel against male authority figures

17. "Thus" (line 18) refers to which of the following lines?

   (A) "Behold, I should answer, the natural effect of ignorance" (line 10)

   (B) "The mind will ever be unstable that has only prejudices to rest on" (lines 10–11)

   (C) "cunning, softness of temper, OUTWARD obedience, and a scrupulous attention to a puerile kind of propriety" (lines 14–15)

   (D) "women are formed for softness and sweet attractive grace" (lines 18–19)

   (E) "he meant to deprive us of souls" (line 20)

18. All of the following techniques may be found in paragraph four (lines 23–33) EXCEPT

   (A) symbolism

   (B) allusion

   (C) example

   (D) metaphor

   (E) rhetorical question

19. Which of these assumptions does the author make in this passage?

   I. Women have souls.

   II. Women are supposed to be virtuous.

   III. Innocence is always a positive trait.

   (A) I only

   (B) II only

   (C) I and II

   (D) I and III

   (E) all of the above

20. The metaphor "fountain of light" (line 38) is extended by which of these phrases?

    (A) "firmest ground" (line 37)

    (B) "mere satellite" (line 39)

    (C) "indefensible right of beauty" (line 40)

    (D) "with perfect beauty adorned" (line 43)

    (E) "woman's happiest knowledge" (line 47)

21. What is the main idea of the passage?

    (A) God has a plan for both men and women.

    (B) Traditional gender roles are wrong.

    (C) Men should not focus on women's appearance.

    (D) Ignorance leads to bad behavior.

    (E) Women should be educated.

22. The author's tone may be described as

    (A) emphatic and ironic

    (B) gently mocking and occasionally sarcastic

    (C) informal and conversational

    (D) passionate and argumentative

    (E) businesslike and formal

Questions 23–30 are based on this excerpt from a memoir about growing up in the 1950s. Read it carefully and then answer the questions that follow.

---

(01) In first grade, no matter where I sit, I can see the board. In second grade things are fuzzier, and I start to squint, but I can still make out the words if I try. I learn to memorize the letters on the eyechart during our annual trip to the nurse's office, where we stand in a line to be weighed and measured, checked for ringworm and nearsightedness. As I wait
(05) (my last name begins with S, so it's always a while), I hear the letters and have no trouble repeating them when it's my turn.

  I know I'm going to need glasses someday, and I desperately don't want them. I've somehow absorbed that "men don't make passes at girls who wear glasses." Nobody tells me how to feel about men with glasses and I'm not into boys yet anyway, but somehow
(10) glasses seem to close off a part of my future in a way I can't explain.

  By third grade I'm in seriously blurred territory, and by fourth I'm having whole conversations with people I can't recognize because they're in a car, perhaps, or across the street. In fourth grade my teacher, Mrs. Ferris, sends a note home about the trouble I'm having seeing the board. It's an arrest warrant, one that I must deliver myself, and my
(15) mother takes me to the eye doctor where, for the first time, I can't memorize the 20-20 line because there's no one ahead of me. He writes out a prescription, which I take as my sentence, head bowed to the inevitable.

  Our usual shopping areas have lots of eyeglass stores, but after some discussion that I am not a party to, we drive to the city and walk into a couple of dingy stores where my
(20) parents ask a lot of questions about prices. I am ready to cry anyway; I don't want the glasses and I don't want to stand around listening to the bargaining, which to me seems

vaguely impolite and totally embarrassing. Finally, in the third or fourth store, the question of cost is settled and all I have to do is to pick out frames. Butterflies are in style (it's the Fifties), and I choose green plastic.

(25)   I formulate a plan, which I actually stick to for the first year or so. I'll put the glasses on only to see the board and otherwise leave them in their case. Because we sit in rows facing forward in my school, a minimum of people will see me with my glasses on. I'll whip them off as soon as I decode what's on the board and they'll never see the light of day in the playground. Outside of school, I'll just sit closer to the television or squint. I won't use
(30)   them when company comes. I know what everyone looks like, and I dread the "don't you look adorable" or "four eyes" comments I'm bound to receive.

Leaving the glasses store, I'm astonished when my father turns away from the car. Suddenly all the signs are in Chinese. Even with my eyes I can tell. We go into a tiny shop filled with exotic trinkets. My father tells me to pick out a doll. I gape for a second. It's
(35)   not my birthday or a special occasion. Could he really know how I feel? My mother looks surprised but nods her head. I can have a doll.

I choose a Chinese dancer in a long red dress, her black hair elaborately styled and her back arched. She comes with a little wooden stand. All the way home I examine her, fingering the silk of her dress, touching the painted porcelain face. She, I note, does not
(40)   wear glasses. In the house again, I put her on my shelf. Every year thereafter I go back to the eye doctor and get stronger glasses, and then just in time for college, contact lenses. I don't remember throwing out the Chinese doll, but at some point I must have, because she wasn't there when my brother and I cleared out the house after my mother's stroke. Everything else in my room was just as I left it when I announced that I was moving to an
(45)   apartment the next day — my makeup, my curlers, my schoolbooks. I tried to pack some of those things when I left home for good, but the atmosphere was soaked with anger and tears. ("You're not stripping that room and leaving us with bare walls for everyone to see," my mother had hissed, ripping the little mirror I thought was mine out of my hand as I packed.) Also everything I wanted to move had to be carried on two subways and a bus,
(50)   and no one would help me because I wasn't supposed to go. So I didn't take much. Not even the only present my father ever gave me, truly from himself.

23. The principal organizing device of paragraphs one through three (lines 1–17) is

(A) chronological order

(B) anecdote

(C) examples

(D) flash forward

(E) flashback

24. The underlying theme of "[n]obody tells me how to feel about men with glasses" (lines 8–9) is

(A) a sign that the narrator has an open mind

(B) a statement about men's attractiveness

(C) a protest against a double standard of beauty

(D) a declaration of freedom

(E) an indication that the narrator is too young to consider people's appearance

25. Which of the following best expresses the meaning of "my sentence" (lines 16–17)?
    (A) a strong statement
    (B) order from the doctor
    (C) a period of time
    (D) a punishment
    (E) fate

26. Overall, the narrator's relationship with her parents may be characterized as
    (A) distant
    (B) warm
    (C) confused
    (D) neutral
    (E) respectful

27. In the first sentence of paragraph five, the subordinate clause ("which I actually stick to for the first year or so" — line 25) marks a shift from
    (A) past to present
    (B) one moment in the past to an earlier period
    (C) one moment in the past to a generalized, later period
    (D) present to future
    (E) present to past

28. Why is the mother's comment (line 47) in parentheses?
    (A) to make the comment more emphatic
    (B) to illustrate the tension of the argument
    (C) to dramatize the comment
    (D) to interrupt the story of the daughter's move away from home
    (E) to distinguish the mother from the daughter

29. In lines 50–51 ("So I didn't take much. Not even the only present my father ever gave me, truly from himself"), how do style and content relate to each other?
    (A) The tone is nostalgic, and the narrator regrets leaving her home.
    (B) The diction is informal, revealing the inner warmth of the narrator's relationship with her parents.
    (C) The diction is formal, echoing the narrator's view that her move away from home was an important event.
    (D) The movement from general to specific reflects the narrator's certainty about her future.
    (E) The sentence fragments mirror the fragmented family.

30. In the context of this passage, the phrase "the only present my father ever gave me, truly from himself" (line 51) serves to

(A) emphasize the doll's value

(B) provide context for the purchase of the doll

(C) exaggerate the importance of the doll

(D) minimize the importance of the doll

(E) reveal the extent of the parent-child disagreement

Questions 31–40 are based on this excerpt from a biography of George Gordon, Lord Byron, a poet.

---

(01) "I was sent, at five years old, or earlier, to a school kept by a Mr. Bowers, who was called 'Bodsy Bowers,' by reason of his dapperness. It was a school for both sexes. I learned little there except to repeat by rote the first lesson of monosyllables ('God made man' — 'Let us love him'), by hearing it often repeated, without acquiring a letter. Whenever proof was

(05) made of my progress, at home, I repeated these words with the most rapid fluency; but on turning over a new leaf, I continued to repeat them, so that the narrow boundaries of my first year's accomplishments were detected, my ears boxed, (which they did not deserve, seeing it was by ear only that I had acquired my letters,) and my intellects consigned to a new preceptor. He was a very devout, clever, little clergyman, named Ross, afterwards

(10) minister of one of the kirks.[1] (East, I think). Under him I made astonishing progress; and I recollect to this day his mild manners and good-natured pains-taking. The moment I could read, my grand passion was history, and, why I know not, but I was particularly taken with the battle near the Lake Regillus in the Roman History, put into my hands the first. Four years ago, when standing on the heights of Tusculum, and looking down upon

(15) the little round lake that was once Regillus, and which dots the immense expanse below, I remembered my young enthusiasm and my old instructor. Afterwards I had a very serious, saturnine, but kind young man, named Paterson, for a tutor. He was the son of my shoemaker, but a good scholar, as is common with the Scotch. He was a rigid Presbyterian also. With him I began Latin in 'Ruddiman's Grammar,' and continued till I went to the

(20) 'Grammar School . . . where I threaded all the classes to the fourth, when I was recalled to England (where I had been hatched) by the demise of my uncle. I acquired this handwriting, which I can hardly read myself, under the fair copies of Mr. Duncan of the same city: I don't think he would plume himself much upon my progress. However, I wrote much better then than I have ever done since. Haste and agitation of one kind or another have

(25) quite spoilt as pretty a scrawl as ever scratched over a frank. The grammar-school might consist of a hundred and fifty of all ages under age. It was divided into five classes, taught by four masters, the chief teaching the fourth and fifth himself. As in England, the fifth, sixth forms, and monitors, are heard by the head masters."

Of his class-fellows at the grammar-school there are many, of course, still alive, by

(30) whom he is well remembered; and the general impression they retain of him is, that he was a lively, warm-hearted, and high-spirited boy — passionate and resentful, but affectionate and companionable with his schoolfellows — to a remarkable degree venturous and fearless, and (as one of them significantly expressed it) "always more ready to give a blow than take one." Among many anecdotes illustrative of this spirit, it is related that

(35) once, in returning home from school, he fell in with a boy who had on some former occasion insulted him, but had then got off unpunished — little Byron, however, at the time, promising to "pay him off" whenever they should meet again. Accordingly, on this second encounter, though there were some other boys to take his opponent's part, he succeeded

in inflicting upon him a hearty beating. On his return home, breathless, the servant
(40) enquired what he had been about, and was answered by him with a mixture of rage and
humour, that he had been paying a debt, by beating a boy according to promise; for that
he was a Byron, and would never belie his motto, "Trust Byron."

He was, indeed, much more anxious to distinguish himself among his school-fellows
by prowess in all sports and exercises, than by advancement in learning. Though quick,
(45) when he could be persuaded to attend, or had any study that pleased him, he was in general very low in the class, nor seemed ambitious of being promoted any higher. It is the
custom, it seems, in this seminary, to invert, now and then, the order of the class, so as to
make the highest and lowest boys change places — with a view, no doubt, of piquing the
ambition of both. On these occasions, and only these, Byron was sometimes at the head,
(50) and the master, to banter him, would say, "Now, George, man, let me see how soon you'll
be at the foot again."

1. A church.

31. The author probably included the introductory quotation (lines 1–28) in order to

(A) validate the author's presentation of Byron

(B) contrast his own view of Byron with that of Byron himself

(C) balance the impartiality of the author's comments on Byron

(D) introduce Byron's voice into the passage

(E) set the scene for his comments on Byron

32. Byron's character is revealed by all of the following EXCEPT

(A) comments by friends

(B) physical description

(C) actions

(D) Byron's own words

(E) setting

33. In the context of this passage, Byron's comment, "seeing it was by ear only that I had
acquired my letters" (line 8) means that Byron

(A) learned to read primarily by listening

(B) memorized letters by repeating them aloud

(C) was better at speaking than writing

(D) preferred to speak rather than to remain silent

(E) was not a good student

34. What does Byron mean when he writes that the battle near Lake Regillus (line 13) was
"put into my hands the first" (lines 13–14)?

(A) The battle near Lake Regillus was the first one Byron understood.

(B) The battle was the first to capture Byron's attention.

(C) The area near Lake Regillus was the site of the first battle of a war.

(D) The area near Lake Regillus was the site of the most important battle known to Byron.

(E) Byron's first reading assignment concerned the battle near Lake Regillus.

35. Byron's tone in lines 1–28 may be characterized as
     (A) conciliatory and regretful
     (B) sarcastic and ironic
     (C) thoughtful and nostalgic
     (D) didactic and condescending
     (E) humorous and self-deprecating

36. The reference to "standing on the heights of Tusculum" (line 14) serves primarily to
     (A) illustrate that time changes one's perspective
     (B) show that Byron has aged
     (C) reveal information about Byron's later life
     (D) promote the benefits of travel
     (E) demonstrate that one can never revisit a place without regret

37. What is the implication in Byron's comments about Paterson (lines 17–20)?
     (A) Unkind tutors are less effective.
     (B) Most people in Scotland are scholars.
     (C) Byron was motivated to serious study by a good tutor.
     (D) Byron believes that scholars seldom come from working-class families.
     (E) Byron would have been a better scholar had he studied longer with Paterson.

38. The dominant rhetorical strategy in paragraph two (lines 29–42) is
     (A) example
     (B) comparison and contrast
     (C) narration
     (D) argument
     (E) cause and effect

39. The author ends paragraph two (lines 29–42) with the Byron motto in order to
     (A) set up a transitional idea for paragraph three
     (B) impress the reader with a strong statement about Byron
     (C) emphasize that Byron keeps his promises
     (D) show that Byron is reliable and loyal
     (E) leave the reader with a positive impression of Byron

40. The anecdote about the exchange between the "highest and lowest boys" (line 48) serves to
     (A) underscore the power of the schoolmaster
     (B) emphasize Byron's deficiencies as a student
     (C) criticize the school's custom of ranking students
     (D) reveal Byron's relationship with the schoolmaster
     (E) explain the reasons why Byron was not a good student

Questions 41–53 are based on this passage, which is adapted from A History of Psychiatry, by Edward Shorter (Wiley, 1997; reprinted with permission of John Wiley & Sons, Inc.). Read the passage and answer the questions that follow it.

(01)   It was not the notion that madness was curable that changed at the end of the eighteenth century, for a kind of therapeutic self-confidence ran throughout traditional medicine with its bleeding, purging, and giving of emetics — all designed to cure. Rather, it was the notion that institutions themselves could be made curative, that confinement
(05) in them, rather than merely removing a nuisance from the vexed family or the aggrieved village elders, could make the patient better. This insight broke in an almost revolutionary way upon the scene.

Yet the eighteenth-century Enlightenment did flatter itself that through the use of reason it could much improve on the therapeutics of previous generations. The notion
(10) of curability was good Enlightenment thinking, part of a larger agenda of improvement through social, political, or medical engineering. If Revolutionary France could be given a constitution and the laws of market economics laid bare, so could illness be systematically treated through right-thinking therapeutic philosophies. Radiating from such centers as Edinburgh, a new therapeutic optimism engulfed the whole world of medicine in the
(15) second half of the eighteenth century, an optimism that psychiatry shared. A new generation of asylum physicians grew up filled with confidence in their ability to heal.

So diffuse was the spirit of change that it is difficult to identify a single individual as responsible for the new-style asylum. Germany's Johann Reil spoke of an international movement to help the plight of the insane. "The physicians of England, France, and Ger-
(20) many," he said in 1803, "are all stepping forward at once to improve the lot of the insane. . . . The cosmopolite sees joyously the untiring efforts of mankind to ensure the welfare of one's neighbor. The horrors of the prisons and the jails are over. . . . A bold race of men dares to take on this gigantic idea, an idea that dizzies the normal burgher, of wiping from the face of the earth one of the most devastating pestilences."[1] Just imagine: Nothing
(25) less than eradicating insanity was what they had in mind, couched in the most delicious of Enlightenment Rhetoric.

It is possible, however, to identify a handful of asylum physicians whose writings became beacons for the rest of the psychiatric world. In view of the great controversy surrounding this subject, one notes that the reform movement in psychiatry was truly inter-
(30) national. There are scholars who associate the rise of psychiatry with various influences, some saying that capitalism was responsible, others the central state.[2] Yet the new therapeutic optimism of psychiatry originated in a wide variety of social and economic settings, making it unlikely that any single social force such as capitalism offers the answer. Enlightenment-style scientific thinking on the other hand spanned continents: Journals
(35) circulated widely, important books were soon translated, and individual physicians undertook trips abroad to learn what was happening elsewhere. It was this kind of scientific thinking, largely independent of social setting, that seems to have launched psychiatry.

1. Johann Christian Reil, Thoughts on Psychology as a Cure for Insanity (Halle, 1803; reprint Amsterdam: Bonser, 1968), pp. 7, 14.

2. Andrew Scull lambasted capitalism strongly in his influential Museums of Madness: The Social Organization of Insanity in Nineteenth-Century England (London: Allen Lane, 1979), pp. 30–31, then returned to gnaw in passing at this bone again in The Most Solitary of Afflictions: Madness and Society in Britain, 1700–1900 (New Haven, Yale U. Press, 1993), a book that is essentially an extensively revised second edition of Museums, see pp. 106, 125.

41. What is the effect of the negative statement ("It was not . . ." — line 1) at the beginning of this passage?

    (A) It sets the stage for a critique of psychiatry in the eighteenth century.

    (B) It introduces a statement about what changed at the end of the eighteenth century.

    (C) It sets up a comparison with a later era.

    (D) It implies a criticism of psychiatry in an earlier era.

    (E) It catches the reader's attention more than a positive statement would.

42. The organizing principle of this passage may be described as

    (A) comparison and contrast

    (B) chronological order

    (C) spatial order

    (D) cause and effect

    (E) deductive argument

43. What is the function of paragraph two: "Yet the eighteenth-century Enlightenment . . . ability to heal" (lines 8–16) ?

    (A) It refutes the statements in paragraph one.

    (B) It supports the statements in paragraph one.

    (C) It qualifies the statements in paragraph one.

    (D) It continues the discussion begun in paragraph one.

    (E) It supplies examples of the situation described in paragraph one.

44. According to the passage, which phrase is the equivalent of "the therapeutics of previous generations" (line 9)?

    (A) "the notion that madness was curable" (line 1)

    (B) "bleeding, purging, and giving of emetics" (line 3)

    (C) "institutions themselves could be made curable" (line 4)

    (D) "a nuisance from the vexed family" (line 5)

    (E) "the use of reason" (lins 8–9)

45. Which statement is closest in meaning to "new therapeutic optimism" (line 14)?

    (A) "It was not the notion that madness was curable" (line 1)

    (B) "This insight broke in an almost revolutionary way upon the scene" (lines 6–7)

    (C) "a larger agenda of improvement through social, political, or medical engineering" (lines 10–11)

    (D) "an optimism that psychiatry shared" (line 15)

    (E) "confidence in their ability to heal" (line 16)

46. In the context of line 20, what is the best definition of "lot"?

    (A) a piece of land

    (B) large quantity

    (C) destiny

    (D) living quarters

    (E) treatment

47. Which statement is true of the first sentence of paragraph four, "It is possible . . . psychiatric world" (lines 27–28)?

    (A) It qualifies the assertion of the first sentence of paragraph three, "So diffuse was the spirit of change . . . new-style asylum" (lines 17–18).

    (B) It refers specifically to Johann Reil (line 18).

    (C) It disputes the idea that change in psychiatry was international.

    (D) It criticizes scholars who see the change in psychiatry as a product of the Enlightenment.

    (E) It connects psychiatric treatment with economics and philosophy.

48. What is the "great controversy" referred to in line 28?

    (A) the writings of asylum physicians

    (B) the new treatments for mental illness introduced in the eighteenth century

    (C) reform movements

    (D) the cause of psychiatric reform

    (E) the theory that mental illness could be cured

49. The author cites many examples of travel and movement of information in order to

    (A) show that mental illness occurs in all societies

    (B) support the theory that many factors influenced the development of psychiatry

    (C) disprove the theory that many factors influenced the development of psychiatry

    (D) reveal the limited role played by Johann Reil

    (E) explain how mental illness spreads

50. Overall, the tone of this passage may be described as

    (A) combative and ironic

    (B) reflective and nostalgic

    (C) critical and didactic

    (D) tentative and superficial

    (E) balanced and informative

51. Which statement is true, according to footnote 1?

    (A) The quotation comes from a book published by Johann Christian Reil.

    (B) The book from which the quotation was drawn was published twice.

    (C) The quotation comes from an article that was reprinted in a book.

    (D) The cited section is 14 pages long.

    (E) The quotation was revised in 1968.

52. Which statement is true, according to footnote 2?

    (A) An article entitled *Museums of Madness: The Social Organization of Insanity in Nineteenth-Century England* is one of the sources referenced by the author.

    (B) Andrew Scull wrote two articles about madness in nineteenth-century England.

    (C) *The Most Solitary of Afflictions: Madness and Society in Britain, 1700–1900* was published in 1993.

    (D) *Museums of Madness: The Social Organization of Insanity in Nineteenth-Century England* was published by a company called London in 1979.

    (E) *The Most Solitary of Afflictions: Madness and Society in Britain, 1700–1900* was published to counter the arguments in Scull's previous book.

53. Overall, the effect of footnote 2 is to

    (A) suggest reading supporting the theory that "capitalism was responsible" (line 31) for the rise of psychiatry

    (B) suggest reading opposing the theory that "capitalism was responsible" (line 31) for the rise of psychiatry

    (C) cite the source of the quotation in this passage (lines 19–24)

    (D) bring other experts into the discussion of psychiatry

    (E) show that the author has done sufficient research

SECTION TWO: ESSAY QUESTIONS

Time: 2:15, divided as indicated below.

Reading Period: 15 minutes

Writing Period: 2 hours

During the reading period, you may annotate the questions and passages. You may *not* write on the answer sheet. During the writing period, you should devote approximately 40 minutes to each of the three essay questions. You may write the essays in any order; place the essay number at the top of each page. At the end of each essay response, write the # symbol.

Do not turn back to the multiple-choice questions during this portion of the exam.

Essay question 1: Synthesis

Directions: The question below is based on the six sources which follow it. To answer this question, you must synthesize information from at least three of these sources. Your essay must present a clear argument supported by information from the sources. Do NOT merely summarize the information or the point of view of the sources.

Be sure to cite information, quotations, or ideas taken from these sources. You may cite them as "Source A," "Source B," or by the descriptions in parentheses.

> **Source A:** (Pew)
>
> **Source B:** (McKenna and Bargh)
>
> **Source C:** (Science News)
>
> **Source D:** (Levine, Young, and Baroudi)
>
> **Source E:** (Howard, Ranie, Jones)
>
> **Source F:** (Charles)

The Question: Although the Internet is relatively new, it has had an enormous effect on modern life. Is that effect positive or negative? Read the following sources carefully and write an essay in which you take a stance on the effect of the Internet on society.

Source A

Pew Internet and American Life Project — Who Uses the Internet?

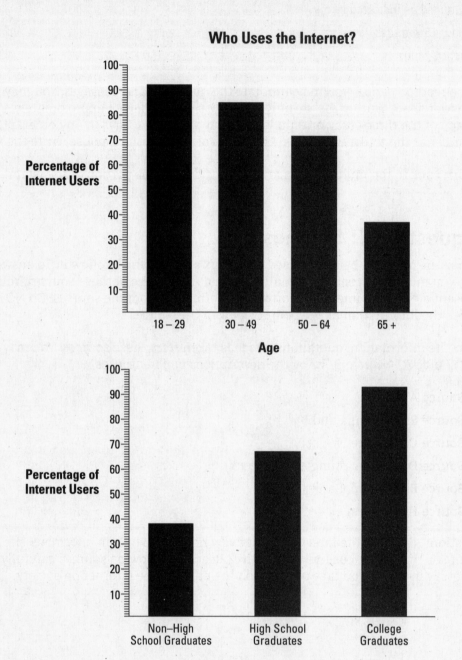

Who Uses the Internet?

Illustration by Wiley, Composition Services Graphics

Source B

Excerpt from *Consequences of the Internet for Self and Society: Is Social Life Being Transformed?*, edited by Katelyn Y. A. McKenna and John Bargh (Wiley-Blackwell, 2002; reprinted with permission of John Wiley & Sons, Inc.)

(01) The events of September 11, 2001, put many aspects of modern life in a new, stark, and poignant perspective. Among their many ramifications was to illuminate some of the positive, as well as the negative, consequences of the emergent Internet as a mode of interpersonal communication. Many of us who had friends, family, and colleagues in the downtown New
(05) York area found ourselves unable to make contact over the telephone, given the damage to vital communications switching and relay equipment. But the Internet was intact, at least enough so that e-mails were sent and received and people could stay in touch during many very dark hours. According to a Pew Foundation report, in the 48 hours after the attack, between four and five million people turned to the Internet to make contact with loved ones
(10) and friends because they could not make contact via telephone.

At the same time, the unfolding investigation into the terrorist attack has revealed that e-mail was a primary mode of communication for the network of conspirators allegedly responsible for it. The use of encryption technology made it especially difficult to decode the messages and so to gather intelligence about the movements and plans of terrorist
(15) suspects — making the Internet a much more effective means of secretive and sinister communication than the telephone or other communication modes.

Source C

Excerpt from "The Social Net," an article by Bruce Bower published in *Science News*, 5/4/2002, p. 282. (Reprinted with permission from *Science News*, copyright 2002.)

(01) Several surveys have probed the social repercussions of Internet use. They offer starkly different portraits of life online.

On the upbeat side, two national surveys of about 2,000 adults each, conducted in 2000 and 2001 by the University of California, Los Angeles Center for Communication Policy,
(05) found that regular Internet users reported spending as much time on most social activities as nonusers did. The online crowd cut back on television time, watching the tube 4.5 fewer hours per week than the no-Net group did.

National surveys in the same years, coordinated by the Pew Internet and American Life Project in Washington, D.C., yielded even rosier findings. Project researchers concluded
(10) that the online world is a "vibrant social universe" in which people widen their contacts and strengthen ties to their local communities.

Data published last November in the *American Behavioral Scientist* supported the Pew findings. In national telephone surveys of as many as 2,500 people conducted annually from 1995 to 2000, Internet users reported more community and political involvement, as well
(15) as more social contacts, than nonusers did, reported sociologist James E. Katz of Rutgers University in New Brunswick, N.J., and his colleagues.

A 1998 survey of about 39,000 visitors to the National Geographic Society web site also noted a social boost from Internet use. In this population, which included many veteran Internet users, online interactions typically supplemented in-person and telephone contacts, says
(20) University of Toronto sociologist Barry Wellman. However, two other national surveys, released in 2000, indicated that regular Internet use may often lead people to spend less time with friends and family; Stanford University researchers directed one survey. The other was a joint project of National Public Radio, the Kaiser Family Foundation, and Harvard University.

Source D

Excerpt from *The Internet For Dummies*, 11th Edition, by John R. Levine, Margaret Levine Young, and Carol Baroudi (Wiley, 2007; reprinted with permission of John Wiley & Sons, Inc.)

(01) Another great thing about the Internet is that it is what one may call "socially unstratified." That is, one computer is no better than any other, and no person is any better than
any other. Who you are on the Internet depends solely on how you present yourself
through your computer. If what you say makes you sound like an intelligent, interest-
(05) ing person, that's who you are. It doesn't matter how old you are or what you look like or
whether you're a student, business executive, or construction worker. Physical disabilities
don't matter — we correspond with deaf and blind people. If they hadn't felt like telling
us, we never would have known. People become famous (and infamous) in the Internet
community through their own efforts.

Source E

Adapted from "Days and Nights on the Internet," by Philip E. N. Howard, Lee Ranie, and Steve Jones, published in
The Internet in Everyday Life, edited by Barry Wellman and Caroline Haythornthwaite (Wiley-Blackwell, 2002), pps.
47–48. (Reprinted with permission of John Wiley & Sons, Inc.)

(01) Ray Oldenburg has described how people use "third places" such as coffee shops, community centers, beauty parlors, general stores, bars, and other hangouts to help them
get through the day. These places were distinct from home and distinct from work, but
were integral parts of social life. As scholars began to look at typical uses of the Internet,
(05) many adopted an analytical frame that the Internet was like one of these third places —
a growing sphere of social interaction where people played games and socialized. They
studied how individuals and small groups behaved within specific environments.

Internet tools have diffused with such speed and depth that many important forms of social
organization — news agencies, business enterprises, charities, and the government — take
(10) care to manage their identity on the Internet, and some have been fundamentally altered by
the organizational opportunities and stresses provided by such technologies. The Internet is
no longer just a third place where people go to escape and play with games and identities.
Today, many of the common forms of daily social interaction can be conducted online, from
checking the news and sports scores to researching and booking travel reservations. However,
(15) there is little consensus about whether the ability of users to conduct personal and professional life through Internet technologies is ultimately good or bad for society at large, local
communities, and individual well-being.

Those who argue that Internet tools have an ill effect make the case that Internet tools
promote the growth of pseudo rather than real communities, breed a new kind of radical
(20) individualism, replicate traditional elites, ideologies, and American cultural hegemony,
facilitate the violation of privacy, abet sound-bite culture, and clutter modern life with
useless data and cumbersome technologies. Others have argued that the Internet shears
social networks and lets individuals disconnect from their families and friends, becoming
loners, if not Internet addicts.

(25) In the other camp are those who contend that Internet tools are good for society. One
argument is that the Internet allows ideas to circulate to a wide audience and thus helps
entrepreneurs with good ideas find capital and bring expertise to bear on marketable
products and services. Others make the case that Internet technologies may help flatten
hierarchies, dilute power from traditional elites who monopolize information, permit new
(30) and interesting forms of community, make citizen activism easier and more effective, and
encourage a generally self-reflective society.

Source F

Excerpt from an unpublished editorial by Henry Charles (pseudonym)

(01) More than 137 million Chinese citizens have access to the Internet, and that number is growing every year. At some point in 2009, China will surpass the United States in the number of Internet users. The Chinese government has tried hard to censor the Internet by blocking content antithetical to its policies. Furthermore, the government actively
(05) pursues and then punishes anyone who posts anti-government comments. However, it is unlikely that the government will be able to control the massive exchange of information between its citizens as they troll the Internet. The Internet is simply too vast to censor effectively. Once they become used to a free exchange of ideas, who knows what the Internet-savvy Chinese will demand of their government?

(10) However, China's access to the Internet is not evenly distributed. Chinese Internet users tend to be young males living in cities. Only .4% of Chinese Internet users are low-income farmers. The Chinese "digital divide" between those who have access to computers and those who don't is similar to the divide in Western countries, where the poor, residents of rural areas, and uneducated are less likely to have the means to go online.

Essay question 2: Paul Robeson

Directions: The following passage is drawn from *The Undiscovered Paul Robeson, An Artist's Journey*, by Paul Robeson Jr. (Wiley, 2000; reprinted with permission of John Wiley & Sons, Inc.). Paul Robeson, an African American, was an actor, singer, and political activist. His father was the Reverend William Drew Robeson, referred to in this passage as "William Drew." Read the passage carefully. Then write an essay analyzing the rhetorical strategies the author employs to illuminate influences on Paul Robeson's character.

(01) When Paul was two, his brother Bill tried to enroll at Princeton University, but he was rebuffed. Refusing as usual to compromise on matters of principle, William Drew appealed in person to Woodrow Wilson, then president of Princeton, for Bill's enrollment. Reverend Robeson refused to accept any of Wilson's repeated and forceful attempts to
(05) avoid a direct response, compelling the future president of the United States to declare angrily that Princeton did not accept "colored." It was long rumored in Princeton's black community that this defiance cost William Drew his pastorate. A wealthy white Presbyterian church had built Witherspoon for its black members after having accommodated them in balcony seats for decades. But ultimate control remained with the white authori-
(10) ties, and one day they took William Drew's pastorate from him on a spurious pretext. Despite his well-argued statement of defense at his hearing and the near-unanimous support of his congregation, the preacher's son's decision to remove him from his pastorate (which he had appealed) was announced as final on November 17, 1900.
Paul was probably in the audience sitting with his mother, brothers, and sister when
(15) Reverend Robeson preached his last sermon at Witherspoon Church on January 27, 1901. Well known throughout the region for his dramatic power and inspiring messages, the reverend filled the sanctuary with his deep, melodious bass voice. Paul would always recall it as the greatest speaking voice he ever heard. On that day, William Drew made no direct mention of his dismissal. But he did intimate that his departure stemmed from his
(20) refusal to curtail his determined criticism of social injustice.
On January 29, 1901, two days after William Drew had preached his farewell sermon at Witherspoon Church, George C. White, of William Drew's home state of North Carolina and the nation's sole remaining black congressman, defiantly addressed the U.S. House of

Representatives. His term was coming to an end, he said, and the electoral rigging legiti-
(25) mized by the U.S. Supreme Court in the service of white rule had denied him any hope
of reelection. His departure, he noted, was "perhaps the Negroes' temporary farewell to
the American Congress; but we say, Phoenix-like he will rise up some day to come again."
So too would William Drew rise again. The Robeson family had to leave the comfortable
Witherspoon Street parsonage and move to a smaller house on Green Street around the
(30) corner. Bill boarded at Lincoln University and two years later enrolled in the University of
Pennsylvania Medical School. William Drew gave himself to making a living. Paul would
write about this period later in his autobiography:

He was still the dignified Reverend Robeson to the community, and no man
carried himself with greater pride. Not once did I hear him complain of the
(35) poverty and misfortune of those years. Serene and undaunted, he struggled to
earn a livelihood and see to our education. He got a horse and wagon, and began
to earn his living hauling ashes. This was his work at the time I first remember
him, and I recall the growing mound of ashes dumped in our backyard. A fond
memory remains of our horse, a mare named Bess, whom I grew to love and who
(40) loved me. My father also went into the hack business and as a coachman drove
students around town and on trips to the seashore. Mostly I played. There were
the vacant lots for ball games, and the wonderful moments when Bill [then in
his mid-twenties], vacationing from college where he played on the team, would
teach me how to play football. He was my first coach, and over and over again on
(45) a weed-grown lot he would put me through the paces — how to tackle a man so
he stayed tackled, how to run with the ball.

Paul chose not to mention that the meager rations of the Robesons in Princeton had
to be supplemented by relatives in North Carolina who sent up "cornmeal, greens, yams,
peanuts and other goodies in bags." From that time on, he relished a good meal in a way
(50) that those who have always been well fed do not.

Essay question 3: Leadership

Directions: French author and critic André Maurois (1885–1967) said that "the most important quality in a leader is that of being acknowledged as such." What do you think is the
most important quality in a leader? That he or she be recognized as a leader, as Maurois
says? Or another quality? In a well-written essay, identify the most important quality of a
leader and support your view with references to history, literature, or personal experience.

18

Answers and Explanations for Practice Exam 1

After you work through the entire practice AP English Language and Composition exam in Chapter 17, you need to take a few minutes to see how you rate. In this chapter, I help you score and evaluate your work. Obviously, the answers to the multiple-choice questions are clear-cut. When it comes to the essays, I offer as much guidance as I can about what test scorers will be looking for, and you may want to enlist an outside reader to help you determine how your writing measures up.

If you score well on the practice test, congratulations! Take a break for at least a day or two and then move on to the next chapter for still another rehearsal for exam day. If you're disappointed in how you performed on the first practice exam, don't be discouraged. A key reason to practice is to figure out which areas are weak so you can reread the parts of this book that discuss them, spend more time practicing, and build your confidence before the exam arrives.

GUIDELINES FOR SCORING AND REVIEWING YOUR PRACTICE EXAM

To check how well you did on Practice Exam 1, follow this plan of attack:

1. **Check the multiple-choice section.** Count only the number of correct answers; that's your score for this section. Ignore the number of incorrect answers and anything you left blank.

2. **Read the explanations for any multiple-choice questions that puzzled you.** This category includes all your wrong answers and any questions you guessed at, even if you ended up with the correct answer. Figure out what types of questions stumped you. Vocabulary? Tone? Rhetorical devices? Once you've pinpointed problem areas, turn to the corresponding chapters in this book for extra review.

3. **Read the scoring guidelines for the essay questions.** These guidelines come in two flavors: general and specific. You need both to score your essays.

   - **The general guidelines:** These guideline appear in the section "How to Grade Your Essay Responses" and apply to all essays.

   - **The specific guidelines:** These are tailored to one particular question. For each essay question, I provide two sample answers and the score each would receive in a real AP-grading situation, along with a breakdown of the essay's rating in four different categories. Understanding how AP graders think helps you evaluate your own essays. You can find the specific guidelines in the sections following the general guidelines.

4. **Score your essays.** After you read both the general and specific guidelines explaining what to look for in evaluating your essay, reread what you wrote, fill in the scoring grid, and add up your efforts with the help of the Essay Scoring Grids. Write the magic numbers in the Essay Conversion Chart at the end of the essay scoring section.

5. **Convert your score.** The Exam Conversion Chart tells you how to turn those raw scores on the multiple-choice and essay sections into AP grades of 1 to 5.

THE MULTIPLE-CHOICE SECTION

When you check your responses in this section, you don't have to read the explanations for questions you answered correctly. However, if you can spare a little more time, you may learn something even from the questions you got right. I've packed the explanations with helpful hints, such as a definition of a literary term or a way to rule out poor choices.

1. **(E).** The "all of the following EXCEPT" questions are easy if you rule out each item as you come across it. First to go is (A), because of the expression "the truth, the whole truth" (line 4). If you're a fan of cop shows, you probably recognized an *allusion,* or reference, to the oath that witnesses swear, which is "to tell the truth, the whole truth, and nothing but the truth." That same phrase is repetitive (two *truths*), as is "will endure as it has endured" (lines 5–6), so you can drop (B). Next to go is (C); *alliteration,* the repetition of consonant sounds, shows up in "the only thing we have to fear is fear itself" (line 7). Hear those "f" sounds? *Direct address* (D) means that the author/speaker is talking to someone, and the "you" in line 11 fills the bill. All that's left — and what's missing — is a simile, a comparison made with the words "like" or "as."

2. **(A).** The second paragraph opens with two general statements — that Americans face "common difficulties" (line 12) that fortunately concern "only material things" (line 13). Then comes the list: loss of value, high taxes, lack of money to pay taxes, savings wiped out, and so forth. Choice (A) fits this pattern perfectly, and (B) has it backward. (C) is a nonstarter because Roosevelt didn't share any individual stories of hardship or triumph. (D) and (E) are appealing because elsewhere in the speech both appear. The key word is *elsewhere.* When the AP asks about a particular spot, focus only on that spot.

3. **(C).** The metaphor "withered leaves" (line 15) is tied to "industrial enterprise" (line 16), and industry relies partly on factories. Another clue pointing you toward (C) is the fact that the metaphor occurs in the middle of a list of problems of the Great Depression. To decide which one matches the metaphor, use common sense. When you're making a list, you're not likely to repeat an item. The list in the long sentence featuring "withered leaves" includes "[v]alues have shrunk" (line 13), which is close to (A), and government's "serious curtailment of income" (lines 14–15), which is another way of saying (B). (D) is out because "farmers find no markets" (line 16), implying that what farmers do sell probably goes at bargain prices. (E) is expressed by "the means of exchange are frozen" (line 15). Once you've ruled out (A), (B), (D), and (E), you know (C) is best.

4. **(B).** Roosevelt has just listed all the problems his new administration is facing. Thus he's implying that he's realistic about the challenges ahead of him. Did I catch you with (A)? That choice is tempting because the opening paragraph of this inaugural address refers to "victory" (line 10) and the firm belief that "this great Nation" (line 5) will not only "endure" (line 5) but "prosper" (line 6). However, the hope of the first paragraph isn't the main idea of the second paragraph, and hope isn't the purpose of Roosevelt's comment about optimism. Choice (C) isn't in the running because "others' views" don't appear in the passage, and (D) is too general. (E) doesn't work because of all the positive stuff in the first paragraph.

5. **(D).** The phrase in the question can be paraphrased as "we're not in trouble because we're lacking material things," the same idea expressed by (D). The other choices don't even come close.

6. **(C).** The third paragraph has a split personality. The first part discusses what the nation has, and the second discusses what went wrong. The shift is in the middle of the fourth sentence, when Roosevelt changes gears from statements about what material advantages the country possesses to a critique of the way in which those advantages were used. The exact spot is marked by the comma following "doorstep" (line 23).

> **TIP**
>
> The word "but" often marks a shift, qualifying or modifying the meaning of whatever precedes it. Whenever you see "but," take a second look.

7. **(D).** "Concession and reply" is the technique of recognizing the opponent's defense, retooling it a little, and using it to support your own argument. In the third paragraph (lines 20–28), Roosevelt indicts the financial biggies, saying that "the rulers of the exchange" (lines 24–25) "have failed" (line 25). He calls them "unscrupulous money changers" (lines 26–27). Then, anticipating the counter argument, Roosevelt concedes, "True they have tried" (line 29). Now for the knockout punch: "[T]heir efforts have been cast in the pattern of an outworn tradition" (lines 29–30). The rest of the paragraph tears them to shreds. (A) may have grabbed your attention, because "True they have tried" does tie the third and fourth paragraph together. However, (D) is much more specific and thus the better answer. The other choices aren't relevant.

8. **(A).** The subject of a verb is the person or thing performing the action or in the state of being expressed by the verb. To find the subject, ask "who have admitted?" or "what have admitted?" The "rulers" (line 24) "have admitted" that they blew the economy.

9. **(E).** The Great Depression was no picnic, and Roosevelt's speech acknowledges that the country is in crisis, so "realistic" certainly applies. However, he takes care to inspire his listeners as well with such phrases as "This great nation . . . will prosper" (lines 5–6) and "our true destiny is . . . to minister to . . . our fellow men" (lines 42–43). Therefore, (E) is the best answer.

10. **(B).** If something is passive, it just sits there, receiving action, words, impressions, and so forth. Something active does the opposite — creates the action, words, and impressions. The lines cited push the listeners into active mode, not passively awaiting government instructions or help. Choice (C) expresses the opposite idea. (A) and (D) are irrelevant, and (E) has nothing to do with active or passive voice.

11. **(C).** Mary Wollstonecraft, the author of *A Vindication of the Rights of Women* from which this passage is excerpted, wasn't shy about sharing her opinions. In the late 18th century, when she wrote this argument for women's education, the prevailing idea was that females should be decorative and ignorant.

12. **(D).** The material after the colon explains more specifically the stuff before the colon. Before the colon, she writes that one of the "ingenious arguments" (line 1) justifying male dominance is that virtue is different in men and women. After the colon, she gets down to the details, explaining that "women are not allowed to have sufficient strength of mind to acquire what really deserves the name of virtue" (lines 3–4).

13. **(B).** The first paragraph briefly explains one of the "ingenious arguments" (line 1) used to "prove, that the two sexes, in the acquirement of virtue" (line 2) go for "a very different character" (line 3). Notice the key word: "different." The sentence you're examining for this question ("Yet it should seem . . . happiness" — lines 4–6) opposes this point of view by stating that "there is but one way" (line 5) to virtue. By the way, the capitalized word, "MANKIND" (line 6), here refers to both males and females. Today, we usually see the more inclusive "humankind" or "human beings," but in Wollstonecraft's day, "mankind" was the word of choice for both sexes.

14. **(E).** The second paragraph of the passage (lines 7–17) is chock-full of big ideas, general statements about men and women that Wollstonecraft supports by logic but no factual information — ruling out (C). This paragraph has no *allusions* (references to literary or historical works), so you can rule out (A). It doesn't present opposing concepts, so (B) doesn't work. (D) doesn't work either because, if anything, Wollstonecraft exaggerates, not understates, her case.

15. **(C).** Paragraph two opens with a rhetorical question — one that the author will soon answer unless the question is so obvious that the author believes that the reader *must* come up with the correct response. Wollstonecraft actually provides an answer, assuming that her reader may indeed favor ignorance for women. (C) contains a little phrase, "I should answer" (line 10), that tips you off.

16. **(B).** The list of traits taught to women by word and example is fairly long, but only one word shows up in capital letters. Why "OUTWARD" (line 14) and not "outward"? Emphasis comes to mind, and (B) implies that unless Wollstonecraft makes a big deal about this point, the reader may not realize that women only *seem* to obey. Inside, they're tearing up the place. (A) is the opposite of what Wollstonecraft is saying. (C) doesn't work, despite the word "emphasize," because Wollstonecraft's disapproval of the traditional female role is plastered all over this passage. She would urge women to reveal, not conceal, their feelings and ideas. Her feminist stance contradicts (D). You may have been tempted by (E), but the word and sentence they're asking you about don't deal with rebellion against male authority figures, or anyone else, for that matter.

17. **(C).** This question is tricky. The word "thus" implies a connection and may be restated as "in this way." Your job is to figure out whether "thus" relates to something before or after it. The first three choices cite lines before "thus," and (D) and (E) cite lines following "thus." So which way do you turn? First, check out the context. Wollstonecraft mentions that "Milton describes our first frail mother" (line 18). Okay, how *does* he describe her? *In this way*, or, as the passage states, "thus" (line 18). Where do you find a list of traits belonging to the "first frail mother? In choice (C).

18. **(A).** The best approach to this question is to skim the fourth paragraph, crossing out each choice as you encounter it. First to be eliminated is (C), which occurs in the sentence beginning "For instance" (line 24). Next out is (E), with the third sentence ("What childish . . ." — lines 25–26). You then encounter an *allusion,* or reference, to Rousseau and the Bible (lines 30 and 31–33), so (B) is a nonstarter. The "tree of knowledge" (line 31) is also a metaphor, which is choice (D). Nothing remains but (A).

19. **(C).** To answer this question, you need to know that "allow" is a synonym for "assume." With this information, it's easy to verify I because of "allowing them to have souls" (line 5) and II because of "For if it be allowed that women were destined by Providence to acquire human virtues" (lines 35–36). You can rule out III when you get to the last paragraph, which counts innocence as positive in children but, "applied to men, or women, it is but a civil term for weakness" (lines 34–35). Only I and II are right, and (C) is your answer.

20. **(B).** A metaphor is an indirect comparison, a way to describe one thing by using another. The "fountain of light" (line 38) is probably the sun. Staying with the solar system motif, the metaphor is extended by the reference to a "mere satellite" (line 39), which is choice (B).

21. **(E).** Main idea questions need to fit *perfectly*. A favorite trap is to provide some choices that are too narrow, such as (D). Yes, the second paragraph discusses the effect of ignorance, explaining that it leads to "follies and caprices" (line 9) in women. But (D) doesn't take into account some of the other arguments the author presents, such as those in the fourth paragraph, which take men to task for "attempting to keep [women] always in a state of childhood" (lines 29–30). (C) is also too narrow, because appearance pops up only occasionally in the passage. The excerpt refers to "Providence" (lines 5–6 and 36), and "Providence" may be interpreted as "God," but those two references don't justify (A). (B) drops out because male roles aren't explicitly addressed. What's left? Choice (E), the appeal for women's education, which is the logical thread running through the whole passage.

22. **(D).** Read this passage with your inner voice and you'll immediately hear the passion in the many exclamation points and the extreme word choices, such as "puerile kind of propriety" (line 15) and "docile blind obedience" (line 21). Argumentative also fits, as the author is trying to convince her readers that women have the same need and ability to be educated as men do.

23. **(A).** Three of the answer choices deal with time, but only (A) fits because in paragraphs one through three (lines 1–17), the narrator moves from first through fourth grade, in chronological order. Other parts of the passage flash forward or back, but not this section. Did (B) tempt you? The author recounts some facts from her childhood, but in a general way. Anecdotes are more specific. Instead of saying that "things are fuzzier" (lines 1–2) and "I start to squint" (line 2), an anecdotal approach would focus on one moment when a line on the blackboard wasn't clear. In the same way, (C) isn't a good answer because the facts cited in this portion of the passage are too general to qualify as examples.

24. **(C).** The second paragraph (lines 7–10) deals with the narrator's reluctance to wear glasses because of concerns about attractiveness. She repeats the old saying, "Men don't make passes at girls who wear glasses" (line 8) just before the line cited in this question — "Nobody tells me how to feel about men with glasses" (lines 8–9). The juxtaposition of these two ideas presents the possibility of a double standard; the culture proclaims that a girl loses something when she wears glasses but says nothing about men in the same situation. Some of the other choices are possible. The narrator doesn't know much about male attractiveness — choices (A) and (E). She is making a statement about men's attractiveness — choice (B). You can even justify (D) on the grounds that no one has told her what to think or feel about this particular situation, though she's "somehow absorbed" (line 8) what she should think about female appearance. However, (C) is the best because it fits this passage most specifically.

25. **(D).** The prescription is for glasses, which the narrator doesn't want to wear. Her head is "bowed to the inevitable" (line 17) because she can't escape wearing glasses. Thus the prescription is the equivalent of the "fifteen years to life" sort of sentence that a judge hands down. In other words, it's a punishment.

26. **(A).** The narrator gives no indication that she talked with her parents about her glass-phobia. She mentions "some discussion that I am not a party to" (lines 18–19) and is surprised when her father buys a doll, asking "Could he really know how I feel?" (line 35). (A) expresses this distance between parents and child. Another serious contender is (C), because the narrator seems puzzled by her parents' actions. However, the bewilderment is a result of the distance, so (A) is better. (D) is not correct because of the tension implied in the last paragraph, when the mother and daughter fight about the daughter's move to an apartment.

27. **(C).** You don't have to know what a subordinate clause is to find the correct answer here. (For the record, a *subordinate clause* is an expression with a subject and a verb that can't stand alone. It depends on another statement to express a complete thought.) Paragraph four (lines 18–24) deals with one shopping trip in the past. The opening line of paragraph five (line 25) starts out at one specific moment of the trip, when the narrator "formulate[s] a plan." The subordinate clause shifts to the "first year or so" (line 25) after she gets glasses. There you go: The passage moves from the past to a bit later, and (C) is the answer.

28. **(B).** The last paragraph of this passage covers a lot of ground, from the arrival home after buying the doll to the narrator's move away "for good" (line 46). The move took place during an argument, which this quotation from the mother illustrates.

29. **(E).** The mother's parenthetical comment and the narrator's statement about an atmosphere "soaked with anger and tears" (lines 46–47) rule out (A) and (B). The same factors point to (E) as the best answer. (C) doesn't work because the diction isn't formal at all; in fact, beginning a sentence with "so" is a fair indication of informal diction. (D) drops out because the narrator doesn't express her views of the future.

30. **(B).** The doll's importance lies not in its intrinsic value (A) or its role in the moving-out fight (E). Nor is the doll's importance exaggerated or minimized, so you can cross out (C) and (D). (B) is best because so much of the story is about buying the doll. Why so much fuss about a doll? Because it's an unusual act. Apart from the fact that the father wasn't much of a gift-giver, the passage reveals very little about the father-daughter relationship.

31. **(D).** Both parts of this passage are multilayered. The portion not written by Byron (lines 29–51) depicts him as someone who wasn't glued to his schoolbooks. Within these lines the author also conveys Byron's pride and willingness to fight. In the quotation (lines 1–28) that begins the passage, Byron jokes about his terrible handwriting, but he also mentions his love of history and his move to England. Validation (A), contrast (B), and balance (C) aren't the best answers because they require simple, straightforward agreement or disagreement. Now you're left with (D) and (E). Of the two, (D) is better because Byron mentions several places and time periods, while the author's exposition concentrates on one time and one place (school) in Byron's life. Rather than setting a scene, the quotation lets the reader "hear" Byron himself — in other words, it introduces Byron's voice into the passage.

32. **(B).** The author tells you that Byron didn't shy away from a fight and that Byron was a "lively, warm-hearted, and high-spirited boy" (line 31). However, Byron's appearance isn't mentioned, so (B) — physical description — is the one you want.

33. **(A).** "[A]cquired my letters" (line 8) means "learned to read." Learning "by ear" (line 8) probably means that he was better at listening than at reading or writing. Byron apparently *wasn't* a good student, the idea expressed in (E), but his failures at school don't come across in that particular line.

34. **(E).** This is a tricky question, because the battle of Lake Regillus was probably the first that Byron understood (A) and did capture Byron's attention (B). However, the line cited in the question is more particular, and "put into my hands the first" (lines 13–14) implies that Byron got homework, which is the subject of choice (E).

35. **(E).** Byron pokes fun at himself in several spots — referring to his handwriting, for example, as a "scrawl" (line 25) and his birthplace as "where I had been hatched" (line 21). "Self-deprecating" is the term appropriate for such comments. Byron's comments won't provoke a belly laugh, but his quotation does contain some humor. The other choices depend partly on your vocabulary knowledge. A "conciliatory" tone (A) aims to make peace, while "didactic" (D) teaches a moral lesson. "Condescending" (also choice D) is the tone of people who think they're much better than anyone else.

36. **(A).** Byron, while gazing on the site of the battle he had read about as a schoolboy, "remembered [his] young enthusiasm" (line 16), a statement implying that he's lost some of that feeling. Thus (A) is true, because the passage of time has altered Byron's view. (B) is true whenever time passes, but the passage doesn't indicate *when* Byron visited Tusculum, other than to say that it was "[f]our years ago" (line 14). Hence you can't tell if he's "aged" or if he's just a bit older. (C) doesn't work because Byron says nothing about his later life, nor does he "promote the benefits of travel" (D). Finally, his comments on Tusculum don't sound regretful, so (E) isn't correct.

37. **(D).** Byron says that Paterson "was the son of my shoemaker, but a good scholar" (lines 17–18). The word "but" is the star here because it gives a tone of surprise. Imagine the sentence with "and": "Paterson was the son of my shoemaker and a good scholar." Now the two facts about Paterson are simply mentioned, with no hidden editorial comment. The other answers fail for various reasons. (A) isn't supported in the passage. Choice (B) gets eliminated because Byron says "as is common" (line 18), an endorsement of Scottish scholarship but not strong enough to justify the phrase "most people." You can cut (C) and (E) because Byron doesn't comment on the quality of his own schoolwork with Paterson.

38. **(A).** The second paragraph (lines 29–42) emphasizes the views of Byron's classmates. They describe him with several adjectives — "lively, warm-hearted . . . passionate and resentful" (line 31), but they also give examples (choice A) to support their characterization. For example, one classmate explains that Byron was "always more ready to give a blow than take one" (lines 33–34) and took time to "pay . . . off" (line 37) a classmate who had insulted him.

39. **(C).** Byron told his servant that he beat a boy "according to promise" (line 41), making (C) a good choice. The motto doesn't link paragraphs two and three, so (A) is out. (B) is way too general; you don't know what kind of statement is being made, other than the fact that it is "strong." (D) and (E) miss the point, because the quality highlighted by the motto is negative — keeping a promise to wallop someone.

40. **(B).** Byron reaches the "head" (line 49) of the class only when the "highest and lowest boys" (line 48) change places, so Byron was probably *not* on the honor role. Even the schoolmaster comments that Byron will soon "be at the foot again" (line 51). Thus (B) works nicely. (A), (C), and (D) are all attractive answers because the schoolmaster appears to have a lot of power, the custom of ranking students is a real pain, and Byron and the schoolmaster were probably *not* on the best terms given that the schoolmaster pretty much says that he expects Byron to fail. However, these three answers don't explain *why* the anecdote is in the passage; they simply comment upon the anecdote. (E) doesn't work because the anecdote has nothing to do with the reasons why one of the greatest poets probably got a poor grade in English.

41. **(B).** This passage begins with a time-honored device, heard most frequently during heat waves, when everyone walks around saying that "it's not the heat; it's the humidity." This pattern — here's what isn't true and now here's what is true — allows the author of this passage to explain that madness was always seen as "curable" (line 1) by such treatments as "bleeding, purging, and giving of emetics" (line 3). Having told you that curability wasn't new, the author assumes your brain replies, "Fine. So what *is* new?" The next portion of the passage explains: The new thing in the 18th century was the idea that an

institution "could be made curative" (line 4). Thus (B) fits best here. The other choices are incorrect. The passage doesn't criticize psychiatry; it simply reports, so (A) doesn't work. The comparison in the first paragraph of the passage (lines 1–7) is with an earlier era, so drop (C). Answer (D) is tempting, because the reader is likely to criticize earlier methods of treating madness. However, the negative ("It was not" — line 1) doesn't set up the criticism; the sentence just glides over the past into the idea of institutions as curative. Choice (E) is just too vague.

42. **(A).** Every idea in this passage is followed by an implied or explicit "on the other hand" statement. *It's not this . . . it's that. You may say this, but then there's the other point. People think x, but don't forget y.* Go back through the passage and look for these comparisons and contrasts. Choice (A) leaps out at you. If it doesn't, try ruling out the other choices. The passage doesn't move forward in time, so (B) is out. Nothing physical is described, so (C) is a bad selection. (D) isn't a terrible answer (though it's not the best one), because the passage tries to explain how Enlightenment ideas led to developments in psychiatry. However, strict cause-and-effect structure just isn't here. Choice (E) is out because the author doesn't lead you through a series of steps to a logical conclusion.

43. **(D).** The easiest way to answer this question is to sum up the first two paragraphs in your head. Paragraph 1: Before the Enlightenment, people tried to cure madness, but not very well. The Enlightenment idea was to make the institution a place of healing. Paragraph 2: The Enlightenment thought it could do better than previous generations in curing the mentally ill. A new generation of asylum doctors arose. Now that you have an outline, measure it against the answers. (A) is out because "to refute" is to show that an idea is wrong, and paragraph two doesn't contradict paragraph one. Answer (B) is possible, for the same reasons that (A) isn't. However, "support" implies additional evidence, and paragraph two is short on facts and long on generalizations. For this reason, (E) also fails. Choice (C) centers on the idea of qualifying. To qualify, in this context, is to build a little fence around meaning, as in "Yes, you can have the car, but only if you mow the lawn first." No fences show up in paragraph two, just a bit more of the same discussion begun in paragraph one — in other words, (D).

44. **(B).** "Therapeutics" are healing methods, clearly identified here as "bleeding, purging, and giving of emetics" (line 3). The other choices are all traps, because all of them are in the passage and all look interesting — wrong, but interesting.

45. **(E).** The "new therapeutic optimism" is optimism about healing, the idea expressed by (E). Did I catch you with (C) or (D)? The words "improvement" in (C) and "optimism" in (D) were the bait, but neither (C) nor (D) says anything about healing.

46. **(C).** The devilish part of this question lies in the fact that (A), (B), and (C) are all definitions of "lot." (D) isn't justified by any statements in the passage, but (E) makes sense. However, only (C) has *two* essential qualities: It makes sense in the passage and also qualifies as an official definition of "lot."

47. **(A).** The author of this passage often puts forth an idea and then the opposing idea, which surfaces somewhere in the middle. Paragraph four lays out the "beacon" metaphor; some physicians pointed the way to knowledge. Paragraph three starts out by saying that "it is difficult to identify a single individual as responsible for the new-style asylum" (lines 17–18). So what do you have? You can't identify a single individual, but you can find a small group of beacons. Therefore, (A) is the best choice.

48. **(D).** The "great controversy" (line 28) is outlined in the sentences following this phrase. Some scholars point to capitalism, and others go for the "central state" (line 31). What are they arguing about? The reasons why psychiatry changed during the Enlightenment. Reasons are causes, so go for (D). None of the other choices even comes close.

49. **(B).** The key here is in lines 32–33, when the author concludes that the "wide variety of social and economic settings" made it "unlikely that any single social force" (line 33) was responsible for the development of psychiatry. These lines point you toward (B) and away from (C). The passage doesn't deal with how and where mental illness occurs, so you can rule out choices (A) and (E). Choice (D), at first glance, may draw you in, because Reil is mentioned and then the author immediately switches to a wider view. However, Reil isn't really the point of the travel/movement examples mentioned in the question.

50. **(E).** The passage examines several possible reasons why treatment of the mentally ill changed during the Enlightenment. The author presents a case, considering several theories and ultimately supporting one. None of the other choices comes close: The author makes a case, but the calmness of his presentation rules out "combative and ironic" (A). There's no nostalgia for the good old days of psychiatry — choice (B). The author isn't criticizing anyone, though he is teaching (making "didactic" a possibility). However, both halves of the pair must be correct for the choice to work. Choice (D) is out because the footnotes alone show the depth of the author's research.

51. **(B).** The italicized title tells you that the quotation comes from a book, not an article. (In this system of citation, the title of an article appears in quotation marks.) So you can rule out (C) immediately. Reil is the author, not the publisher; choice (A) is wrong. The page numbers tell you where the quotation appears, not how long the section is. Therefore, you can dispense with (D). The book was reprinted in 1968, but nothing indicates that the quotation was revised. What's left? A book that was published in 1803 and reprinted in 1968.

52. **(C).** You can drop (A) and (B) because the italicized titles indicate books, not articles. "London" is a place, not a company, so (D) doesn't make the cut. The footnote also says that the second book restates the argument of the first, so (E) isn't appropriate. (C) is what you want, because the publication date is 1993.

53. **(B).** To "lambaste" is to scold sharply. The second footnote points out that the author twice made the same argument against the theory that capitalism and psychiatry were related, so (B) is best.

HOW TO GRADE YOUR ESSAY RESPONSES

To score AP exam essays, the College Board gathers college professors and high-school English teachers for a week of nonstop grading. All the graders read and rate the same few essays, discussing their answers according to the College Board's criteria. The goal is to come up with a rubric, which is a set of standards for great, good, fair, and poor essays, along with several gradations in between. The evaluators are charged with awarding a number from 0 to 9 to each essay, with 9 being the best.

This section explains the general guidelines the AP applies. Before you score your own essays, however, turn to the sample answers I provide — along with a detailed analysis of the good and bad points of each. Examining how the samples are graded helps you rate your own work.

AP standards

During each AP exam grading session, statisticians calculate the norm for every question they ask, including the essay questions. The statisticians tweak the standards a bit every year, adjusting for extra-easy or super-tough questions. Tweaking aside, year after year the same general guidelines apply:

7–9 The College Board calls essays in this category "effective" in both content and style. The essay answers the question, digs deeply into the text or topic, includes appropriate support for the ideas it asserts, and shows a mature command of language. Supporting evidence is strongly linked to the topic and appropriately cited (if needed).

4–6 In this slot, the College Board rates your essay "adequate." The essay makes some good, but not great, points. It includes some supporting evidence and is generally clear. The supporting points are linked to the topic, but not perfectly. The writing is a little less fluid and may contain some errors in diction (word choice), grammar, spelling, or citation (if needed).

1–3 The essay resides in "inadequate" territory. Instead of analysis or argument, the essay may simply summarize or restate ideas. Little or no supporting evidence appears. The language is flawed, with incomplete sentences or enough grammar and spelling errors to distract the reader.

0 The essay is left blank or does not address the question.

Professional AP grading is holistic. The evaluators don't award 10 percent for grammar, 15 percent for supporting evidence, and so forth. They just stick a number on the whole thing. That method works fine for the pros, but not for anyone else. To give you a little more guidance, I've divided the grading for each essay into four categories. The categories are tailored to the specific question you're answering. Give yourself a number from 0 to 9 for each category.

> **TIP**
>
> If the score for any essay is below 4, turn to Chapter 16 for additional practice. Also, if you notice that one type of essay stumped you — say, for example, the synthesis essay — check out the relevant section of Chapter 15 for the best approach to that sort of essay.

You've probably noticed that a range of scores applies to an effective, adequate, or inadequate essay. Here's how to decide which of the three numbers is best for your essay:

- **If you think that your answer almost, but not quite, deserves the next higher category:** Give yourself the highest number. In other words, if you can glimpse but not reach the 7–9 slot, give yourself a 6.

- **If your answer barely escapes the next lower category:** Award yourself the lowest number.

- **If you're squarely in one slot:** Go for the middle number.

Your final essay score

For each essay on the practice test, I provide a grid (in the next section) to help you sort through the scoring. Here's what to do:

1. **Fill in the Essay Scoring Grid for each essay.** You should end up with four numbers assessing how you answered the question, analyzed the passage or topic, employed evidence, or conveyed your thoughts to the reader. (The categories vary slightly depending upon the question you're answering.)

2. **Add up your grades for each essay and average your scores.** The answer is your score for that particular essay.

3. **Complete the Essay Conversion Chart at the end of the chapter.** Now you know your score for the entire essay section.

> **TIP**
>
> Only an essay that does *not* address the question or is left blank scores a zero. If your essay is in that category, turn to Chapter 15 for some essay-writing help. Then try again.

SCORING ESSAY 1: SYNTHESIS ESSAY ON THE INTERNET AND SOCIETY

The prompt inquires about the effect of the Internet on society. Is it positive or negative, or something in between? You've got six possible sources, including a set of bar graphs — the "visual source." Rate your essay by asking these questions:

■ **Have I communicated a clear point of view?** You have to take a position on the effect of the Internet on society. Mind you, the position doesn't have to be one-sided. You can — and most likely should — allow for complexity, explaining both good and bad effects of the Internet. However, by the end of the first paragraph, the reader should know where you stand.

■ **Have I supported my viewpoint?** The question requires you to draw upon at least three of the six sources, though you can refer to more, if you wish. The information from the sources should clearly relate to the views you express.

■ **How complex is my analysis?** How good is your *interpretation* of the data or ideas presented in the sources? It's not enough to mention that China has a lot of Internet users. What's the significance of that fact?

■ **How well have you presented your ideas?** Your writing should be organized, coherent, and reasonably correct in terms of spelling and grammar. Because this is a synthesis essay, the graders also want to see that you understand what has to be cited and that you know how to cite sources. (For help with source citation, turn to Chapter 12.)

The College Board instructs its graders to give no more than 2 points to any essay with enough grammar and spelling errors to distract the reader from the point the writer is trying to make. If you fall apart in the last category, your scores in the other three will *not* raise your grade. (Grammar-challenged? Chapter 6 comes to your rescue.)

Scoring grid for the synthesis essay

Clear point of view _____

0   The essay does not answer the question or is left blank. **Note:** If the essay doesn't an-swer the question, the *overall* score is zero, even if the essay is nicely written and would receive high marks in the "writing" category.

1–3   The essay simply summarizes the ideas in several sources without taking a recogniz-able position on the effect of the Internet on society.

4–6   The essay presents a position about the effect of the Internet on society, but the reader has to work to find it or to understand it. Or the position may be clear but not consistent throughout the essay.

7–9   The essay clearly and effectively presents a position on the effect of the Internet on society.

Evidence _____

1–3   The essay repeats information from the sources, but the information selected doesn't relate to the central argument of the essay — whether the Internet has helped or hurt society. The evidence is *not* drawn from the required minimum of three sources.

4–6   The essay provides evidence, either quoted or referred to indirectly, but these points are not the most effective choices from the given source material. The evidence may be linked only weakly to the central argument about the effects of the Internet.

7–9   The evidence is particularly well chosen and is clearly and effectively linked to the writer's position on the effects of the Internet.

Analysis _____

1–3   The essay stays on the surface, merely restating information from the sources about the Internet and its effects. No attempt is made to interpret the data in or to consider the consequences of a given statement or position.

4–6   The writer goes a little deeper, considering somewhat effectively the meaning of sta-tistics about Internet use or the significance of facts about how the Internet has been used. Positions taken in the sources are analyzed, though the writer may miss the main idea or oversimplify the situations described.

7–9   The statistics about Internet use or other facts, as well as the positions taken in the various sources, are analyzed in depth. The writer demonstrates the ability to under-stand complex ideas about the effects of the Internet on society.

Writing _____

1–3   The essay may be marred by many errors in grammar, spelling, or punctuation. **(Note:** If the essay is hard to read because of these errors, the highest score the essay may receive *overall* is a 2. Higher scores in other categories do not lift the overall score!) Ci-tations may be missing or misplaced. The writing may sound immature, perhaps with choppy or repetitive sentences. The essay may be disorganized.

4–6 The writing is competent and reasonably correct, but the structure may be confusing or the citations may be incorrectly placed. The diction and tone may be uneven. An essay in this category doesn't have the fluid, mature sound of an essay in the highest category.

7–9 An essay in this category demonstrates a command of language, the ability to make a point clearly and concisely. Diction, tone, and structure are handled well. Though the essay may contain errors in grammar, spelling, punctuation, or citation, the errors are minor and infrequent.

Fill in each blank in this Essay Scoring Grid with your score, and then add your scores to determine the total.

Clear point of view _____

Evidence _____

Analysis _____

Writing _____

Raw score total _____

Divided by 4 _____

Rounded to nearest whole number for final score _____

Check the end of the chapter to see how to combine the scores for essays and multiple-choice questions.

Sample answer A

As McKenna and Bargh report in source B, the terrible events of September 11, 2001 showed both the good and bad effects of the Internet. Between 4 and 5 million people sent e-mails to each other when the telephone system failed, comforting each other and checking to see that friends and family had come through without injury. But the Internet also gave the attackers a "place" to meet and plan their deadly attacks (source B). The question of the Internet's effect on society, therefore, is complicated. Overall the Internet has been an extremely positive development, but only so long as the potential dangers are taken into account and controlled by authorities.

The Pew Internet and American Life Project found that most adult Americans are on the Internet, although people over the age of 65 and people who did not finish high school have less access (source A). Because most Americans now have what Oldenburg calls a "third place" to meet away from work and home (source E), ideas can be exchanged freely and people who would never be able to talk in real, personal, face-to-face situations can potentially become friends. Factors that might become a barrier in person aren't important on the Internet, which is "socially unstratified" (source D) and where "how old you are or what you look like or whether you're a student, business executive, or construction worker" doesn't matter (source D). True, some surveys show that Internet use can cut the amount of time spent on personal encounters and "can lead people to spend less time with friends and family" (source C). However, other surveys point to the opposite trend, reporting "more community and political involvement, as well as more social contacts" (source C). As people become more used to the Internet, it is likely that they will find a way to have both personal and Internet contacts.

The level playing field referred to in source D also affects governments. In China, a state where the government is rather strict and tends to control everything it can, the Internet is a possible tool for democracy (source F). Yes, the government "actively pursues and then punishes anyone who posts anti-government comments" (source F). But how can any government check up on 137 million users? It can't. The "Internet savvy" (source F) Chinese are probably more educated, and educated people have higher expectations in life and make more demands. As the Internet becomes even more popular in China and people who live in rural areas or have less education go online, their expectations will rise and they will want more say in how their country is run.

Some experts worry that the Internet will create a "sound-bite culture" and encourage "the violation of privacy" (source E). Television already encourages sound bites, so the Internet is no different. In fact, because the Internet is under the control of the users, they can go to many different sites to check up on the facts. Less power is given to television, and sound-bites may even be lessened by the Internet. Privacy is a problem, but when you check out at the supermarket or buy a magazine subscription, you already become part of someone's database. The Internet isn't different in that effect. If we want privacy and more depth in our news and more complex thinking, we have to work for it. The medium is not responsible. The way we use it is. The attackers of September 11th were responsible for their actions, not the Internet.

Analysis of sample answer A

This AP test taker did a fairly good job on the synthesis question, though you can easily spot a few areas for improvement. Take a look at how this essay rates in each of the four categories.

Clear point of view: 6

Right away you know what this writer thinks about the effect of the Internet on society. The introductory paragraph states that "the Internet has been an extremely positive development, but only so long as the potential dangers are taken into account and controlled by authorities." I can hear you asking: If the writer has stated a point of view, why only a 6? The problem is that one part of the statement is never really addressed in the essay. The essay makes several points about the Internet's positive effects and a couple of points about dangers. The idea that "potential dangers" must be "taken into account and controlled by authorities" isn't developed. The "clear point of view" has to be true of the whole essay, not just the introduction.

Supporting points: 6

The writer throws in quite a few facts from five of the six sources, noting Internet use in the United States (source A) and China (source F) and surveys about the effect of the Internet on life outside the computer (sources C and D). The writer also mentions possible negative effects and answers those objections (sound-bite culture already exists on television, for example). However, the comments about negative effects don't relate to the thesis in paragraph one, which calls for control by authorities, because the writer points out that the Internet is just too big for effective monitoring.

Analysis: 5

The information presented is analyzed fairly well. The second paragraph, for example, attempts to explain the significance of the statistics about who uses the Internet, how the Internet provides a neutral forum, and so forth. Similarly, the writer analyzes the information about China in paragraph 3. A better essay would go a little further, perhaps discussing the gap between the educated and uneducated presented by source A and its potential to create a larger gap in income and experience between those who use the Internet and those who don't.

Writing: 8

This writer tucks the quotations into the text neatly and efficiently and moves well from point to point. The essay is organized, and the mechanics (grammar, spelling, punctuation) are good. Why isn't this a 9? The nine-essay "sings," in the words of one experienced AP grader. This essay speaks well, but the song isn't there.

Overall score: 6

Math time: Add up the four scores

$$6 + 6 + 5 + 8 = 25$$

and divide by 4

$$25 \div 4 = 6.25$$

which rounds down to 6.

Sample answer B

The Internet is everywhere these days, from school to home to business. You can hardly find anyone who hasn't had a chance to buy airline tickets. They also research a report, or even meet a date by going online. The activity in this computer world has been very helpful, it is speeding up our transactions and making modern life easier, but some people don't have a chance to go on the Internet at all. They're left out, and they are on the other side of the "digital divide" (source F). I think the Internet has some good points and bad points.

As Henry Charles says, people in China may have more chance at democracy because of the Internet (source F). Because so many people in China are on the net talking to each other, the government can't keep track of what everyone is saying. The government does arrest some people who talk about democracy, but not all of the people. So in the years to come people in China may get more used to freedom and may have some demands for their government – they will want freedom!

The Internet is also a place where people meet each other. Not just dating. Ray Oldenburg says that the Internet is a "third place" (source E) away from home and work where people make friends. I know when I'm on the Internet, I am part of a virtual reality game that has thousands of players. I don't know the people personally, but I feel like I know them because I spend so much time "talking" to them. Oldenburg thinks that the Internet can make an elite, make ideologies grow, and have other bad effects (source E). But the Internet also lets people form new businesses and takes power away from the "traditional elites" (source E). So overall the effect is positive.

The Internet lets people who have things they like meet each other. About 39000 visitors to the National Geographic Society Web Site began to talk with each other on the telephone and in person after they met on the web site (source C). But if you spend too much time on the web, you will probably spend less time with your family and friends and watching television (source C.

It may be good or bad, but the Internet is not going to go away. It is here to stay, and we have to get used to it. When you look at source A, you see that most people from age 18 to age 64 are on the Internet in America. Older people aren't on as much, but they will probably get onto the net more if someone helps them make the first connection. Also, people on the net are more educated, so they can have a greater effect on American society. That also proves my point, that we may as well get used to the internet because it is permanent.

Analysis of sample answer B

This essay doesn't do the job on any number of levels. Here's how it rates in each of the four categories.

Clear point of view: 3

The writer of this essay is so muddled that she contradicts herself in the very first paragraph, stating that "you can hardly find anyone" who's not on the Internet and then explaining that "some people don't have the chance to go on the Internet at all." The thesis seems to be that "the Internet has some good points and bad points." Okay, that's a point of view, but a vague one. Contrast this thesis statement with the one in sample answer A to see how a qualified "yes, although" thesis can be handled better. The last paragraph of the essay seems to contain a different thesis: The Internet is here to stay. Fine, but that's not what the question asked.

Supporting points: 4

The writer refers to four sources, but one reference to source E confuses Oldenburg, who is mentioned, with the writers of the passage. Also, the writer misread the information about the *National Geographic Society* poll. Furthermore, the writer relies heavily on personal experience, as in the third paragraph when she discusses her participation in an online game. You don't have to exclude every bit of personal experience in the synthesis essay, but it should be a *tiny* part of the essay. The information in the source material is there for a reason: You are supposed to use it, and this writer didn't get much out of the provided material.

Analysis: 3

Here's the biggest problem in an essay filled with problems. The writer mostly summarized information from the sources but did not interpret it — an error the AP considers so horrible that the directions specifically prohibit it. For example, the writer gives some data from source A, but doesn't explain why the reader should care that "older people aren't on as much."

Writing: 3

The writing is okay, but the essay rambles from point to point without much of a logical progression. True, the paragraphs stay mainly on point, but most of the information is just thrown in without any connections or transitions. The essay has some grammar errors, but it is readable.

Overall score: 3

Add up the four scores

$$3 + 4 + 3 + 3 = 13$$

and divide by 4

$$13 \div 4 = 3.25$$

which rounds down to 3.

SCORING ESSAY 2: ANALYTICAL ESSAY ON PAUL ROBESON

The prompt for the second essay asks you to analyze "the rhetorical strategies the author employs to illuminate influences on Paul Robeson's character." So you have two jobs: You have to figure out what influenced Paul Robeson's character, and you have to determine which writing techniques the author — Robeson's son — used to convey those influences. Start by asking these questions about your essay:

- **Have I answered both parts of the question?** An essay that talks only about the influences on Robeson's character is only half-finished, as is an essay that discusses the writing techniques and nothing else.

- **How complex is my analysis?** An essay that describes the passage (for example, that it includes a passage from Robeson's autobiography) doesn't make the grade. A better essay explains the significance of the author's tone or diction or inclusion of anecdotes and quotations.

- **Have I included evidence from the passage?** You can't analyze a piece of writing without quoting from it or referring to it very specifically.

- **Is my essay well written?** Is your writing organized and clear? Have you flubbed the grammar and spelling or aced what English teachers call the "mechanics" of writing?

Scoring grid for the Robeson essay

Addresses the question _____

0 The essay does not answer the question or is left blank. **Note:** If the essay doesn't answer the question, the *overall* score is zero, even if the essay is nicely written and would receive high marks in the "writing" category.

1–3 The essay merely summarizes or lists factors that formed Paul Robeson's character. No attempt is made to discuss how these factors are presented or the rhetorical strategies that the author employed.

4–6 The essay effectively presents the factors that formed Paul Robeson's character. Some portion of the essay deals with rhetorical strategies, but only in a superficial or incomplete way.

7–9 The essay effectively presents the factors that formed Paul Robeson's character and addresses the rhetorical strategies of the passage in depth.

Analysis _____

1–3 The essay stays solely on the surface. Influences on Paul Robeson's character are simply listed, with no analysis of what the passage implies. If writing style is mentioned, it isn't tied to content in any way.

4–6 The essay offers an interpretation of Robeson's character. The essay addresses rhetorical strategies and style fairly well, but does not relate style to content in a meaningful way.

7–9 The essay digs into the text, unearthing and exploring the factors that shaped Paul Robeson's character. The author's writing style is analyzed in depth and clearly linked to content.

Evidence _____

1–3 The writer makes only general statements with no or very few specific references to the text.

4–6 The writer's interpretation is supported by some references to the text. The references may not be the best or most sophisticated choices. Some quotations may be overly long, too short, or not supportive of the writer's point.

7–9 The writer provides strong support for his or her interpretations by choosing specific and relevant evidence from the text. Quotations are excerpted so that the point is made clearly and concisely.

Writing _____

1–3 The essay is disorganized or filled with distracting grammar and spelling errors. Transitions between one point and another are awkward or missing entirely.

4–6 The essay has a logical structure. The writer's thesis (main idea) and supporting points are easily defined. The writing does not always flow smoothly or may contain repetitive or wordy statements. Quotations are inserted awkwardly.

7–9 The essay demonstrates clear, fluid style with a good command of language. The essay moves from a clear thesis through supporting points, each accompanied by evidence, to a logical conclusion.

Fill in each blank in this Essay Scoring Grid with your score, and then add your scores to determine the total.

Addresses the question _____

Analysis _____

Evidence _____

Writing _____

Raw score total _____

Divided by 4 _____

Rounded to nearest whole number for final score _____

Check the end of the chapter to see how to combine the scores for essays and multiple choice questions.

Sample answer A

Paul Robeson grew up to be a civil rights activist, and from the very beginning, he was surrounded by people who cared about justice. Paul was too young to know about his brother's rejection from Princeton University, but he must have been influenced by his father, William Drew Robeson, who protested the rejection and demanded a response from the president of Princeton, Woodrow Wilson. Paul must have heard, throughout his childhood, how his father preached and how he protested. William Drew is described as having "dramatic power and inspiring messages", and the author mentions William's "determined criticism of social justice."

The excerpt also mentions a black congressman, George C. White, who lost his election because of "electoral rigging." This second example of racial injustice also took place when Paul was little. Though he could not have understood it at the time, the congressman's statement that there was only a "temporary farewell to the American Congress" from blacks turned out to be true. The hope expressed by George C. White was justified, and Paul probably picked up some hope from White too.

After the information about William Drew Robeson and George White, the author turns to William's career in his later years. William drew carried ashes and sometimes other things in order to earn a living. However, he was always dignified and respectable. Paul must have understood that a man should behave with dignity no matter what happens, because that's what his father always did. The excerpt from Paul Robeson's autobiography emphasizes the father's dignity and gives the reader Paul's own words, which makes his personality come alive.

The essay also spends some time talking about Paul Robeson's brother, the one who couldn't go to Princeton. Paul must have understood that you shouldn't give up, even when things don't go well, because his brother didn't give up after Princeton rejected him. Instead, Bill went to another college and to medical school. Bill taught Paul how to play football. It says in the introduction to the excerpt that Robeson was an athlete. Bill taught Paul how to be an athlete.

The writing style of this passage is very clear. The author uses little stories about Bill and William to make his point. The author also brings in a quotation as evidence and to allow the reader to hear Paul "in person." All these things make you see how Paul grew up and what influenced him.

Analysis of sample answer A

This essay has quite a few holes in it, making it at best a below-average effort.

Addresses the question: 3

This essay talks about the content of the passage, listing several elements: Bill's rejection from Princeton and William Drew's demand for answers from Wilson, William Drew's dismissal from his church, the statement of George C. White to congress, William's work as an ash collector, his son's autobiography, and the sports skills that Bill taught Paul. However, the essay says almost nothing about *how* the passage is written other than a short list in the last paragraph.

Analysis: 2

The essay attempts a little psychological analysis, trying to draw a line from William Drew's protest to Paul's activism, for example. However, the essay doesn't discuss the effects of the author's rhetorical devices — the writing techniques employed — and makes very little use of the information presented about Robeson's family or the time in which he grew up.

Evidence: 2

The essay pulls in some evidence in the form of brief quotations, but they don't make much of a case for any particular rhetorical strategy. The essay calls the passage "clear" without giving any examples.

Writing: 3

The writing isn't terrible, though the essay has a few grammar errors and at one point calls the passage an "essay" instead of a biography. The essay has a reasonable structure, moving more or less chronologically through the passage and then making a couple of basic points about writing style in the last paragraph. Nevertheless, this essay is a long way from a mature, AP-level effort.

Overall score: 3

Here's how to calculate the score for the sample A. First, add up the four scores

$$3 + 2 + 2 + 3 = 10$$

and divide by 4

$$10 \div 4 = 2.5$$

which rounds up to 3.

Sample answer B

Paul Robeson's life as a civil rights activist undoubtedly had many roots, chief among them the examples from his own family and the terribly unfair era in which he grew up. In this excerpt from a biography of Robeson, written by his own son, the author paints a picture of a determined father, a loving and helpful brother, and a son who appreciated both. The author also includes an anecdote about a black congressman who loses his election because of "electoral rigging" and who prophesizes, correctly, that blacks will overcome and return to Congress.

The author's chief strategy is anecdote. First he presents the anecdote about Bill's rejection from Princeton and then one about William Drew's dismissal from his church. Next there is an anecdote about George C. White, and finally a bit of description of William Drew's life after his dismissal and Paul's interaction with his brother. The anecdotes are the kind of family history that gets passed down from one generation to another. Although Paul was only two when Bill was not allowed to enroll in Princeton, one can imagine that the Robeson family often told and retold that little story as a moral lesson to Paul. Is it a surprise that he became an activist for civil rights? The story of George C. White is from the world outside the Robeson family. This widens the scope of the passage and shows the influence of the climate in the United States when Robeson was growing up. Although the White story isn't the kind that gets passed down within a family, it does show what Paul had to deal with when he wasn't in the family home. (The dismissal of his father was probably only one injustice that Paul witnessed personally.)

The author's diction also reveals a lot about Paul Robeson's early influences. Reverend Robeson didn't just ask Wilson for an explanation of his son's rejection; he "refused to accept" Wilson's attempt to avoid a confrontation. William Drew is described as "refusing as usual to compromise on matters of principle." The words "refused" and "refusing" hammer home the point that William Drew was a strong man, as was his son. Other words associated with William Drew in this passage include "defiance," "dramatic power," and "determined criticism of social injustice." These are forceful words for a forceful man, who raised a forceful son.

Another element of style in this passage is the long quotation from Paul Robeson's autobiography. There the fruit of his father's strength comes across clearly. Paul describes his father as "dignified" and says that "no man carried himself with greater pride." He tells of his father's hard work and then notes that "mostly I played." His father's struggles allowed the son to have a happy childhood — something the quotation emphasizes. Even within the quotation, there is an anecdote. The anecdote tells about Paul's lessons in football, when Bill taught his "how to tackle a man so he stayed tackled." Again, strength is emphasized, and that strength carried Paul Robeson to his work in civil rights.

Analysis of sample answer B

Now we've got some AP-level work! This essay is a winner.

Addresses the question: 8

This essay addresses the question very well; it stays on topic and goes right to the point about the factors that influenced Paul Robeson's development. The essay also addresses the way in which the passage is written — the rhetorical strategies employed by the author.

Analysis: 8

Sample answer B does a fine job explaining what's going on in the passage. The essay talks about the anecdotes, diction, and quotation and explains what each contributes to the passage. These elements of writing are discussed in relation to the content of the passage, and everything is tied to Paul Robeson's character.

Evidence: 7

The essay uses quotations fairly effectively, especially in the paragraph about diction. A few more quotations might have been helpful, but this writer knows how to make a point and back it up from the passage.

Writing: 8

This exam-taker created a logical structure and shows a good, though not excellent, command of language. The point about George C. White is made in two places; combining these points in one spot would have been better. The essay has very few mechanical problems (errors in grammar).

Overall score: 8

Add up the four scores

$$8 + 8 + 7 + 8 = 31$$

and divide by 4

$$31 \div 4 = 7.75$$

which rounds up to 8.

SCORING ESSAY 3: LEADERSHIP

With this sort of essay, you don't have to read anything except the prompt. You do, however, have to unearth information (about history, literature, or your own life, for example) that doesn't appear on the test in order to answer this question. To rate your answer, ask yourself these questions:

- **Have I answered the question?** First you need to explain what quality you see as essential to leadership. If you differ from Maurois, no problem. You can acknowledge and respond to Maurois's ideas, but most of your energy should go toward proving your own case, not demolishing Maurois's.

- **Have I provided supporting points?** If you selected "excellent speaking skills" as the essential leader-quality, you have to make a case for that characteristic. The case consists of reasons why "excellent speaking skills" are important.

- **Have I included evidence?** For your discussion of speaking skills, for example, you need to be able to cite (though not necessarily quote from) powerful speeches given by outstanding leaders.

- **Is my essay well written?** Check structure, organization, clarity, grammar, spelling, and punctuation.

Because this is an open-ended question, I can't even imagine which quality of leadership you chose to write about. The sample answers here will help you score your own effort, but keep in mind that it's possible to differ greatly from these samples and still do well on this question. Be extra careful applying the general guidelines to your own work.

Scoring grid for the leadership essay

Addresses the question _____

0   The essay does not answer the question or is left blank. **Note:** If the essay doesn't answer the question, the *overall* score is zero, even if the essay is nicely written and would receive high marks in the "writing" category.

1–3   The essay partially answers the question. For example, an essay that proves Maurois wrong and hints at other important leadership qualities is in this slot. So is an essay that contains a lot of off-topic material, straying from leadership into, for example, techniques to identify leadership.

4–6   The essay answers the question by choosing the important leadership quality but buries that fact in a mass of detail or generalities. Key rule: You don't want to have to read the thing twice to find the thesis. An essay in this category may contain some off-topic material, but not much.

7–9   The essay chooses the most important leadership quality and stays focused on it.

Supporting points _____

1–3   The essay provides few reasons other than "I think so" for the chosen leadership quality. Or the essay muddles all the arguments for the most important leadership quality into one undifferentiated mass.

4–6   The essay contains two or three reasons why the chosen leadership quality is essential. The reasons are only loosely linked to the leadership quality.

7–9   The essay identifies three or four reasons why the chosen leadership quality is the most important. Each reason is strongly and logically tied to leadership.

Evidence _____

1–3   The essay contains few or no examples from history, literature, or personal experience to back up the claim that a particular quality is most important in a leader. Or the examples are poorly explained.

4–6 The essay contains a couple of solid examples from history, literature, or personal experience. The examples are fairly well explained but could be discussed at greater length or in greater detail.

7–9 An essay in this slot has very good examples of the chosen leadership quality. Each example clearly shows why the quality is essential.

Writing _____

1–3 The essay is disorganized, hopping from one idea to another or repeating something already stated. Or the essay has many distracting errors in grammar and spelling.

4–6 The essay is fairly well written, with a logical structure and some — but not many — mechanical errors. The writing sounds less polished than an essay in the next higher category.

7–9 Essays in this range sound mature. The sentences vary in length and pattern, the diction and tone are consistent, and the logical structure of the argument is easy to follow.

Fill in the blanks below to determine your total score:

Addresses the question _____

Supporting points _____

Evidence _____

Writing _____

Raw score total _____

Divided by 4 _____

Rounded to nearest whole number for final score _____

Go to the end of the chapter to convert your essay and multiple-choice scores into an AP-exam score.

Sample answer A

Andre Maurois said that "The most important quality in a leader is that of being acknowledged as such." Maurois's comment is practical. What use is a leader if no one is following. But sometimes a leader's followers take a long time to emerge – even after the leader's death. Also, sometimes a small number of people follow a particular leader, and a great many people reject him or her. The number isn't necessarily crucial to leadership, because a committed group with a dedicated leader can change the world. Therefore, to judge a leader by his or her acceptance is a good standard, so long as that standard isn't applied too narrowly.

The former mayor of my town was, I believe, a very good leader, even though he served only one term and was strongly defeated by the current mayor in the last election. Why did the former mayor lose? He had a lot of great ideas — he really cared about the environment, for example, and he pushed for many regulations to create a "greener" town government. Under his leadership, stores had to ask you whether you wanted a bag or not, and recycling went to a whole new level, with large fines for unrecycled trash. Of course this made him many enemies in the business community, because their only concern was profit. Did this make the mayor less of a leader? I don't think he could have convinced the business owners to like him or to reelect him, and he wasn't their leader. But he did inspire my grade to press for "good-on-one-side" printing paper (reused scrap paper) and biodegradable lunch containers. He was our leader, even if he lost the election, and the ideas he put into place will last for generations and even be extended. There are more people in my high school who followed the former mayor than in the business community. So by numbers, and by impact, the mayor fits Maurois' definition.

History has many examples of leaders who <u>were</u> acknowledged by some people, though maybe not by enough, during their lifetimes. Rachel Carson, for example, wrote about "the silent spring" that would happen when pesticides had killed too many animals and plants. She wrote in the 1920s, and not many people paid attention to her. However, many years later, in the present time, she is now seen as a visionary. Was Rachel Carson a leader. I think she was. Another person who became a leader only later was Betty Friedan, the author of <u>The Feminine Mistique.</u> She described the way that women were limited by their roles as housewifes, and advocated for more power and equality for women. Her ideas in the 1950s weren't really accepted, but now they are. Friedan was a leader too.

Andre Maurois was only partially right in his definition of leadership. He should have said more to define "acknowledged." Once the definition of "acknowledged" is widened, you can include more true leaders in that category. Your influence can go on even in the face of opposition and sometimes even after you die, if you are a true leader.

Analysis of sample answer A

This is a fairly good essay, by a writer who has some complexity in his thinking. Yes, the essay isn't perfect, but the writer has conveyed his ideas and made a case for his definition of leadership. Now for the details.

Addresses the question: 7

The writer accepts Maurois's idea about leadership but qualifies it a little. The introductory paragraph says it all: "to judge a leader by his or her acceptance is a good standard, so long as that standard isn't applied too narrowly." The essay stays on this topic throughout.

Supporting points: 6

The writer has two supporting points: (1) sometimes a leader is recognized only later and (2) a leader may be recognized by some but not all people and still be effective. Not bad! I wouldn't mind seeing one other supporting point, perhaps about the way acknowledgment is measured — by re-election? by bills passed? by lives changed? Still, two good supporting points are present in this essay.

Evidence: 6

The examples of the mayor, Rachel Carson, and Betty Friedan are all good, though the writer has a couple of facts wrong. (For example, Carson didn't write in the 1920s!) The AP graders, fortunately, are told to recognize that writers can't check their facts in the middle of an exam. Happily for you, mistaking a date won't hurt your score. The example of the mayor is more fleshed out than the other two examples. A little more on Carson and Friedan would have raised this score.

Writing: 6

The essay is reasonably well written. The writer has made a couple of spelling errors ("mystique," not "mistique," for example), and some of the sentences are awkward. The last paragraph is not as polished as the first, probably because the writer was tiring.

Overall score: 6

To calculate the overall score for the leadership essay, add the four scores

$$7 + 6 + 6 + 6 = 25$$

and divide by 4

$$25 \div 4 = 6.25$$

which rounds down to 6.

Sample answer B

"The most important quality in a leader is that of being acknowledged as such." That's what Andree Marois said, but he was wrong. The most important quality in a leader is honesty. If you aren't honest, you can't be a leader. Case closed. Maybe you will have some success for a while, but then you will fail. To prove this point, look at King Claudius in Hamlet, which was written by William Shakespeare, and many other literary works. Also, think about the people you have known who have been honest or dishonest.

Claudius was Hamlet's uncle, and he became king because he murdered Hamlet, the old king who had the same name as the character who is the most important one in the play. Claudius murdered the king because he wanted to take over the throne and also marry Gertrude, Hamlet's mother, who loved her husband but was fooled by him and ultimately died because of him. Claudius in the first act seems to be doing okay as a leader, but pretty soon you see the cracks in his facade. He says that he can't repent of his actions without giving up the kingship and his wife, so he doesn't repent, and in the end Hamlet killed him. Gertrude dies when she drinks from a poisoned cup, which Claudius had ready to kill Hamlet (the son). Was Claudius a leader? For a little while he is in charge, but he isn't really a leader because no one likes him, and no one likes him because he wasn't honest. He started and ended with murder.

Other literary works show characters who try to be leaders but who aren't honest, and then they aren't really leaders. In Great Expectations written by Charles Dickens, Uncle Pumblechook wants to be the important leader in the neighborhood, but he fails because he claims to have made Pip a gentleman and to have liked him all along, even though really he was mean to Pip when Pip was little. Uncle Pumblechook isn't a leader because he lies. In Their Eyes Were Watching God by Zora Neale Hurston, Joe Starks thinks he is the leader of the town just because of his store and his position as mayor, but he tries too hard to control Janey and loses her to Tea Cake. Joe isn't a real leader either.

In my family, one of my uncles always wants to be the leader. He was the first to start a business, and he has done well. At dinners on holidays, he is the one to say when we are finished or what the topic of conversation will be. But then we found out that he had taken some money from my grandmother after she died without sharing it equally with his brother and sisters. So he isn't a leader, we don't listen to what he has to say.

Analysis of sample answer B

This essay doesn't represent a very strong effort. Here's the breakdown.

Addresses the question: 3

The writer takes a stab at defining leadership, choosing honesty as the crucial quality. So far, so good. The essay wanders into all sorts of off-topic paths — murder, for example — and spends far too much time summarizing plot.

Supporting points: 2

The writer doesn't really explain why honesty is the most important quality of a leader. She might have said, for example, that dishonest leaders eventually find themselves in disgrace (or in jail). She could have discussed the way that people relate to leaders and how honesty facilitates that relationship. The essay has several examples (see "Evidence," below) but no real support for the idea of honesty as a crucial component of leadership.

Evidence: 4

The examples of Claudius and the uncle are reasonable, though the discussion of Claudius has way too much plot summary and not enough commentary on Claudius as leader. The catch-all paragraph about Dickens and Hurston is not very helpful. Yes, the writer shows that Uncle Pumblechook is a liar, but what does that have to do with leadership? The comments about Hurston are even more problematic because Joe's wish to hold onto his wife has little to do with leadership.

Writing: 4

This essay, if it were a boat, would be leaking from several spots but not quite sinking. The points the writer wants to make are conveyed with some errors but reasonable clarity.

Overall score: 3

To calculate the overall score for the leadership essay, add the four scores

$$3 + 2 + 4 + 4 = 13$$

and divide by 4

$$13 \div 4 = 3.25$$

which rounds down to 3.

EXAM CONVERSION CHART

Now that you've checked the multiple-choice and essay responses, you're ready for the final number. Fill in the accompanying chart, drawing upon the numbers you calculated for the multiple-choice section and for each essay.

Multiple Choice

Multiple-choice score _____ × 1.23 = _____ (final multiple-choice score)

Essays

Essay 1 score _____ + Essay 2 score _____ + Essay 3 score _____ = _____ (essay raw score)

Essay raw score _____ × 3.06 = _____ (final essay score)

Final Score

Final multiple-choice score _____ + final essay score _____ = _____ (final raw score)

AP Score

Now find your AP score, using the following table:

Final Raw Score	AP Score
104+	5
92–103	4
76–91	3
50–75	2
Below 50	1

19

Practice Exam 2

If you're working through this book from front to back, this chapter is your second stab at a full-length practice exam. Chapter 20 provides answers and explanations. Before you begin this exam, read the general directions for how to prepare for the exam in Chapter 17, which contains Practice Exam 1. Those directions help you simulate real AP exam conditions.

THE AP ENGLISH LANGUAGE AND COMPOSITION TEST

This test consists of two parts:

> **Section One:** Multiple choice — one hour
>
> **Section Two:** Essays — fifteen-minute reading period plus two hours for writing

At any time you may write in the margins of the exam, annotating as you wish. However, nothing but the scoring grid and the essay answer sheets will be graded. Answers or remarks written next to the question receive no credit. During the fifteen-minute reading period, you may not write on the answer sheet.

SECTION ONE: MULTIPLE CHOICE

Time: 60 minutes

This section contains five selections, each of which is followed by a set of questions. Section One has a total of 53 questions and counts as 45 percent of the exam score.

You have one hour for this section. Work carefully and quickly. Not all students will finish the multiple-choice questions. Blank and wrong answers receive no credit.

Do not turn to another section if you finish early.

For each multiple-choice question, choose the best answer. Fill in the corresponding oval, being sure to darken the entire oval. Do not select more than one answer. If you erase an answer, take care to do so completely. Questions with more than one answer are automatically scored as wrong.

Questions 1–10 are based on the following passage, which is a letter written by Pliny, an ancient Roman writer, lawyer, and philosopher, to a friend. Read the letter carefully and answer the questions following it.

---

(01) To SOCIUS SENECIO:

This year has produced a plentiful crop of poets: during the whole month of April scarcely a day has passed on which we have not been entertained with the recital of some poem. It is a pleasure to me to find that a taste for polite literature still exists, and that
(05) men of genius do come forward and make themselves known, notwithstanding the lazy attendance they got for their pains. The greater part of the audience sit in the lounging-places, gossip away their time there, and are perpetually sending to enquire whether the author has made his entrance yet, whether he has got through the preface, or whether he has almost finished the piece. Then at length they saunter in with an air of the great-
(10) est indifference, nor do they condescend to stay through the recital, but go out before it is over, some slyly and stealthily, others again with perfect freedom and unconcern. And yet our fathers can remember how Claudius Caesar, walking one day in the palace, and hearing a great shouting, enquired the cause: and being informed that Nonianus was reciting a composition of his, went immediately to the place, and agreeably surprised the author
(15) with his presence. But now, were one to bespeak the attendance of the idlest man living, and remind him of the appointment ever so often, or ever so long beforehand; either he would not come at all, or if he did would grumble about having "lost a day!" for no other reason but because he had not lost it. So much the more do those authors deserve our encouragement and applause who have resolution to persevere in their studies, and to
(20) read out their compositions in spite of this apathy or arrogance on the part of their audience. Myself indeed, I scarcely ever miss being present upon any occasion; though, to tell the truth, the authors have generally been friends of mine, as indeed there are few men of literary tastes who are not. It is this which has kept me in town longer than I had intended. I am now, however, at liberty to go back into the country, and write something
(25) myself; which I do not intend reciting, lest I should seem rather to have lent than given my attendance to these recitations of my friends, for in these, as in all other good offices, the obligation ceases the moment you seem to expect a return.

Farewell.

1. The expression "their pains" (line 6) is equivalent to which of the following?

   (A) "a taste for polite literature" (line 4)

   (B) "lazy attendance" (lines 5–6)

   (C) "agreeably surprised the author with his presence" (lines 14–15)

   (D) "persevere in their studies, and to read out their compositions" (lines 19–20)

   (E) "write something myself; which I do not intend reciting" (lines 24–25)

2. Pliny uses all of the following techniques to characterize the audience at poetry readings EXCEPT

   (A) thoughts

   (B) setting

   (C) actions

   (D) dialogue

   (E) description

3. The chief rhetorical strategy of this letter is

   (A) narrative

   (B) cause and effect

   (C) comparison and contrast

   (D) definition

   (E) description

4. The author most likely includes the anecdote about Claudius Caesar in order to

   (A) show that the quality of poetry has declined

   (B) reveal the author's knowledge of history

   (C) establish that poetry was once appreciated

   (D) reveal the author's connection with nobility

   (E) link himself to nobility

5. The statement that "he had not lost it" (line 18) may best be restated as which of the following?

   (A) Poetry is not a lost art.

   (B) Every activity has some value.

   (C) It is never too late to change.

   (D) He could always change his plans.

   (E) He participated in a valuable activity.

6. Lines 18–19, "[s]o much the more do those authors deserve our encouragement and applause," imply a comparison between

   (A) authors with appreciative and unappreciative audiences

   (B) poets and aristocrats

   (C) poets and their audiences

   (D) authors who work hard on their creations and those who don't

   (E) people who attend poetry readings and people who stay home

7. Pliny's purpose in mentioning that "the authors have generally been friends of mine" (line 22) is probably to

   (A) brag about his literary connections

   (B) reveal that his motives for attending readings are not purely literary

   (C) explain his sole reason for attending literary events

   (D) pressure the reader to attend Pliny's readings

   (E) show that most people need extra incentives to appreciate literature

8. Lines 23–24 contain the statement that "It is this which has kept me in town longer than I had intended." What is the meaning of "this"?

   (A) that Pliny's friends are authors

   (B) that Pliny's friends have given readings

   (C) attending literary events

   (D) increasing the audience at literary events

   (E) writing poetry

9. Why is the author of this letter unwilling to recite his own work?

   (A) He is afraid that it is unworthy.

   (B) He feels that modern audiences do not appreciate art.

   (C) He does not want his attendance at his friends' readings to be misinterpreted.

   (D) He will be too isolated in the country.

   (E) He wants to concentrate only on writing.

10. The tone of this letter may be characterized as

   (A) didactic and ironic

   (B) sarcastic and pedantic

   (C) nostalgic and regretful

   (D) critical and serious

   (E) formal and somber

Directions for questions 11–20: Read this excerpt from The Souls of Black Folk, *a book of essays by W. E .B. DuBois. Then answer the questions that follow.*

---

(01)   In a wee wooden schoolhouse, something put it into the boys' and girls' heads to buy gorgeous visiting-cards — ten cents a package — and exchange. The exchange was merry, till one girl, a tall newcomer, refused my card, — refused it peremptorily, with a glance. Then it dawned upon me with a certain suddenness that I was different from the others;
(05)   or like, mayhap, in heart and life and longing, but shut out from their world by a vast veil. I had thereafter no desire to tear down that veil, to creep through; I held all beyond it in common contempt, and lived above it in a region of blue sky and great wandering shadows. That sky was bluest when I could beat my mates at examination-time, or beat them at a foot-race, or even beat their stringy heads. Alas, with the years all this fine contempt
(10)   began to fade; for the words I longed for, and all their dazzling opportunities, were theirs, not mine. But they should not keep these prizes, I said; some, all, I would wrest from them. Just how I would do it I could never decide: by reading law, by healing the sick, by telling the wonderful tales that swam in my head,— some way. With other black boys the strife was not so fiercely sunny: their youth shrunk into tasteless sycophancy, or into silent hatred of
(15)   the pale world about them and mocking distrust of everything white; or wasted itself in a bitter cry, why did God make me an outcast and a stranger in mine own house? The shades of the prison-house closed round about us all: walls strait and stubborn to the whitest, but relentlessly narrow, tall, and unscalable to sons of night who must plod darkly on in resignation, or beat unavailing palms against the stone, or steadily, half hopelessly, watch the
(20)   streak of blue above.
   After the Egyptian and Indian, the Greek and Roman, the Teuton and Mongolian, the Negro is a sort of seventh son, born with a veil, and gifted with second-sight in this American world,— a world which yields him no true self-consciousness, but only lets him see himself through the revelation of the other world. It is a peculiar sensation, this double-
(25)   consciousness, this sense of always looking at one's self through the eyes of others, of measuring one's soul by the tape of a world that looks on in amused contempt and pity. One ever feels his twoness,— an American, a Negro; two souls, two thoughts, two unreconciled strivings; two warring ideals in one dark body, whose dogged strength alone keeps it from being torn asunder.
(30)   The history of the American Negro is the history of this strife,— this longing to attain self-conscious manhood, to merge his double self into a better and truer self. In this merging he wishes neither of the older selves to be lost. He would not Africanize America, for America has too much to teach the world and Africa. He would not bleach his Negro soul in a flood of white Americanism, for he knows that Negro blood has a message for
(35)   the world. He simply wishes to make it possible for a man to be both a Negro and an American, without being cursed and spit upon by his fellows, without having the doors of Opportunity closed roughly in his face.
   This, then, is the end of his striving: to be a co-worker in the kingdom of culture, to escape both death and isolation, to husband and use his best powers and his latent genius.

11. Which phrase best expresses the main idea of the first paragraph (lines 1–20)?

(A) the role of race in one boy's life

(B) causes of hatred

(C) experiences in school

(D) striving for excellence

(E) reactions to prejudice

12. All of the following phrases are equivalent EXCEPT
   (A) "see himself through the revelation of the other world" (lines 23–24)
   (B) "double-consciousness" (lines 24–25)
   (C) "twoness" (line 27)
   (D) "self-conscious manhood" (line 31)
   (E) "double self" (line 31)

13. What is the meaning of "like" in the context of line 5?
   (A) affection
   (B) the same
   (C) almost
   (D) for example
   (E) similarity

14. The phrase "this fine contempt" (line 9) is illustrated by which of the following?
   (A) "when I could beat my mates at examination-time" (line 8)
   (B) "the words I longed for" (line 10)
   (C) "all their dazzling opportunities" (line 10)
   (D) "tasteless sycophancy" (line 14)
   (E) "mocking distrust" (line 15)

15. The "blue sky and great wandering shadows" (lines 7–8) may symbolize the narrator's
   (A) attempt to rise above his situation
   (B) inability to change others' views of him
   (C) yearning for freedom
   (D) competition with his schoolmates
   (E) imaginary world

16. In lines 13–14 ("With other black boys . . .") the passage shifts from
   (A) third-person limited to third-person omniscient
   (B) nostalgia to bitterness
   (C) description to narration
   (D) rebellion to acceptance
   (E) personal narration to general observation

17. The narrator refers to a "veil" in several places (lines 5, 6, and 22). Which of these statements are true in the context of this passage?

   I. The veil excludes blacks from the world of white people.

  II. The veil comes into effect during elementary school.

 III. The veil impedes the formation of identity.

   (A) I only

   (B) I and II

   (C) II and III

   (D) I and III

   (E) all of the above

18. The sentence beginning "One ever feels . . . asunder" (lines 27–29) achieves its effect primarily by

   (A) metaphor and simile

   (B) parallelism and repetition

   (C) symbolism and hyperbole

   (D) irony and imagery

   (E) allusion and apostrophe

19. Lines 32–35 ("He would not Africanize . . . message for the world") serve to

   (A) explain the effects of "strife" (line 30)

   (B) state the goals of the writer

   (C) lead into the main idea of the following sentence

   (D) illustrate "twoness" (line 27)

   (E) allay the fears of the reader

20. The attitude of the author may be described as

   (A) conciliatory and philosophical

   (B) argumentative and sarcastic

   (C) passionate and committed

   (D) realistic and cautious

   (E) resigned but hopeful

Directions for questions 21–30: After carefully reading the passage below, answer the questions that follow.

(01)   The personal character and career of one man are so intimately connected with the great scheme of the years 1719 and 1720, that a history of the Mississippi madness can have no fitter introduction than a sketch of the life of its great author John Law. Historians are divided in opinion as to whether they should designate him a knave or a mad-
(05)   man. Both epithets were unsparingly applied to him in his lifetime, and while the unhappy consequences of his projects were still deeply felt. Posterity, however, has found reason to doubt the justice of the accusation, and to confess that John Law was neither knave nor madman, but one more deceived than deceiving, more sinned against than sinning. He was thoroughly acquainted with the philosophy and true principles of credit. He
(10)   understood the monetary question better than any man of his day; and if his system fell with a crash so tremendous, it was not so much his fault as that of the people amongst whom he had erected it. He did not calculate upon the avaricious frenzy of a whole nation; he did not see that confidence, like mistrust, could be increased almost ad infinitum, and that hope was as extravagant as fear. How was he to foretell that the French people,
(15)   like the man in the fable, would kill, in their frantic eagerness, the fine goose he had brought to lay them so many golden eggs? His fate was like that which may be supposed to have overtaken the first adventurous boatman who rowed from Erie to Ontario. Broad and smooth was the river on which he embarked; rapid and pleasant was his progress; and who was to stay him in his career? Alas for him, the cataract was nigh. He saw, when
(20)   it was too late, that the tide which wafted him so joyously along was a tide of destruction; and when he endeavoured to retrace his way, he found that the current was too strong for his weak efforts to stem, and that he drew nearer every instant to the tremendous falls. Down he went over the sharp rocks, and the waters with him. He was dashed to pieces with his bark, but the waters, maddened and turned to foam by the rough descent, only
(25)   boiled and bubbled for a time, and then flowed on again as smoothly as ever. Just so it was with Law and the French people. He was the boatman, and they were the waters.
    John Law was born at Edinburgh in the year 1671. His father was the younger son of an ancient family in Fife, and carried on the business of a goldsmith and banker. He amassed considerable wealth in his trade, sufficient to enable him to gratify the wish,
(30)   so common among his countrymen, of adding a territorial designation to his name. He purchased with this view the estates of Lauriston and Randleston, on the Frith of Forth[1], on the borders of West and Mid Lothian[2], and was thenceforth known as Law of Lauriston. The subject of our memoir, being the eldest son, was received into his father's counting-house at the age of fourteen, and for three years laboured hard to acquire an insight into
(35)   the principles of banking as then carried on in Scotland. He had always manifested great love for the study of numbers, and his proficiency in the mathematics was considered extraordinary in one of his tender years. At the age of seventeen he was tall, strong, and well made; and his face, although deeply scarred with the small-pox, was agreeable in its expression, and full of intelligence. At this time he began to neglect his business, and be-
(40)   coming vain of his person, indulged in considerable extravagance of attire. He was a great favourite with the ladies, by whom he was called Beau Law; while the other sex, despising his foppery[3], nicknamed him Jessamy John. At the death of his father, which happened in 1688, he withdrew entirely from the desk, which had become so irksome, and being possessed of the revenues of the paternal estate of Lauriston, he proceeded to London, to see
(45)   the world.

1. A body of water in Scotland. 2. Areas of Scotland. 3. The quality of a man who pays too much attention to clothes and manners.

21. How may the rhetorical purpose of the first sentence in the passage (lines 1–3) best be described?

    (A) It provides background information on John Law.

    (B) It justifies an exploration of John Law's life.

    (C) It exonerates John Law.

    (D) It explains why historians have been divided in their view of John Law.

    (E) It informs the reader about "Mississippi madness" (line 2).

22. In line 3, "its" refers to which of the following?

    (A) "character" (line 1)

    (B) "career" (line 1)

    (C) "scheme" (line 2)

    (D) "history" (line 2)

    (E) "introduction" (line 3)

23. The frequent use of "he" in lines 9–15 serves to

    (A) introduce a list of Law's faults

    (B) make the references to John Law more universal

    (C) focus the reader's attention on Law

    (D) qualify Law's guilt in "Mississippi madness"

    (E) create a list of reasons why Law is blameless

24. The fourth sentence ("Posterity . . . sinning" — lines 6–9) is characterized by

    (A) parallel structure

    (B) an ironic tone

    (C) circular reasoning

    (D) sensory details

    (E) a nonjudgmental stance

25. The "fine goose" that produced "so many golden eggs" (lines 15–16) is an example of

    (A) morality

    (B) metaphor

    (C) figurative language

    (D) paradox

    (E) allusion

26. In lines 17–26, the author employs an extended metaphor for what purpose?

    (A) to illustrate the dangers of river travel

    (B) to portray Law as a force of nature

    (C) to show that Law wasn't fully in control of the situation

    (D) to blame the people of France

    (E) to show that Law didn't understand the trouble he was in

27. The abrupt shift between paragraphs one (lines 1–26) and two (lines 27–45) may best be described by which of the following?

    (A) biographical to philosophical

    (B) argumentative to expository

    (C) concrete to metaphorical

    (D) descriptive to explanatory

    (E) third to second person

28. In the context of line 37, what is the meaning of "tender"?

    (A) soft

    (B) young

    (C) innocent

    (D) advanced

    (E) teenaged

29. The author's observation that Law was "nicknamed . . . Jessamy John" (line 42)

    (A) contrasts with Law's attractiveness to women

    (B) shows that Law had many male friends

    (C) reveals that Law was popular

    (D) creates an informal tone

    (E) relies on a knowledge of eighteenth century history

30. The author's purpose in this passage is probably to

    (A) mock John Law

    (B) show that history is subject to interpretation

    (C) place Law's actions in context

    (D) caution against hasty judgments

    (E) illuminate a particular period in French history

Directions for questions 31–43. The passage below is excerpted from Gandhi: A Life, *by Yogesh Chadha (Wiley, 1997; reprinted with permission of John Wiley & Sons, Inc.). The events described take place in 1930 when Mohandas K. Gandhi, a leader of the nonviolent protest movement attempting to free India, then a British colony, led a group of marchers to the sea coast to protest the Salt Tax. Gandhi's plan was to extract salt from the sea, an illegal act, and to accept the ensuing punishment.*

(01) Gandhi marched at the head of the procession like a conqueror. Behind him the administration was silently crumbling as scores of village headmen resigned. On his arrival at Borsad on 18 March, large-scale resignations by village administrators were announced. Gandhi reiterated the significance of this noncooperation to the assembled crowd:

(05)   Today we are defying the salt law. Tomorrow we shall have to consign other laws to the waste-paper basket. Doing so we shall practise such severe non-cooperation that finally it will not be possible for the administration to be carried out at all. Let the government then, to carry on its rules, use guns against us, send us to prison, hang us. But how many can be given such punishment? Try and calculate how much time
(10)   it will take of Britishers to hang three hundred million of persons.[1]

The spectacle of this sixty-year-old man, staff in hand, striding vigorously along the dusty roads of India with his khadi-clad followers, to challenge peacefully the mighty British Empire, aroused the interest and sympathy of millions all over the world. "For me there is no turning back, whether I am alone or joined by thousands," he declared. "I would rather
(15) die a dog's death and have my bones licked by dogs than that I should return to the ashram a broken man."[2] In the course of his speech at Navsari a few days later, he proclaimed: "I shall return with what I want or my dead body will float in the ocean."[3]

At first the authorities expected the salt march to fizzle out but when the tempo began to increase and the movement to spread, the Bombay government sought to persuade
(20) Lord Irwin to take action against Gandhi. The Viceroy was not in favor of Gandhi's arrest, though he knew he would have to act eventually. He was marking time, for he was more inclined to rely on the reports of his agents and advisers than on those in the world press, which was being fed by Indian nationalist sources. "The will-power of the man must have been enormous to get him through his march," he wrote to the Secretary of State for India
(25) a few days later. "I was always told that his blood pressure is dangerous and his heart none too good, and I was also told a few days ago that his horoscope predicts that he will die this year, and that is the explanation of this desperate throw. It would be a very happy solution."[4] This was a rather harsh verdict, coming from a Viceroy who regarded himself as a man of principle. In any event Lord Irwin's sources of information were grossly inac-
(30) curate since they were primarily based on rumors.

Meanwhile the villagers joined the column as it surged on, and when on 5 April, after a march of twenty-four days, it reached the sea coast at Dandi, the original group of seventy-nine had swelled to thousands. Among them were many women — not only the poor, but wealthy ladies from the cities. Asked what he hoped to achieve by breaking the salt laws,
(35) Gandhi answered: "I want world sympathy in this battle of Right against Might."[5]

1. Mohandas K. Gandhi, *The Collected Works*, XLIII (New Delhi: Publication Division of the Government of India, 1958-84), 100.
2. Ibid, 149.
3. Ibid.
4. D. G. Tendulkar (ed.), *Gandhiji: His Life and Work III* (Bombay: Karnatak Publishing House, 1945), 30.
5. Gandhi, *Works*, XLIII, 149.

31. Given the information in the introduction and in the passage, what is the likely identity of the "administration" (lines 1–2)?

    (A) local dissidents

    (B) opponents of the British government

    (C) supporters of the Salt March

    (D) part of the British colonial administration

    (E) the British Empire

32. The indentation of lines 5–10 indicates that

    (A) these are Gandhi's exact words

    (B) Gandhi's words have been paraphrased

    (C) this material is more important than anything else in the passage

    (D) Gandhi himself separated this material from other information

    (E) these words address the reader directly

33. The content of the indented material (lines 5–10) is intended to

    (A) lay out a plan of action

    (B) answer critics of the Salt March

    (C) justify defiance of the salt law

    (D) explain the purpose of the Salt March

    (E) motivate Gandhi's followers

34. Which of the following rhetorical devices is present in the indented material (lines 5–10)?

    (A) rhetorical question

    (B) comparison and contrast

    (C) allusion

    (D) understatement

    (E) apostrophe

35. Throughout this passage, the tone of Gandhi's comments may best be described as

    (A) angry and regretful

    (B) passionate and rebellious

    (C) resentful and somber

    (D) indignant and sarcastic

    (E) formal and ironic

36. The first sentence of paragraph three ("The spectacle . . . all over the world" — lines 11–13) serves to

    (A) emphasize the difficulties Gandhi faced

    (B) show the magnitude of the problem

    (C) elicit sympathy from the reader

    (D) place the Salt March in a larger context

    (E) create a contrast

37. The antecedent of "which" (line 23) is

    (A) time

    (B) reports

    (C) agents

    (D) those

    (E) press

38. The effect of the quotation from the Viceroy (lines 23–28) is to

    (A) show the attitude that Gandhi hoped to change

    (B) give equal time to the opposing position

    (C) illustrate the frustration of British officials

    (D) explain why Gandhi began the Salt March

    (E) foreshadow Gandhi's death

39. Which statement best describes the purpose of the word "[m]eanwhile" (line 31)?

    (A) It gives background information on the Salt March.

    (B) It provides a time frame for the Viceroy's remarks.

    (C) It returns the narrative to the Salt March.

    (D) It emphasizes the Viceroy's misreading of the situation in India.

    (E) It extends the narrative beyond the Viceroy's point of view.

40. What statement may be made about footnote 1?

    (A) The quotation cited comes from a book about Mohandas K. Gandhi.

    (B) The publisher of *The Collected Works* is a company called "New Delhi."

    (C) The book referred to in the footnote was published in 1943.

    (D) The book referred to in the footnote was published over a period of 26 years.

    (E) The book cited contains everything Gandhi wrote between 1958 and 1984.

41. What statement may be made about footnote 2?

    (A) The quotation cited comes from the same book and same page cited in footnote 1.

    (B) The author of the source cited may not be identified.

    (C) The quotation comes from the same book cited in footnote 1, but a different page.

    (D) The source of the quotation is unknown.

    (E) The quotation appears in a book entitled *Ibid*, on page 149.

42. Footnote 4 most likely refers to

(A) a book of short essays or articles by various authors

(B) a book of writing by Mohandas Gandhi, edited by D. G. Tendulkar

(C) an article edited by Gandhiji

(D) the thirtieth volume of *Gandhiji: His Life and Work*

(E) the third volume of a work by *Gandhiji*

43. Overall, the footnotes indicate that

(A) the author values opposing viewpoints

(B) the author considers Gandhi the best source of information

(C) Gandhi wrote very little

(D) the author consulted many secondary sources

(E) the author relied heavily on Gandhi's own words

Directions for questions 44–53: Read the passage below, an excerpt from A Fool and His Money: The Odyssey of an Average Investor, *by John Rothchild (Wiley, 1998; reprinted with permission of John Wiley & Sons, Inc.) and answer the questions that follow.*

---

(01)   What used to be known as acquaintances, relatives, children, husbands, and wives have all become investments. A few years ago — though I'm not certain when — we began calling children "our investments in the future." Soon we found ourselves investing in their education, which used to be called putting them through school. Some people invest
(05) in relationships, as opposed to just having friends over for dinner. My wife, of course, is a perpetual investment, as I am to her. It's possible to invest in pets and sell the offspring, though I doubt we could pay anybody to take our cats. Lately I've begun to think of the hereafter as the Keough Plan and life after death as the tax-deferred IRA. Once I regarded my car as simple transportation, and now it is a depreciated holding. The roof over our
(10) heads has become an inflation hedge, next-to-useless in a deflationary cycle. Every other week we're debating whether to sell out or stay, whether to refinance or hold out for lower rates, whether to rent the place and move into something with a bigger mortgage-interest deduction.

    The dining room table is a fixed asset; the dishes set down upon it are collectibles. The
(15) smart money, I realize now, would have divested the dishes in the early 1980s, when collectibles were at a premium, and gone into paper plates. The last spike in silver prices destroyed all feelings of loyalty for the family flatware, which now serves only as a reminder of our missed opportunity to cash in at $41 an ounce. Ditto the silver backgammon cube, which I transported to the safe-deposit box but which is no longer worth protecting.

(20)   The silver samovar is corroded, but we maintain it in spite of no sign of inflation. Its ultimate purpose may depend on whether the Federal Reserve continues to lower the discount rate. Looking through our closets, I see dozens of examples of poor market timing, things that were bought too early or held too long: the $2,000 Apple computer in the former category, the art deco water pitchers in the latter. The old train set and the base-
(25) ball cards thrown away long ago by mistake once had sentimental value, but since prices of such items are now common knowledge, I now remember them as hundreds of dollars lost in the restructuring of my childhood closet.

    A couch was once a place on which to sit, and a chest of drawers a place in which to put things, but these, too, have evolved into collectibles — the claw marks, the jelly stains,
(30) the rips, the tears, the broken handles, the gouges in the record cabinet, the scratches in

the marble table, the mildew spots on stuffed armchairs left outside in the rain are no longer simple repair jobs. They're threats to the bottom line, and a great deal more fuss is made over mishaps these days.

(35) Our clothes are a continual source of fiscal disappointment, especially during frequent catastrophes when they are soiled, ripped, or otherwise damaged. Having spaghetti dumped in one's lap is the dinner-party equivalent of a 30 percent drop in a stock or the cancellation of a dividend. The same can be said for high heels that are sheared off by a hidden sprinkler head.

Since clothes have become investments, many of the hand-me-down items that we once (40) kept in paper bags for Halloween costumes or used as car rags are now hung in the closets. This includes old Pucci dresses and houndstooth coats too big in the shoulders, feather boas worn by relatives from cafe society, discarded kilts from Scottish festivals, Hawaiian shirts retained since college, scarves, trout vests, riding jodhpurs, and smocks from Panamanian molas. Someday, we assure ourselves, there'll be a bull market in molas.

(45) Have we just gotten greedy, or have we been forced into it: routed from our passbooks by fantastic opportunities; lured by the irresistible increases in the price of gold, silver, grandfather clocks; convinced that it is highly speculative not to speculate; millions of us and our loose cash, wandering from chance to chance, desperate for good advice yet almost always confused; our net worth vacillating with the monetary system, the fiscal sys-(50) tem, the balance of trade; our futures papers in CATS funds and zero-coupon bonds; our very daily moods tied to the discount rates. Is it possible not to be financially obsessed? I find time for little else.

44. How may the tone of this passage be described?

   (A) informal and annoyed

   (B) regretful and apologetic

   (C) mocking and nostalgic

   (D) self-righteous and authoritative

   (E) pedantic and ironic

45. Overall, this passage may be described as

   (A) narrative

   (B) exposition

   (C) argument

   (D) description

   (E) anecdotal

46. Which of the following best describes the organizing principle of this passage?

   (A) example and analysis

   (B) comparison and contrast

   (C) chronological order

   (D) spatial order

   (E) cause and effect

47. In line 17, what is the antecedent of the pronoun "which"?
    (A) spike
    (B) silver prices
    (C) loyalty
    (D) flatware
    (E) the fact that silver prices went up

48. What is the theme of paragraph three (lines 20–27)?
    (A) the importance of keeping childhood possessions
    (B) the importance of sentimental value
    (C) decreasing value
    (D) increasing value
    (E) changing value

49. Which statement is true of paragraph four (lines 28–33)?
    (A) It marks a shift from general to specific.
    (B) It follows a cause-and-effect pattern.
    (C) It represents a digression from the main point of the passage.
    (D) It presents an exception to the main point of the passage.
    (E) The information is presented without interpretation.

50. The extended discussion of clothes (lines 34–44) serves to
    (A) reveal the author's main concern
    (B) emphasize the need to spend wisely
    (C) show how money is wasted
    (D) heighten the sense of absurdity
    (E) illustrate the importance of fashion

51. The last paragraph (lines 45–52) marks a shift from
    (A) anecdotes to generalities
    (B) examples to interpretation
    (C) personal to universal
    (D) universal to personal
    (E) economics to philosophy

52. Which of the following is parallel to "the monetary system" (line 49)?
    (A) "desperate for good advice" (line 48)
    (B) "the balance of trade" (line 50)
    (C) "in CATS funds" (line 50)
    (D) "tied to the discount rates" (line 51)
    (E) "for little else" (line 52)

53. In the context of lines 50–51, what is the meaning of "our very"?

   (A) even our

   (B) our extreme

   (C) except our

   (D) yet our

   (E) not our

SECTION TWO: ESSAY QUESTIONS

Time: 2:15, divided as indicated below.

Reading Period: 15 minutes

Writing Period: 2 hours

During the reading period, you may annotate the questions and passages. You may *not* write on the answer sheet. During the writing period, you should devote approximately 40 minutes to each of the three essay questions. You may write the essays in any order; place the essay number at the top of each page. At the end of each essay response, write the # symbol.

Do not turn back to the multiple-choice questions during this portion of the exam.

Essay question 1: Synthesis

Directions: The question below is based on the six sources which follow it. To answer this question, you must synthesize information from these sources. Your essay must present a clear argument supported by at least three of the sources. Do NOT merely summarize the information or the point of view of the sources.

Be sure to cite information, quotations, or ideas taken from these sources. You may cite them as "Source A," "Source B," or by the descriptions in parentheses.

> **Source A:** (Senate)
>
> **Source B:** (Broun)
>
> **Source C:** (National Association of Broadcasters)
>
> **Source D:** (Goodman)
>
> **Source E:** (Anderson et al.)
>
> **Source F:** (Snyder)

The Question: It is widely agreed that the media has power to influence children. However, controversy surrounds the extent of that power and what, if any, restrictions should be placed upon the media in order to promote children's well-being. Should government play a role? Should the media self-regulate? Are parents to take full responsibility? After reading the following sources carefully, develop a position regarding freedom and regulation of the media, taking children's well-being into account. Then write an essay in which you support your position with references to these sources.

Source A

"Children, Violence, and the Media: A Report for Parents and Policy Makers," prepared by the Majority Staff of the Senate Committee on the Judiciary, 9/14/99.

(01) Americans have grown increasingly alarmed about youth violence. Far too many of our children are killing and harming others. This report identifies and begins to redress one of the principal causes of youth violence: media violence. . . .

It has been estimated that more than 1000 studies on the effects of television and film
(05) violence have been done during the past 40 years. In the last decade, the American Medical Association, the American Academy of Pediatrics, the American Academy of Child and Adolescent Psychiatry, and the National Institutes of Mental Health have separately reviewed many of these studies. Each of these reviews has reached the same conclusion: television violence leads to real-world violence. The National Institute of Mental Health
(10) reported that "television violence is as strongly correlated with aggressive behavior as any variable that has been measured." A comprehensive study conducted by the Surgeon General's Office in 1972, and updated in 1982, found television violence a contributing factor to increases in violent crime and antisocial behavior; a 1984 US Attorney General's Task Force study on family violence revealed that viewing television violence contributed
(15) to acting-out violence in the home; and recently, the National Television Violence Study, a 3-year project that examined the depiction of violent behavior across more than 8200 programs, concluded that televised violence teaches aggressive attitudes and behaviors, desensitization to violence, and increased fear of becoming victimized by violence. The majority of the existing social and behavioral science studies, taken together, agree on
(20) the following basic points: (1) constant viewing of televised violence has negative effects on human character and attitudes; (2) television violence encourages violent forms of behavior and influences moral and social values about violence in daily life; (3) children who watch significant amounts of television violence have a greater likelihood of exhibiting later aggressive behavior; (4) television violence affects viewers of all ages, intellect,
(25) socioeconomic levels, and both genders; and (5) viewers who watch significant amounts of television violence perceive a meaner world and overestimate the possibility of being a victim of violence.

Source B

Excerpt from "Nonsensorship," by Heywood Broun, written in the 1920s.

(01) Of course, it may be argued that motion pictures are not an art and that it makes little difference what happens to them. We cannot share that indifference. Enough has been done in pictures to convince us that very beautiful things might be achieved if only the censors could be put out of the way. Not all the silliness of the modern American picture
(05) is the fault of the producers. Much of the blame must rest with the various boards of censorship. It is difficult to think up many stories in which there is no passion, crime, or birth. As a matter of fact, we are of the opinion that the entire theory of motion picture censorship is mistaken. The guardians of morals hold that if the spectator sees a picture of a man robbing a safe he will thereby be moved to want to rob a safe himself. In rebut-
(10) tal we offer the testimony of a gentleman much wiser in the knowledge of human con-
duct than any censor. Writing in *The New Republic*, George Bernard Shaw advocated that hereafter public reading-rooms supply their patrons only with books about evil characters. For, he argued, after reading about evil deeds our longings for wickedness are satis-
fied vicariously [experienced indirectly]. On the other hand, there is the danger that the
(15) public may read about saints and heroes and drain off its aspirations in such directions without actions.

Source C

Excerpt from "Reply Comments of the National Association of Broadcasters before the Federal Communications Commission," 11/15/04.

(01) The National Association of Broadcasters filed this report with the Federal Communications Commission (FCC), the government agency charged with overseeing the airwaves. The FCC was at the time considering mandating a "safe harbor" — relatively nonviolent programming during times when children are likely to watch television.

(05) The National Association of Broadcasters (NAB) submits this reply to certain comments on the Commission's *Notice of Inquiry* seeking comment on numerous issues relating to violent programming on television. In the *Notice,* the Commission requested comment on numerous issues relating to violent programming on television, including its effects on children, how violent programming could be defined for regulatory purposes, and the

(10) statutory and constitutional limitations on the Commission's and Congress's authority to regulate this programming. The *Notice* specifically sought comment about a "safe harbor" approach similar to the Commission's regulation of broadcast indecency, which would restrict violent programming to airing in very limited hours. The record in this proceeding provides little empirical or legal support for the imposition of a safe harbor or other

(15) regulation of violent content on television.

The frequently alleged link between violence in the media and violence in the "real world" is not in fact supported by existing empirical research. A new report submitted in this proceeding confirms that the overall scientific evidence fails to support the hypothesis that exposure to violent media content causes people to act aggressively. Thus, the record

(20) fails to provide the evidentiary underpinning necessary for the adoption of a safe harbor or similar regulation of television programming based on a rationale that violent depictions cause real world aggression.

But even among commenters who expressed concern about media violence, the support for a safe harbor was strikingly muted. Several of these commenters admitted the dif-

(25) ficulty of identifying the specific types of violent depictions that are actually harmful. Certainly the record provides no assistance to the Commission in the virtually impossible task of defining violent (or excessively or gratuitously violent) television programming in an intelligible way that is narrowly tailored and not unconstitutionally vague and overbroad. Because any definition would inevitably encompass a wide array of highly

(30) valued speech, including many of the finest and most popular shows in television history, a safe harbor or similar restriction on violent content would violate both the rights of broadcasters as speakers and the rights of viewers to receive constitutionally protected speech. No commenter, moreover, satisfactorily explained how the Commission could properly assert the authority for it to regulate television programming due to its

(35) violent content.

Source D

Cartoon by Sam Goodman

Cartoon by Sam Goodman

Source E

Excerpt from *Early Childhood Television Viewing and Adolescent Behavior: Monographs of the Society for Research in Child Development*, by Daniel R. Anderson, Aletha C. Huston, Kelly Schmitt, Deborah Linebarger, and John C. Wright (Wiley-Blackwell, 2001; reprinted with permission from John Wiley & Sons, Inc.)

(01) Historically, each new medium of mass communication has, within a few years of its introduction, been condemned as a threat to the young people who use it most. Typically the new medium has been blamed for capturing excessive time and interest of children and youth, for corrupting their values, for wasting time that would otherwise have been
(05) spent more constructively, and for causing a decline in taste, morality, self-discipline, learning, and socialization. Whether the new medium has been paperback books, telephones, comic books, movies, radio, television, video games, or the World Wide Web, it has been assumed to have homogeneous use and content. It has therefore been held responsible for captivating the younger generation with a level of passive engagement that was
(10) close to addiction and for generating an indiscriminate fascination with all its messages regardless of their content, validity, merit, or relevance to the life of the child. On the heels of fears about the medium itself have come concerns about content that will corrupt moral values and stimulate undesirable behavior. In the United States, we vacillate between alarms about violence and concerns about sex on the media, with each new
(15) medium raising alarm that it poses greater threats than those that preceded it.

At the same time, new media have been greeted with optimism about their potential for expanding the horizons of the young and for offering powerful new tools for teaching and learning. With respect to television, the focus of the *Monograph,* educators and others saw its potential for providing information in an interesting and engaging form. By the end
(20) of the 1960s, two pioneering educational programs for young children, *Sesame Street* and *Mister Rogers' Neighborhood,* had established the power of broadcast television for informing and educating young children.

Source F

Excerpt from personal essay by Jean Snyder (pseudonym).

(01) Eight months pregnant, I wander through the electronics store and imagine the world that will descend upon my child. She (or he — in the old-fashioned way, I've chosen surprise) can learn how to be a car thief with one video game or blast the heads off an alien and obliterate a bad guy with another. What will he see? Steroidal muscles on the males,
(05) and silicon-enhanced impossible proportions on the females, who, by the way, never seem to wear more than two cents' worth of clothing.

Okay, I think. No video games in my house! But then I picture a lonely child, sitting in the corner with a no-one-will-play-with-me frown, excluded from the conversation of classmates. Friendless. Outside the loop. Besides, television and film aren't much better,
(10) with their Bo-toxed faces and air-brushed bodies. If the message doesn't get through from video games, it'll come through the airways.

At home, I decide to write to my congressman. Don't let them make those games, I plan to write. Don't let them make those movies! Take back the television frequencies. Return the world to natural goodness. Of course, I never write the letter. My favorite show is on. I
(15) settle down with the popcorn, lamenting every single minute that I'm glued to the screen.

Essay question 2: Paired passages

Directions: Read these passages, both of which deal with leave-taking. The narrator in Passage One is a man leaving his boarding school, where he has been a student for many years. The narrator in Passage Two is a woman embarking on a career as a governess. In a well-written essay, discuss how the rhetorical devices in each passage convey the narrator's attitude toward the change that is about to take place in his or her life.

Passage One

(01) I dressed myself, took my hat and gloves, and lingered a little in the room. For the last year and a half this room had been my "pensive citadel": here I had read and studied through all the hours of night, and though true it was that for the latter part of this time I, who was framed for love and gentle affections, had lost my gaiety and happiness during
(05) the strife and fever of contention with my guardian, yet, on the other hand, as a boy so passionately fond of books, and dedicated to intellectual pursuits, I could not fail to have enjoyed many happy hours in the midst of general dejection. I wept as I looked round on the chair, hearth, writing-table, and other familiar objects, knowing too certainly that I looked upon them for the last time. Whilst I write this it is eighteen years ago, and yet at
(10) this moment I see distinctly, as if it were yesterday, the lineaments and expression of the object on which I fixed my parting gaze. It was a picture of the lovely_____ , which hung over the mantelpiece, the eyes and mouth of which were so beautiful, and the whole countenance so radiant with benignity and divine tranquility, that I had a thousand times laid down my pen or my book to gather consolation from it, as a devotee from his patron
(15) saint. Whilst I was yet gazing upon it, the deep tones of the clock proclaimed that it was four o'clock. I went up to the picture, kissed it, and then gently walked out and closed the door for ever!

Passage Two

(01) This testimonial I accordingly received in about a month, forwarded a copy of it to Mrs. Fairfax, and got that lady's reply, stating that she was satisfied, and fixing that day fortnight as the period for my assuming the post of governess in her house.

I now busied myself in preparations: the fortnight passed rapidly. I had not a very large (05) wardrobe, though it was adequate to my wants; and the last day sufficed to pack my trunk, the same I had brought with me eight years ago from Gateshead.

The box was corded, the card nailed on. In half-an-hour the carrier was to call for it to take it to Lowton, whither I myself was to repair at an early hour the next morning to meet the coach. I had brushed my black stuff travelling-dress, prepared my bonnet, (10) gloves, and muff; sought in all my drawers to see that no article was left behind; and now having nothing more to do, I sat down and tried to rest. I could not; though I had been on foot all day, I could not now repose an instant; I was too much excited. A phase of my life was closing to-night, a new one opening to-morrow: impossible to slumber in the interval; I must watch feverishly while the change was being accomplished.

Essay question 3: Friendship

Directions: Roman historian Gaius Sallustius Crispus (1st century B.C.E.) said that the "firmest friendship is based on an identity of likes and dislikes." Must friends share common interests and enemies? How important is "an identity of likes and dislikes"? In a well-written essay, develop your own position on the importance of shared interests and beliefs in friendship. You may refer to history, literature or other arts, or personal experience to support your assertion.

20

Answers and Explanations for Practice Exam 2

I n this chapter, I help you score and evaluate your work on the second practice exam that's found in Chapter 19. While the multiple-choice questions are easy to score, the essays are tougher to evaluate. My goal in this chapter is to provide guidance regarding what the AP test scorers generally look for. For more detailed instructions on scoring and reviewing your practice exam, turn back to Chapter 18. If you struggle to evaluate your own essay writing, ask for help from a teacher or another good writer you can trust.

THE MULTIPLE-CHOICE SECTION

Most of the explanations that follow answer why one response is right and why others may be tempting but are wrong. I encourage you to read the explanations for every answer because you may learn or reinforce information that can help on the exam, but pay special attention to the explanations for answers you get wrong.

1. **(D).** The Roman poets played to a tough crowd, according to Pliny. Not many people showed up for poetry readings, and those who did spent more energy seeing and being seen than listening to the verse. The expression "their pains" (line 6) refers to the energy the poets have put into writing and reciting their work — the same tasks described by (D).

2. **(A).** Pliny lets you see a bit of the setting ("in the lounging-places" — lines 6–7), their actions (they "go out before [the recital] is over" — lines 10–11), a strand of dialogue ("lost a day!" — line 17), and description ("they saunter in with an air of the greatest indifference" — lines 9–10). You never get to crawl inside the spectators' heads, so (A) is your answer.

3. **(C).** Pliny yearns for the good old days, when "Claudius Caesar, walking one day in the palace, and hearing a great shouting . . . went immediately to the [poetry reading] and agreeably surprised the author with his presence" (lines 12–15). That golden era is in direct contrast to the audience that Pliny describes in lines 6–11, who don't even enter the recital hall or arrive late and leave early. Comparison and contrast rules this piece, making (C) a winning answer.

4. **(C).** If you answered question 3 correctly, you probably got this one as well. You can almost hear old Pliny groan: "Audiences aren't what they used to be!" Listeners were apparently so caught up in the verse that they let loose with a "great shouting" (line 13) that drew the most powerful person in Rome to the reading. In other words, poetry was once appreciated, as (C) states.

5. **(E).** Pliny's a poetry fan; Pliny hates people who hate poetry. These two facts are obvious. Therefore, the type who regrets losing a day to poetry is, according to Pliny, complaining because a day of poetry has value — a concept expressed nicely by (E). Did I catch you with (B)? It's similar but a little too general. (E) is the most specific answer supported by the passage.

6. **(A).** To answer this question, finish reading the sentence. Notice that Pliny refers to authors "who . . . read out their compositions in spite of this apathy or arrogance on the part of their audience" (lines 19–20). Pliny compares the poor guys who read to empty rooms to the ones who fill a coliseum with poetry lovers.

7. **(B).** Pliny is bragging a little in this letter; in the very next sentence, he says that "there are few men of literary tastes" (lines 22–23) who aren't his friends. However, consider the context. He's telling the reader that he goes to readings, so he's a fan of great writing. But he qualifies that statement by revealing that he has an extra motive — friendship. Hence (B) is the best answer.

8. **(C).** Pliny tells the reader that he "scarcely ever miss[es] being present upon any occasion" (line 21), the occasion being a reading of some sort of literature. Thus (C) fits the meaning of "this" nicely. Granted, he says that the authors "have generally been friends of mine" (line 22), but he mentions that fact almost as an unavoidable coincidence ("as indeed there are few men of literary tastes who are not" — lines 22–23). Therefore (A) and (B) don't make the cut. (D) and (E) aren't serious contenders, because Pliny isn't talking about declining attendance at that spot in his letter, and he's going to the country in order to write poetry.

9. **(C).** Pliny writes, "I do not intend reciting" (line 25) because his friends may then believe that he attended *their* readings only because he wanted their attendance at his own recitals. He says that he would "seem rather to have lent than given my attendance" (lines 25–26). A loan has to be paid back, but a gift does not.

10. **(D).** The key to a double question is to find two answers that work. One is not enough. In this letter, Pliny is *not* happy with the literary world of his day, as you see in his remarks about audiences who prefer to gossip rather than to listen. He's not teaching anything to Socius Senecio, the letter's recipient; (A) and (B) are therefore bad choices because "didactic" and "pedantic" apply to educators. (C) is a possibility because Pliny does refer positively to a previous era, when Caesar attended a literary event. However, "nostalgia" implies personal participation, and that element isn't present in Pliny's letter. Pliny isn't draped in mourning, so you can rule out (E) because "somber" is too strong.

11. **(E).** The first paragraph begins with an unpleasant incident — the narrator's exclusion because of race from a greeting-card exchange and his reaction to the realization that he "was different from the others" (line 4) and "shut out from their world by a vast veil" (line 5). The second part of the paragraph (lines 13–20) discusses the way "other black boys" (line 13) handle prejudice. Choice (E) perfectly suits these two halves of paragraph one. (A), (C), and (D) are too narrow, and (B) is too broad.

12. **(D).** DuBois describes a split between a person's inner self and the way one is perceived by others. All of the choices refer to this double nature except for (D), which describes a goal, "to attain self-conscious manhood" (lines 30–31), which is equated with the merging of the "double self" (line 31) into a "better and truer" (line 31) and more importantly, *single* self. Therefore (D) is the choice you want.

13. **(B).** The narrator understands that he was "different from the others" (line 4) but immediately follows this statement with a speculation. Perhaps he's the same in heart and life and longing. You can easily eliminate (A), (C), and (D), which all express common definitions of "like." The problem is to differentiate between (B) and (E). Of the two, (B) is stronger. The narrator's comment fits (B) better because he isn't just similar in his heart and longing; he's the same as his classmates.

14. **(A).** The narrator explains that he rises above prejudice by living "in a region of blue sky" (line 7), which is bluest when he demonstrates his superiority over his classmates with activities such as "beat[ing] my mates at examination-time" (line 8). These activities are immediately followed by his comment that "this fine contempt" (line 9) faded after a time. Clearly, the activities, including being the best at exams, are equated with "fine contempt" (line 9). Choices (B) and (C) express what the narrator wants but doesn't have. (D) and (E) express other reactions to prejudice, not the "contempt" claimed by the narrator.

15. **(A).** The narrator says that he was "shut out" from "their [white] world" (line 5) and that he had "no desire to tear down that veil" (line 6). Therefore, he "lived above it" (line 7) in the blue sky. (A) fits perfectly; as he tries to "rise above his situation." The only other answer remotely in the running is (C), because the veil limits the narrator's freedom, and the sky is a traditional symbol of freedom. However, in the context of this passage, (A) is more specific and thus the better answer.

16. **(E).** Take another look at paragraph one. The first part concerns the narrator's experience. At line 13, the narrator, with broad statements, describes how "other black boys" react to prejudice. The shift is from the narrator's own story ("personal narration") to others' and ends with a startling conclusion: The "prison-house closed round about us all" (line 17).

17. **(D).** Because of the veil, the narrator is "shut out from their world" (line 5). Though whites aren't named in that sentence, the implication is clear, and statement I is correct. Statement II isn't correct, because while the narrator becomes aware of race in elementary school, he doesn't claim to describe a universal experience. Statement III is correct because line 23 relates the veil to "a world which yields him no true self-consciousness," another way of saying that forming an identity is tough when the veil is around. Add the whole thing up, and you've got (D).

18. **(B).** Parallelism means that parts of the sentence performing the same function have the same grammatical identity. In other words, your favorite hobbies can't be hang-gliding, windsurfing, and to go bowling. They have to be hang-gliding, windsurfing, and bowling. Even without the grammar terminology, you can hear the difference in the two sentences. One matches, and the other doesn't. The sentence beginning "One ever feels . . ." contains a series of nouns: "American," "Negro," "souls," "thoughts," "strivings," and "ideals" (lines 27–29). The repetition comes with the word "two," which pops up in front of several of these nouns. No other choice is even close.

19. **(C).** The sentence in the question — "He would not Africanize . . . message for the world" (lines 32–35) — explains what the goal of the "American Negro" (line 30) is *not*. The next sentence states what the goal *is* ("to make it possible for a man to be both a Negro and an American" [lines 35–36] on an equal basis). The first sentence sets the stage for the next, as (C) says.

20. **(C).** The author is committed to a cause, and he's not shy about revealing it. He wants a fairer world, where he and everyone, regardless of race, can be "a co-worker in the kingdom of culture" (line 38). His passion comes through in his diction; many words are extreme. He refers to "genius" (line 39) instead of "talent," for example. The other choices are incorrect because at least one word is not appropriate. In (A), for example, you can make a case for "philosophical," because the author discusses important ideas. However, he's not "conciliatory" because there's no hint of an apology. Similarly, (B) doesn't work because the passage isn't sarcastic. (D) is eliminated as an option because of the word "cautious," and (E) makes no sense because the two words contradict each other.

21. **(B).** The passage as a whole concerns John Law — his life, his reputation among historians, and his close ties to "Mississippi madness" (line 2), which was *the* financial scandal of the 17th century. (Law sold nearly worthless shares in a project to develop trade on the Mississippi River.) The question, however, does not concern the passage as a whole. Instead it focuses only on the first sentence, which links John Law and Mississippi madness, stating specifically that a discussion of that historical event "can have no fitter introduction than a sketch of the life of . . . John Law" (lines 2–3). Clearly, sentence two justifies the biographical information that follows.

> **TIP**
>
> You don't need to know anything about history to answer question 21, or any other AP English Language and Composition question. The selections you read may be from history, science, or other disciplines, but the answers deal only with rhetoric and comprehension of the information supplied in the passage.

22. **(C).** In grammatical terminology, you have to find the *antecedent* of "its" (line 3). You can answer this question using logic. Which word does "its" replace? John Law is referred to as an "author" (line 3), but he didn't write anything. Instead, he created a "scheme" (line 2) that became "Mississippi madness" (line 2). "Scheme" is an answer choice, but "Mississippi madness" isn't.

23. **(D).** In lines 10–16, many sentences or parts of sentences follow a "*he* plus verb" pattern. You're almost reading a list. All you have to do is figure out the nature of the list. Law knew "philosophy and true principles of credit" (line 9) and grasped "the monetary question" (line 10). He didn't "calculate" (line 12) the "avaricious" or greedy "frenzy" (line 12) of the French, nor did he see that "hope was as extravagant as fear" (line 14). Some of these statements are against John Law (he knew what he was doing) and some aren't (he didn't see the big picture). The overall effect, therefore, is to "qualify" or limit his guilt.

> **TIP**
>
> Remember the word "qualify." In the essay section, you're often asked to take a position that supports, opposes, or qualifies the views expressed in a quotation or passage.

24. **(A).** Sentence four resembles an old-fashioned scale where weights are placed on each side until the two halves match. Look at the balance in this sentence: Law was "neither knave nor madman" (lines 7–8) and was "more deceived than deceiving, more sinned against than sinning" (lines 8–9). Grammatically, "knave" balances "madman" because both are nouns. Even if you don't know the terminology, you can see how the meaning balances also, because both words describe character. Similarly, "more deceived . . . sinning" balances two participles (a grammar term for verbs that are used as descriptions). And again, you can hear how these two statements match. Pairing up

grammatical elements is called *parallelism* or the use of *parallel structure,* the answer you find in (A). The other choices aren't even close. The sentence has no *irony,* a literary term for a gap between what you say and what you mean, so (B) is out. *Circular reasoning* ("Michelangelo is great because he's in my art history textbook. He's in my art history textbook because he's great," for example) isn't in this passage, so (C) doesn't work. Sensory details don't appear, and the author does make judgments about Law's actions, so (D) and (E) are out.

25. **(E).** The passage tells you that the French, "like the man in the fable" (line 15), destroy the source of their future wealth. The word "fable" is key here. An *allusion* refers to a literary work or a historic event and brings all the ideas involved into the piece of writing in which the allusion appears. Once you see *fable,* and even if you never read the story of the goose that laid golden eggs, you know you have an allusion. Did I catch you with (A)? Yes, the golden egg fable strongly condemns greed, but the AP exam isn't going to test your ideas of right and wrong. It tests literary terms, such as *metaphor* (B), an implied comparison, and *figurative language* (C), writing that leaves the land of realism for a venture into imaginative territory. A *paradox* is something that seems impossible or contradictory, such as the famous statement from Yankee legend Yogi Berra that "nobody goes there anymore because it's too crowded."

26. **(C).** Law starts out on a "broad and smooth" (lines 17–18) river, but the "current was too strong" (line 21), and he goes over the "tremendous falls" (line 22) and is "dashed to pieces" (line 23). Sound like a man in control of his destiny? I don't think so. As the last line of paragraph one states, Law was "the boatman" but the French people were "the waters" (line 26). The nature metaphor emphasizes that Law isn't fully in control; no one zooming down a river is, if the river has waterfalls, rocks, and rapids in it. Therefore (C) is best. Were you fooled by (D) and (E)? (D) is tempting because the French people, as "the waters" (line 26), bear some responsibility. However, (D) doesn't take into account all the statements about Law. (E) is out for a similar reason. True, Law is clueless, but (E) refers only to him and ignores the French.

27. **(B).** The author has a strong point to make in paragraph one: Law, an almost legendary conman of the 18th century, wasn't the only bad guy in the mess known as "Mississippi madness" (line 2). The first paragraph portrays him as a mixture. He's not a "knave or a madman" (lines 4–5), and the greed of the French people played a role. In paragraph two (lines 27–45), the author jumps to Law's birth and takes the reader through Law's early years. The author makes some judgments about Law — "he was tall, strong, and well made" (lines 37–38), for example. However, most of paragraph two is simple exposition — laying out the facts of Law's life. Therefore the shift is from argumentative to expository, expressed by choice (B).

28. **(B).** The word "years" tells you that you're in the age category, so you can rule out (A) and (D) immediately, even though Law is described as way ahead of his peers in math ability. (C) is the next to go, because the association of innocence with youth isn't good enough to make this the correct answer. (E) is very tempting, because in the next sentence Law is said to be 17 years old. However, you can't tell whether the author is moving forward in time to age 17, and "tender" is a more general word. Go for (B), or "young."

29. **(A).** You don't have to know the meaning of "Jessamy John" (line 42) in order to see that women like Law and men don't. Law is "a great favourite with the ladies" (lines 40–41) "while" he is despised by "the other sex" (line 41). (The word "while" often signals a contrast.) Nicknames are associated with each gender, with "Beau Law" (line 41) contrasting with "Jessamy John" (lines 42). Therefore, (A) fills the bill here.

30. **(C).** The passage occasionally pokes fun at John Law (A), as in the last line, when Law is described as going to "London, to see the world" (lines 44–45). However, most of the selection is more serious. (B) is tempting because the first paragraph discusses how history has mellowed the condemnation of Law that he experienced "in his lifetime" (line 5). Overall, (C) is the best answer because the passage links Law to those around him — to the French in paragraph one and to acquaintances and relatives in paragraph two. Choices (D) and (E) aren't even close.

31. **(D).** The introduction and the passage point you to (D) in several ways. The introduction tells you that Gandhi wanted to free India from British rule. The "administration was silently crumbling . . . as scores of village headmen resigned" (lines 1–2). If they're crumbling but Gandhi isn't — and in fact his group is growing larger, as noted in lines 18–19 — they're his opponents, not his allies. Therefore you can easily rule out (A) and (B). Choice (C) is tempting; maybe the resignations occurred because the "headmen" (line 2) support what Gandhi's doing. But (D) is best because it identifies, not describes, the administration. Choice (E) is just too broad.

32. **(A).** Lines 5–10 are "blocked" — set apart from the rest of the test. Blocked material is a long quotation. The block takes the place of quotation marks in signaling the reader that these words are quoted.

33. **(E).** This is a particularly tricky question. Most of the answers are possible, but only one — (E) — is best. You may have chosen (A) because Gandhi's words address future actions. However, "plan of action" implies specifics, and the "severe non-cooperation" (line 6) is never detailed. Choice (B) is also tempting because you can imagine someone saying, "Okay, what can one march accomplish?" However, no criticism is cited in the passage, so (B) fails. (C) doesn't make the cut because Gandhi doesn't waste any time here explaining why salt shouldn't be taxed. Similarly, (D) fails because the purpose of the march — to force the British government to change — is implied but not stated. (E) works because Gandhi motivates the weary marchers, showing them that they are part of an unstoppable and huge force.

34. **(A).** A *rhetorical question* doesn't need a reply; the answer — at least in the general sense — is already there. When Gandhi asks, "But how many can be given such punishment?" (line 9), he isn't looking for a number, though he himself supplies one in the very next line ("three hundred million of persons" — line 10). Instead he is telling his followers that they can't be defeated if enough people join the movement. The more activists there are, the less likely the British will be able to control them. Of the other answers, choice (B) is out because Gandhi isn't comparing their march to any other. Nor is he referring to a historical event or literary work — an *allusion*, choice (C). *Understatement* is way out of bounds because if anything, Gandhi is overstating the number of followers he can expect. He was hugely popular, but three hundred million is a bit steep. *Antithesis*, or contradiction of ideas, isn't present either, so (E) is out.

35. **(B).** The extreme statements — "to hang three hundred million of persons" (line 10), "battle of Right against Might" (line 35), "I would rather die a dog's death and have my bones licked by dogs" (lines 14–15), and so forth — reveal Gandhi's passion. The content shows that he is rebelling against the government. Thus (B) is a perfect fit. Choice (A) fails because Gandhi shows no regret; nor is he "somber," as choice (C) states, "sarcastic" — choice (D), or "ironic" — choice (E).

36. **(E).** On one side is an old man walking with a staff "striding vigorously" (line 11) along with followers dressed in homemade cloth. On the other side is the "mighty British Empire" (lines 12–13). These two definitely contrast, so (E) fits nicely here. The only other contender is (B), but the sentence doesn't show the magnitude of the problem but rather the incongruity of these two extremely different adversaries.

37. **(E).** An *antecedent* is the noun that a pronoun refers to. When you're searching for an antecedent, try inserting the choices for the pronoun. See which one makes the most sense. In the given sentence, you have to figure out what was being fed by Indian nationalist sources. In this case, "which" refers to "world press."

38. **(C).** The Viceroy is described as someone who "regarded himself as a man of principle" (lines 28–29), yet in his quotation he expresses the hope that Gandhi will die and says that the death "would be a very happy solution" (lines 27–28). Such a comment probably comes from frustration, as the Viceroy "was not in favor of Gandhi's arrest" (line 20) but clearly wanted him out of the way. The only other answer remotely in the running is (A), because I imagine most human beings would prefer *not* to have an official hoping that their death is just around the corner. However, if you put the Viceroy's quotation together with Gandhi's, Gandhi sees his struggle as "Right against Might," not an issue of sensitivity or personal safety.

39. **(C).** The passage begins and ends with the Salt March, with a small digression into the British response to Gandhi's protest. The word "meanwhile" (line 31) provides a transition from the paragraph about the Viceroy to the march.

40. **(D).** The Publication Division of the Government of India, which is located in New Delhi, collected all of Gandhi's writings. The volume number cited is 43, so this is a long book — so long that its publication date covers a span of 26 years, from 1958 to 1984. Apply these facts to the choices given, and only (D) works.

41. **(C).** Footnotes and endnotes often drag in some Latin. *Ibid* tells you that the citation refers to the preceding source. If *ibid* is alone, the cited material comes from the same source and page as the preceding foot- or endnote. If *ibid* comes with a number, the source is the same, but the page is different — exactly the situation described in (C).

42. **(A).** The abbreviation "ed." is the tipoff: D. G. Tendulkar is an editor. The text in question is a book, because article titles are enclosed by quotation marks and book titles are italicized or underlined. The roman numeral "III" indicates that the citation is to the third volume of the work. Who wrote the book? If it were Gandhi (or Gandhiji, his affectionate nickname), Gandhi would be listed first, because the author's name precedes the editor's. Therefore, you're looking at a book of writing by various authors, edited by D. G. Tendulkar.

43. **(E).** Four of the five footnotes refer to the same book, *The Collected Works by Mohandas K. Gandhi*. Clearly, the author relied heavily on Gandhi's own words. Secondary sources, by the way, are those that interpret someone else's work or writing. The fourth footnote cites a secondary source, but one out of five doesn't qualify as "many," so (D) isn't the answer you seek. Choice (B) may have caught you. Because the author has so much from Gandhi himself, you may guess that he considers Gandhi the best source of information. However, you don't know for sure. Stick with what you *do* know, which is that the author relied on Gandhi's own words.

44. **(C).** The author of this passage is speaking with his tongue solidly planted in his cheek, as you see in the very first line when he refers to "children, husbands, and wives" (line 1) as investments; hence "mockery" is a good bet. The many references to the way things used to be ("Once I regarded my car as simple transportation" — lines 8–9) can be the basis for "nostalgic," the second term of (C). The only other serious contender is (D), because the author adopts an air of authority, pronouncing his opinions as fact. However, "self-righteous" would remove him from the group that he is criticizing, and he includes himself in the "financially obsessed" (line 51) category.

45. **(C).** An author making an argument doesn't always tell you his or her thesis in the beginning of the passage. This author waits until the end, when he concludes that it isn't possible "not to be financially obsessed" (line 51). Yet the whole passage yearns for a different era, when not everything was evaluated in terms of its investment value. (Yes, he's kidding around, but a serious point underlies his jokes.) The implied argument is that the author — and the readers — should pull some of those dollar signs away from their possessions and relationships.

46. **(A).** In this passage the author starts off with a ton of examples of items that used to be valued for themselves and are now seen as investments — the couch, clothes, and even children. What's the point of all those examples? You don't find out until the last paragraph, when the author analyzes *why* this attitude has taken hold: "routed . . . by fantastic opportunities . . . lured by the irresistible increases" (lines 45–46) in value. No doubt about it: (A) is the answer you want. Were you trapped by (B)? The author does compare older and current attitudes when he says, for example, "[w]hat used to be known as acquaintances" (line 1) "have all become investments" (line 2). However, the question asks you to consider the whole passage, not just the first paragraph, and (B) falls apart in the last paragraph.

47. **(D).** An *antecedent* is the word a pronoun replaces. To answer this question, all you have to do is figure out what "which" means. What "now serves only as a reminder of our missed opportunity to cash in at $41 an ounce" (lines 17–18)? The flatware, or silverware.

48. **(E).** Paragraph three (lines 20–27) is all about changes. The Apple computer was bought too soon, and the water pitchers weren't sold at the height of their market value. The silver samovar may increase or decrease in value depending upon the actions of the Federal Reserve. Choices (C) and (D) are too limited, but (E) encompasses both.

49. **(B).** Paragraph four (lines 28–33) begins with a series of statements about furniture: It was once a place to sit or to keep things, but now furniture is an investment. All the little mishaps of daily life are "threats to the bottom line" (line 32). Do you see the cause-and-effect pattern? The cause is "furniture = investment" and the effect is "a great deal more fuss is made over mishaps these days" (lines 32–33). The other choices just don't fit. The passage moves from specific to general, the opposite of (A). Paragraph four is similar to the paragraphs before and after it, so it's not a digression or exception. There you have it: (C) and (D) are eliminated. The last line of the paragraph is an interpretation of the information presented, so (E) is also out.

50. **(D).** The assertion that "spaghetti dumped in one's lap" (lines 35–36) is equal to "a 30 percent drop in a stock or the cancellation of a dividend" (lines 36–37) should point you immediately toward (D).

51. **(B).** The passage piles on the details, taking you through family relationships, furniture and clothing, baseball cards and silver samovars. The last paragraph puts everything into perspective, explaining the point of all those examples: We're obsessed with investments, but our obsession is understandable.

52. **(B).** In English grammar, *parallels* are words or expressions doing the same grammatical job or having the same grammatical identity. In line 49, "the monetary system" is the object of the preposition "with" (line 49). The same preposition has other objects, including "the balance of trade" (line 50).

53. **(A).** The word "very" generally intensifies meaning, and this "very" is no exception. However, the "very" in line 51 is used in an unusual way. Here it indicates that *even our* "daily moods" are tied to our finances.

HOW TO GRADE YOUR ESSAY RESPONSES

If this is the second practice exam you've completed, you already know how to proceed. Here's a short refresher:

- **Check out the general guidelines for each essay.** First I tell you what to look for in the three essay questions — and your goals differ depending upon the type of essay you're writing. Then I break the grades into three categories, each with a range of three or four scores.

- **Read the two sample answers.** For each of the three essays, I provide two answers, graded and accompanied by explanations of *why* a particular score is appropriate. These essays won't match your own, but the samples do help you see what works and what doesn't in an AP essay, and you can apply those principles to your essay.

- **Assign a number from 0 to 9 for each scoring category.** First decide which scoring slot you're in. Give yourself the highest score in the range if your essay almost, but not quite, qualifies for the next higher category. If you can see but not reach a 7, give yourself a 6. Give yourself the lowest score if you barely escape the next rung down. That is, if you think about the 4-5-6 slot but decide against it, go for a 7. Essays solidly in one category receive the middle number.

- **Fill in the Essay Scoring Grid for each essay.** You need a little arithmetic here, but not much. Just plug in the numbers and follow the directions.

- **Enter your essay scores in the Exam Conversion Chart at the end of the chapter.** Here's where the multiple-choice and essay scores mix together and turn into a number from 1 to 5.

If this is your first practice AP exam, or if you've forgotten how to rate your work, turn back to Chapter 18 for a more complete explanation of AP exam grading.

SCORING ESSAY 1: SYNTHESIS ESSAY ON REGULATING THE MEDIA

The prompt inquires about regulation of the media "in order to promote children's well-being." Your task is to decide what sort of regulation is appropriate, if any. Then you must support your position from at least three of the six possible sources. The problem facing you with this question is that the sources feature wildly divergent points of view and a ton of possible evidence. Rate your essay by asking these questions:

- **Will my reader (grader) easily grasp my position on the regulation of the media?** This topic invites you to consider various types of media, from television and film to video games and the web. You also have to figure out what kind of regulation you favor. Should government be involved, as in "put this on the air and do ten years in the penitentiary"? Should the media regulate itself? Or do parents bear the entire responsibility for monitoring their kids' media exposure? You may argue for any position, including one I haven't mentioned here, so long as you actually *have* a position. Also, though you don't have to announce yourself in the very first sentence, in most cases the reader should be able to determine where you stand on media regulation before the end of paragraph one.

■ **Have I subdivided my argument into logical supporting points?** When you're working with a complex set of ideas, organization matters. This question covers the media, and that term includes everything from television and films to video games. The sources cover violence, smoking, unrealistic body image, and other elements. You have to untangle what's been served up so that your argument makes sense.

■ **Have I used evidence effectively?** The sources for this synthesis question contradict each other (a situation familiar to anyone who's ever researched a controversial topic). You have evidence to back up pretty much anything you want to say. As always, the question requires you to draw upon at least three of the six sources. The evidence from the sources should be strongly tied to your argument.

■ **How good is your writing?** This is an English test, and your evaluator is an English teacher or professor. He or she wants to see good spelling and grammar at least most of the time, organized thoughts, and appropriate citations. (If you need help with source citation, check out Chapter 12. Grammar assistance arrives in Chapter 6.)

Scoring grid for the synthesis essay

Clear point of view _____

0 The essay does not answer the question or is left blank. **Note:** If the essay doesn't answer the question, the *overall* score is zero, even if the essay is nicely written and would receive high marks in the "writing" category.

1–3 The essay simply summarizes the ideas in several sources without taking a recognizable position on media regulation for the well-being of children.

4–6 The essay presents a position about media regulation, but the reader may have trouble finding or understanding the writer's point of view. Or the position may be clear but not consistent throughout the essay.

7–9 The essay clearly and effectively presents a position on media regulation and the well-being of children.

Supporting points _____

1–3 The ideas and information are scattered haphazardly throughout the essay.

4–6 The ideas and information are grouped into subtopics, but these subtopics may not be the most effective or the most logical choices possible.

7–9 The ideas and information are grouped logically into subtopics, which help the reader understand the writer's point of view.

Evidence _____

1–3 The essay paraphrases or quotes from the sources, but the information selected does not relate to the central argument of the essay — how the media should be regulated in order to protect kids. Or fewer than the required three sources are cited.

4–6 The essay provides evidence, either quoted or referred to indirectly, but these points are not the most effective choices from the given source material. The evidence may be linked only weakly to the central argument about media regulation and children's well-being.

7–9 The evidence is particularly well chosen and clearly and effectively linked to the writer's position on media regulation and protecting children.

Writing _____

1–3 The essay may be marred by many errors in grammar, spelling, or punctuation. (**Note:** If the essay is hard to read because of these errors, the highest score the essay may receive *overall* is a 2.) Citations may be missing or misplaced. The writing may sound immature, perhaps with choppy or repetitive sentences.

4–6 The writing is competent and reasonably correct, but the sentences may be choppy or repetitive. The citations may be incorrectly placed. The diction and tone may be uneven. An essay in this category doesn't have the fluid, mature sound of an essay in the highest category.

7–9 An essay in this category demonstrates a command of language, the ability to make a point clearly and concisely. Diction, tone, and structure are handled well. Though the essay may contain errors in grammar, spelling, punctuation, or citation, the errors are minor and infrequent.

Fill in each blank in this Essay Scoring Grid with your score, and then add your scores to determine the total.

Clear point of view _____

Supporting points _____

Evidence _____

Writing _____

Raw score total _____

Divided by 4 _____

Rounded to nearest whole number for final score _____

Check the end of the chapter to see how to combine the scores for essays and multiple-choice questions.

Sample answer A

Violence has been a concern throughout history, and modern times are no exception and are even worse. No victim of violence draws more sympathy than a child, especially when the child has been harmed by another child. The school shootings that take place every year or so bring this issue to national attention, and that is a good thing. However, we do not always know how to respond to tragedies such as Columbine. One possible reason for violence in children is the violence directed at children by the media, including television, movies, and video games. Drugs, alcohol, and body image are also effected by the media, when children watch them. So is smoking (Source D). That's why the media should be regulated by the government. A time when nothing unsuitable for children is shown should be established, a "safe harbor" (Source C).

According to Source A, 1000 studies have shown that violence on television has caused violence in real life. If you have a child watching television, they will almost certainly react to the aggressiveness that they see there. "Televised violence teaches aggressive attitudes and behaviors" (Source A). So if you are going to take care of children, you have to keep them away from television or you have to regulate television. Keeping a child away from television is tough on the child, as Source F explains. A child wouldn't be able to talk with friends about television shows. Besides, even people who worry about children like to watch television (Source F), and if their children are in the room, they will watch too. You can have a safe harbor which is a time when violence on television is not allowed. The National Association of Broadcasters believes that the studies showing violence on television are not valid (Source C), but many organizations such as the American Academy of Pediatrics disagree with that idea (Source A).

Once you know that television must be regulated, you can easily accept the idea that movies and video games must be regulated also. Movies already have a label saying that children of a certain age should not see them if they have violence and sexual scenes, but what about tobacco? Source D mocks the idea that children's film should not have smoking. However, regulation is the answer. No one says that everything in the media should be sanitized, but at least some of the content can be controlled during the peak viewing hours of children. Smoking does so much harm that it is better left out of children's films.

Some people make the point that violence in film substitutes for violence in real life (Source B). Others point out that "each new medium of communication has, within a few years of its introduction, been condemned as a threat to the young people who use it most" (Source E). However, these condemnations may be justified by the violence that we see in our society. Why take the chance? Why not allow the government to step in so that children can grow up in a safe world.

Analysis of sample answer A

This AP test taker did an adequate but not great job on the synthesis question. The writer did understand the sources and did refer to them correctly. However, the essay badly needs reorganization, and the writing style is unsophisticated.

Clear point of view: 4

The writer calls for government regulation of the media, including the so-called "safe harbor" concept. However, the writer doesn't explain what kind of regulation he or she favors and how the regulations would affect the broadcasters' first amendment right to free speech. The first paragraph spends so much time on violence that it almost seems to be an essay on just that subtopic — a trap that's easy to fall into because several sources refer to violence. A better approach would refer to a variety of issues (violence, tobacco, body image, and so forth) in a more balanced way in the introductory paragraph and throughout the essay.

Supporting points: 3

The writer hasn't really broken down this topic into effective subtopics. A couple of approaches would have made sense here. For example, if the writer is calling for government regulation, one paragraph might make the case for new laws by pointing out the perils facing children exposed to violence, drugs, tobacco, and so on through the various forms of media. Another paragraph could answer likely objections to the writer's plan, explaining how the proposed regulations do not unfairly limit freedom of speech. Still another paragraph could address how these regulations might be implemented — a rating code with specific penalties, for example. Or the essay might have been organized by media type, discussing films in one paragraph, video games in another, television in a third, and so forth.

Evidence: 4

This essay does make use of the sources, though not very well. The information from the sources is thrown into the essay without much thought. In the second paragraph, for example, the contradictory views about the effect of televised violence on children are simply plopped there. No attempt is made to reconcile or even to discuss which evidence seems more credible.

Writing: 4

The grammar isn't perfect here, but it isn't terrible either. The style is competent, though no one would mistake this essay for a mature piece of prose.

Overall score: 4

Math time: Add up the four scores

$$4 + 3 + 4 + 4 = 15$$

and divide by 4

$$15 \div 4 = 3.75$$

which rounds up to 4.

Sample answer B

As Heywood Broun explains, "it is difficult to think up many stories in which there is no passion, crime, or birth" (Source B). Yet many people, alarmed by perceived threats to children, want to do exactly that. By censoring or otherwise regulating film, television, and other media, critics of the entertainment industry hope to create what the Senate calls a "safe harbor" (Source A). Children could sail into that harbor, these critics say, and rest there in a state of innocence. But is that innocence ever permanent? And how can we square the idea of official censorship with the American ideal of free speech? In my opinion, I think that regulation of the media should come from parents, for the most part. The media themselves should also consider how their words and images affect the audience, especially children, and then make their own standards of what is right and wrong in children's programming.

True, the situation is complicated. Scientists can't even agree on how the media affects children. A report for the Senate Majority Committee says that "more than 1000 studies on the effects of television and film violence have been done during the past 40 years" (Source A) and those studies, according to the National Institute of Mental Health, show that "television violence is as strongly correlated with aggressive behavior as any variable that has been measured." (Source A) However, violence has been part of the world since way before the age of film and television. The Bible even shows a murder, when there were only four people in the world, and one of them killed another. Cain wasn't influenced by the media. According to Source E, all new media are first suspected of causing harm to children. "Typically, the new medium has been blamed for capturing excessive time and interest of children and youth, for corrupting their values" (Source E). After the new medium "ages," people see it as safer.

The pregnant woman in Source F is typical in that she first thinks of safeguarding her child from the media and then realizes that media is all around and must be dealt with. If she doesn't let her child watch tv or play video games, the child will be "sitting in the corner with a no-one-will-play-with-me lunch box." Next she decides that the government should regulate and sanitize *all* media, which lets her off the hook. Now no one will have objectionable media to talk about and her child will not be left out.

The National Association of Broadcasters thinks that the studies equating media violence with real violence aren't proved. "The frequently alleged link between violence in the media and violence in the "real world" is not in fact supported by existing empirical research" (Source C). The Broadcasters have a reason to feel this way. They don't want the government telling them what to do. But they also point out that creating a "safe harbor" is something that can be interpreted. "Several of these commenters admitted the difficulty of identifying the specific types of violent depictions that are actually harmful." (Source C)

With so much disagreement, it's better to let parents decide for their children what is safe and isn't. It's also better to let broadcasters take responsibility, with the government left out.

Analysis of sample answer B

This writer started off strongly and then hit a wall, as many test-takers do because they run out of time or energy. Thus the first part of the essay is good, and the second part not so good. Here's how this effort would be graded.

Clear point of view: 5

Right away you know what point of view the writer takes: parents are primary, broadcasters secondary and self-regulating. Government regulation isn't mentioned except as a negative, something contrary to "the American ideal of free speech." The first paragraph also opens with a snappy quotation from Broun, stating that every story has something objectionable in it. Clearly this writer is an individualist who favors decentralized power. However, as the essay moves along, the point of view is a little muddied. The writer says that the situation is "complicated." Does that statement mean that the issue of regulation is complicated also? Divergent views on the link between media- and real-life violence aren't fully addressed, and the reader wonders what the writer believes. The essay restates the thesis in the last paragraph: "With so much disagreement, it's better to let parents decide" and "to let broadcasters take responsibility."

> **TIP**
>
> When you state an idea or opinion in an essay, don't label it ("In my opinion I think"). Doing so simply wastes time and words because the reader already knows it's your opinion.

Supporting points: 5

The essay has several supporting points, but they aren't laid out in a logical way and none is fully developed. The writer jumps from the idea that no story lacks "passion, crime, or birth" (Source B) to the difficulty of creating a safe harbor. So far so good. Paragraph two begins an idea — the media violence/real violence link is controversial — but the writer doesn't develop it until the fourth paragraph, when the possible bias of the National Association of Broadcasters is mentioned. Paragraph two seems to come down against the media/real-world link, explaining that Cain murdered Abel without being influenced by a video game and that new media are always criticized, as Source E points out. Paragraph three jumps to another supporting point, that keeping your child away from media harms the kid's social life. So far, the arguments against government regulation are piling up. Not bad! But then paragraph four moves backwards, to the real-world/media link. The information here should be combined with the information in paragraph two. The last paragraph is just tacked on and weakens the whole essay because it is repetitive.

Evidence: 5

This essay analyzes the sources at times and at times just summarizes. The first three paragraphs do a good job with the information, and then paragraphs four and five fall apart. In paragraph four, for instance, quotations pop up, but they aren't linked to the central argument. In fact, paragraph four sails perilously close to something the directions tell you to avoid — summary. Paragraph five accomplishes nothing.

> **TIP**
>
> AP exam graders know they're reading a first draft, and they understand the time pressure you're facing. They don't expect a fully developed conclusion. However, they don't want a fake wrap-up either — repetition of something you've already written or the "in this essay I have proved" ending. When you get to the end of the essay, make your point and then stop writing.

Writing: 4

The essay begins with a reasonably mature command of language but deteriorates as it goes along.

Overall score: 5

Math time: Add up the four scores

$$5 + 5 + 5 + 4 = 19$$

and divide by 4

$$19 \div 4 = 4.75$$

which rounds up to 5.

SCORING ESSAY 2: PAIRED PASSAGES

The prompt asks you to compare two short passages, each of which features a narrator heading off to a new life. The first is an excerpt from *Confessions of an English Opium-Eater*, a thinly disguised autobiographical novel by Thomas de Quincey. The second comes from *Jane Eyre* by Charlotte Brontë.

> **TIP**
>
> Don't be disturbed by the fact that these passages are fiction. Approach both passages the same way you deal with memoir or biography as you analyze the authors' rhetorical techniques.

As you evaluate your essay, consider these questions:

- **Have I identified the narrators' attitudes toward "the change that is about to take place"?** The first passage looks backward. The narrator reminisces about "familiar objects" he won't see again. He doesn't tell you where he's going, just that he's leaving, as he "closed the door forever!" He acknowledges that he hasn't always been happy, but he's nostalgic about the life he's had. The second passage is much less sentimental. The narrator lists her preparations in a no-nonsense, straightforward way. Only at the very end do you see emotion, and it's all for the future: a "phase of my life was closing to-night, a new one opening to-morrow." This narrator is excited about what comes next.

- **Have I discussed how the passages convey these attitudes?** It's not enough to identify the narrators' emotions. You have to explain what rhetorical devices get those feelings across. You may mention diction, syntax, tone, and other aspects of the writing. (The sample essays show you some solid points you can make about these two passages.)

- **Have I used evidence effectively?** You can't just state that the narrator in passage one is sentimental. You have to dig into the text and quote the words that create this impression ("many happy hours," for example). When you discuss diction, you need to mention "lingered" or "radiant" or other words and analyze how they contribute to the overall effect of the passage.

- **Have I produced a well-written essay?** Check your grammar, spelling, and punctuation. Read the sentences aloud. Do they sound fluid and mature or choppy and simplistic?

Scoring grid for the paired-passage essay

Identifies narrators' attitudes _____

   0 The essay does not answer the question or is left blank. **Note:** If the essay doesn't answer the question, the *overall* score is zero, even if the essay is nicely written and would receive high marks in the "writing" category.

  1–3 The essay mischaracterizes the attitude of one or both narrators.

  4–6 The essay accurately presents the attitude of each narrator, but in an overly simple or general way.

  7–9 The essay explores the complexities of the narrators' attitudes, correctly identifying each.

Analyzes rhetorical devices _____

1–3 The essay does not discuss the way in which the passage is written, or it misidentifies elements of style. It may list rhetorical devices without explaining how they convey the narrators' attitudes.

4–6 Various rhetorical devices (diction, syntax, tone, and so forth) are identified, and some analysis of how they convey the narrators' attitudes is included.

7–9 The essay effectively analyzes the rhetorical devices in each passage, explaining what is present and how each element contributes to the reader's perception of the narrators' attitudes.

Evidence _____

1–3 The essay quotes from the passages, but the quotations selected don't relate to the central argument of the essay — how these devices convey the narrators' attitudes.

4–6 The essay provides examples of various rhetorical devices, but these examples may not be the most effective or may be poorly linked to the writer's point.

7–9 The evidence is particularly well chosen, clearly and effectively conveying how the rhetorical devices convey the narrators' attitudes.

Writing _____

1–3 The essay may be marred by many errors in grammar, spelling, or punctuation. The writing may sound immature, perhaps with choppy or repetitive sentences.

4–6 The writing is competent and reasonably correct, but the sentences may be choppy or repetitive. The diction and tone may be uneven. An essay in this category doesn't have the fluid, mature sound of an essay in the highest category.

7–9 An essay in this category demonstrates a command of language and the ability to make a point clearly and concisely. Though the essay may contain errors in grammar, spelling, punctuation, or citation, the errors are minor and infrequent.

Fill in each blank in this Essay Scoring Grid with your score, and then add your scores to determine the total.

Identifies narrators' attitudes _____

Analyzes rhetorical devices _____

Evidence _____

Writing _____

Raw score total _____

Divided by 4 _____

Rounded to nearest whole number for final score _____

Check the end of the chapter to see how to combine the scores for essays and multiple-choice questions.

Sample answer A

The narrator plays an important role in any piece of writing. All the reader's perceptions are filtered through the narrator, and although the reader can disagree with the narrator and understand more than the narrator, in the end it is the narrator's voice that the reader hears and the narrator's impressions that the reader gathers. In these passages, the narrators are both on the brink of leaving a place they have lived for a long time. The narrator in Passage One is nostalgic for the past and preoccupied with what he's losing, while the narrator in Passage Two is optimistic and excited about the future.

In passage one, the narrator reflects on his room while packing. The diction shows his ties to the room. He "lingered a little" before leaving. He calls the room his "citadel," a fortress, which implies that he felt protected there. All the words he uses to describe his time in the room are extreme: "passionately fond of books", "radiant" (not just "shining"), and "divine tranquility." These extremes show a romantic and idealistic nature, which in the passage is all directed at the past. In fact, the narrator never mentions the future at all.

One particularly interesting part of Passage One involves a picture of "the lovely _____" — someone who isn't even named. The narrator looks at the picture and appreciates its beauty, like the woman in Byron's poem, "She Walks in Beauty," her physical appearance is less important than what is inside. The sentence about the portrait only devotes a few words to "the eyes or mouth" which were "beautiful," but more of the sentence talks about her "benignity" and "divine tranquility." It's significant that as the narrator looks at the picture, he hears the clock chime. Time is running out for him, another idea that means nostalgia. He won't be here, appreciating her, as he has in the past. He even kisses the picture goodbye before he "closed the door forever!" He is sadly leaving her and also the room, where he has looked at her picture "a thousand times."

Passage Two is much more matter of fact. This narrator doesn't feel anything until the end, when she says that she "tried to rest" but couldn't despite her tiredness because "I was too much excited." The excitement isn't related to what went on in the room or in her previous life. She says, "A phase of my life was closing" and a "new one opening." True, she mentions the past, but it is parallel in syntax to the future. The last part of the sentence, after the semicolon, has her "watch feverishly while the change was being accomplished." For her the fact of change is exciting ("feverishly" means with excitement).

Other syntax shows her attitude. She makes a list of all she has done, all with "I-verb" statements: "I now busied myself . . . I had brushed my black stuff travelling-dress . . . I sat down." Things are stated matter of factly, not exaggerated. She has no sentimental feelings about her room, only about the change she's making. Her diction is plain and unemotional also. She says her wardrobe was "adequate" and a day "sufficed" to pack her trunk. This narrator couldn't be more different from the other, though they are both doing the same thing.

Analysis of sample answer A

Though it isn't perfect, this is a very fine AP essay with many good points about style and content. The details follow.

Identifies narrators' attitudes: 8

The essay immediately contrasts the two narrators. One is sentimental, and the other matter-of-fact about leaving but excited about making a change. The one point this writer missed was the reference to sadness. Though the writer is correct in saying that the narrator of Passage One is nostalgic, the narrator also says that in that room he "had lost my gaiety and happiness during the strife and fever of contention with my guardian" and at another point refers to "general dejection" — what today would probably be termed depression.

Analyzes rhetorical devices: 7

The essay mentions diction and syntax and gives several very good examples of each, though more could be made of the syntax. In a general way the test taker tackles point of view in the introductory paragraph; more specifics on point of view would be better. The essay doesn't explicitly say anything about tone, though some points are implied ("Things are stated matter of factly [sic], not exaggerated.") The essay could also discuss structure. Passage One is arranged according to the furnishings in the room — a spatial organization pattern. Passage Two relies more on narrative, a list of what the narrator did.

> **TIP**
>
> Did you notice the word *sic* in brackets in the preceding quotation? That's one of the most useful words in the language. Sic indicates that you're quoting exactly what's there, even though you know something is wrong with the spelling, grammar, or punctuation. In the quotation above, *sic* follows "matter of factly," which should be written "matter-of-factly."

Evidence: 7

I like the writer's use of quotations. A few more would be nice. I know that time is tight, and that's why I'd remove the reference to Byron, which is interesting but irrelevant here. Take that out and you have room — and time — for a few additional quotations. What is here is nicely tied to the point the writer is making.

Writing: 8

The essay is organized, the quotations are tucked into the sentences nicely, and only a few errors mar the prose.

Overall score: 8

Here's the calculation:

8 + 7 + 7 + 8 = 30

and divide by 4

30 ÷ 4 = 7.5

which rounds up to 8.

Sample answer B

How does one feel when leaving home? The two passages in this question have first-person narrators, but the narrators give very different impressions of their feelings about home. The tone of the first narrator is sad because he is leaving behind something he loved, even though it was not perfect. The tone of the second narrator is serious and determined. She is also excited about the future, not sad as the first narrator is. The tone, diction, imagery, and the way the stories are told convey the narrators' views of the change about to take place in their lives.

The tone of the first passage is sad. The narrator has only spent a year and a half in his room, but he talks about it with affection. He remembers the books he read there and the things he learned. He talks of all of these things in an affectionate way. He explains that he remembers this moment, when he left, "distinctly," after eighteen years have passed. He spends a lot of time talking about a picture of someone he loved, probably someone he knew while he was living in that room. At the end of the passage, he realizes that he is going away "for ever!" The exclamation point emphasizes his sadness. The tone of the second passage is very different. The narrator explains what she has done to get ready for the trip. She packs her things in a box and nails a card on it. She gets her dress ready and her bonnet, gloves, etc. She checks the room one more time. All of this comes across like a report. At the last minute her excitement leaks out. She "could not now repose." She was "too much excited" about the new things coming in her life. She looks ahead. She nails a card on a box. This shows her determination.

The diction of the passages are also important in conveying the narrators' attitudes toward the changes ahead. The first narrator is extreme. He calls his room a "pensive citadel," not just a plain bedroom. He is "passionately fond of books," not just interested in reading. He thinks of the girl in the picture as "his patron saint," not a normal girl-friend. You get the sense that he feels bad about leaving. The diction of the second passage also tells alot about the narrator. Her dress is "stuff" not precious to her but ordinary. She doesn't tell you anything about the contents of the room. She just says that she "had not a very large wardrobe." A wardrobe is something you take with you, but it doesn't tell you anything about the place she is leaving.

Imagery also says something about the narrators. In passage one you see the picture, the desk, the hearth, the chair, and you can almost picture the room. In passage two you see the clothes the narrator will wear. You don't see the room at all. The first narrator is attached to the room. The second isn't. The second narrator is closing a "phase" of her life and the first has "closed the door for ever!" You know what's behind the first narrator's door, but not the second.

Overall, you get much more information about the first narrator. But he doesn't tell you where he is going. He goes "for ever" to someplace. The second narrator doesn't tell you what she is leaving. She tells you where she is going (to Mrs. Fairfax). The way these passages are arranged, you know that the first narrator doesn't want to leave or has mixed feelings. The second narrator does want to leave and "must watch feverishly while the change was being accomplished."

Analysis of sample answer B

This essay has some strengths and some weaknesses. The strengths lie in some surprising observations; the weaknesses mostly concern overly general statements and repetitious or unnecessary explanation. Also, the essay is a little disorganized. This writer would have done better with a little advance planning. Take a look at these details.

Identifies narrators' attitudes: 6

The narrators' attitudes are correctly identified in the first paragraph, though "sad" is less specific than "nostalgic" or "sentimental." Also, the statement in the first paragraph of the essay that "[s]he is also excited about the future, not sad as the first narrator is" may imply that the first narrator is sad about the future, and the passage says nothing about what lies ahead for that narrator and how he feels about the future. The "serious and determined" statement about the second narrator is also accurate, as is the idea that she is "excited about the future." However, these ideas are not fully developed.

Analyzes rhetorical devices: 4

The writer of this essay makes some good points about the rhetorical devices without developing them fully. For example, the third paragraph deals with diction, or word choice. The writer gives some good examples from the first passage, but not enough, and relates the word choices to the narrator's attitude only weakly. The writer also misinterprets "stuff," a synonym for fabric, in the discussion of the second passage. Furthermore, the writer confuses diction with imagery — the details the writer selects to "show" the scene. Many of the observations in paragraph three concern imagery (for example, the comments about the wardrobe).

Evidence: 4

If you're in the mood, count the number of quotations in this essay and in the sample answer A. This essay has far fewer. Passage-based essays rely on close reading. This essay would benefit from more examples from the passages.

Writing: 5

A couple of grammar errors are evident, but the grammar and spelling aren't bad. Many sentences could be more concise, and some could be combined. For example, the second paragraph ends with a series of short, choppy sentences.

Overall score: 5

Here's the calculation:

6 + 4 + 4 + 5 = 19

and divide by 4

30 ÷ 4 = 4.75

which rounds up to 5.

SCORING ESSAY 3: FRIENDSHIP

In some ways, the comment-on-a-quotation essay is easier than the synthesis essay because you grasp the question immediately. But in some ways, it's harder because you have to generate ideas and evidence for your response.

TIP

The prompt mentions "history," and that's a clue. You don't have to define friendship as a relationship between individuals. Countries can be allies or enemies, for example.

As you evaluate your essay, consider these questions:

- **Have I communicated a clear point of view on the importance of shared interests and enemies in friendship?** You can say, "Yes, friends must be similar in their tastes," or "No, opposites attract." You can also say something in between, along the lines of "Usually . . . but sometimes . . . ." However, you have to take a stance that the reader can recognize.

- **Have I provided sufficient evidence?** Why do opposites attract? Perhaps what is lacking in one person is present in another, and together they make a whole. Or, friendship relies on similarity because people are most able to understand each other when they have like ideas. You don't have to agree with these ideas, but you do have to present *some reasons* in support of your main argument. Once you have the reasons, also known as supporting points, you still have work to do. Do you have an example of a pair created by two people (or countries) that compensated for each other's weakness? Or an example of a strong bond that arose between people on the same wavelength?

TIP

Though the prompt states that you *may* refer to history, literature or other arts, or personal experience, you actually *have* to tap into one or more of those areas in order to make a case for your view of friendship. The "may" is a disguised command and pops up on the AP exam from time to time. Be sure to read it as "must."

- **How's my writing?** Check your grammar, spelling, and punctuation. Look at your sentences. Are they complete? Are they varied in length and pattern? Do you have any repetition or unnecessary words?

Scoring grid for the friendship essay

Clear point of view _____

- 0 The essay does not answer the question or is left blank. **Note:** If the essay doesn't answer the question, the *overall* score is zero, even if the essay is nicely written and would receive high marks in the "writing" category.

- 1–3 The point of view is muddled. The writer may contradict him- or herself or wander away from the topic.

- 4–6 The point of view is defined, but poorly communicated. The reader has to work to find the test taker's idea about friendship and "identity of likes and dislikes."

- 7–9 The essay effectively communicates the author's point of view on friendship.

Evidence _____

1–3 The main idea is presented without support, or the supporting arguments are weak, vague, or confusing.

4–6 The writer's stance on friendship is supported by two or three acceptable but not great points. Or the supporting points are presented adequately or are only loosely tied to the central argument. The evidence is fairly specific, though more examples or details would be desirable.

7–9 The main idea is supported effectively and clearly by two or three supporting points. The essay contains specific and detailed examples in support of the writer's position on friendship.

Writing _____

1–3 The essay may be marred by many errors in grammar, spelling, or punctuation. The writing may sound immature, perhaps with choppy or repetitive sentences.

4–6 The writing is competent and reasonably correct, but the sentences may be choppy or repetitive. The diction and tone may be uneven. An essay in this category doesn't have the fluid, mature sound of an essay in the highest category.

7–9 An essay in this category demonstrates a command of language and the ability to make a point clearly and concisely. Though the essay may contain errors in grammar, spelling, punctuation, or citation, the errors are minor and infrequent.

Fill in each blank in this Essay Scoring Grid with your score, and then add your scores to determine the total.

Clear point of view _____

Evidence _____

Writing _____

Raw score total _____

Divided by 3 _____

Rounded to nearest whole number for final score _____

Check the end of the chapter to see how to combine the scores for essays and multiple choice questions.

Sample answer A

According to Gaius Sallustius Crispus, "the firmest friendship is based on an identity of likes and dislikes." History proves that Crispus was correct, because countries that are allies often join together because they have common interests and common enemies. Novelists also affirm the truth of Crispus's statement. In Jane Austen's book, <u>Northanger Abbey</u>, it says that Isabella and Catherine are friends. Really they aren't, because they have little in common.

During the 1950s through the 1990s, the countries of Eastern Europe were under the control of the Soviet Union. These countries had little freedom, and they had to do everything the Soviet Union ordered. The United States was locked in a "Cold War" with the Soviet union because our way of life and idea of freedom was the complete opposite of The Soviet's. Because they felt threatened by the Soviet Union, the countries of Western Europe were happy to join with the United States in the NATO alliance. Also, attitudes of the people in those Western European countries were pro-United States, because the countries were afraid of the Soviets. The common enemy, the Soviet Union, made many allies for the United States. The common interests were in building a strong trading partnership and a strong defensive alliance. Once the Soviet Union collapsed, the countries of Eastern Europe were free. Now the Western European countries drifted away from their traditional friendship with the U.S. They were more interested in joining the European Common Market than in working with the U.S. The loss of a shared enemy harmed the relationship.

In Austen's <u>Northanger Abbey</u>, a young girl named Catherine Morland goes to Bath, where she meets Isabella. At first it appears as though the girls are firm friends. Isabella is going to marry Catherine's brother, and Capt. Tilney, an officer who flirts with Isabella, is a common enemy. Later Captain Tilney and Isabella form a relationship and Isabella breaks off her engagement with Catherine's brother. Catherine loses a friend. But she doesn't, really. She thought that her own values — honesty and loyalty — were shared by Isabella, which was a mistake. The values that Catherine saw in Isabella were illusions. Isabella cared only about money and about making a good "match." In the end, Catherine finds a true friend in Eleanor Tilney, who really does have the same ideas and values. Their friendship will last, not fall apart.

I have had several experiences with friendship also. Some friends that I thought I would be with forever aren't a part of my life anymore, and some remain. The ones I care about the most are those that, while on the surface may be different, in reality are just like me on the inside.

Analysis of sample answer A

This writer has come up with a fairly good essay, with a defined argument and reasonable support for it. The essay has a fair amount of detail and competent writing. Overall, a good effort. Following are the details.

Clear point of view: 6

By the time you hit the end of the first paragraph, you know that this essay-writer agrees with Gaius Sallustius Crispus. The essay stays on that note throughout the first three paragraphs. However, the last paragraph strays into general statements and is a little confusing.

Evidence: 5

This test taker gets points for thinking outside the box. Countries can be friends or enemies, not just individual people. The Soviet Union/NATO point, therefore, is a good one, though it's not particularly well developed. Isabella and Catherine, the characters from *Northanger Abbey*, are a more obvious choice, but this writer has interpreted their bond in an interesting way. They *appear* to have similar interests, but their values don't match. The last supporting point ("I have had several experiences with friendship . . .") is the weakest. It's obvious, and it's also presented almost as an afterthought.

Writing: 5

If you read this one aloud, you hear some awkward sentences. It sounds good but not great. On the other hand, the essay has a logical structure and fairly correct grammar and spelling.

Overall score: 5

Here's the calculation:

6 + 5 + 5 = 16

and divide by 3

16 ÷ 3 = 5.33

Which rounds down to 5.

Sample answer B

The Roman historian Gaius Sallustius Crispus (1st century B.C.E.) was wrong when he said that the "firmest friendship is based on an identity of likes and dislikes." Just imagine a pair that never disagrees about anything. How can they maintain any sort of interest? The old saying, opposites attract, is true for friendship, not only for love. Challenging a friend, disagreeing vehemently, adds spice to life, and brings life to any relationship. This is true in the arts, in Shakespeare's play, <u>King Lear.</u> It is also true in my own life with my friend.

In Shakespeare's great play, <u>King Lear,</u> the old king divides his kingdom among his three daughters. All three appear to be friends with the king. They are his daughters and his subjects, so they are bound to him by two bonds. When the king is ready to divide the kingdom, he asks each daughter to speak about her relationship with the king. Two of the daughters, Goneril and Regan, offer loving tributes to the king. They appear to agree with everything he says. He feels close to them, and he wants to give them power. Cordelia, on the other hand, faces the king in a different way. She's not afraid to disagree with him, and she won't offer him any love. So what happens? The foolish old king divides the kingdom in half and Cordelia is left with nothing. At the end of the play the king has been betrayed by his older daughters and realizes that Cordelia is the one he should have listened to. Though she disagrees with him, she is loyal to him, she is a true friend.

Another example of friendship that is strong because the participants don't resemble each other too much occurs in my own life. When I was five years old, I was sitting outside my house when a young girl a year older, skated by. She literally fell on my feet. I helped her up, and that started a friendship that lasted all my life. From that day on we played together constantly. But we didn't ever want to do the same things. She likes athletics, so she is always taking me along to tennis, softball, and other sports. When it's my turn to decide what we're doing, we go to poetry readings or to see films. She complains about the "boring stuff you make me do" and I complain about the sore muscles I have after one of our marathon exercise sessions. However, I still want to see her and she still wants to see me. She challenges my body, and I challenge her mind. Not only that, but we don't agree on politics either. We joke that when we go to vote, we cancel each other out — in school elections or in (when we're old enough) national elections — we are against each other. I get angry at her ideas sometimes, but I always think about them. Sometimes I change my own position because of something she said. The reverse is also true.

Next year my friend and I will part. I hope that I will find someone like her in college, even though I know I'll be up late arguing. King Lear didn't value argument, and he paid the price.

Analysis of sample answer B

This writer tried, but the essay falls short of its goals in all three categories. Take a look at this analysis of its strengths and weaknesses.

Clear point of view: 4

Right away you know that this essay writer disagrees with Gaius Sallustius Crispus. However, the problem is that the writer didn't fully understand the ancient Roman's point and therefore didn't develop her point of view as she should have. The test taker goes on and on about disagreement in *Lear* and pastimes in her personal friendship. Thus the writer addresses the importance of shared interests *or* beliefs, not shared interests *and* beliefs. She's chopped the question into two halves and allowed one example to answer each half. That's not terrible, but it's not the ideal response.

Evidence: 3

This essay provides two examples, one from literature and one from personal experience. The *King Lear* paragraph is seriously flawed. In the play, Lear asks for flattery from his daughters, not agreement on a serious issue. Cordelia refuses to flatter; she simply states what she thinks. The conflict doesn't arise from a lack of "likes and dislikes." Instead it arises from honesty/dishonesty issues. The personal example is better, though some of the material (such as how they met) is off topic.

Writing: 3

This essay is marred by quite a few grammar errors — not quite enough to make the overall score a 2, but almost. (The College Board requires graders to give no more than 2 points *total* to an essay with distracting grammar and/or spelling errors.) Read the essay aloud; it sounds choppy and awkward, the product of an immature writer.

Overall score: 3

Add the scores together

$$4 + 3 + 3 = 10$$

and divide by 3

$$10 \div 3 = 3.33$$

which rounds down to 3.

EXAM CONVERSION CHART

It's time to tally your final score, using the numbers you calculated as you checked the multiple-choice and essay responses. Fill in the chart that follows to see how you fared.

Multiple Choice

Multiple-choice score _____ × 1.23 = _____ (final multiple-choice score)

Essays

Essay 1 score _____ + Essay 2 score _____ + Essay 3 score _____ = _____ (essay raw score)

Essay raw score _____ × 3.06 = _____ (final essay score)

Final Score

Final multiple-choice score _____ + final essay score _____ = _____ (final raw score)

AP Score

Now find your AP score, using the following chart:

Final Raw Score	AP Score
104+	5
92–103	4
76–91	3
50–75	2
Below 50	1

ANSWER SHEET FOR PRACTICE TEST 1

Use this bubble sheet to mark your answers for Section One of the exam.

1 Ⓐ Ⓑ Ⓒ Ⓓ Ⓔ	31 Ⓐ Ⓑ Ⓒ Ⓓ Ⓔ
2 Ⓐ Ⓑ Ⓒ Ⓓ Ⓔ	32 Ⓐ Ⓑ Ⓒ Ⓓ Ⓔ
3 Ⓐ Ⓑ Ⓒ Ⓓ Ⓔ	33 Ⓐ Ⓑ Ⓒ Ⓓ Ⓔ
4 Ⓐ Ⓑ Ⓒ Ⓓ Ⓔ	34 Ⓐ Ⓑ Ⓒ Ⓓ Ⓔ
5 Ⓐ Ⓑ Ⓒ Ⓓ Ⓔ	35 Ⓐ Ⓑ Ⓒ Ⓓ Ⓔ
6 Ⓐ Ⓑ Ⓒ Ⓓ Ⓔ	36 Ⓐ Ⓑ Ⓒ Ⓓ Ⓔ
7 Ⓐ Ⓑ Ⓒ Ⓓ Ⓔ	37 Ⓐ Ⓑ Ⓒ Ⓓ Ⓔ
8 Ⓐ Ⓑ Ⓒ Ⓓ Ⓔ	38 Ⓐ Ⓑ Ⓒ Ⓓ Ⓔ
9 Ⓐ Ⓑ Ⓒ Ⓓ Ⓔ	39 Ⓐ Ⓑ Ⓒ Ⓓ Ⓔ
10 Ⓐ Ⓑ Ⓒ Ⓓ Ⓔ	40 Ⓐ Ⓑ Ⓒ Ⓓ Ⓔ
11 Ⓐ Ⓑ Ⓒ Ⓓ Ⓔ	41 Ⓐ Ⓑ Ⓒ Ⓓ Ⓔ
12 Ⓐ Ⓑ Ⓒ Ⓓ Ⓔ	42 Ⓐ Ⓑ Ⓒ Ⓓ Ⓔ
13 Ⓐ Ⓑ Ⓒ Ⓓ Ⓔ	43 Ⓐ Ⓑ Ⓒ Ⓓ Ⓔ
14 Ⓐ Ⓑ Ⓒ Ⓓ Ⓔ	44 Ⓐ Ⓑ Ⓒ Ⓓ Ⓔ
15 Ⓐ Ⓑ Ⓒ Ⓓ Ⓔ	45 Ⓐ Ⓑ Ⓒ Ⓓ Ⓔ
16 Ⓐ Ⓑ Ⓒ Ⓓ Ⓔ	46 Ⓐ Ⓑ Ⓒ Ⓓ Ⓔ
17 Ⓐ Ⓑ Ⓒ Ⓓ Ⓔ	47 Ⓐ Ⓑ Ⓒ Ⓓ Ⓔ
18 Ⓐ Ⓑ Ⓒ Ⓓ Ⓔ	48 Ⓐ Ⓑ Ⓒ Ⓓ Ⓔ
19 Ⓐ Ⓑ Ⓒ Ⓓ Ⓔ	49 Ⓐ Ⓑ Ⓒ Ⓓ Ⓔ
20 Ⓐ Ⓑ Ⓒ Ⓓ Ⓔ	50 Ⓐ Ⓑ Ⓒ Ⓓ Ⓔ
21 Ⓐ Ⓑ Ⓒ Ⓓ Ⓔ	51 Ⓐ Ⓑ Ⓒ Ⓓ Ⓔ
22 Ⓐ Ⓑ Ⓒ Ⓓ Ⓔ	52 Ⓐ Ⓑ Ⓒ Ⓓ Ⓔ
23 Ⓐ Ⓑ Ⓒ Ⓓ Ⓔ	53 Ⓐ Ⓑ Ⓒ Ⓓ Ⓔ
24 Ⓐ Ⓑ Ⓒ Ⓓ Ⓔ	
25 Ⓐ Ⓑ Ⓒ Ⓓ Ⓔ	
26 Ⓐ Ⓑ Ⓒ Ⓓ Ⓔ	
27 Ⓐ Ⓑ Ⓒ Ⓓ Ⓔ	
28 Ⓐ Ⓑ Ⓒ Ⓓ Ⓔ	
29 Ⓐ Ⓑ Ⓒ Ⓓ Ⓔ	
30 Ⓐ Ⓑ Ⓒ Ⓓ Ⓔ	

ANSWER SHEET FOR PRACTICE TEST 2

Use this bubble sheet to mark your answers for Section One of the exam.

1 Ⓐ Ⓑ Ⓒ Ⓓ Ⓔ		31 Ⓐ Ⓑ Ⓒ Ⓓ Ⓔ
2 Ⓐ Ⓑ Ⓒ Ⓓ Ⓔ		32 Ⓐ Ⓑ Ⓒ Ⓓ Ⓔ
3 Ⓐ Ⓑ Ⓒ Ⓓ Ⓔ		33 Ⓐ Ⓑ Ⓒ Ⓓ Ⓔ
4 Ⓐ Ⓑ Ⓒ Ⓓ Ⓔ		34 Ⓐ Ⓑ Ⓒ Ⓓ Ⓔ
5 Ⓐ Ⓑ Ⓒ Ⓓ Ⓔ		35 Ⓐ Ⓑ Ⓒ Ⓓ Ⓔ
6 Ⓐ Ⓑ Ⓒ Ⓓ Ⓔ		36 Ⓐ Ⓑ Ⓒ Ⓓ Ⓔ
7 Ⓐ Ⓑ Ⓒ Ⓓ Ⓔ		37 Ⓐ Ⓑ Ⓒ Ⓓ Ⓔ
8 Ⓐ Ⓑ Ⓒ Ⓓ Ⓔ		38 Ⓐ Ⓑ Ⓒ Ⓓ Ⓔ
9 Ⓐ Ⓑ Ⓒ Ⓓ Ⓔ		39 Ⓐ Ⓑ Ⓒ Ⓓ Ⓔ
10 Ⓐ Ⓑ Ⓒ Ⓓ Ⓔ		40 Ⓐ Ⓑ Ⓒ Ⓓ Ⓔ
11 Ⓐ Ⓑ Ⓒ Ⓓ Ⓔ		41 Ⓐ Ⓑ Ⓒ Ⓓ Ⓔ
12 Ⓐ Ⓑ Ⓒ Ⓓ Ⓔ		42 Ⓐ Ⓑ Ⓒ Ⓓ Ⓔ
13 Ⓐ Ⓑ Ⓒ Ⓓ Ⓔ		43 Ⓐ Ⓑ Ⓒ Ⓓ Ⓔ
14 Ⓐ Ⓑ Ⓒ Ⓓ Ⓔ		44 Ⓐ Ⓑ Ⓒ Ⓓ Ⓔ
15 Ⓐ Ⓑ Ⓒ Ⓓ Ⓔ		45 Ⓐ Ⓑ Ⓒ Ⓓ Ⓔ
16 Ⓐ Ⓑ Ⓒ Ⓓ Ⓔ		46 Ⓐ Ⓑ Ⓒ Ⓓ Ⓔ
17 Ⓐ Ⓑ Ⓒ Ⓓ Ⓔ		47 Ⓐ Ⓑ Ⓒ Ⓓ Ⓔ
18 Ⓐ Ⓑ Ⓒ Ⓓ Ⓔ		48 Ⓐ Ⓑ Ⓒ Ⓓ Ⓔ
19 Ⓐ Ⓑ Ⓒ Ⓓ Ⓔ		49 Ⓐ Ⓑ Ⓒ Ⓓ Ⓔ
20 Ⓐ Ⓑ Ⓒ Ⓓ Ⓔ		50 Ⓐ Ⓑ Ⓒ Ⓓ Ⓔ
21 Ⓐ Ⓑ Ⓒ Ⓓ Ⓔ		51 Ⓐ Ⓑ Ⓒ Ⓓ Ⓔ
22 Ⓐ Ⓑ Ⓒ Ⓓ Ⓔ		52 Ⓐ Ⓑ Ⓒ Ⓓ Ⓔ
23 Ⓐ Ⓑ Ⓒ Ⓓ Ⓔ		53 Ⓐ Ⓑ Ⓒ Ⓓ Ⓔ
24 Ⓐ Ⓑ Ⓒ Ⓓ Ⓔ		
25 Ⓐ Ⓑ Ⓒ Ⓓ Ⓔ		
26 Ⓐ Ⓑ Ⓒ Ⓓ Ⓔ		
27 Ⓐ Ⓑ Ⓒ Ⓓ Ⓔ		
28 Ⓐ Ⓑ Ⓒ Ⓓ Ⓔ		
29 Ⓐ Ⓑ Ⓒ Ⓓ Ⓔ		
30 Ⓐ Ⓑ Ⓒ Ⓓ Ⓔ		

Index

N

narrative passage
  chronology rhetorical strategy, 34, 62,
    76–78, 108
  defined, 108
  elements of, 108–110
  topic sentence use, relationship to, 58
narrator, defined, 63
"The Negro Artist and the Racial Mountain"
  (Hughes), 122
nonessential *versus* essential sentence
  element, comma usage, 90–91
nonfiction passages, 5, 108, 115, 120
Northanger Abbey (Austen), 146–148
note-taking for AP English course, 27–28
no-verb rule for pronoun antecedents, 86–87

O

observation-leading-to-conclusion essay,
  121–122, 128–129
"Of Innovations" (Bacon), 182–185
"Of Studies" (Bacon), 122
omissions from passages, making note
  of, 111, 133
omniscient third-person point of view,
  defined, 64
"On Envy" (S. Johnson), 126–127
"On Keeping a Notebook" (Didion), 123
"On Lying in Bed" (Chesterton), 123
online *versus* real-world research activity, 36
onomatopoeia, defined, 170
opinion piece as essay assignment, 234–235
organizing information, 34, 111
outlining, 34
oxymoron, defined, 187

P

page numbers in citations, 157
paired-passage essay
  analyzing, 34, 70–72, 122
  decoding prompt for, 209
  overview, 4
  practice examples, 229–232
  strategies for, 217–218
paradox, defined, 57, 184, 188
paragraph construction, 58–62
parallelism
  defined, 56, 172
  in Johnson's State of the Union speech, 151
  sentences, 56–58, 88
paraphrase, defined, 213
parenthetical citation, 157, 158–159, 160, 216

passage-order essay structure, 218
passages
  analyzing essay
    anecdote-and-interpretation type, 121
    Big Idea type, 122, 126–127
    characteristics of an essay, 119–121
    compare-and-contrast type, 122
    inductive, 34, 121–122
    mosaic type, 115, 123
    nonfiction, 120
    observation-leading-to-conclusion type,
      121–122, 128–129
    paired-passage type, 4, 70, 209, 217,
      229–232
    samples, 123–129
    structure, 121–123
  argument
    elements of, 113–115
    essay, compared to, 120
    topic sentence, relationship to, 58, 59
  defined, 107
  descriptive
    biography and autobiography, 132
    elements of, 110–112
    topic sentence use, 58, 59
  expository. *See also* patterns of exposition
    characteristics and examples, 115–117
    practice reading of nonfiction, 17
    third-person point of view in, 64
    topic sentence, relationship to, 58–59
  fiction, 5, 64, 108, 115
  narrative
    chronology rhetorical strategy, 34, 62,
      76–78, 108
    defined, 108
    elements of, 108–110
    topic sentence use, relationship to, 58
  nonfiction, 5, 108, 115, 120
  omissions from, making note of, 111
  overview, 5
  paired-passage essay
    analyzing, 34, 70–72, 122
    decoding prompt for, 209
    overview, 4
    practice examples, 229–232
    strategies for, 217–218
  poetry, 5
passive compared to active vocabulary, 30
passive vocabulary, defined, 30
past perfect tense, defined, 82
pathos argument, defined, 113
patterns of exposition
  anecdote and example, 72–74
  cause and effect, 34, 62, 68–69
  chronology (process), 34, 62, 76–78, 108

T

table, statistical, 100–102
table of contents for citing research
    as you go, 38
tables and charts, analyzing, 100–102
A Tale of Two Cities (Dickens), 57
Tan, Amy (author)
  "Mother Tongue," 122
tense, verb, 80, 82–84
terminology
  figurative language
    allusion, 50, 95, 184
    apostrophe, 50, 188
    in descriptive passage, 111
    elements of, 49–51
    hyperbole, 50, 149, 172, 187, 188, 201
    interpreting, 29
    letters, 146
    metaphor, 49, 188
    metonymy, 49
    personification, 50, 172, 184, 187
    quotation usage in discussing, 214
    simile, 49
    synecdoche, 49
    understatement, 50, 172, 187
  syntax
    adjective, 81
    adverb, 81
    agreement, verb, 82
    antecedent for pronoun, 85, 175
    complement, 80
    complex sentence, 56
    dependent clause, 56, 80
    essential sentence element, 90
    helping verbs, 80
    imperative mood, 84
    independent clause, 56
    indicative mood, 84
    infinitives, 80
    loose sentence, 56
    nonessential sentence element, 90
    past perfect tense, 82
    periodic sentence, 56
    present perfect tense, 82
    pronoun, 85
    subject, 80
    subjunctive mood, 84
    subordinate clause, 56, 80
    syntax, 5, 45, 53, 179
    tense, 80, 82
    verb, 80
    verbal, 55, 81
test day countdown, 17–20
theme multiple-choice questions, 177–179
thesaurus, defined, 43

thesis statement, 34, 113, 211
thesis-and-proof essay, 123, 124–126
third-person point of view, 63–64, 108, 132
Thomas, Lewis (author), 58
Thoreau, Henry David (author)
  "Civil Disobedience," 124
time management
  duration of exam, 4
  essay section, 12–13, 207–208, 223–224
  multiple-choice section, 165–169
time shifts in narrative passages, 108
title(s) in citations, 157
tone
  biographical passages, 133
  defined, 45
  letters and speeches, 144
  questions on, 9, 189, 197–198
  quotation usage in discussing, 213
  words and phrases, 30, 45, 46–49
topic sentence position within paragraph,
    58–60, 115
transitions, 62, 76
translating quoted material, avoiding, 214
translations, citations to, 161
Treaster, Joseph (author), 173
  Paul Volcker: The Making of a Financial Legend,
    46, 61
Treatise on Old Age and Friendship (Cicero), 27, 33
Two Years Before the Mast (Dana), 46, 190–194

U

understatement, defined, 50, 172, 187

V

verbals
  defined, 55, 81
  as descriptive element, 89
  tense of, 83
verbs
  agreement, 82, 85–86
  defined, 80
  helping, 80
  tense, 80, 82–84
  usage, 81–85
visual details in descriptive passage, 111
visual sources
  advertisements, 98–100
  AP English course, 38–39
  cartoon analysis, 95–96
  charts and tables, 100–102
  graphs, 102–103
  photograph analysis, 97–98
  step-by-step interpretation, 93–95

Prepare for your AP Exam

with these titles from Wiley

Visit Wiley.com for more information

WILEY

AP*

Geraldine Woods

ENGLISH LANGUAGE
& COMPOSITION

- Two full-length practice tests to help you score your highest

- Review questions with complete answers and explanations for the most popular themes on the test

- Study strategies and expert test-taking tips to keep you calm and focused on test day

978-1-118-49017-4